Johan Cruyff: Always on the Attack

Johan Cruyff: Always on the Attack

THE BIOGRAPHY

Auke Kok

Translated from the Dutch by Liz Waters

**SIMON &
SCHUSTER**

London · New York · Sydney · Toronto · New Delhi

First published in Great Britain by Simon & Schuster UK Ltd, 2022

Copyright © Auke Kok, 2019
English translation copyright © Liz Waters, 2022

The right of Auke Kok to be identified as the author
of this work has been asserted in accordance with
the Copyright, Designs and Patents Act, 1988.

1 3 5 7 9 10 8 6 4 2

Simon & Schuster UK Ltd
1st Floor
222 Gray's Inn Road
London WC1X 8HB

www.simonandschuster.co.uk
www.simonandschuster.com.au
www.simonandschuster.co.in

Simon & Schuster Australia, Sydney
Simon & Schuster India, New Delhi

The author and publishers have made all reasonable efforts
to contact copyright-holders for permission, and apologise
for any omissions or errors in the form of credits given.
Corrections may be made to future printings.

A CIP catalogue record for this book
is available from the British Library.

Hardback ISBN: 978-1-3985-0165-2
Trade Paperback ISBN: 978-1-3985-1471-3
eBook ISBN: 978-1-3985-0166-9

Typeset in Bembo by M Rules
Printed and bound by CPI Group (UK) Ltd, Croydon, CR0 4YY

MIX
Paper from
responsible sources
FSC® C171272
FSC
www.fsc.org

'In a certain sense I'm probably immortal.'

– H. J. CRUYFF (1947–2016)

CONTENTS

FOREWORD

The first contact between us was unforgettable – for me, not for him. I remember precisely where it happened. I was standing amid the commotion of the Ajax restaurant after a league game against FC Den Bosch. It must have been half past five on the afternoon of Sunday 9 November 1986. I was there to report on a new phenomenon, the 'skybox'. Rooms had been hung from the roof of the main stand at De Meer, so that VIP spectators could watch the football while enjoying salmon and champagne. The outcry against the elitism of the arrangement had been going on for months, and that was reason enough for an article in the weekly *Haagse Post*, where I'd started work as an intern three years earlier. The atmosphere in the packed restaurant was excellent. Ajax had won 3–1 and Marco van Basten had scored one of the most beautiful goals of all time, firing the ball into the net with an overhead volley.

Out of nowhere, Johan Cruyff appeared to my left. In trying to get past, he gently pushed me aside. I felt his hand on my stomach and naturally made way for the Ajax coach. A trivial incident, you might think, but I stared after him for a minute or more, watching as he was swallowed up by the throng of businesspeople, board members, footballers and their wives and girlfriends, and put my hand on the place he'd touched. Well, I'll be damned. A shiver ran through me. I immediately knew why.

For a moment I'd been Geert Bals, or Heinz Stuy, the Ajax goalkeepers who in the late 1960s and early 1970s had been tapped on the stomach by teammate Cruyff just before the start of every match. I'd read a lot about that and it had somehow appealed to me. Such an intimate moment in the stadium between the striker and his goalie, a ritual gesture; it had seemed like something out of a children's book and now I'd experienced a comparable moment with the best Dutch footballer of all time. Nobody could never take that away from me.

Thirteen years later I felt the touch of his hand again. We'd greeted each other and now I was sitting across a table from Cruyff. One to one. In the intervening years I'd interviewed countless famous players and coaches, CEOs and politicians, but at that moment I was as excited as a child on Christmas Eve. He talked about his latest projects as a philanthropist and I wrote it all down. Or, rather, my pen moved. Listening was hard, because I kept looking at my hand, the hand that had shaken his.

I still have my notes – entirely illegible.

Was I infatuated with Cruyff? My head was of course full of memories of the Number 14 dribbling, pointing and shouting, leaping like a ballet dancer. I'd watched him play in Amsterdam, against Benfica (1972, 1-0), CSKA Sofia (1972, 3-0), Bayern Munich (1973, 4-0), Bayern Munich again (in his farewell match in 1978, 0-8 – yes, really), Haarlem (his comeback match in 1981, 4-1), even against Ajax, in a Feyenoord shirt (1983, 8-2 to Ajax). Each occasion had been an extraordinary experience, whether in De Meer or in the Olympic Stadium. But my bedroom hadn't been plastered with Cruyff posters and, like many people, I'd sometimes been irritated by his unfathomable arguments, his smart-aleck chatter, his stubborn refusal to admit he was wrong. All the same, he was a phenomenon impossible to ignore, the only Dutch sportsman to be ranked among great artists. I'm merely stating that as a fact. Many of his inner circle, when I spoke to them for this book, used the word; he has often been called a 'performer', but 'artist' expresses his creative urge rather better. As does 'businessman', incidentally, but we'll come back to that.

His indomitable creativity, along with the occasionally puzzling things he came out with, made it seem almost as if what he created was fiction, intangible, impossible to nail down. He misled his opponents on the pitch and he misled the public whenever he deemed it necessary. Because, to paraphrase one of his most amusing sayings: if he'd wanted you to understand it, he would have explained it better.

It had often been claimed that Cruyff was a visionary, that as an analyst on Champions League nights he could watch several football matches at once. I refused to believe it. On Tuesday, 7 December 1999, several days after our interview, I was present at one such evening. In Studio 7 in the Media Park in Hilversum, Cruyff sat directly in front of me, in the middle of his usual group, which included his childhood friends Rolf and Frans Grootenboer. Biting his nails, the 52-year-old match analyst watched four games simultaneously. Feyenoord were playing Olympique Marseille and with every backward pass by the Dutch side he started to grumble; the ball must be passed forward without delay and he knew precisely how. Not just on that one screen but on all four of them. My scepticism subsided by the minute.

Cruyff knew the current score, he knew the style of play of each of the eight teams – and he knew what each of them was doing wrong. Yet he was also chatting with those around him and he even had to go out for a moment – 'Back in a sec' – to record an advert for his foundation.

At half-time he nipped into the live studio to tell television viewers, without any preparatory consultation with interviewer Mart Smeets, what had so far gone well and badly in the Feyenoord vs Olympique match.

Cruyff was a competitor in every sense. There was a sweepstake; all those present in the studio had forked out five guilders for the pot and written four results on a sheet of paper, signed with their initials. So who won? Stupid question. When it was over, 'JC' swept all the coins together and pocketed them with a satisfied expression on his thin face.

Then he glanced at the piece of paper again and asked in a stern voice, 'Who is AK?'

For a moment I was the child in the class who is unexpectedly asked a question. I believe I even raised my hand.

'Er, me.'

He looked at me.

'He hasn't got a clue.'

That was where I stood with him. Just so you know.

We already had our coats on when I found myself watching a replay. Cruyff popped up beside me out of nowhere and berated a player who was approaching the goalkeeper in slow motion. 'Look,' he said. 'That guy's running sideways, which means he's making his angle smaller. They all do that. Unbelievable. Why make things harder for yourself?' To be honest I had no idea how a striker could be so foolish, but, before I knew it, we'd been talking for several minutes. Or, rather, he talked and I listened. He appeared to be taking me, the numbskull of the sweepstake, completely seriously.

Cruyff didn't seem to care what sort of person he was speaking to and perhaps it was only while researching this book that I came to understand why. I uncovered countless anecdotes of people who'd bumped into him, on the street, at airports, in bars and restaurants, and found him to be a thoroughly down-to-earth, regular guy. What he said about himself was true: in daily life he didn't look up to anyone and he didn't look down on anyone. He was available and at the same time unreachable. He was certainly a man of flesh and blood and that's how I've tried to describe him, based on 170 interviews with friends and foes in the Netherlands, Spain, Britain and the United States, with intimates and advisers, with classmates and friends from his neighbourhood, with former players, board members, trainers and relatives. I also undertook extensive archival research and watched an endless number of matches and other footage.

*

Please note:

- If a quote is followed by a verb in the present tense – 'he says', 'she remembers' – then it comes from one of my own interviews. 'He said' and the like indicate pre-existing sources.
- Foreign currencies referred to before the introduction of the euro have been converted into guilders, according to the exchange rate at the time.

CHAPTER ONE

What do we do with Johan?

In the sporting goods shop where he worked, because a 15-year-old has to do something, they knew him as a quiet, rather unhappy-looking boy. He was working because he had not been a success at school, and he wasn't making tremendous headway with this first job either. Johan Cruyff had work to do, but that was probably the most positive thing to be said about his time at Perry van der Kar. At its branch on the Ceintuurbaan in Amsterdam there was a strict hierarchy, and for a stockroom employee that was discouraging. Johan was an assistant. The cleaner was the only person lower down the pecking order. There was no sign of the training as a sales clerk that he'd been promised.

He'd started in January 1963, during the coldest winter in living memory, when snowstorms lashed past the shop and the nearby River Amstel was frozen over for weeks. There was barely a chance for Johan to enjoy skating, or even to stare dreamily out of the window as he had done at school. In the basement he helped unpack deliveries from wholesalers: football kits and other sporting gear, toys, or casual wear for ladies and gents. Johan checked that the deliveries were in order, then attached price labels to items and put them on the correct shelves in the storeroom.

It was a sizeable shop, in a working-class neighbourhood of

Amsterdam known as De Pijp, and he trudged back and forth from nine to five, up the stairs and down again. He was shut away in a world that bored him.

His index card in the employee records office reflects the position in which he found himself. The black-and-white photo shows a boy with a vulnerable, lacklustre look, suggesting a teenager who would rather be almost anywhere else. The photo also seems to illustrate the norms and values of his upbringing. As in his school photos, he looks clean and neat, in a buttoned-up shirt with an impeccable white collar, his sweater equally spotless, his shiny hair in a side parting. Despite his discomfort, there need be no doubt Johan was polite to the customers. On the street in Betondorp, the neighbourhood where he lived with his mother and his older brother Henny, he could be a show-off, even a pain in the neck, but at school he had generally shown respect for the teachers and here, in the largest sporting goods shop in the city, five storefronts wide, he was never heard to say a rude word. Or many other words either, in fact.

He looks into the photographer's lens as a boy with slightly questioning eyes, in complete contrast to his reputation in the street where he lived and utterly different from the way the world would later come to know him.

Later. Fifteen-year-old Johan Cruyff must have wondered whether, in a social sense, there ever would be a 'later'.

Three years before, the employment office, which gave careers advice to schoolchildren from quite a young age, had not been particularly positive about his chances. Johan had been held back in his first year at the Oosterpark ULO school and so had to leave. (ULO stood for *uitgebreid lager onderwijs*, or advanced primary education, and such schools were intended to turn out broadly educated workers and administrators for trade and industry.) Pupils were not allowed to repeat the first year. It seems this was sufficient reason for his mother to have him examined by a psychologist. At home he was restless and at school had clearly achieved little. So where to go from here?

Vocational training perhaps? The careers advice department at the employment office came to the conclusion that Johan was 'still too childlike' to choose a specific path in life. 'Careers in trade', the report said, 'or in the transport sector, or retail and warehousing' might suit him. The same could not be said for technical occupations or precision work in general, since for those he lacked 'patience, thoughtfulness, neatness and exactitude'. He definitely didn't excel at languages either, but arithmetic came naturally to him. Mentally and physically, Johan was still 'far from adult', which possibly had to do with his playful and 'emotional' attitude. Unless he began concentrating more intensively on his schoolwork, his performance would remain below par. 'He has the intellect to deal with the ULO material, if only he showed sufficient dedication.'

The impression that Johan had failed to apply himself to his studies is confirmed by his final report at primary school. Beside a list of many sixes out of ten, a seven (for arithmetic) and one nine (gymnastics) is written in firm strokes: 'Johan can do better!'

Johan might well have been able to do better, but if so he cunningly hid the fact from the next set of teachers to take him on. Perhaps Nel Cruyff was still optimistic when in 1960 she registered her 13-year-old son at the W. Y. Bontekoe School. It was what was known as a vocational school, where manual skills and carpentry were a major part of the curriculum and where pupils often merely sat out their time until the end of compulsory schooling (at fourteen in those days). How often, if at all, Johan showed up there is unclear. At any rate, he made another fresh start a year later, after his fourteenth birthday, once more at a ULO school. Frankendael was a school where everything was highly structured, for children who found it hard to concentrate. His performance improved, but as at the Oosterpark ULO school he was fully present only during gym lessons.

The strict regime at the Frankendael school helped, and Johan made it into the second year. At last he met with success,

although not of the kind the teachers were hoping for. 'In class
he was a quiet, self-contained boy,' a classmate remembers. 'You
might easily overlook him. But after the weekend, if he'd done
something remarkable at Ajax, a whole gaggle of children would
cluster around him. He was the centre of attention then.'

At Christmas, after three and a half years of worry, encouragement and scolding, his mother decided to take him out of
school. Three secondary schools, three failures: it was pointless
to keep ploughing on.

For Nel Cruyff-Draaijer, a 45-year-old widow, this was a
difficult time. But, fortunately, Ajax offered help. Since her
husband's death she had worked as a cleaner at the stadium
and, on seeing that there were problems with Johan, the club
officials put their heads together. That son of Nel's was a terrific
footballer, as everyone had known since he became a member
at the age of ten, but the way things were going, he'd amount
to nothing. So what now? What do we do with Johan?

Leo van der Kar knew the answer. The director of Perry van
der Kar, a man as amiable as he was vain, from a Jewish family
of merchants and diamond dealers, was on good terms with the
board at Ajax. In the role of masseur he had kept the calf muscles
of top athletes like Fanny Blankers-Koen supple, and since setting
up his retail business he'd given jobs to skaters and footballers so
that they had an income to facilitate their unsalaried sporting lives.
Jopie, as Johan was called at the club, would be able to join them.

Leo van der Kar undoubtedly wanted the best for his
youngest employee. Although Johan was clearly bored on the
Ceintuurbaan, his monthly wage was raised as of 1 August 1963
from eighty guilders (roughly £8) – not bad in itself for a teenager with hardly any work experience – to a hundred. The new
lad was also allowed to help the players of the Ajax first eleven
in the shop on Saturdays, if they needed new football boots, say.
He thought it was great just to be able to fetch the new boots
from the shelves. Those immaculate laces! Those shiny steel

studs! But after the men left, Johan had to go back down to his windowless basement.

The one promising thing in his life was a youth contract with Ajax, which he'd wheedled out of the club by his own efforts. Johan wanted to earn money by playing football and because in 1962 Ajax had not been willing to accommodate him, or not quickly enough as he saw it, he'd declared himself, as a 15-year-old, ready to go off and play in Amsterdam-Noord instead. There a club called De Volewijckers had held out the prospect of a new moped. The Ajax board managed to block that move at the last moment, but in that same period the English trainer of Ajax 1, Keith Spurgeon, was eager to take the budding talent with him to his new club, Blauw-Wit. All this tugging at Johan caused panic; the lad must of course stay at Ajax and so he was offered a 'special youth contract', as club chairman Jan Melchers would later cryptically call it. Special because his age was raised to sixteen. 'Everyone in the club knew that story,' says Johan's teammate at the time, Hennie Heerland. 'And everyone understood it too; it was Ajax's way of helping a family that had fallen on hard times. But it wasn't talked about.'

The rules of the Royal Dutch Football Association (KNVB) said that no young player could be paid until he reached the age of sixteen. That had been made very clear when paid youth football was introduced in 1961. The signature of Johan's first youth contract caused problems at home as a result. Uncle Dirk, the brother of Johan's late father, who had been appointed as his guardian, refused to go along with the faking of his age. Dirk's daughter Dorie would never forget it, such was the impression made on her by her straitlaced father's refusal to cross that particular moral boundary. With Dirk Cruyff, 'no' meant 'no', so if Johan was determined to persist he would have to look for a different guardian.

One was soon found. Barend Tak, also an uncle, married to Nel's sister Riek, was less troubled by the deceit. Barend Tak was active in Ajax as a youth-team manager. A tough character, he lived a stone's throw away from Nel in Betondorp. So it was that Johan's youth contract came to be signed by Nel Cruyff and Barend Tak.

This first contract included a special clause. If Johan studied hard and got his ULO diploma, Ajax would pay him a bonus of 500 guilders, a considerable sum in those days. It showed how much importance the board, and especially his mother, attached to the creation of a broader social foundation for Johan than purely the scoring of goals – something he did with improbable regularity, incidentally. Despite the prospect of a generous reward, however, he continued to do little schoolwork.

On top of his wages from the sports shop he was now earning several tens of guilders a month by doing the one thing in the world that interested him. He was almost certainly the only 15-year-old Amsterdammer in possession of a football contract. Not for the first time, and certainly not for the last, an exception had been made for Jopie.

Ajax, and above all Johan's mother, had reason to be worried. The chances of the boy being able to pay his own way in the long term by playing football were slim. He was short and skinny for his age, and he was often plagued by headaches. 'He sometimes went about with an elastic band round his finger,' his friend of those days Leo Happé remembers. 'His mother used to tell him it would take the pain away. He was sometimes sent to a doctor of alternative medicine, too.' Nothing helped. The headaches, which probably had to do with his nervousness, kept coming back. He also had some kind of problem with his insteps. They were rather broad, which his doctor said had to do with weak muscles and flat feet. Add to that a lack of self-control and you would hardly think he was cut out for a career in sport, of whatever kind.

Even if Cruyff were to overcome his physical and mental limitations and mature into a professional footballer, how far might that get him? Life as a professional player in 1962 didn't amount to much. Eight years after the introduction of paid football, the Netherlands still had not a single full-time professional. Players in the premier division – the Eredivisie – trained in the evenings. In the daytime they were reps, bookkeepers, insurance agents, barkeepers or builders. At Ajax, often called a tradesman's club, many of the players ran shops. It seemed clear that once he passed the age of about thirty, Johan would find himself doing something like that. As a self-employed retailer of cigarettes or sporting goods, you could convert your local footballing fame into cash. Still, if that was what he wanted, he would need qualifications, diplomas, and he had none, aside from a certificate to say he had completed primary school, a swimming certificate and a road safety certificate.

Not even the country's greatest postwar footballing heroes were able to live from the sport alone. The graceful forward Faas Wilkes, for instance, had earned serious money for a few years in Italy and Spain, but after living the good life, driving sports cars on the boulevards of southern Europe, he had to knuckle down as the owner of a clothes shop in Rotterdam. The legendary dribbler Abe Lenstra had never wanted to abandon the security of his job working for the Heerenveen local council. In 1962, by then in his early forties, Lenstra was still turning out for the Enschedese Boys, which soon afterwards merged into FC Twente. Later he became a brewery rep. Haarlem goal-getter Kick Smit, on whom, along with Wilkes and Lenstra, the cartoon strip character in *Kick Wilstra* was based (extremely popular when Cruyff was a boy), was likewise unable to earn enough through his footballing exploits. He spent his days as a sports teacher.

In short, a life built on his sporting talent alone did not look like a viable option for Johan. Everything that was expected of a footballer in the early 1960s – grit, modesty, quiet determination – was to be found in the big blond ball-heading Kick Wilstra, but apparently not in the restless stockroom employee from Betondorp.

*

Johan was quite often ill and his health did not improve when, as a young teenager, he took up smoking. If he was able to get outside for a moment during breaks at Perry van der Kar, he often went into Piet Ouderland's tobacconist's shop nearby in De Pijp. In the company of Ajax footballer Ouderland, Johan could briefly escape the boredom of stockroom work. He would chat and cadge cigarettes, and Ouderland – 'Ought you to be doing that, lad? I don't smoke myself, you know' – gave him the smoking materials he asked for. Puffing away, Johan seemed to be trying to calm his nerves, a struggle that only grew worse.

At Ajax he was becoming more rebellious by the week. Shorts flapping round his matchstick legs, there was no sign of the shy shop worker of the Ceintuurbaan. That questioning look in the photo was not in evidence when he played with the B1 juniors at Ajax. Sometimes he coolly stubbed out a cigarette on the sole of his boots, and he would give referees lip as readily as he did his teammates. They often didn't understand the game at all, he believed, and he told them so. During training Jopie talked almost incessantly. 'Hey, Johan, try playing!' youth coach Jany van der Veen often shouted at him. He would shut up for a bit then, but rarely for long. Van der Veen believed that Johan had everything it took to become a top-class player – everything except for the necessary discipline.

At Ajax they put a great deal of effort into Johan. Otherwise the lad would come to no good and that, of course, would be to the detriment of the club, which had no choice but to fine him, first five guilders, later ten guilders and later still, when the board began to get desperate, to make him write out fifty times, 'I must behave myself during matches and always play fairly.'

Fifty times over, Johan promised to control himself and respect the codes of the sport, as if he was still at school. He closed with 'Respectfully yours' and his signature.

CHAPTER TWO

Daddy's boy

Johan often had the feeling he was living in a village. His home neighbourhood was called Betondorp, literally 'concrete village', and most of its street names referred to the countryside: Hooistraat, Graanstraat, Sikkelstraat. There was also the Akkerstraat (field street), around the corner from the Tuinbouwstraat (horticulture street), where Johan grew up, having been born in the local hospital, the Burgerziekenhuis. In this eastern corner of Amsterdam, across the road from the Ajax stadium, you could see farmland as soon as you got beyond the houses. Next to Betondorp was the Oosterbegraafplaats, a huge cemetery with tall trees, and all around was the green of sports fields, gardens, market gardens and woodland.

Yet Johan was a street boy. Between the low, rectilinear housing blocks of Betondorp were streets and pavements where restless youngsters like him could do as they pleased. There were hardly any cars and Johan didn't need to ring any doorbells; via the backyards, people simply walked into each other's houses. You might almost call the neighbourhood a paradise for children, since a great effort had been made, by socially engaged architects, to provide 'light, air and space', a 'radical alternative' to the often miserable living conditions of the overcrowded city.

It was for that reason that Nel and Manus Cruyff had left

the cramped and poverty-stricken Amsterdam neighbourhood known as the Jordaan in December 1945 for this small, close-knit community. In recognition of their good deeds during the German occupation, they had been given the chance to move into Akkerstraat 32, a shop with living space that had lain empty for some time. The ground-floor apartment behind the shop could not be described as spacious, but they made it a happy home. Their first child, Henny, born on 11 December 1944, during what has gone down in history as the Hunger Winter, would grow up healthier there than in the Eerste Lindendwarsstraat, where Nel and Manus had sold potatoes and vegetables ever since they were married in 1941. Like the Jordaan, Betondorp had a shop on almost every corner, and with the arrival of the Cruyffs there were now four greengrocers. But although Nel and Manus's shop was modest, by working hard they were able to make a living from it. They both put in long days. There was no money to hire staff.

When, at one in the afternoon of 25 April 1947, the family rejoiced at the arrival of their second child, Hendrik Johannes, known as Johan, the municipal social services department sent a teenage girl to help with the housework. Babysitter Etty cooked and mashed the brown beans for Henny and bottle-fed Johan so that Manus and Nel were free to serve customers.

Etty had a tough time of it in the Akkerstraat. Henny was not the quietest of children and Johan was out-and-out boisterous. They were both adventurous, a fact that had already cost the life of a kitten. The scene of the crime was a milk boiler, a tall pan with holes in the lid in case the milk frothed up too high. It was used to sterilise milk and toddler Johan wanted to see what would happen if you put a kitten in the hot milk. A horrified Etty intervened, but not in time to save the poor creature.

A few years later, Johan would often ride along the pavement, standing on the pedals of his mother's bicycle, sending anyone who dared get in the way packing with a loud, 'Sod off.' His head only just above the handlebars, fearing no one, Johan was the little tearaway of the street then. On other occasions he might shriek, 'You're rubbish at football!' if he wanted to settle an argument with a friend. He flattened the plants in the front gardens with his ball, or smashed neighbours' windows with it, and in winter he used snowballs to knock milk bottles off a window ledge. His father Manus tended to be laconic in his response. Even when it cost him customers, he usually laughed off the havoc wreaked by his sons. 'Rightly or wrongly, we always got the blame in the neighbourhood,' Johan said later.

For Mr and Mrs Nuis, these were signs that the family across the street was of a different standing, as it was called in those days. What on earth was to become of Johan, that 'Cruyff brat'? 'My parents preferred me not to mix with him,' their son Bert remembers. Everything revolved around respectability and social progress in the Nuis household, and in that sense Bert's family may have been more typical of Betondorp than the Cruyffs. Most of the residents were socialists, and for them the norm was not elementary technical training but a more general education, the ULO at the very least. A quite remarkable number of local children went on to attend high school and then to become entrepreneurs, scientists, writers, architects, lawyers or the editor of a national newspaper. Leo van Wijk, who played football with Johan but spent far more time than he did with his nose in a book, became CEO of KLM.

The Cruyffs were not leftists; the tone of Akkerstraat 32 was set by the mores of the market. That was how it had been for generations in the Jordaan, where Nel Draaijer's parents and grandparents ran a shop selling potatoes, vegetables and fish. In 1844 Johan's Frisian great-great-grandfather had left Leeuwarden for Amsterdam to earn his keep, starting out there as a road-mender. With his wife Griet van Oort, Hendrik Draaijer had a son in 1855 who was named Gerrit. Gerrit Draaijer married Gerritje Laroo, who bore him a son in 1879, and they called him Hendrik Johannes. It was this Hendrik Johannes Draaijer, Nel's father, a greengrocer and diamond cutter, who later became the source of Johan's name. The Draaijers had a reputation in the Jordaan for intransigence. They either liked you or they didn't, and once the door had been shut to you it rarely opened again.

Manus Cruyff's family was likewise made up of small entrepreneurs, and it too had its roots in the northern province of Friesland, but in general the Cruyffs had a rather more relaxed manner. Both families excelled at trade and at exchanges of wit, as well as at speaking plain truths to the point of rudeness. You could find Cruyffs and Draaijers working market stalls on the Lindengracht and the Westerstraat, in shops and in long narrow storage rooms. For the countless small traders of the Jordaan, it was a tough life of rising early to get the best deals, hawking your wares all day and then counting your money at night. Whoever was smarter and busier than the neighbours earned more, but if a competitor fell prey to debilitating illness you would take round a pan of soup. That principle of what goes around comes around, and the need to fight for a foothold, along with a certain distrust of the powers that be, was passed on undiluted to Johan Cruyff. He grew up in a family that was a long way from being socialist but was highly socially aware all the same.

Many children, like those of the Nuis family, were educated outside the 'village', attending the best state schools. But Henny and Johan simply went to the Groen van Prinsterer School, a Protestant primary on the edge of Betondorp that, as Henny said later, had something rural about it. The atmosphere was friendly, but there were clear lines of authority. Although the Cruyffs were not religious, at school the boys were taught about the afterlife and the wrath of God. Psalms were sung and stories from the Old Testament read out. Prayers were always said at the start of the school day.

One day Johan noticed that the teacher was surveying the class during prayers. After saying 'Amen' he promptly stuck up his hand.

'Sir?'

'Yes, Johan?'

'When you pray, you're not supposed to have your eyes open, are you?'

'That's right . . .?'

'Yours were open. I saw them.'

'Yours too, in that case,' the teacher countered in his own defence.

'Yes, but I'm allowed. I never go to church on Sundays. And that's what makes all the difference, see.'

Johan liked to challenge authority from time to time, but he was rarely truly insolent and that may have had to do with the character of the Groen van Prinsterer, where a lot of attention was paid to music, crafts and sport. If the boys were having a good game of football on the patch of grass next to the school, called 't Zandje, then breaktime might last a little longer.

That progressive approach suited Johan. His restlessness – 'These days it's called ADHD,' he said decades later – was steered on to the right track, not suppressed. Since he was constantly playing with a ball, he was the only boy in the class with permission to bring one into the classroom. As a general rule, or as a pedagogical ritual, he had to put it into the metal litter bin before he went to sit down. At the start of breaktime or when school finished, Johan picked up the ball and showed off his mastery of it outside. There were even days when he was allowed to keep the ball with him during a lesson. His class-mates would watch perplexed as he rolled it constantly under his foot while staring dreamily out of the window.

It was a five-minute walk from Johan's house to the Groen van Prinsterer. Nel Cruyff regularly came to the school to discuss her younger son's behaviour with Mr Ritchi, Johan's teacher in year six. 'He never would settle,' Nel Cruyff said later about that time. 'He couldn't really sit still for a moment.' Sometimes, when his parents felt driven crazy by his boister-ousness in the house, his father would offer him a bet, saying he'd get a chocolate bar if he could sit quietly for five minutes in a row. Johan never won. Other times Manus sent him out into the garden with a ball, telling him to practise with his left leg, which he found difficult, so that he and Nel could catch their breath.

One thing Johan concealed from his mother was that he occasionally skipped school, and something else Nel Cruyff was better off not knowing about were the treats Johan took to school from his parents' shop. The 'what goes around comes around' principle, so deeply ingrained in him, was handy when it came to raising his marks at school. 'Across from us was a studious boy who wore glasses,' classmate Ria Lagrand remembers. 'He wrote something on a scrap of paper during an oral test and handed it to me. I passed it on to Johan. If the boy did his best for us, he'd get a half-tube of liquorice drops that Johan nicked from his parents' shop. That's what Johan was like: everything has its price. Liquorice for a crib sheet.'

Henny Cruyff generally behaved rather better. He attended school regularly and got good marks. At home he often had to look after his little brother, which according to neighbours and relatives wasn't always easy. They were 'fire and water'.

The 'hot-headed' Johan, who might well kick out during an argument, had another side to him too. 'He was one of the few boys who acted normally towards girls,' Riet Glashouwer recalls. 'Before school he joined in when we did handstands against a wall. He was interested in my father's work as a clergyman, and he even wrote something in my poetry album, the only boy to do that. When I got it back from him there was a rhyme inside. But there was also a page torn out. It seems he was dissatisfied with his first attempt. He wanted a good result.'

Dear Rietje
A seal once lay on the strand
and rubbed its nose clean in the sand.

Rietje let your heart be as pure
as the seal's nose there on the shore.
In memory of Johan Cruyff

After reading that, another girl in the class wanted a verse from him. Three days later, in February 1959, Johan wrote,

Dear Anneke,
I wasn't born to be a poet
And it's hard for me to rhyme
I don't want to parrot others,
At least not this time
So a verse or song I haven't got
Only a wish: 'Forget me not!'
In memory of Johan Cruyff

All very sweet, but for Johan, as for so many boys in the 1950s, everything revolved around football. Whenever he was asked what he wanted for his birthday he would say: a ball. If there wasn't a game going on in the street or on the Betondorp recreation ground then he simply played by himself. He walked to school in the mornings messing with a tennis ball, often singing as he did so, or imitating a barrel organ, which he could do rather well. In the afternoons he walked home doing the same thing. On the little open space behind the house, he kept balls in the air with his feet – right, left, right, left – or with his head, arms wide for balance. He played football with friends in the street, laying coats on the ground to make goals; he played the ball between his opponents' legs, and if it was raining they would hold heading contests in the underpass on the Tuinbouwstraat.

On other days, older boys might tell him to kick the ball into the top right corner of a goal drawn on the side wall of the greengrocer's shop. The ball went to the top right corner. 'Top left corner.' The ball hit the top left corner. They might put a brick on a low wall and Johan would knock it off from 5 metres away. 'Lamp post!' Johan kicked the ball against the lamp post from a distance of 10 metres. Nobody else in the neighbourhood could do that, only Johan. So while he was a 'problem child' to adults, Johan became a hero to other children. On the street they called him 'Abe' because of his endless dribbling, which reminded them of the evasive moves by Abe Lenstra, the quiffed striker at Heerenveen. Johan with a string of friends behind him, none of them able to get the ball off him, became a familiar sight in the Akkerstraat and surrounding streets.

Losing the ball – or indeed any form of losing – was the worst thing in the world for Johan. Whether he was playing ludo at home, draughts in the street with his friend Leo Happé, or football with his mates, as soon as the prospect of defeat loomed, the board game would fly through the air, or the draughts would be swept off the board as if by accident. He could spend so much time yammering on while roughly equal teams were being picked that it was impossible for the worst player to end up in his team. If it nevertheless looked as if he might lose a game in the street, on the gravel pitch at the recreation ground, on the grass between the blocks of housing or the car park next to the Ajax stadium, then to the astonishment of the others he was capable of walking away with the ball under his arm. They could all get stuffed.

Anyone who dribbled around Johan ran the risk of bruises and anyone who seemed to be better than him, like his equally skinny friend Wim van Laar, might find himself flat on his face. Sometimes they ended up fighting it out, without anyone understanding why. Card-playing evenings with his brother Henny occasionally developed into major battles. 'Losing affected me deep inside,' Johan admitted later in the book *Boem*. 'I couldn't stand losing, not even the little games I played in the street as a boy. Winning was confirmation. Losing undermined my self-confidence. It meant I was no longer what I wanted to be.'

The boy who sat staring out of the window at school came

to life whenever there was a prize to be won. In a football tournament for primary schools during the Easter holidays, he was
impossible to stop. 'Johan was all over the pitch,' his mother
remembered later. 'He took everything, did everything. Free
kicks, goal kicks, corners, everything! When the ball rolled into
the ditch, he was the first to get to it and pull it out.' When it
was the turn of the Groen van Prinsterer School team, fathers
and sons from the district got on their bicycles and rode to the
sports field to see if it was true, if there was indeed a scrawny
little kid who could do exceptional things with a football. It
was. In midfield a spindly boy in a green shirt got possession,
slalomed past three or four opponents and then past the keeper
before slipping the ball into an empty goal. Someone shouted
that there had been four goals already. 'Ah, that's nice for those
little kids. Still 3-1 then,' said a spectator who had just arrived.
At which another turned round and said, 'No, it's 4-0 to the
Groen van Prinsterer. That little bugger pulls it off every time.'

Here and there in the neighbourhood lived people who sneered
at Ajax. They could see the stadium from their windows but
never went there. Football was vulgar, the antithesis of studying and building a career. But greengrocer Manus Cruyff
thought very differently. In the Jordaan he'd been a supporter
of nearby Blauw-Wit, where his brother Dirk had made a name
for himself as a player. But since the move to the Akkerstraat,
blue-and-white Manus had become a full-on Ajax fan. His
brother-in-law, Nel's brother Gerrit Draaijer, had played several matches for Ajax 1 in 1945 as a left-winger, and that had
further strengthened the bond. As a donor and as deliverer of
fruit baskets to sick players, Manus became 'a true *Ajacied*', as
the Ajax club magazine called him.

Manus knew for certain that his son Johan would play for
Ajax 1 someday. That was clear to him at an early stage, so
on 25 April 1957, for his tenth birthday, he gave Johan a club
membership. Other boys first had to show what they could do

before being allowed to join, but not the skinny dribbler who had so often hung around on neighbouring fields, kicking balls against the walls of the stadium. He was welcomed without having to demonstrate his aptitude.

Football wasn't all that happened at Ajax. The club also had baseball and cricket teams. It wasn't long before Johan was able to show his ball skills in those games as well. 'When the two of us were allowed to take part in an Ajax youth cricket team he did everything he could to win,' says Leo Happé. 'I found it a scary sport, I was afraid of the hard ball, but Johan wasn't bothered by anything.' For years little Cruyff played baseball in the street, with drain covers as bases. He enjoyed it almost as much as soccer.

It seems incredible now, but some friends and relatives regarded Henny as more likely to become a famous footballer than skinny Johan. Henny was more solidly built; he was good with the ball and he too was immediately allowed to join the club at the age of ten. Henny proved a good defender in the B1 juniors, and with his self-confidence and charisma he seemed made for stardom. His wavy black hair and infectious laugh made him 'a real Cruyff'. But Manus expected great things from the weedy-looking Johan. He had no problem with the way his younger son endlessly rolled little balls back and forth across the dining table and kept heading footballs against his bedroom wall. He told the boy to go right ahead. Loyal and good-humoured, Manus provided Johan's team with drinks and apples, and on Saturday mornings he drove them to away games in his van, whether for soccer or baseball. The smallest among them clearly had the edge.

The adoration was mutual. 'I loved my father and admired him, because he worked terribly hard,' Johan said later. 'If he asked for something, I'd fly to get it. But he wasn't strict.' Johan respectfully called Manus 'father'. His mother was simply Nel.

He was a daddy's boy precisely because he resembled his mother. Like Nel Cruyff-Draaijer he was forthright, inflexible and persistent. For Johan, football was more than just a way of attracting attention, or having a bit of fun. That made him 'a real Draaijer'. His enthusiasm was irresistible to football-mad Manus Cruyff. Sometimes Johan was allowed to go with him in the early morning to the Centrale Markthallen in Amsterdam-West, where they stocked up on fruit and vegetables for the shop. Manus was regarded as a nice bloke; he treated the children of the neighbours upstairs to horror stories about his glass eye (the result of a childhood incident with a catapult) and adults knew him as a bit of a wag and a cheery beer drinker. Moreover, on family evenings exciting tales were told about the wartime courage of Manus and his brother Dirk, who provided food for people in hiding. Such stories can only have increased Johan's adoration of his father.

How hard and unforgettable then was the blow that came when Johan was plucked from the stage in the school hall one summer's evening in 1959. Parents and pupils nudged each other and watched as he walked across the packed hall of the Groen van Prinsterer on his way to the exit. Something had happened to his father. The farewell evening for year six, the excitement and joy of plays and songs, ended abruptly for Johan. He left behind on the stage the gift for Mr Ritchi that he'd been holding when the message came.

His mother had already hurried home and Johan arrived shortly after her. People were standing on the pavement outside. Johan saw an ambulance and police cars. Dashing through the hallway, where the family's suitcases were standing ready for a holiday in Luxembourg, he entered the living room. There he found his father moaning about a pain in his chest. The family doctor was standing beside him. Henny and Johan were sent to Mr and Mrs Happé across the street, on the first floor, next to the underpass. Even before he got there Johan cried out, profoundly distressed, 'My father is dead!'

Later in the evening that proved indeed to be the case. His

father would not be coming home. The previous evening Manus had brought juice and fruit to Henny's baseball team. To the boys what had happened must have been inconceivable; from one moment to the next your father could simply die.

At the age of forty-five, Manus Cruyff had succumbed to heart failure.

'Why me?' Johan heard his mother shout, smashing a glass in the kitchen. But he doesn't remember her crying. 'As far as that goes she's just like me,' he said later.

On the morning of the funeral he insisted on saying goodbye to his father. 'Do you think you should?' Nel Cruyff asked him. 'Just hold on to the image of your father the way he was.' But the 12-year-old insisted, and although his mother continued to protest they eventually went to the chapel of rest together. Johan walked up to the open coffin, looked at his father's pale face, his big lifeless hands, and whispered, 'Bye, Dad.'

REST IN PEACE

LOVING HUSBAND AND FATHER HERMANUS C. CRUYFF

30 OCTOBER 1913 – 8 JULY 1959

Johan was devastated by the loss. It made him ill. He was tormented by migraine attacks. When Ria Lagrand, a friend from year six, called by to visit him several months after the funeral he wasn't at home. Go and see if he's at the grave, she was told.

Ria walked from Betondorp to the Oosterbegraafplaats and after searching for a while she found her friend, sitting next to his father's gravestone, silent and lonely, intensely sorrowful under the tall trees. 'Just come with me, Johan,' Ria said. 'Johan stood up and came with me,' Ria remembers. 'What we went off to do I no longer recall. But you can be sure we didn't talk at any length about his father. We were young.'

CHAPTER THREE

A special case

After Manus's death, Johan felt drawn to father figures. Whether in his home life or at Ajax, it didn't seem to matter to him as long as he had someone to talk to. He usually sought the counsel of older men, as if their worldly wisdom calmed him, making everything fall back into place. He sought fatherly advice until long after he became an adult. He would go to see a close acquaintance, a club doctor, a masseur or a coach, and, whoever it was, the door would be opened to him. The older man would pour him a cup of tea or fry him an egg, and after a chat about something that had been on his mind, Johan would get up and leave – he never stayed long.

Johan's first father figure after Manus died was Bertus Happé, the father of his friend Leo. It was the obvious choice, since the Cruyffs and the Happés had got along well for years. To Johan, Bertus ('Appie') Happé and his wife Cor were Uncle Ap and Auntie Cor. The two fathers had both been Ajax men and if Johan's mother was very busy in the shop, Auntie Cor would briefly step in to help. The way Uncle Ap and Auntie Cor threw open the door of their nearby flat in 1959 to a family in mourning, as if it was the most natural thing in the world, made a great impression on Johan. Now that his mother was at her wits' end and the shop had to be transferred to a new owner, Uncle Ap provided a refuge just by being there. Appie, who worked at a canteen in the docklands of Amsterdam-Noord, spent all his free time helping his neighbour Nel. Auntie Cor assisted Johan's mother in the shop for those final weeks and Ap showed the new owner the ropes.

Without the help of 'family' the world can look a desolate place when you're twelve and broken by grief.

There were other friends around who offered support, but, for Johan, Uncle Ap was special. He spent hours in the Happés' flat, comforted by Leo's father. Not that much happened there – a game of Monopoly, a sandwich – but it was enough. Johan gave back, too. For example, when Leo was told at the age of thirteen that he'd have to leave Ajax because he wasn't good enough, Johan thought, 'They can't do that.' Leo had joined at the same time and they belonged there together. To Leo's amazement, Johan went to the board and said, 'If Leo has to leave, then I'm leaving too.' And he meant it.

Leo was allowed to stay. A few years later his friend was dropped all the same – he was always a reserve player and there was no future in that – but Johan had made his point. Anyone messing with Leo would be messing with him.

After the sale of the shop, Nel and the boys moved to a small ground-floor apartment at Weidestraat 37, also in Betondorp. The two families were no longer neighbours, but they stayed in touch. Decades later, when Uncle Ap and Auntie Cor flew to Barcelona at the invitation of coach Johan, Ap was introduced to Romário in Camp Nou. 'This man here was a kind of second father to me,' Cruyff told the famous player.

Another father figure, no less important than Ap, was Arend van der Wel, a friend of the Cruyffs. Johan had known him since he was a toddler. In the early 1950s, Van der Wel played in the Ajax first eleven, and because he was still attending school in the centre of town and often had to train at De Meer in the evenings, Manus arranged for him to have dinner with the Cruyffs on weekdays. It saved Arend a lot of travelling back and forth between Amsterdam-Oost and his parental home in Amsterdam-Noord. As a result, a warm friendship grew up and so Van der Wel found it natural to invite Nel and the boys to his house in Enschede in the summer of 1959. Now twenty-six and married, he played for Sportclub Enschede, having chosen it because it meant he could be in the same team as his idol Abe Lenstra.

Much to their delight, 12-year-old Johan and his brother Henny were allowed to watch training sessions at Sportclub Enschede and, even better, to have a kickabout with veteran Abe, who was thirty-eight. The Cruyffs spent some hugely enjoyable weeks in the east of the country, where Nel and the boys were able to put worries at home out of their minds. After 1959, they also had some cheerful summers holidaying as a harmonious family in the province of Twente. In those years even the Enschede coach František Fadrhonc became a father figure for Johan. Fadrhonc was a friendly man, a former refugee from Czechoslovakia, who later became the Dutch national coach. It seemed he couldn't resist the skinny lad with the vulnerable look in his eyes, because in no time Johan was visiting his house for a sandwich and a glass of milk. After Fadrhonc moved to Deventer as coach at Go Ahead, Johan continued to visit him.

There was a new father in Johan's life back home too. His name was Henk Angel and Johan had known him for years as Uncle Henk, the groundsman at Ajax. Uncle Henk was always to be found in or around the stadium, and he tended to turn a blind eye when on rainy days Johan and his friends played football in the gym (transformed into a restaurant on match days). Johan had often helped Henk pump up the balls, sweep the terraces, thread new laces, hang out flags and do practically everything else that was needed to keep professional footballers happy. The high point for Johan was scattering sand at the mouth of the goals when they got muddy in winter. The stadium would already be filled with people, and the buzz of the stands and the heroism of the players came very close then.

Some Sundays a little devil in Johan whispered to him as he scattered sand and he would shake his head dejectedly, hoping the spectators might be impressed by his expertise and think the match was about to be called off. Later, in an interview, he smiled at the memory of that impishness.

When Henk Angel's wife died in December 1961, two and a half years after the death of Manus Cruyff, it was Johan who proposed that Uncle Henk should come and eat at their house. He came, it clicked between Henk and Nel, and before very long the groundsman moved in with the Cruyffs on the Weidestraat. At fifteen Johan had a new father.

Uncle Henk was a quiet drinker of *jenever*, Dutch gin. He was eleven years older than Johan's mother, and in an atmosphere that resembled that of the Jordaan, with lace curtains at the windows and sills lined with porcelain knick-knacks, he felt comfortable from the start. The living room was often crammed with family members. Nel had nine brothers and sisters, and there were always neighbours and acquaintances who happened to be passing and were beckoned inside. Uncle Henk made his roll-ups and tossed back his bottles of bitters and found it all most convivial. As Nel's partner (they never married) he didn't create too many difficulties for Johan. The worst he might do was to growl at the nervous nail-biter – 'easy now, Johan' – from the depths of the velour-upholstered sofa. Over dinner Uncle Henk, active at Ajax since 1945, would string together anecdotes about the first eleven, and Johan listened with bated breath.

When Johan crossed the long, busy Middenweg, he stepped out of Betondorp with the De Meer stadium filling the sky before him. In the attractive 1934 building and on the training pitches around it, he was as much at home as with his mother on the Weidestraat. Small houses stood at the corners of the stadium and from an early age Johan knew which one was the home of the groundsman (who would give him hot chocolate to drink in winter), which was the home of the administrator and which the head coach. For young Johan the club was one big family with many football fathers. He knew the staff and the adult players and they knew him, calling him Jopie or Tiddler. And at the top of the list of football fathers was youth coach Jany van der Veen. All his life Cruyff would point to him as the man who made him what he became.

Trainer and former Ajax player Van der Veen, a man in his forties with dark-rimmed glasses and a sharp eye for talent, lived on the edge of Betondorp, where he'd watched 8-year-old Johan play right outside his window, on 't Zandje next to the school. It had struck him that when Johan moved, the ball barely left his feet. Later he saw the lad with incredible ball control at the club. 'I was watching the sixth eleven playing in front of the stadium,' Van der Veen said later. 'The secretary came over to me and said, "Jany, we've got ten players, do you know anyone?" At that very moment Johan rode up on his bicycle and I said to him, "Go and fetch your boots and you can join in." Ajax 6 usually lost by a long way, but that afternoon, with 14-year-old Johan playing, they won 6-0. I was promptly called in to explain myself, because of course it was strictly forbidden to let a lad like that play with the seniors.'

Johan was lucky that it was Van der Veen who took an interest in him. The youth trainer was seen as the guardian of the 'better football' that Ajax had championed since the pre-war years of English coach Jack Reynolds. Following the example of the legendary Reynolds, Van der Veen advocated technically skilful, intelligent attacking play and the club congratulated itself on his fruitful policy of using home-grown players. The youth trainer insisted on receiving the ball adroitly and thoughtful passing. Difficult situations on the pitch needed to be resolved by 'footballing', with no hint of panic or violence. 'We grew up with that,' says Johan's teammate of the time Hennie Heerland. 'After a while it was all we knew.'

So Johan's identity merged with that of Ajax; the club seeped

into his very being. As a child he put the towels out ready for
the first eleven and from time to time he ran errands for goalkeeper Eddy Pieters Graafland. He hung around at the stadium
for hours, especially on the days when his mother was cleaning
the changing rooms or the restaurant. Johan was the boy who,
during Ajax 1 training sessions, fetched balls out of the bushes
and kicked them back on to the pitch. Ajax usually had British
head coaches and occasionally they took him aside, long before
he became a senior player. Keith Spurgeon or Vic Buckingham
might get him to do power training, or give him extra hot meals
at lunchtime in the hope it would help him gain weight. Often
Johan's mother was there too, tidying the coach's house, and
would unexpectedly come upon her son eating brown beans.

Van der Veen, Spurgeon and Buckingham: three football
fathers at one club. Johan could hardly complain of a lack of
attention. According to Gerrie Splinter, who was a fellow player
in the youth team for several years, that attention was a result of
the social intelligence that enabled Johan to get his own way, to
profit from his appearance as an endearingly skinny lad, a boy
who always did his best and wanted to know everything. Later
Cruyff would admit as much, in veiled terms. There were advantages to the disadvantage of being thin and small and vulnerable.
Meanwhile, youth coach Van der Veen improved Johan's running technique and got him to exercise his weaker left leg over
and over again. The idea was that, as a two-footed player, Johan
wouldn't have to shift the ball to his right foot in order to shoot;
he would be able to act more quickly and have simpler ways to
evade opponents. Johan did Van der Veen's exercises for as long
as it took, until he dared to shoot with full force using his left.
He eventually became virtually two-footed. Hesitation, never
really a tendency of his, was rare from that point on.

Dribbling had been Cruyff's hallmark for years. Dribbling and
scoring goals. He was 'as egotistical as hell', as he later admitted.
'Because I felt I was better than the others. We needed to win,

after all. Wasn't it better if I did that alone rather than let the others spoil our chances? Exasperating, perhaps, but because of all the goals I scored, I felt again and again that I was right.'

No doubt his hogging of the ball also arose from his short-comings. You might say that his limitations forced him to invent his own game. He wasn't capable of the kind of kick that was so characteristic of the game in the early 1960s. Everywhere players kicked the ball as hard and straight as they could with their instep. It was all about 'scorching the grass'. But since that was too much to ask of his thin legs, Johan did something com-pletely different. As on the street, he dribbled past his opponents all the way to the goal. When still a small boy, in the sandpit in the recreation ground on the edge of Betondorp, he had learnt to flip the ball into the air – no one could match him at that. Elsewhere in the neighbourhood, on the gravel pitch, he had taught himself to make the ball curve with the help of the inside or outside of his foot. Falling on gravel was not to be recommended, since it resulted in cuts and grazes, and so Johan learnt to stay on his feet during quick and deft manoeuvres. At the same time, he had to avoid the legs of boys trying to block him from all sides. Curving shots, flick-ups and evasive jumps were the signature of Johan the Dribbler. At the end of a solo run, he often dribbled around the goalkeeper as well and was able to run with the ball into an empty goal. He was effective without having to shoot hard, using ingenuity in place of power, the sides of his feet instead of the instep. 'Many of our players were capable of really thwacking it with the instep,' Sjaak Swart remembers. 'The only one Van der Veen didn't insist on that with was Johan.'

He was a special case, and that was how he posed among his fellow players who, in April 1962, stood together in merry disarray on the pitch of Blauw-Wit, right next to Amsterdam's Olympic Stadium. The Ajax junior team had just won an international Easter tournament. In the background are bare poplar trees like plumes against a lead-grey sky, under Johan's

feet the flattened grass. This was his life. In the midst of his
exuberant teammates, he stands there frowning, arms crossed,
body at an angle to the lens, as if to say, 'Whaddya want?' He
looks both smaller and more serious than the other B1 juniors,
having scored two goals in the final. Below his elbow is a big
dirt mark and his fingers are grubby from falling and scram-
bling upright. Because he had to move forward. Because playing
football wasn't just a nice way to pass the time, it was the most
important thing on earth.

The difference between a photo of Johan as a stockroom
assistant at Perry van der Kar and a photo of Johan in a football
shirt is the difference between a question mark and an exclama-
tion mark. Between not being there and being there. Between
feeling browbeaten and browbeating others.

'You keep playing the ball to my left foot, but with my right
foot I can take it with me more easily and the attack gets more
pace.' Such compelling advice would still echo decades later in
the head of his then teammate Hennie Heerland. Anyone who
didn't keep their promise to pass the ball to him in the correct
manner from then on could not expect to receive any more
balls from Johan. Laziness made him furious. Sometimes the
other players stood listening to him open-mouthed when he
brought up details they weren't yet taking into account at all.
They might be annoyed by his chatter, but nevertheless they
understood that Johan was at a more advanced stage than they
were. 'He was ahead of us all,' says Heerland. 'As if he was years
older.' Where others made jokes about the exercises the coach
got them to do, Johan thought along with him, or asked questions that demonstrated a mature form of curiosity. 'Sometimes
he knew better than Van der Veen and showed as much during
the match,' Heerland says. 'After scoring a goal he'd take a long
look to the side, as if to say, "See what I mean?"'

Nice guy, that Johan, but there was rarely any fooling around,
certainly not during football.

*

The only people he respected were the Ajax 1 players he watched on Sunday afternoons along with his brother Henny. There was a platform near a stairwell at De Meer that they'd made their sacred spot. There the brothers gazed at their foot-balling heroes and later they were sometimes able to go to the Olympic Stadium, if the Dutch team was playing there. Johan would study the beautiful evasive manoeuvres and accelerations of forward Faas Wilkes. 'It was as if it didn't cost him any effort at all,' he said of Wilkes later. 'He accelerated and got past.' On the street Johan was often called Abe, but he preferred to model himself on the casual finesse of Wilkes.

But no matter how important such examples were for Johan, 2 May 1962 was the day on which he found the Great Inspiration of his life. Led out by Dutch referee Leo Horn, the teams of Real Madrid and Benfica ran on to the pitch of the Olympic Stadium in Amsterdam that Wednesday evening. They had come to compete for the European Champion Clubs' Cup. Real Madrid had won the European Cup five times in a row since the tournament began, in 1955–56, and then in 1960–61 it had gone to Benfica. Now the two top clubs were to play each other in the final of the seventh season. In the Netherlands there had been hardly any major international football since the 1930s, so anyone who dreamed of heroic deeds wanted to be there. And Johan was in that stadium. He watched every move.

DWS and Blauw-Wit always played in the Olympic Stadium, and Ajax were able to provide them with a few ball boys. Fifteen-year-old Johan and Rolf Grootenboer, already a friend of his, were among the chosen. Johan even managed to get a spot close to Real Madrid's left-winger Francisco Gento during the match and could feast his eyes on the experienced attacking winger's dribbling skills. He also soon spied Alfredo Di Stéfano, the 35-year-old centre forward who moved all over the pitch as a playmaker and was easy to recognise by his balding pate. 'I watched everything he did,' Cruyff said years later, looking back on that extraordinary evening in Amsterdam-Zuid.

He gazed in admiration at the deft leaps and blistering, accurate shots by Real's world-famous striker Ferenc Puskás and memorised all his moves. He also watched the smooth ball control of Eusébio, the Portuguese striker, only twenty years old, whose two goals helped Benfica to their 5–3 victory. Six of the eight goals were scored right before the eyes of ball boy Cruyff, and Eusébio emerged as a new European star.

In 1962 it was not yet particularly difficult to approach famous footballers in a stadium, even if they were playing in the final of the European Cup. So what did the 15-year-old Ajax junior do? 'Believe it or not, Johan simply walked over to the changing rooms,' fellow ball boy Rolf Grootenboer remembers. 'Other boys really wouldn't have dared, but he stood there talking and gesturing with the players as if it was the most normal thing in the world. He didn't seem the slightest bit starstruck.'

A few months after the European Cup final, Johan joined the A juniors, with his special youth contract. He started in September 1962 in the A2 but he soon made a magnificent debut in the top junior team, where his brother Henny was centre back at that point. Despite being only fifteen, and the youngest player, he volunteered to take a penalty in his first match, and scored. After that he regularly made his mark in the A1 juniors with artful midfield play. The high point of that season full of care-free dribbling came on 7 March 1963 at half past ten in the morning, when Johan signed his first official youth contract. The next month he would turn sixteen and then, as he put it, he'd be able to earn 'thirty a week basic'. It added up to a fairly impressive salary of fifteen hundred guilders a year. He bought a moped and rode to the cinema in the centre of town with his mother on the back. Shortly after signing his contract, he broke his leg playing football and realised the importance of a secure income, since he still got his thirty a week.

After signing the contract, he was obliged to concentrate fully on soccer. Ajax insisted he must give up baseball. That was a disappointment; Johan was mad keen on baseball. With his feel for the ball and his spatial awareness he had been a permanent member of the top junior baseball team, which won the Amsterdam championship in 1961 and 1962. He'd also won a major baseball tournament with the school team at the Frankendael ULO. He couldn't throw particularly far or hard, but as catcher he was good at thinking ahead, and once he'd got hold of the ball he could throw it lightning fast to the strategically correct baseman. Although engulfed by his chest protector, Johan had astonishing reflexes, often managing to catch even the balls that glanced off the batter's bat.

When baseball player Johan was in action, he occasionally got a walk because the distance between his knees and shoulders, already the shortest on the field, became even smaller if he bent a little. He was a cunning 'stealer' of bases and as a runner he didn't shrink from performing intimidating dives. In this popular summer game, too, Johan was a 'winner', even a 'brat', as the famous pitcher Herman Beidschat called him. Beidschat played for VVGA, close to the Ajax stadium, and he would never forget how Johan, at about the age of twelve, came up to him after a match and started asking all kinds of questions. Nineteen-year-old Beidschat could see that the 'little bastard' was genuinely interested. He decided to help him and teach him a few tricks about spinners and batting stances.

But despite his talent and passion for the summer game, he now had to stop. He didn't protest. Deep down he felt that if he wanted to make something of his life, then aside from his work at Perry van der Kar he should play football and nothing else.

So, after the summer of 1963 Johan played with the 'paid youth', the crack troops of the Ajax juniors, which didn't exactly diminish his status. The team took part in an interregional tournament in which the best Dutch juniors aged sixteen or above played each other. The KNVB was hoping to use this competition to lift professional football – still lagging behind the game played in other countries – to a new level. For Johan it meant more opposition on the pitch, because practically everyone was bigger than he was, but that didn't affect how he played. He always impressed opponents by barely needing to look at the ball when he had it in his possession, leaving him able to watch the whole field: Who's standing where? Who's running where? Where's the free space? At the same time, and this was something his teammate Barry Hulshoff in particular would never forget, he remained intensely focused on the game when the ball was far away from him. He might use a severe glance to convey to one of the team standing near him that he'd do better to go and stand somewhere else, or that next time he should pass the ball to him more quickly, since then there would be more space for him to get around his opponent. Or he might signal that his teammate should run not *here* but *there*, because Johan himself was on his way *here*.

The next day, if he was playing in the top Ajax amateur team – which wasn't officially permitted – then Johan would make his presence felt no less firmly. That was simply how it worked for him; if a team was a man short, then he'd put on his boots and join in. Different norms applied than for all the others on the Middenweg and the wunderkind always did more talking than anyone else.

There was none of that chatter when Johan was out on the town on a Saturday night. The paid youth players of Ajax all used to go to Saint-Germain-des-Prés, a revue café on the Rembrandtplein that had been converted into a bowling alley. Most of them went there for good company, to talk, and for all the other things 16- and 17-year-olds find important in life. Not Johan. All evening he would concentrate almost exclusively on the ball and the pin. For him going out meant smoking and bowling, and above all smoking and winning at bowling. He pulled out all the stops to come first, including, here too, cheating. It didn't always make him popular. 'Does that little guy really have to come with us again?' some of his teammates grumbled when the young, pale fanatic joined them at the start of the evening. Yes, that little guy, Henny's brother, had to come with them again. So he would sit all evening looking intently at the bowling balls while Henny looked at the girls.

If Johan did happen to get talking to a girl in Saint-Germain-des-Prés, there was a good chance she would later walk out on the arm of one of the other Ajax juniors. At this point, he was not the one to make conquests. Even his relationship with Ria Lagrand had got no further than the occasional stroll holding hands and the sending of touching postcards from holiday addresses:

> *Dear Ria*
> *How's it going?*
> *I wanted to ask if you're still going out with me.*
> *Yes or no if you want to write to me this month this is the address.*
> *Marisstraat 23*
> *Zandvoort*
> *Johan Cruyff*

That's how it goes when you put all your energy into football. Of course, his play steadily improved – even though he was still regularly criticised for his lack of self-control. It even got to the point where his mother had to prevent the skinny goal-getter from being deployed in the Ajax first eleven at the age of sixteen. 'I don't know whether my Johan can deal with it psychologically,' she told the club management. 'He only needs to play badly twice and his whole footballing life will be wrecked.' No matter how plagued by injuries Ajax 1 might be, the club would just have to have a bit of patience.

In May 1964 the Ajax paid youth team won the national championship. In the final, a two-legged affair, Volendam were beaten 4-1 at home and Johan's goal in particular was 'a gem' according to the club magazine. A month later he shone in a prestigious youth tournament in The Hague. Foreign clubs took part in that competition and they often had more pace, forcing Cruyff to anticipate approaching tackles and collisions even more quickly than usual. With thousands of people gathered around the main pitch of premier division club ADO, Johan had to prove his worth in short, intensive matches. Which he did. In the final, Ajax triumphed 3-0 over Dinamo Zagreb and Johan was named the tournament's best player. Afterwards the photographers immortalised him as a boy among almost-men, his sleeves rolled up, right at the front, in a white football shirt that looks big enough for two of him. From his forehead a cowlick sticks straight out, as if the effort and the sweat had stiffened his hair. Wet and proud, he stands with his team in the shadow of the stand; he has been the cleverest and quick-est, perhaps also the most cunning. In his right hand he holds a bunch of flowers, blooms casually pointing downwards. The other players went into town more often than he did, they paid less attention during training, they practised less fanatically with their weak foot, as a general rule they gave less of themselves, and now Johan Cruyff was the best of the lot.

Work was now going well too. Halfway through the season he'd got a new job, in which he felt considerably more at home than in the Perry van der Kar sporting goods shop. From among the circle of businessmen around the club, the Ajax board had found him a new employer, at the request of Cruyff's mother. In January 1964 Johan had started working for Harry Blitz. Cruyff never said much about this job, but the eighteen months he spent at Blitz's textile wholesaler Litrico, in the city centre, had quite an influence on him, especially when you consider how much importance Johan attached all his life to that other form of sport that held a ceaseless attraction for him: business. True, again it was a matter of spending the whole day packing and unpacking, sorting, labelling, checking packaged socks and sheets, under-wear and pyjamas, but there were far fewer formalities than at

Perry van der Kar. A messy kind of mercantile spirit prevailed and Johan was treasured as the little footballer of whom a great deal would be heard in the future.

Litrico was in the Nieuwe Hoogstraat, a narrow shopping street dominated by Jewish textile businesses. Less than twenty years after the war, this lively, run-down district had developed a culture of mutual help and mutual leg-pulling. Almost everyone had lost friends and relatives in the war, but, with hard work and humour, many succeeded in hiding their scars. In an atmosphere of joking and deal-making, of trust and trickery, Johan learnt more than he had at school – now that he was paying attention. As the son of retailers, he was of course already familiar with money. He had dabbled in business at a young age in Betondorp. He'd sold children's stamps door to door – 'I was determined to bring in the most profit of the whole class' – and on Saturday mornings he'd delivered bread for a local baker. He'd become good at arithmetic at the counter in the greengrocer's and had a piggy bank where he put all his earnings. He never raided the piggy bank if he could avoid it. He was always 'reluctant' to spend money, as he later admitted, and he never enjoyed buying rounds of drinks.

In a world without a father, without certainties, earning money was the same as being the strongest. 'Make sure you get with the strength,' he thought. In the Nieuwe Hoogstraat that attitude made him an able pupil, eager to learn, along with Ed Tanis, a Litrico rep and Ajax back. 'We learnt about reusing things that other people threw away, like old wrapping paper and bits of string,' says Tanis. 'The motto was: the money is lying on the street; you just need to learn to see where it is. Blitz let us sell small batches of textiles and we enjoyed the little deals we managed to make. Repeat your message again and again until you've talked someone round: I often saw him do that later.'

A born salesman, Johan – like Ed Tanis – took textile goods home with him and in front of his mother he worked out on paper how cheap the sheets, towels and face cloths had been. But before Nel Cruyff could put the things away in the linen cupboard, Johan would have cycled off with them, working his way through the neighbourhood in search of people he knew who might buy them from him at a few cents' profit. He would return deeply satisfied with the proceeds and be met with compliments from Nel. 'You're a proper businessman already!' At weekends Johan would see many Jewish businesspeople at Ajax and he loved raw beef sausage. To friends and acquaintances, he might say with a serious face, 'I'm Jewish too!' Two of his mother's older sisters, Aunt Riek and Aunt Leen, were married to Jewish men and one of them, Barend Tak, was not only a youth leader at Ajax but nowadays also his guardian.

Johan was doing increasingly well in the football business too. His fame spread all over the country and he stood out during training sessions for the KNVB youth in Zeist. Feyenoord, from Rotterdam, made a secret attempt to sign him up, which was blocked at the last moment. So, on 1 September 1964 Cruyff was number one on the agenda when the Ajax board met for the first time following the summer. The decision was made to raise his salary. Henceforth he would be paid sixty guilders a week. Even his ever-worried mother could no longer hold him back. She benefited too. With his improved football contract, plus his pay from Harry Blitz, 17-year-old Johan was able to persuade her to give up her job. He insisted that she must no longer clear up other people's mess, which he found embarrassing. No more toiling away in the changing rooms and the restaurant; from the start of the new season he would support her financially.

One of the tasks Nel did of course have to keep doing, like the other mothers, was wash his football kit. By hand, because the Cruyffs didn't yet have a modern electric washing machine. Still, even that – Johan was now beginning to gain confidence – was certain to come before long. He was part of the squad. The door to the first eleven was open.

CHAPTER FOUR

The debut

The national press made its first mention of footballer Johan Cruyff in August 1964. At the start of the new season, many newspapers printed the player selections made by premier division teams, and under the heading 'Ajax' they displayed his name, with the comment 'home grown'. But however sensational it may have been for the 17-year-old to see himself up there among the country's best senior players, as far as competition football was concerned he began the season with the juniors again. For the moment, his inclusion in the squad was limited to training sessions. Of course, he couldn't wait to make his premier division debut, but in the paid youth team he went on the offensive immediately at the end of August, scoring the first goal of the season, after just seven minutes, against Cambuur in Leeuwarden. He was also immediately injured. 'After little more than half an hour, Cruyff, who had probably suffered slight concussion in a collision with keeper Arie Mud, was taken off, which had an obvious effect on both the match and the spectators,' reported the *Leeuwarder Courant*, praising the inside right for his ability to read the game.

Excellence and seeking out danger: there you had Cruyff's play in a nutshell. For someone of his build he showed a bullish kind of courage, as if the goal was a magnet he couldn't resist. On this particular occasion he probably got into an aerial duel with the keeper rather too enthusiastically, as he continued to do for years to come, with both risks and goals as a consequence. This despite the fact that his nightmare scenario was embodied by Piet Keizer, who was four years his senior. In March 1964, Keizer, a technically skilful left-winger, had suffered a serious head injury in a collision with a defender. He almost died. Even now, at the start of the new season, he had still not fully recovered.

Cruyff knew him well. For some time there had been a special understanding between the two of them. Johan called Piet 'my example' and followed all his moves. He loved Keizer's laconic attitude, something he himself lacked. The starting point of their friendship must have been a prank Johan played on him. While Piet was training with the first team, Jopie would sometimes take his scooter, a Solex, and ride it in circles around De Meer. Several times Keizer stood beside his scooter after training swearing and cursing, having found it completely out of petrol. One day Johan was caught in the act and from that moment on they often went about together: both born in Amsterdam-Oost, slightly unusual characters, both of them shy and cheeky by turns, heavy smokers, too, one of whom could talk your ear off whereas the other, Piet, might spend minutes on end in unfathomable silence. Piet taught junior Johan how to give the ball more pace and watched over him like an older brother.

Johan's real brother Henny had not made the squad. Too much 'fun and frolics', as youth coach Jany van der Veen put it. 'Henny doesn't regard football as number one,' Johan said two years later. 'I do. There's nothing I like more.' Henny found a place for himself in the first team at Blauw-Wit, where according to Johan he was a modern left back who often moved forward. 'I think he's a magnificent player. Do you know he's twice as fast as I am?'

The damage to Johan's head wasn't serious. Shortly after the collision in Leeuwarden he was back, although again in the youth team. According to *Ajax Clubnieuws*, he engaged in 'adroit combinations' with teammates, helping them to a 7-1 victory over Elinkwijk of Utrecht. After that he spent weeks in relative anonymity, but on 25 October his moment came. Cruyff was included in the first eleven, although not in a serious league match but in a friendly against Helmondia '55.

There was every reason to insert a practice match. Partly because of Keizer's absence, Ajax 1 had started the season poorly. They had recently been defeated 4-1 at home by Heracles and in the KNVB Cup competition the team had already been knocked out by RCH, a small club from Heemstede that played in the second division, the lowest level of paid football. The papers described Ajax as 'not even a shadow of the team it was last season', even though the club had managed to finish only fifth in the league in 1963. 'For the time being we don't dare speak of a lucky Ajax,' wrote one sports reporter. Indeed, ten national championships in the bag (a record) and now in twelfth place: it was almost embarrassing.

There was hope that Cruyff could create a new impetus in Helmond and, the way he did with the juniors, 'make a great leap like a jack-in-the-box', as the club magazine put it affection-ately. As well as Keizer, several other players were injured and so, under the watchful eye of youth coach Van der Veen, who had travelled with him to North Brabant, Cruyff was allowed to taste the atmosphere for forty-five minutes. Helmondia '55 played in the second division; it seemed a sensible decision.

Jacques van der Schoot was rather disappointed when he heard which player he was to mark that afternoon. The Helmondia left back was hoping to be put up against the famous right-winger Sjaak Swart, thereby gaining an experience worth talking about at parties. Instead, in the first half, he was pre-sented with a scrawny lad whose name was new to him. His marking was effective, incidentally. Cruyff, who had been put on the right wing to keep him out of the turmoil at the centre, didn't achieve very much. Nevertheless, in the Helmondia dressing room all the talk was about him: such a grasshopper, gesturing to his teammates all the time – was that normal in Amsterdam maybe? 'So young, and such a presence, we'd never seen anything like it before,' Van der Schoot recalled later.

That aside, Cruyff failed to make any impression on the thousands of spectators who came to the stadium on that cold Sunday. Three weeks later it was to be a very different story.

On the windy morning of 15 November 1964, Johan Cruyff reported to the Centraal Station in Amsterdam. As was their usual habit with distant away games, the players, coach Vic Buckingham and several of the team's other staff took seats in the restaurant car of the wagons-lits. Despite Ajax's poor season, Johan had little to fear from the English coach. There was no way 'father figure' Buckingham was going to take any resentment out on the youngest; the coach had often given Johan extra hot meals and protected him. No problem there. Even before the train got to Amersfoort and playing cards appeared on the table, followed by steak, Buckingham told Cruyff this was going to be his big day.

His debut in the premier division.

Of course, it was a pity his mentor and friend Piet Keizer was not yet fit to play. Piet's presence in Groningen would certainly have given him moral support. Still, Keizer's injury was one of the reasons he'd been picked to take part. In the squad everyone was fighting for Keizer's place and now Johan had been given his chance.

It was hardly a matter of having to prove himself, since everyone had known for a long time what he could do. In any case, his Protestant schooling had left Cruyff with the idea that there were more things in heaven and earth. His father Manus, who he could feel watching over him, had declared until his death that Johan would be one of the greats, a player for Ajax 1. And behold, the favourite son was on his way to GVAV (later part of FC Groningen), regarded by top clubs like Ajax and Feyenoord as tough opponents. In the Oosterpark Stadium a bumpy pitch awaited the Amsterdammers, along with a hostile crowd and a strong defence. The combative eleven in Groningen were on fine form, having reached a good fourth place in the premier division, far above the hesitant Ajax, who had now fallen to thirteenth. It was the world turned upside down. But Johan had every faith. Manus was watching. Not for nothing had his father been buried right beside the De Meer stadium, close to the cemetery fence, so he could hear the cheers after every Ajax goal. And not for nothing did Johan always speak to his father briefly whenever he went past the park on the Middenweg. 'Hi, father, everything's going well at home,' he would say. Or, 'Mother's working really hard, but we're managing fine.' Manus was always nearby at important moments, so he was undoubt-edly present now.

The clock ticked towards two-thirty. The match could begin. The 16,000 spectators sat close to the pitch and the flags above the stands flapped on their poles as Cruyff ran on to the pitch from below a main stand that was full of noisy anti-Amsterdam feeling. He was wearing number 8 and playing as a striker along with Klaas Nuninga, part of a four-man forward line. As is commonly the case with struggling teams, it was a matter of waiting every week to see which formation would be deployed. This afternoon Buckingham had opted for the relatively new 4-2-4 system.

As soon as the first whistle blew, the atmosphere grew grim. While the Groningers put the visitors under pressure and created chances, there were howls of derision here and there as Johan gestured to his teammates and issued instructions. A skinny young unknown with flapping hands was acting the leader – the sober Groningers found that ridiculous. 'No sense putting him up against us,' Wilko Koning, standing at the fence at the age of twelve, remembers thinking. 'Cruyff was mocked. And I joined in with full conviction. After a while we switched to jeering.' All the same, Johan calmly ran for free balls, was agility personified and sprinted forward as soon as he saw space.

Tense-faced beforehand in the dressing room, sneaking a quick cigarette in the toilets to steady his nerves, then fluid and self-aware on the pitch – that's how it went in Groningen and that's how it would go throughout his career.

Johan evaded his opponents, who were out to get him that afternoon, as easily as if he was playing street football in Betondorp. Among them was left back Dick van Vlierden. When he found Cruyff directly ahead, he realised that tackling him would be pointless. It was as if the young forward had antennae everywhere that enabled him to keep jumping away just in time. As a result, 'that sprig', as Van Vlierden called him later, remained in one piece to the end. Johan could even feel kicks from behind before they reached him; if he'd insulted someone and they wanted to take revenge with a whack to his calves he would spring into the air like a girl with a skipping rope and run on without looking back.

The debutant's unflinching attitude caused some surprise, because Ajax were clearly inferior to GVAV and the match grew steadily scrappier – an unfavourable situation for Johan, who barely got to do any proper dribbling. The referee frequently turned a blind eye and irritation mounted on both sides. In this atmosphere of intimidation and aggressive play, few held back, and after an Ajax player had been stretchered off the Amsterdammers had to continue with ten men, since in those days no substitutions were allowed. The cause seemed hopeless. Yet for Cruyff it was not an unpleasant afternoon. He had the good fortune to be fully supported by his fellow striker Klaas Nuninga, who was back on top form for the first time since his arrival at Ajax the previous summer. Nuninga, a 24-year-old former teacher from a small town near Groningen, was an altruistic player with an old-fashioned sense of decency, who on this stormy November day did all he could to help Johan survive. 'It was natural,' he still recalls. 'You only had to give him a slap on the back if he'd missed a chance or lost possession of the ball: don't worry, Johan, just keep it up. The others did the same. Of course, it helped that he already knew what he needed to do.'

Oddly, Cruyff was left with little recollection of this 'old-time spectacle', as the local paper described it. Just three incidents stayed with him. Situation one: Nuninga cleverly plays him free in the GVAV penalty area. Cruyff attempts to strike but kicks the ball so softly towards the goal that keeper Tonnie van Leeuwen makes a show of catching it with exaggerated ease. The young and ambitious Cruyff feels humiliated.

Situation two: a corner. The ref points to the corner flag and, since Cruyff is close to the GVAV goal line at that point, he's the obvious man to take it. But until a year earlier he simply couldn't take corners; he lacked the strength to get the ball high into the penalty area. Even in the paid youth team he preferred to leave corners to others. He now had the strength, as long as he was fit, but at this point, well into the second half, he no longer was. The solution? Limp a little, grab a knee to feign an injury, until a teammate comes running up to take it. Cruyff feels both relief and embarrassment. How often does it happen that a player in the premier division lacks the nerve to take a corner? A historic moment in Cruyff's mind.

Situation three. The best of all. Four minutes before full time, with Ajax finally mounting a traditional type of attack to do something about being 3-0 down, Nuninga takes a shot at goal. Keeper Van Leeuwen, still rather shaken by his collision with Muller, only half parries the ball. Johan does what has been his trademark for years with the juniors. He dashes up and kicks the ball into the net from close range. It's his first premier division goal.

There it ended. GVAV won 3-1.

Johan had survived a battle in Groningen and it was just as well Nel Cruyff hadn't travelled there with him. She would have been shocked to the core by the rough atmosphere and might have demanded that her son stick with the youth team for now.

Instead, he was in Ajax 1 again the following week, at home against PSV. Again, the pitch was bumpy, even muddy, and there was fog and drizzle, but right from the start Johan displayed his sharp ball technique, spatial awareness and depth of thought. It felt as if he owned the main pitch at De Meer. He'd cleared it of stones along with Uncle Henk and played pre-match games there as a junior. That familiarity seemed to pay off in his first official home game. *De Telegraaf* wrote that Cruyff played 'like a field marshal'. 'It was thanks to sublime play by Klaas Nuninga and the seventeen-year-old Johan Cruyff (a promising home-grown technician) that Ajax avoided the risk of falling behind early on.' Because 'in the eighth minute the duo mounted an evasive attack that produced a chance beautifully taken by Nuninga (1-0)'.

In the remaining eighty-two minutes a harmony developed between the thoughtful, always serious-looking Groninger and the nervous Betondorper that was quite moving to watch. The former passed, the latter flew in all directions and took a shot at goal as soon as he saw an opening, whether with the right or left foot – sometimes too hastily and far from always perfectly, but at least there was no sign of any fear of failure. Everything about the little number 8 was dynamic and bouncy; halfway into the PSV half he attempted to take a free kick even while the ball was still rolling, such was his eagerness to surprise the opposition. The referee stopped him, but it illustrated his fanatical determination to reach the goal.

At 2-0 he shot from close range and hit the bottom of the bar (once more with his left foot), at which point Sjaak Swart put the ball into the back of the net on the rebound. Involved again in a goal, Cruyff raced out from between the posts, jumped up with delight and swung his arm high into the air, his loose sleeve flapping around his wrist, which made him look slightly feminine, as if he had a long scarf around his shoulder. For the rest of the match he continued to make himself available to his teammates and where necessary braced himself to prevent a PSV defender from mounting a counterattack (something that became common only years later). In the second half the 'slender, diligent young man' decided the match with a move of beautiful initiative. In a rapid counterattack he got possession of the ball with an empty pitch ahead of him. He touched the ball lightly to give it pace and then sprinted to the goal with his hands out in front of him, as if pulled along by the misty air of Amsterdam. One more light touch of the ball with his right foot for control, an upward glance for a precise assessment of goal and obstruction, of posts and keeper, then immediately a medium-high lob over the goalkeeper's head – 4-0.

He came free of the ground, and when he landed he was surrounded by his fellow players, who ruffled his hair, lifted him up for a second and addressed a few words to him as if he was a son to them all, their Jopie.

Partly because of Cruyff's profound understanding of the game, Ajax, who won 5-0, were finally playing well enough again to make the fans at De Meer, who were usually reserved, even sceptical, clap and cheer exuberantly. When it was over, youth coach Van der Veen felt quite emotional as he walked through the stadium corridors. All that dedication, all those punishing hours of practising and sweating it out with Jopie, had been worthwhile.

It was time for Cruyff's first interview. It was published in *De Tijd* with the by-line of Koos de Boer, one of a new generation of sports journalists who had decided to focus attention on a sportsman or sportswoman's character. De Boer was convinced it would be a good idea to interview this amazing new man Johan Cruyff for the regional edition. After a week of phone calls to the chairman of Ajax, Jaap van Praag, who was somewhat wary of so much attention being paid to a nervous adolescent like Jopie, he received permission. His invitation was for the day after Ajax vs PSV. On Monday 23 November 1964, De Boer walked from his editorial office to the textile wholesaler Litrico in the centre of Amsterdam.

The interviewer shook hands with a bashful lad, his shiny hair combed to one side, slightly ill at ease in a rather loose-fitting suit. It was one o'clock in the afternoon. 'Ajax is happy for you to be here,' said owner Harry Blitz, on good terms with Van Praag for years. 'But they'd like me to stay.' De Boer described Johan as 'shy, with downcast eyes', and he looked pale, younger than seventeen, waiting for his first question 'wringing his hands in his lap and glancing shyly at the photographer'.

The journalist soon noticed something remarkable. Johan's diffidence seemed to evaporate as soon as he started talking, as if the footballer was a machine he had switched on. Suddenly he didn't seem younger than seventeen but older.

When asked how it felt to become famous overnight, Cruyff laughed. 'It's all very nice,' he said. 'But how long does fame last? I've seen it with Sjaak Swart. First he was the man to watch and then last year when it didn't go so well the crowd whistled at him.'

Harry Blitz nodded his approval: sensible talk.

Johan told the interviewer about becoming a member of Ajax and how, as a 10-year-old, he hadn't needed to play a selection match. About his mother, too, who had prevented him from making his debut in Ajax 1 at the age of sixteen. And about his youth coach, Jany van der Veen, who had been so important to him. 'It's his profession, don't you agree it's a success if he's got four or five guys into the first eleven in one year?' That showed Johan was able to look beyond his own situation and had an understanding of, or at least a firm opinion about, established, nationally famous footballers. He also had an answer ready for a question as to why Ajax had given him his debut. 'Probably because I scored twelve goals in four selection matches for the UEFA youth team.'

Koos de Boer wanted to know why things had been going so badly with Ajax lately. Cruyff undoubtedly had an opinion about that, but he used a diplomatic expression rarely heard from him in future years: 'I don't know.'

The coming weekend Ajax were due to go to Rotterdam
for a confrontation with Feyenoord. Didn't that make Cruyff
nervous, given that their archrivals' stock stood so much higher?
'Those Feyenoord players are human too,' he answered. 'And on
Sunday the ball rolls in every direction.' He then volunteered
a snippet of business insight. 'Incidentally, by beating PSV, and
therefore being "in" again, we've bolstered the Feyenoord coffers by around five thousand guilders.' True enough, Ajax's 5-0
victory might well draw more people to De Kuip.

As for his own future, 'All the football cash goes into the
bank. I can't get at it until I'm twenty-one. Maybe I'll eventually be able to set up my own business. A distillery sounds like
a good option.'

There was one final pearl of wisdom about the essence of his
game: 'For me, attacking is a matter of getting free.' Plain enough.

The young footballer smiled as he posed holding a folded
and packaged pair of pyjamas. His eyes fixed expectantly on
the camera, wearing a shy grin, his tie straight: a stockroom
employee could hardly make himself any more presentable than
that. Cruyff's employer Harry Blitz will have been delighted
with the free publicity for his wholesale business, and Johan's
mother must have concluded with satisfaction that her sometimes unruly son was on the right track. That engaging photo,
that reassuring face. 'Ajax is watching carefully over talent Joh.
Cruyff.' That hopeful caption: '. . . a promise . . .'

The piece appeared on the Friday, in the run-up to the tie
with Feyenoord. To the left of Johan's interview was a preview
of 'the match of the year'. Sure enough, tickets for Feyenoord
vs Ajax had been snapped up.

It certainly was the match of the year. For Feyenoord. In De
Kuip, Ajax suffered a devastating 9-4 defeat and most of the
attention focused not on Cruyff but on the young Rotterdam
attacker Hans Venneker, who scored five goals against an Ajax
defence generally agreed to have been 'disorderly'. The players'

faith in Buckingham, already less than firm, diminished further after that painful rout. The chaos at Ajax grew, the commitment to training weakened. This was bad news for Johan, who was furthermore faced with the return of a recovered Keizer to the attack. For the time being he had to revert to the youth team or the second eleven.

On Friday 22 January 1965, Buckingham returned to Britain to manage the London club Fulham. Nobody doubted the Ajax board had asked him to go. Ajax were still rated as weak. It had been impossible to detect any logic in the composition of the team or its tactics and the players found his training sessions mind-numbing. It was time for a coach with organisational skills and authority.

When Buckingham left, Johan lost a trainer who had put extra hot meals in front of him, who had made him stronger and treated him as a special case. Such an attitude could not be expected of the new coach. When Rinus Michels arrived he didn't seem the type to give anyone preferential treatment. He was still young, just short of thirty-seven, and he didn't yet have much experience as a coach, but he did have authority. At the nearby amateur club JOS, Michels had built a reputation as an ambitious, consistent and reliable Amsterdammer. Since the summer of 1964 he had spent his free afternoons (he was a gym teacher) training the young cubs of AFC in Buitenveldert. So he was available, and in professional competitions in neighbouring countries he had seen all the ways in which those countries were more advanced than the Netherlands. The former Ajax player therefore knew both the club culture and the latest tactical developments in top-level soccer.

Michels made his debut on 24 January 1965 with a home game against MVV. For Cruyff it was good to be able to take part immediately that Sunday – Keizer had the flu. It was equally good to get two goals and a decisive pass to his name in a resounding 9–3 victory. Less good was the fact that shortly afterwards he turned up late for training. *Can happen*, he thought. After all, he'd had a dental appointment. He was told to clear off right away. Dentists, Michels said, were to be visited by professional footballers in their free time. These were working hours. Cruyff was ordered back to the dressing room. Later he had to make up the training session on his own, so that he knew the consequences of failing to behave like a professional.

Michels dealt firmly with many things and not least the behaviour of the promising, if not always thoroughly disciplined, 17-year-old he called 'that tiddler'.

CHAPTER FIVE

Go easy on Johan

In the summer of 1965 Johan Cruyff, now eighteen years old, was still not a regular player in the Ajax first eleven. Since the arrival of Michels in January he had been in the Ajax 1 team for only five of their twelve matches. His total for the 1964–65 season amounted to ten premier division matches and four goals. On occasions he had displayed 'a very good class of play', according to the club magazine, only to find himself the following week back in the second eleven. As in the juniors, he was both an outstanding talent and a source of concern. He was underweight, with a lack of self-control and a skinny frame, and he had developed an 'unhappy foot', as he called it. As the result of a neglected contusion in March, the little toe on his right foot had become inflamed and, because nothing was done about it, after a while his foot wouldn't fit into any boot. 'We briefly considered amputating the toe,' Michels said later. 'But because I don't like seeing teenagers faint, we left it at that one suggestion. Fortunately, an orthopaedist in Haarlem knew what to do. He was able to make special boots. Beautiful museum pieces, but heavy as lead. I've always been amazed that Johan could play in clogs like that.'

Happily for Cruyff, for Ajax and for the history of international football, that little toe, by now almost as thick as his big toe, was left in place. The heavy footwear was also needed to support Johan's insteps, which club doctor John Rolink described as 'too wide'. His new boots, extra broad, with lead tips and reaching above his ankles, looked old-fashioned, but Cruyff felt safer in them.

He also felt safe enough to stage a performance of his own in the Ajax boardroom. Jaap van Praag, a man as conceited as he was enterprising, who had become chair of the board a year earlier, had offered him a new contract that he couldn't accept. It had been good of the board to give him a bonus of 250 guilders at the end of the season – possibly as an incentive to behave better – but this new proposal would mean he was earning less than some of the others. He refused to swallow that. His mother had pointed out to him that an apprentice salesman earns less than an experienced rep, but that argument made little impression.

'I'm not signing,' he said in the boardroom on the first floor, where other footballers entered with deference but where he'd sat down as if he was at home. Which of course he was.

The board members looked at him in bewilderment. 'Without Ajax you'd be nowhere,' Van Praag tried. That was true; Johan had in part been brought up by the club. But for Cruyff it was no reason for humility, and when the adults across the table from him continued to defend the contract, Johan could no longer restrain himself. He became 'aggressive', as he would put it himself later. He tore it in two. His heart was thumping. 'Suit yourselves,' he said. 'And if you don't give it a reasonable second look, I'm off. There are plenty of other football clubs in the Netherlands.'

Later he wondered where he had found the 'brazen cheek' to tear up the contract. 'I think it was because I'd been part of the football world from an early age, because I'd so often heard the players in the changing rooms talking about these kinds of problems.' For as long as anyone could remember, Ajax had been a club of gossip and of shady connections, a snake pit where secret deals took place. 'You never knew what was being decided behind your back,' says former goalkeeper Jan van Drecht. 'If you didn't have influence, in the form of a father who was a club donor and could fix things for you, for instance, then you just had to do as you were told.'

Since Johan no longer had a father who could hand out jen-ever in the boardroom, and because his mother had too much respect for the top brass, he needed to do everything for him-self. His simple method was to threaten to leave. That was how he'd secured his special youth contract at the age of fifteen and now he was determined to get his own way again. 'No matter how wonderful you find football when you're young,' Cruyff reflected later, 'you'd better be very businesslike at the same time, otherwise you're finished. The whole problem is that there aren't any fixed norms in football. You have to establish the norms yourself.'

So it was that Johan rewrote the rules and shortly after the confrontation in the boardroom a new contract was drawn up for him. Along with three experienced fellow players, including Piet Keizer, from the summer of 1965 onwards he was one of Ajax's first batch of full-time professionals. He received the pay of a skilled craftsman. For the next four years he would earn 10,000 guilders a year, roughly the same amount as a pastrycook, and on top of that came the match bonuses. In return he was obliged to train more often, not only in the evenings but during the day. Plus – and this was an unusual clause – if he gained his business diploma, he would be paid an additional 5,000 guilders. That was a fabulous sum for the time. Various teammates already had a diploma and his brother Henny had passed the exam with no difficulty at all, but Johan always found it hard to concentrate on anything for long if it didn't involve a ball. He had no interest in the subject matter and the lessons gave him a headache. Ajax and his mother hoped that the generous bonus would enable Johan to overcome his aversion – or was it a disorder? Only then would he have more security for the future and more peace of mind.

Nel Cruyff and Uncle Henk Angel insisted that first of all Johan must undergo psychological testing. According to the resulting report, the top talent was 'sometimes extremely tense' and could respond with 'unease' that was hard to reconcile with his 'otherwise balanced nature'. The psychologist expected that now he was able to focus entirely on football as a full-time professional, he would be less nervous. He demonstrated that he was capable of taking the initiative 'very calmly', thereby showing himself to be mature for his years, but at the same time he was 'not yet mentally strong enough to progress without leadership'. In his daily training sessions, he was going to be given 'a bit of upbringing', by 'a man', in other words Michels. 'This will be a facing up to life that Johan has so far missed out on and which he quite badly needs if he is to have the capacity to find his way entirely independently before long,' the report went on. There were 'no psychological objections' to a life as a professional footballer, so Johan could give up his job with Harry Blitz in the centre of Amsterdam.

At last he was what he'd wanted to be all along and believed he could be: a full-time professional.

If anyone had it in him to be the father figure Cruyff needed, it was Rinus Michels. The former gym teacher would not be quick to lay a protective arm around Johan's shoulders – their relationship was too detached for that – but he provided clarity and a structured approach with predictable patterns. Rules were rules. Anyone who asked Michels for an explanation would receive a terse reply, such as 'it's best for the team'. The in-crowd mentality was a thing of the past. Michels' living arrangements were the first illustration of this. His predecessors Spurgeon and Buckingham had lived in one of the corner houses at the stadium, cosy and convenient in view of the continuing postwar housing shortage. That way they were always close by, where juniors like Johan Cruyff could easily find them. Michels, by contrast, simply drove from his own house to the stadium every morning, and after a long working day he drove back home.

To the astonishment of several of his former teammates, the Ajax centre forward of the 1940s and 50s, who had a reputation for indolence and conviviality, turned out to have become an authoritarian. Rinus was now 'Mr Michels', and he issued orders that had to be acted upon without delay. The players needed to understand that they weren't just involved in a fun game but were carrying out their assigned tasks for the good of the enterprise as a whole. A true professional served the team first, not himself. For Ajax, and in fact for all of Dutch football, this was new, a minor revolution. Michels was educated and well read – highly unusual qualities for a coach of his generation – and able to explain with perfect clarity his analyses of opponents and tactics. Drawing upon his experience at a school for deaf children, he managed to get a squad of shopkeepers, driving-school instructors and bookkeepers to repeat certain exercises for as long as it took for their combined play to become quicker and more effective. In doing so Michels explained what he was after IN-TER-MIN-AB-LY-AND-IN-A-LOUD-VOICE.

The pioneering coach sometimes resorted to downright childish punishments in his efforts to 'educate' his players. Especially at the expense of 'the tiddler', who learnt a great deal from him every day but at the same time didn't always accept everything he was told. That was the case right from the start, with preparations for the new 1965–66 season. Like the other players in the squad, Cruyff had his nose held to the grindstone. To his horror, in the summer programme the emphasis was put on running, and as far as he was concerned that turned the Amsterdamse Bos into a hell on earth. Cruyff loathed trotting through the woods in herd formation and after a while he knew every bend, every hill and every bush on the route where he could cut corners. He developed tricks for reducing the distances, making it a game he could win. 'He'd start in one of the last groups,' Sjaak Swart remembered later. 'Then he would vanish. He knew every inch of the way.' Sitting in the bushes, Johan would wait until the rest of the pack had completed a circuit before joining them at the rear, unnoticed.

One day Michels found him out. As a penalty Cruyff had to come back on his day off for extra training in the Amsterdamse Bos. As the coach had ordered, he turned up at the Bosbaan rowing lake at eight in the morning. At that same moment Michels drove up in his car and wound down the window. The collar of his pyjamas was visible under his coat. 'It's far too cold for me,' said Michels. 'I'm going back to bed.' The coach drove away leaving Johan alone beside the windy lake, Michels hoping his squad's biggest talent would stop cheating during distance running in future. It proved a vain hope.

In contrast to many of his fellow players, Cruyff did not find being drilled by Michels humiliating. He was even able to laugh about it. One day Michels said, 'Lads, all into the bath this afternoon.' Cruyff thought that was ridiculous. He'd just got out of the bath. He was keen to go and play pool and made no secret of the fact.

'If I tell you to do something, you do it,' Michels told him.

'Yeah, that's great,' Cruyff answered back. 'If you tell me to jump into that filthy ditch, I'm not going to do that either.' A fine for Cruyff. When he arrived late for training: a fine for Cruyff. When he was asked to come back in the afternoon to run circuits and coolly sat on the ball for a bit: a fine for Cruyff. Cheating at distance running, wrong training kit: fines for Cruyff. He became the most frequently punished Ajax player of the 1960s.

Yet deep down Cruyff knew that he needed discipline if he was to achieve his goal. He needed a character like Rinus Michels, the coach who assumed countless powers in the organisation and managed to create clarity and structure as a result. The 'bull', the 'slave driver', modernised the game and the club (with the help of chairman Van Praag) and its greatest talent knew perfectly well that he could make that work to his advantage. He'd given up his job with Harry Blitz for this career as a professional. No matter how often the coach barked at him and handed out fines, he saw it as 'a new phase in my life'.

Still looking for fixed patterns of play, from the first match of the season onwards Michels picked the same team. As yet he had no place for the tiddler. Still weighing just 62 kilos, Cruyff first needed to 'mature' in the second eleven. That led to some formidable initiatives in the reserve team, to some disastrous arguments with referees and to hat-tricks. After he yet again demanded an umpire should intervene because his thin legs had been kicked and was sent off as a result, the club magazine addressed him directly: 'Mouth shut!' It was too much to ask of the garrulous striker and so it would always remain.

But on the glorious Sunday afternoon of 24 October 1965 he got his chance. Klaas Nuninga was unable to play because of the flu and Cruyff seized the opportunity to attract attention nationwide. In front of 55,000 spectators in the Olympic Stadium in Amsterdam, he scored twice against the city's own DWS. First, he headed a casually curving lob from Keizer into the goal and ten minutes before time he ran past a defender, jumped adeptly over the goalkeeper who was sliding towards him and, as soon as he landed back on the ground, hit the ball into the net with his left foot. With his 'artificial' left leg, in other words. Building on Keizer's advice, he'd learnt to use his weaker leg by jumping into the air a little as he took the shot and at the same time turning his body so that he was facing in the best direction. It looked entirely natural, but it was the product of endless practice.

Johan celebrated in his own way by running off and leaping into the air, wheeling his arms. He launched himself high and forwards through the thin air of autumnal Amsterdam like a grasshopper. When the others finally got hold of him, they picked him up and carried him triumphantly above their heads like a surfboard. Of course, Johan had botched several chances in his haste to score, and some of the players had again been driven mad by his yackety-yacking, but, as one commentator observed, he was also their little brother, their pet.

Following that 2-0 victory, Cruyff was congratulated from all sides, by board members, trainers and journalists. Even Michels, not usually given to bestowing compliments, stressed that Johan had found out only that morning that he was going to play, and in light of his lack of preparation he'd delivered an extraordinary performance. Experts were lost for words, and some would later remember that Sunday afternoon as the occasion on which Johan Cruyff rose to stardom.

It was decided that, in the period after his breakthrough, the new star would play in the first team on alternate weeks. It led to extravagant compliments and an equal number of conflicts. 'One of the strongest elements of his game is playing without the ball,' a journalist contended. 'He's one of the few footballers in this country who have an ability to spot free space and he's not too lazy to throw himself into it. Cruyff could become a "great", but he needs to keep his jaws locked together during the game and refrain from gesturing to his fellow players as much as to say, "Boys, boys, what a lot you still have to learn."' In matches with the second eleven in particular, Cruyff was accused of arrogance. He sometimes kicked opposition players after losing the ball and occasionally tapped his finger to his head to confront referees with their limited brainpower.

In between times, Cruyff appeared in the newspaper *Het Parool* as a male model of sorts. The Spijkerbroekenhuis in the centre of town was having a sale and Johan, 'eighteen years old and a professional player in Ajax 1', was happy to advertise it. He was photographed wearing a coquettish cap, in a nonchalant stance with his hands in his pockets, like a pop star. As befitted a celebrity, he told *Parool* readers that his first car was a red Morris 850, the fashionable Mini made in England, which he'd bought second-hand after taking his driving test (nine lessons; passed first time). The identity of Johan's favourite singer was public knowledge now, too – Dave Berry, who, with 'This Strange Effect', had been at number one in the Top 40 for weeks. He was working hard for his business diploma, he claimed, and of course soon, in May, Ajax would be national champions.

He might be right about that. The players in the first eleven were becoming more attuned to each other by the week and gradually they were managing to stick to the 'tasks' assigned to them. In an interview Michels talked optimistically of the 'total football' that Ajax were going to play in the future, with defenders who could attack and attackers who could defend. All players must keep moving non-stop and be capable of taking the initiative in any situation, adjusting their tactics if necessary. But, ironically, the key player who rarely needed correction in this regard was seen as problem number one. The club leadership feared things might go badly wrong with the much-praised 'tiddler'. All those headlines, those lyrical commendations: Johan acted as if he was the only person on earth who understood football. He found it practically impossible to admit mistakes and he was uncommonly quick to see fellow players as rivals. His aggressive reactions might sometimes be alarming. 'During training he could be thoroughly unpleasant,' recalls goalkeeper Wim de Wit, a member of the squad at the time. 'I remember him deliberately kicking sand into my face as I dived for a ball, he was so eager to score. As if his life depended on it.'

In the boardroom at De Meer the Cruyff problem was broached yet again in late 1965. Michels said that his sanctions were having little impact on Cruyff. He had no doubt the young striker was extremely well suited to the fast-paced football of the future, but his attitude was a cause for concern time and again. Moreover, he was increasingly troubled by headaches, especially after matches, as if they placed too much strain on his nerves. The fact that he had recently been rejected for military service because of his chronic migraines was hardly a good sign. Michels therefore put an unusual suggestion to the board. He

would take the budding talent to a psychologist. The proposal
was accepted with open arms.

The psychologist was called Jan Slikboer and, as part of efforts
to make Ajax more professional, he held a weekly surgery at the
stadium. In early January 1966, Johan knocked on his door. As
requested, the striker took a number of psychological tests and had
his handwriting analysed. Slikboer was also a graphologist. The
final result was unambiguous. The report compiled by Slikboer,
who had no previous experience in sport but was able to observe
the players in a range of different situations, includes some fairly
powerful assertions. Among other things the psychologist concluded that his client had a tendency to superficiality and an
overestimation of his own abilities. 'His subjectivity prevents
him from seeing things in their proper proportions,' the file says.
In a visual sense his client was 'good, at least in theory', but that
capacity was unfortunately 'not always used in an appropriate
manner, since his attention quickly evaporates'. As was already
well known, Cruyff's speed of reaction was 'high', since he 'generally reacts impulsively or even instinctively'. The 18-year-old's
'aggression' was addressed in the report too. It was 'considerable',
and the explanation should be sought in an 'overcompensation for
a sense of inferiority and the accompanying insecurity'.

One unsurprising conclusion was that Cruyff had more talent
for attacking than for defensive play. That fitted neatly with his
'assertiveness', his 'competitiveness' and his 'impudence'. 'He
has a thoroughly egocentric-materialist mindset,' Slikboer went
on, adding that Cruyff was no more than 'reasonably' capable of
thinking of the interests of the team. He also expressed his sportsmanship more in words than in deeds. 'In adversity he makes
excuses and cannot easily acknowledge error or incapacity.' At
the same time, 'He is a very good footballer, as long as he sees
in the game an opportunity to achieve something for himself.'
There was 'little sign' of a 'tight bond' with Ajax, apparently. 'He
wants to sell himself to the highest bidder, preferably abroad.'

*

Slikboer's report cannot have encouraged Michels to give a place in the squad to the young rising star. The psychologist seemed rather to advocate putting a foot on the brake, approving of the 'go easy on Johan' approach so often heard in the boardroom. But events intervened. Cruyff was deployed in the very first important match of the year, on 9 January against Feyenoord. Henk Groot had suffered a groin injury and Jopie was put in to replace him. In a hostile De Kuip, against a team that wanted to reduce its six-point deficit at any cost, he wasn't exactly being given an easy ride.

The night before, Johan readied himself at home in the Weidestraat almost meditatively. A short time later he would describe his mental preparation for the Feyenoord vs Ajax match as follows: 'You lie in bed and walk into the stadium. Not once but ten times. You turn over and think: the ground is frozen, so watch out tomorrow. You see tens of thousands of people in the stands, who are very quiet, but after all it's only Saturday evening. And then you think: now Sjaak's going into that corner and now I move away from him, if Nuninga takes a man with him, that is, and of course you also need to see where Piet Keizer's got to. Well, see? It's more a matter of feeling, of intuition. You want to know everything precisely, but that getting unmarked that I do, I can't quite explain it, even to myself. When I have to describe it, I mean. On the pitch it all goes by itself, especially on Saturday night when I've yet to make it a reality, but that'll be the same for all players, I think. It's a nice bit of fantasising before I have a good sleep, and they call it concentration.'

The next day De Kuip was packed with 60,000 people and a raw January wind whipped across the hard, slippery pitch. But even in those tough conditions, Cruyff showed what he could do. The newspapers later praised his 'technical skill', his 'speed, ability to read the game and his firepower'. The 'youth player' had 'inexhaustible energy; he popped up everywhere in the forward line and even when he didn't have the ball, the

Feyenoord defenders were unable to take their eye off him even for a fraction of a second'. He was 'indisputably the best player on the pitch', 'swerving left to right, always in place when a Feyenoorder gave the slightest impression of not having the ball entirely under control'. Cruyff was always alert, as practically all those in the press box noted – and that in a team whose mental acuity was still described by coach Michels as below par.

But however much the journalists indulged in superlatives, the high point came with just over fifteen minutes left and with Feyenoord 1-0 ahead. Piet Keizer crossed the halfway line with the ball at his feet. The left-winger, who had dropped back into midfield as he often did, made dummy moves with his hips that threw his opponents off balance while in reality carrying on straight ahead. Then, nonchalant as a rambler kicking a stone off a woodland path, Keizer passed the ball to Johan. He did it without looking, as if he knew that his 'little brother' had taken his place out on the left and the laws of nature decreed that the ball could go only there, nowhere else. As if they'd been playing together all their lives, Keizer kicked the ball and Cruyff took it with him between two Feyenoorders into the penalty area before shooting without any hesitation with his left foot from 15 metres – 1-1. Keizer had passed an effective ball and Johan had shot it past the keeper with 'countereffect', Cruyff explained later. 'That was effect twice over. The goal could be made that way only because we always work together in training.'

There was no stopping him now. Without Cruyff, Ajax played slowly and stiffly. With him, Ajax won matches in a fluid, attacking style. When centre forward Henk Groot, brought back to Amsterdam for a considerable fee, was uninjured for once and Michels promptly deployed him, the newspapers wrote that reserve player Johan was 'the great absence'. Even the club magazine, which had so often called him to order, now described Cruyff as 'Ajax's most popular player'.

From mid-March 1966 onwards he had a permanent place

in the squad. The ideal forward line that Michels had in mind for that season – Swart–Nuninga–Groot–Keizer – would never appear on the pitch again. 'The tiddler' had benefited from the team's injuries and loss of form, and had performed optimally whenever he needed to prove himself. Perhaps psychologist Slikboer had been right to conclude that Cruyff was struggling with excessive aggression, fierce ambition and a sense of rivalry. Perhaps Johan was overcompensating for all sorts of things and had fallen prey to deplorable egocentrism. But for the time being it seemed he might actually be using those characteristics to his advantage. Everything went smoothly in the second half of the season as far as he was concerned, and there were no more negative reports. One might almost think his visits to a psychologist had done him good.

In the end he played nineteen of the thirty league matches of his breakthrough season 1965–66 and four cup matches, scoring a total of twenty-five goals, more than anyone else in the squad. As if that wasn't enough, he scored eleven times in five friendly matches. Furthermore, he was no longer stick thin. Power training had given him reasonably adult thighs, and at 1.78 metres he was no longer so short either; one reporter even wrote that he made a 'lanky impression'. Even so, 'man of class' Cruyff would need to 'get a bit more solid', because 62 kilos was still rather light.

On 15 May 1966, Ajax secured the premier division championship with a win in Enschede against FC Twente. That Sunday 'great class' was once more attributed to Cruyff. After Keizer opened the scoring at the start of the second half with an improbably hard and effective distance shot, Johan made it 0-2 with a volley. That was the final score. The club had won the national title as a result of 'a better class of football', according to *De Tijd* – and because of Cruyff, 'the most remarkable talent presented on any pitch this season'. Johan, several other players and even coach Michels were carried off the pitch shoulder high. Countless celebrations followed, which was only to be expected. This national title had come immediately after the disastrous 1964–65 season, and Ajax ended 1965–66 with a record fifty-two points in the league, one of the most remarkable performances in Dutch footballing history.

In Amsterdam, Van Praag, the Jewish chairman for whom football was showbusiness, threw one party after another. There was limitless champagne and folk singers performed typically sentimental Amsterdam songs. During a big reception in the Hilton Hotel, Cruyff felt a tap on his shoulder. There was a phone call for him. A certain Mr De Vos wanted to know whether his car had been fixed yet. 'I'll come right away,' said Cruyff. He had every reason to respond quickly. Two weeks earlier he'd been driving along the Ferdinand Bolstraat far too fast in his Mini when he hit a car coming from the right. It brought him to an abrupt standstill. The front wheel of the other vehicle, a Citroën 2CV driven by Hans de Vos, stood at right angles to the road, the mudguard almost completely wrenched off. Pedestrians rushed to the scene from all sides and someone called out, 'Well, he's better at football than at driving.' That afternoon Cruyff had been forced to admit he was in the wrong. It may well have been the first time he discovered the disadvantages of fame. If you kept appearing in the newspapers, you had to watch your step. The police showed up and Cruyff immediately offered to pay for repairs. The police officer eventually decided not to fine him, which given the long skid mark Johan's Mini had made along the tram tracks could perhaps be put down to the advantages of fame. The 2CV was driven to the Citroën garage on the Stadionplein in Amsterdam-Zuid.

Shortly after that phone call to the Hilton, Cruyff picked up victim Hans de Vos from his home in the Mini. With some difficulty, De Vos squeezed into the passenger seat and observed that his knees were above the dashboard. 'Well, that's nice if you have a girl in the car,' he said, in a reference to the miniskirt rage of the day. 'You can see everything.'

'That's partly why I drive this thing,' Cruyff said.

They arrived at the garage on the Stadionplein. To the amazement of De Vos, Cruyff was charged only 200 guilders for the repair, even though his wallet was bulging with banknotes.

'You sure that's right?' Cruyff asked. It was. Another advantage of fame.

From one day to the next, Cruyff had money. Each of the players received a bonus of almost 8,000 guilders at the end of their surprisingly successful season, so he could do without the 5,000 he would have earned by getting his business diploma. Cruyff had managed little in the way of study, despite the virtuous things he'd said to the media, and now he could forget it. The acquisition of abstract knowledge didn't appeal to him, although he would rarely admit it in public, and sustained concentration was still difficult because of his migraines. He was a professional footballer and could get through life perfectly well without diplomas.

His life was looking exciting, too. In the summer, the number of full-time professionals at Ajax grew further. With the arrival of Yugoslav Velibor Vasović, a physically and mentally seasoned central defender aged twenty-six who had a lot of international experience, the next major challenge could be faced with confidence. Michels intended to drill the players until they were able to behave like 'robots'. The team was raising its sights, and the ambitious and restless Cruyff, who wanted to show what he could do beyond the Dutch borders, could hardly wait. The European Cup tournament between national champions was about to begin.

CHAPTER SIX

A hitting motion

Johan Cruyff's first European adventure was not with Ajax but with Oranje. On 7 September 1966, at nineteen years old, he stood in line as the orchestra played the Dutch and Hungarian national anthems. It was half past eight in the evening and Johan, in black shorts and an orange shirt, looked fragile. He felt deeply moved. A few months later, when he talked about his life with his first biographer, Frank Bonte, the memory of that moment brought tears to his eyes once again. A hint of that emotion was visible in his stance as the 'Wilhelmus' echoed through De Kuip. While fellow players to his left and right stood to attention, Johan bent forward slightly. He held a hand to his mouth, as if he was secretly speaking into a microphone. Was he talking to his late father? He sometimes did that at important moments, and had Manus Cruyff still been alive there can be no doubt that he would have driven to Rotterdam to watch the match. He had always said the scrawny boy would be big one day, and there stood his son, in a packed De Kuip, listening to the national anthem as one of the greats, an international.

There was a lump in Johan's throat that he found hard to shift.

Of course, he'd worn an orange shirt before. He'd played youth matches for Oranje (and been praised for his 'easy control of the ball'). In early 1966 the persistent attempts of the national coach to have him take part – and the dogged efforts of Ajax to prevent it – had led to an informal practice game in The Hague. Against Racing Strasbourg, playing as centre forward, he'd scored three of the seven goals on 9 February. (He'd also been one of the reserves for the Oranje match against Eintracht Frankfurt in the Olympic Stadium on 2 March.) But now, as part of the Ajax squad, he was playing so well – and at 66 kilos no longer a 'shrimp' either – that resistance to giving him his official debut was abandoned.

In Rotterdam he was up against strong opponents. Hungary had a brilliant eleven that had defeated reigning champions Brazil in the 1966 World Cup. As for Oranje, the national side had failed to qualify that year. Since 1938 the Netherlands had always fallen short at the crucial moment. A draw against Hungary this Wednesday evening would be fine, a more than acceptable start to qualification for the 1968 European Championship. Expectations were low and on the Monday there were still 10,000 unsold tickets, reason enough for the football association to refuse permission for a live television broadcast. That was how it worked in those days. Despite rising prosperity levels, the masses might stay at home if they could watch the match for free from their sofas.

Cruyff was slightly dreading the game. The Hungarian striker Flórián Albert was a hero of his, he greatly admired players like Ferenc Bene and János Farkas, and during the World Cup he'd been captivated by the Hungarian team. When the match began, it showed; his play was nervous and he made mistakes. The advantage he had was that the entire Dutch attack was made up of Ajax players, with Ajax midfielder Bennie Muller behind them. To the surprise of practically everyone in Rotterdam, the Dutch played more fluently by the minute and Johan gradually got into his rhythm. After half an hour he turned adroitly away from his opponents several times, made a number of good crosses and cheered exuberantly along with the rest when PSV player Miel Pijs made it 1–0.

In the second half things got even better. Oranje set out on

an 'overwhelming offensive', according to one reporter. Johan
flashed past his opponents and took a shot at goal. Then again,
and again. With his agility and his skill at reading the game, he
caused continual unease in the opposition defence. Even after
losing possession he kept moving, looking for ways to disturb the
Hungarians as they mounted attacks of their own. It would later
be called closing gaps – and Johan had already been doing that
during training at Ajax, and in practice games with the Oranje
youth team in Zeist. To quote Ajax youth trainer Jany van der
Veen, 'A footballer like that simply feels what the coach wants.'
In the words of Cruyff, years later, 'What was demanded on the
pitch was actually what I was cut out to do.' It was as if he did
whatever he liked, one newspaper wrote. Clearly national coach
Georg Kessler – taking his cue from Michels – had sent him on
to the pitch without too many instructions and allowed him to do
what struck him as right. Although he didn't always manage to
keep his balance, De Kuip fell under the spell of the eager and persistent centre forward. The crowd shouted, 'Cruyf-fie, Cruyf-fie!'

In the fifty-second minute, it happened. The troublemaker,
'that cheeky Amsterdam youngster', intercepted a ball at the
halfway line that had been kicked away by the Dutch defence.
The interception took the form of a volley to Klaas Nuninga,
who was standing diagonally behind him. By the time the ball
landed, Cruyff had turned round and sprinted forward, past an
opponent for whom it was all going too quickly. And he kept
running, because Nuninga would now naturally give the ball
back to him, which is exactly what Nuninga did, at precisely the
right moment and between two astonished backs, so that Johan
could approach the Hungarian goal unhindered. The crowd
rose in a cloud of desire – yessss! – and then Cruyffie scored
with his left, quick as a flash, without the slightest hesitation.

Two-nil. How was it possible? The debutant vanished into a
mass hug, then pulled free to thank nearby Nuninga for the successful one-two before disappearing into another group of huggers.

As so often happens when players are unused to getting the

better of top teams, Oranje were paralysed and the match ended 2-2. A good result all the same, everyone agreed. 'My debut exceeded my expectations,' Cruyff told journalists as he stuffed his sweaty kit into his sports bag. 'At the start I was a bit nervous, but later I felt just as comfortable as with Ajax. Shame I didn't score that goal a bit earlier in the match; then I might have been able to get a few more in. Hearing the crowd shout "Cruyf-fie, Cruyf-fie!" was fantastic.'

Everything about this season was fantastic, it seemed, at Ajax too. He was in the squad right from the first league match, and the team gradually adopted a fixed form. It wasn't long before the fans knew it by heart. Bals–Suurbier–Pronk–Soetekouw–Van Duivenbode–Muller–Groot–Swart–Nuninga–Cruyff–Keizer formed a tight crew whose members understood each other better by the week. It was good for their symbiosis that the older, thoughtful Henk Groot, squeezed out of the forward line by Cruyff, now usually played in midfield. 'Jopie' had just as good a rapport with him as with Keizer. The midfielder was adept at passing and had an eye for free space, so an intelligent triangle quickly developed: Groot–Keizer–Cruyff. 'I liked to pass the ball to Johan or Piet,' Groot remembers. 'They saw it. And they saw that I saw it. Players recognise that in each other. But if I'm honest I liked best of all to slip the ball to Piet. He was more socially minded than Johan by nature and more often passed the ball back. Johan had rather too many egotistical traits for my liking.'

The team functioned almost like a harmonious family, with the 'egotistical' Johan as the youngest who could get away with a lot. His chatter only increased as he gained in confidence. Groot would sometimes shout, 'Shut your gob for once, Tiddler.' But it never lasted for long. 'After a while he just went on yackety-yacking,' Groot remembered later. 'The tiddler was a bundle of nerves who meddled in everything and always had an opinion. I have to admit he was almost always right, but he

really did blather on too much.' Cruyff was so garrulous that
the players called him Flipper, after the popular television series
about a clever, cheerfully chattering dolphin.

In the premier division Ajax collected victories as if they
were postage stamps. A pattern emerged, on the pitch but also
beyond. No point changing something that works, so preparation for matches was increasingly made up of fixed rituals, and
nervy Johan perhaps stuck to them more doggedly than the rest.
He always had uncleaned football boots with him that could be
touched only by defender Ton Pronk. He always changed fifteen minutes before the start of the match. With three minutes
to go, he was last but one to get on to Salo Muller's massage
table and when he was done the masseur would grip his hands,
so that the tension flowed out of him. When Cruyff got to his
feet, Muller was to hold up two fingers, the number of goals
the striker was certain to score.

Then he would wait until all the other players had left the
changing room. He didn't want to arrive on the pitch any
sooner than that. 'To check everyone was there,' he said later.
'Seriously, I mean it. I always need to have everything under
control. You can't have someone still sitting on the toilet or
something when you go out.' His superstition also dictated that
he ran on to the field last, bouncing the ball, with fresh chewing
gum in his mouth. On entering the centre circle, where the
others lined up side by side and greeted the crowd, he would
give goalkeeper Bals an almost invisible pat on the stomach. The
goalkeeper brought serenity to the team, perhaps that was why.
After a while the calm Utrechter and the restless Betondorper
began sharing a room at training camps, as yin and yang.

When the match was about to start and Bals had positioned
himself in his goal, Cruyff would kick the ball into his hands.
On hearing the referee's whistle, he would spit out his gum
and kick it into the opposition half. All these rituals had to be
observed, otherwise things would go wrong.

*

The European Champion Clubs' Cup, commonly known as the European Cup, interrupted the established rhythm. In the first round Ajax was to play Beşiktaş, a relatively unknown club from Turkey that nevertheless worried Michels because of its tough, defensive game and the intimidation his players could expect. So, on Sunday 25 September 1966, three days before the match in the Olympic Stadium, the Ajax squad withdrew to Zeist. Cruyff was generally far from keen on attending training camps. He referred to it as 'going camping'. He always enjoyed training as long as it meant practising with a ball, but a training camp usually involved many hours of waiting around at the KNVB sports complex. Other players spent their time playing pool, table tennis or cards, but Johan stood little chance of winning at those, so if money was at stake he preferred to watch how others got on. 'Which gets boring,' he admitted later. 'I'm a nervous type. That's why I talk so much, that's why I eat four times a day, and that's why I'm too impatient to sit in my chair for more than half an hour at a training camp.'

Then there were the walks. To improve their concentration, Michels took the Ajax squad into the woods. The first few minutes weren't too bad. The players pelted each other with pine cones and acorns, even with toadstools – they thought that was great. But before long, when the fun of horsing around wore off, Johan would sigh, 'Mr Michels, are we going far?'

'A lot further yet, lad,' the coach would growl. He was passionate about training camps, if only because they meant he didn't need to cycle to the Leidseplein in the evenings to check on his players. At the start of the competition, he'd found Piet Keizer in a bar at midnight and had given the left-winger a three-match ban.

'But then we'll have to walk all the way back,' said Cruyff. A little later he said, 'It's crazy to drag yourself all this way across the sand. Is that any way to get fitter?'

Johan could say what he liked. Michels, for whom explaining amounted to surrendering authority, trudged on in silence.

Like his first international for Oranje, Johan's debut in the European Cup was not shown live on television. Again there were thousands of unsold tickets two days before the match in the Olympic Stadium. When the stadium filled up after all, it was too late to reverse that decision. Cruyff walked through the double row of ball boys on 28 September surrounded by no fewer than 60,000 spectators. Will he have cast his mind back to that beautiful evening in 1962 when he was a ball boy here at the final between Real Madrid and Benfica? A sense of triumph would have been appropriate, but it seems more likely that, as usual, he was as tense as a coiled spring. Rightly so, as it turned out, because his first European Cup match was a disappointment. Beşiktaş, dressed in aggressive black-and-white striped shirts and black shorts, put more emphasis on defence than Michels had predicted. For Cruyff that meant he was continually shadowed and had little space to get around his opponents. There was always a push to his back, a raised thigh, an elbow or a pinch to his belly that threw him off balance. Nuninga later called the irritating time-wasting by the Turks 'unsporting'. Swart said he was 'sick to death' of all the thuggery and after a while Keizer, who'd had enough, lay down and stretched out on the grass, disillusioned. Even the English referee Jack Taylor said it had been an 'exceptionally annoying' match.

So these were the 'different norms' in international football that Michels had warned them about. The Ajax players responded by playing too hastily, making minor errors as a result, and consequently getting more and more nervous. Cruyff created unusually few chances and at one point shot a ball high over the goal from close range. Even after Keizer made it 1-0 from a free kick, Ajax remained agitated. The team's nervousness increased the more the Turks slowed the game down, with tactics that included lying on the pitch for an unnecessarily long time after collisions and firing the ball into the crowd, behaviour rarely seen in the Dutch premier division.

Although Ajax made it 2-0 in the second half with a goal

by Muller, the players felt bewildered when it was over, tormented by the Turks' rock-hard defensive football. While Swart and Keizer were still stumbling about in the changing room, Cruyff, already dressed, said, 'Those guys were so mean. They closed in from behind, and then those sneaky elbows . . . What a shambles. I can't play football like that.'

A week later, on 5 October, Cruyff created an artwork of historic beauty. It lasted ten seconds. The away game in Istanbul had not proven 'hellish' after all, partly because the match took place in the afternoon and Michels had strengthened his midfield. Aside from an initial offensive, the fanatical Turkish attacks hadn't been so bad (even though players were thumped and punched, and soldiers with carbines were stationed behind the fence). But fifteen minutes into the second half, after Beşiktaş scored and as a result gained sufficient courage to put the Dutch under pressure, something needed to be done. Lone striker Johan Cruyff did what he had to do. The start of a Turkish attack was interrupted near the halfway line and Keizer immediately turned a speculative ball his way. In the second it took the ball to reach him, Cruyff surveyed his surroundings. He was able to transform receiving the ball into a kick ahead, an acceleration that surprised two Turks simultaneously. Leaning forwards, he ran between them and gave the ball a tap with his left, then, because a Turkish leg was approaching, he immediately gave the ball another tap, but a very different one this time, as if he and the ball together were a startled deer springing over a fallen log to freedom. Out of the corner of his right eye he saw two backs running towards him. He almost overreached himself but, half falling forwards, remained on his feet. He suddenly slowed, to fool an opponent, then took the ball to the left with him after all, running into the left side of the penalty area. There he accelerated again and then fell – deliberately, since that got him to the onward rolling ball slightly ahead of a defender – and as he slid he shoved the ball sideways across the goal, where Swart savoured putting it in the net.

Cruyff ran out of the penalty area as if chased by a bear and did one of his arm-wheeling jumps, proud of his preparation, his seven touches of the ball in a 50-metre run. His teammates stretched to their full height with joy as they leapt into the air all around him in mad disarray: 1-1. Just before the final whistle, Keizer sent a Turkish defender off in all directions and, skidding on his right foot, brought salvation – 1-2. Ajax were through to the second round. Michels had been right. In Europe you had to play realistically, as it was termed, awaiting your moment and knowing when to strike. Cool and hard. There was no place in the modern game for romanticism, as even Cruyff, 'always difficult and plugging away to the last metre', understood. The future belonged to players with the mentality of soldiers – Michels was now more convinced of that than ever.

Soldier Cruyff understood what Michels meant. He regarded the coach, with his sometimes childish punishments interspersed with drily comical jokes, as a 'great guy'. Michels gave Johan valuable tips: keep an eye on fellow players and on the use of space when on the attack, make the space small when you're defending, and always concentrate. He further increased the intensity of training sessions and made cynical remarks about players who disappointed him. They had to be able to take it. As in the youth team, Cruyff had no difficulty absorbing all those comments and criticisms, even though Michels continued to think him too egotistical during matches. 'Michels paid attention to detail,' Cruyff said later. 'Pay attention, that's where it starts. If you don't, you can't see the details. You learn to watch for things like: is one of your team in the match or not? Should you help him? What are the opponent's strong points?'

The toughness Michels wanted in his players fitted well with the year 1966 in some ways. The whole of Dutch society seemed to be hardening and nowhere in the traditionally law-abiding Netherlands could the atmosphere be as grim as in Amsterdam. The wedding between Princess Beatrix of the Netherlands and her German fiancé Claus von Amsberg in March 1966 was marked by major riots. Young people plastered the walls of the city centre with 'Claus *raus!*' and 'Clausewitz', references to the new prince's former membership of the *Wehrmacht* and the Hitler Youth. To the dismay of law-abiding citizens, smoke bombs were thrown in front of the royal coach, and when the wedding was over the city became a scene of violence and chaos. In the months that followed, street battles broke out between construction workers, students, young people and the police. The joviality of 'magic centre' Amsterdam, inspired by the pro-vocative postwar generation, seemed to have come to an abrupt halt. Even the 'happenings' around the Lieverdje statue on the Spui had grown bigger and bigger, until they were eventually tackled with brute force by the police.

Disruption became a reality in the football stadiums too. The 'sport-crazed' on the terraces pelted opponents and referees with leather cushions and beer bottles as if they were just having a bit of fun. Spectators had lost control of themselves, the board in De Meer concluded, so there was no other option but to protect players and officials with a movable fence. Caging off the stands from the pitch, the board felt, was a necessary response to the recent collapse of moral standards.

These excesses, or 'South American practices', occurred even at Oranje matches. People would be talking about them for months to come, and on 6 November 1966 the instiga-tor was none other than Johan Cruyff. At first little seemed to be happening that Sunday afternoon. The Netherlands vs Czechoslovakia was a friendly match. Long shafts of sunlight were cast across the pitch in the Olympic Stadium and the Czechs felt no obligation to show the 56,000 spectators more than a few well-judged crosses. Johan alone was truly doing his best. He stood at the tip of the attack formation and fought a lonely battle there, watched from a distance by his fellow attack-ing players. For almost the entire match he'd been faced with having to compete, on his own, against the three best Czechs:

two wily and experienced central defenders and goalkeeper
Ivo Viktor. Every time the backs failed with their pushing and
pulling to prevent him from shooting, there was the damned
keeper, who kept flicking the ball away from the corner of the
goal. The Dutch found themselves an undeserved 2-1 down and
thirteen minutes before the end Cruyff's fuses blew. The mean-
tempered little bastard from the paid youth team and the Ajax
second eleven suddenly surfaced in him, like a bright flash in
the stadium, from which the sunshine had already disappeared.

Yet another hopelessly high ball arrived from the Dutch
defence. It flew unreachably over Cruyff's head and that must
have been what caused the short circuit. Several metres short of
the penalty area, he gave a vicious kick to a Czech defender who
was running between him and the ball. He missed. A Czech
leg swished upwards with the shock. Horror spread across the
stands in waves. Goalkeeper Viktor easily caught the bouncing ball, and the referee blew his whistle and stormed angrily
towards Cruyff.

Facing away from the goal, Cruyff gave a backwards kick in
the direction of one of the opposing backs. Again he missed.
He then turned round like a startled horse – suggesting that he
was the one being kicked, or perhaps wanting to set about his
tormentor but restraining himself.

The Czechs pointed at him: there he is, the man-kicker.
Cruyff bent over guiltily to fiddle with his boot, and when he
straightened up and saw the referee approaching he made a kicking motion to demonstrate what had been done to him. The
37-year-old ref from East Germany, Rudi Glöckner, gestured
to him to beat it.

Johan looked like a schoolboy caught in the act and did as
he was told. But after a few paces he decided once again to
check the condition of his boot, because his mate Piet Keizer
had now gone over to Glöckner to point out what a hard game
the Czechs were playing. Cruyff straightened up for the second
time, walked over to the pair and looked Glöckner in the eye

from very close. He said something, signalled something, and then Keizer resolutely pulled him away. Too late. Brisk and authoritative, Glöckner pointed to the main stand, where the dressing rooms were. For the first time in history, a Dutch player was sent off in an official international.

At the touchline Johan felt his temple and closed his eyes. He was back at square one, despite all his resolutions: a brat with no self-control. Awkward and immature. And it was on television too. He neatened his hair, looked to one side for a moment, then ahead again, before disappearing in the direction of the changing rooms. In the path between the stands he heard applause from left and right and shouts of 'Cruyf-fie, Cruyf-fie!'

For the rest of the match he sat with an assistant national coach in the Olympic Stadium's dressing room, behind a closed door. So he could not see, even if he could perhaps hear, that on the pitch it was all getting totally out of hand. A Czech foul went unpunished, after which dozens of spectators angrily ran on to the pitch, followed by photographers and stewards. When the match ended the pitch was invaded again and punches were thrown. An attack on the referee was narrowly averted. Glöckner needed police protection as he left the field, cushions and bottles raining down on him. Shouts of '*Schweinhund!*' and '*Sieg Heil!*' were also hurled at the East German.

The following morning the newspapers described the scenes as 'unworthy of sport', a 'scandalous, shameful display'. Action would have to be taken. There was talk of fencing off the spectators even at the Olympic Stadium and the decision was made to deploy more police officers, dogs and attendants at future matches.

It was the first 'Cruyff affair'. The central character in the tragedy had twice kicked out at a player, but oddly that had not been the reason for his sending-off. On the match registration sheet Rudi Glöckner wrote that the Dutch number 9 had hit him. 'I most certainly did not send Cruyff off for kicking out at opponents,' the referee said. 'The Czechs had got up to quite a few things themselves. But when I tried to separate the gentlemen, Cruyff hit me right in the face.' For his part, the culprit, whom Glöckner described as 'a very good but dangerously undisciplined player', responded by saying, 'Of course I'm not going to hit the referee. Who would take such a thing into his head?' And, 'When I felt something I pulled free. It's certainly possible I touched him, but I don't remember anything about that. It all happened so quickly.' So *if* he had hit the ref – who was 'upset' – then 'it certainly wasn't deliberate'.

The term 'hitting motion', consistently used in the Dutch press coverage of the incident, would follow Cruyff for the rest of his life. He was so troubled by it that in his autobiography, which appeared shortly before his death, he suggested his sending-off was a result of talking back to the referee. In this particular match, unlike others, that was definitely not the case.

In the trams, bars and shops, the 'Cruyff affair' was explored from all angles. Maybe he didn't hit the ref, but he was certainly a difficult young man, 'swollen-headed' even, as one newspaper wrote, whose behaviour was a 'flagrant violation of the norms of civility'. He needed to be reined in, otherwise Cassius Cruyff, as *Voetbal International* called him, would come to grief. Ajax chairman Jaap van Praag had a word to say on the matter too. He assured newspaper readers that Johan was a pleasant young man, a sweet young man even, and that he was absolutely not too big for his breeches. Of course Cruyff must be punished, but Van Praag feared that the disciplinary committee would blame the youngest player for everything that had gone wrong in the Olympic Stadium, including the verbal abuse and the flinging of cushions. He was far from wrong.

On the evening of Friday 11 November, the Cruyff affair was addressed in the Hotel Terminus in Utrecht. In a rented room the defendant, neatly dressed in a suit and tie, explained once more that he hadn't hit anyone. At least, a minor tap might have taken place, not deliberate but as a reflex amid the commotion.

'On the pitch I'm simply nothing but movement,' he said. 'Maybe I even touched him slightly, but then that's pure chance. Hit the man ... Nonsense!' Again the television pictures were shown and, as had been determined in room 21, even in slow motion there was no sign of a blow to the referee's face.

It seems the football association's disciplinary commission smelt a rat. It tried to turn the attention to Cruyff's kicking out at players – precisely what Jaap van Praag was keen to avoid. Eventually, after hearing from three witnesses, the committee settled upon a remarkably harsh punishment. It didn't speak of specific kicks or punches, it was all a matter of Cruyff's behaviour in general. It had been unacceptable and so as a penalty he could not play for Oranje for a period of twelve months

It seemed Johan Cruyff had been chosen to set an example for everything that was in danger of going wrong in football, on the stands, in the stadiums and far beyond.

The scapegoat was utterly downcast. His closed eyes as he left the pitch had been enough to show he was deeply ashamed. The footballer who was seen as a rebel regarded playing for the Dutch team as an honour. 'It's terrible that I can't be part of Mr Kessler's team any longer,' he said meekly.

On Sunday 13 November, two days after the meeting in Utrecht, Cruyff had to play against Feyenoord at home again. Once more there were disturbances. The police turned out in Watergraafsmeer in large numbers that Sunday, charged at crowds near the stadium and made arrests. Several black-marketeers were led away. The police seemed to seize upon any pretext, this time a conflict between Ajax and Feyenoord over tickets, as sufficient reason to get stuck in. The initially so idyllic De Meer looked like a 'fortress', one newspaper wrote. Five minutes before the start of the match the Feyenoord song 'Hand in Hand' sounded from the speakers, part of a desperate attempt to preserve honourable sportsmanship. Then Van Praag spoke to the crowd, requesting the fans to greet the Feyenoord players with warm applause when they came on to the pitch.

For the first half-hour of the match, Cruyff was even more nervous than usual. He was timid, he later admitted, 'a bit afraid', because he felt 'all eyes were on me'. 'It was lucky I got lots of balls, but it was only when I noticed that I could trick an opponent again that I got real self-confidence.' He fooled Feyenoord defender Rinus Israël by acting as if he was about to pass him on the inside and instead going out around him, at which point Israël tumbled backwards and Johan sent in a cross from the left that enabled Swart to make it 2-0. His humiliating evasive move had produced a goal: food for Johan's soul. He got into his stride immediately then and later that afternoon made it 4-0 and 5-0. 'I'm the type that likes to trick people,' he said. 'Twice over, if I can. Then a defender or a back thinks: I say, I've just been made fool of by that whippersnapper. It may be hard to take, but I enjoy being quicker or niftier.'

After twelve matches, Ajax were three points ahead of Feyenoord at the top of the premier division. They had scored forty-five goals in the process, almost four per match. The forward line of Swart–Cruyff–Nuninga–Keizer was grabbing all the headlines. Two matches and twelve goals later, Liverpool FC awaited, national champions of the country that had won the World Cup the previous summer. It seemed unthinkable that the Netherlands' most highly rated striker could come up with a comparable performance against the English side in the Olympic Stadium. A modest victory would be quite wonderful enough, and from early December onwards, they also had to contend with a persistent thick fog that hung over the Dutch capital.

CHAPTER SEVEN

Gadabout of the Leidseplein

Tickets for the European Cup match between Ajax and Liverpool were sold out well in advance and therefore the game was shown live on television. But most viewers saw little of it. Even the spectators in the Olympic Stadium, now behind fences and barbed wire, had difficulty following Ajax (in an all-white strip) and Liverpool (all red). The fog was so dense that the match should really have been abandoned. For reasons that remain unclear, the referee, a sun-tanned Italian called Antonio Sbardella, gave the go-ahead. Beforehand, everyone at Ajax was on edge. Chairman Van Praag seemed to faint in the afternoon and then Piet Keizer withdrew with an ankle injury. Nevertheless, the ball was in the goal in the third minute. Substitute Cees de Wolf, a player almost unknown to the fans, headed in a high cross from Henk Groot: 1-0. Fifteen minutes later Nuninga, after a clever solo effort by Swart, took a shot. Keeper Tommy Lawrence deflected the ball back and Cruyff, alert as ever, slipped it into the empty goal: 2-0. In the voice of television commentator Herman Kuiphof – 'and a goal!' – you could hear joyful astonishment and, on the stands, full-grown men almost jigged themselves out of their winter coats.

Nuninga scored from a free kick by Swart: 3-0. Swart delivered a cross from the right, Cruyff leapt from the back line in front of a defender to move the ball onwards and Nuninga shot from close range: 4-0. 'This is great!' Kuiphof shouted, and so it was. The stadium echoed to the sound of 'De Zilvervloot', an old song by Jan Pieter Heije about the capture by the Dutch of the Spanish fleet in 1628. A choir of 62,500 kept itself warm at three degrees Celsius by repeating the chorus over and over: 'He has won, the silver flee-ee-ee-eet.' Those who could see little or nothing of this historic victory through the fog could still raise their voices for the song of triumph of seventeenth-century seafarer Piet Hein. It was spontaneous. Two months earlier, an attempt at communal singing during Ajax vs Beşiktaş had failed. But this evening, without a band or any other preparations laid on, people clearly got a lot more fun out of it. A tradition was born.

In the sixtieth minute, Henk Groot scored from a free kick: 5-0. Just before the end defender Chris Lawler made it 5-1 with a header, but that was not enough to prevent Liverpool going down to the biggest ever defeat of an English team in the European Cup.

Afterwards Cruyff beamed, his eyes, wide with adrenaline, contrasting with his narrow tie. 'Magnificent,' he said to the press. 'Fantastic.' The huge bruise on his left buttock, caused by a collision with defender Ron Yeats, was of secondary importance now. The same went for the injuries suffered by his teammates in their encounter with the hard-playing Brits. The first ever Dutch demolition of a top foreign team made the pain fade quickly. 'This 5-1 victory is the first bit of evidence that our team is a force to be reckoned with at an international level,' Michels claimed.

The away game was scheduled for just a week hence. So off to Beatle City, as the newspapers wrote. Fourteenth December 1966 would be the moment of truth, even more than 7 December had been. Liverpool would of course be determined to erase the shame of Amsterdam. If the fog had caused any underestimation of the Dutch team, that was over now. It was foggy again, but the atmosphere could not have been more different. The crowd made a tremendous racket. Ajax were not allowed to warm up on the pitch, so Michels sent them out an hour and a quarter ahead of the opening whistle to get used to the ambience. These were the 'different rules' elsewhere in Europe that the coach had so often told the players about. Coins were thrown on to the pitch and when Michels picked up a few of them he saw they had been sharpened. From the feared stands behind one of the goals, Spion Kop, came a roar that made 'De Zilvervloot' seem like a lullaby. From 'God Save the Queen' to 'She Loves You' by The Beatles, everything seemed intimidating and bloodthirsty. Shouts for striker Ian St John echoed across the pitch, thundering through Ajax diaphragms. They'd never experienced anything like this, not from such close proximity.

The match had barely begun before some of the Liverpool fans lay pale and retching against the advertising hoardings, so great was the crush. With ambulance men walking back and forth, Michels could not even see Johan as he glided through the Liverpool defence, dynamic and fearless. Michels was further distracted by unconscious spectators who were passed down over the heads of the crowd like sacks of flour. Ajax manfully withstood the Liverpool attacks and managed to reach half-time with the score at 0–0. Then came the miracle. Twice Ajax broke out to the left via Piet Keizer. Both times the ball ended up low in front of the goal and the entirely unmarked Cruyff scored with his right. The goal-getter sprang into the air, arms wheeling, and the six hundred Ajax supporters who had made the trip sang the song about Piet Hein and yelled, 'Cruyf-fie, Cruyf-fie!'

Asked twenty years later about the best goal of his career, Cruyff said, 'Those two away against Liverpool, in 1966, they made a great impression. Those were two identical goals.'

The result was 2–2, in truth a greater achievement than the 5–1 in Amsterdam. As if they were well aware of that fact, the players sat in the dressing room after the match, 'naked on the benches' as a reporter noted, 'with blue and yellow bruises, hematomas, and trickles of blood flowing from shins, heads and eyebrows'. Michels watched in silence. His team was through to the next round. 'It's the best day of my life,' he mumbled to journalists. 'I cannot recall a single day, no, even single hour when I've been so happy.'

Johan Cruyff – 'that went nicely' – got into the shower singing. Along with the others he struck up a song about Liverpool coach Bill Shankly, who had bragged that Ajax would be beaten 7-0. It was like the soundtrack of a school trip: 'Shankly better pack his bags, hi–ha–ho.'

Some 5 million Dutch people (out of a population of 12 million) had watched the match on TV. Only the wedding of Beatrix and Claus that same year had drawn more of them to their television sets. Cruyff's brilliance and his goals made an impression on many and so, partly because of his reputation as an exceptional talent with explosive tendencies, he began to rise above the domain of sport. Cruyff became a national figure, a phenomenon. He couldn't walk off the training field in the afternoons without children crowding around to get their idol's autograph. Every day, fan mail landed on the doormat in Betondorp, letters and cards from boys who wanted to be him and girls who wanted to be with him. Even adults came up to him more and more often, their demeanour suggesting they'd known him for years. But he showed more reserve with them than he did with children: What does that man want from me? Is he interested in me or in the name I've made for myself?

There was something to be said for that hesitancy. Outsiders were trying in various ways to earn money from Ajax's success, a fact that had not escaped Cruyff's attention. Records with radio fragments from the Ajax vs Liverpool match and with Ajax songs came on to the market, for instance. Singers and the music trade did well out of sales of records featuring 'In One Slipper and One Old Football Boot' and 'Cruyffie', but none of it earned the players anything. 'Johan, want to try a bit of cheese?' went an advertisement on the sports pages. Everyone knew which Johan was meant, but was Cruyff getting a cut? Meanwhile, even serious weeklies like *Elsevier Weekblad* put the Ajax forwards on the cover, like cool-looking beat musicians. But however enjoyable that may have been, 'the carefully nurtured, delicate hothouse plant Johan' got little more than small change out of it. So when a man called Frank Bonte walked up to him and proposed writing a book about his life, the shopkeeper in Johan was wide awake. His reaction consisted of four words:

'What do I get?'

Bonte didn't have an answer ready. He was a freelancer who worked for the *Leidsch Dagblad*, a sports fan with a law degree who was simply mad about Cruyff. Bonte consulted the publishing company. It was willing to spend 10,000 guilders, a sum that made Cruyff willing to talk about his life and his brief career. In the thirty-page *Oog in oog met Johan Cruyff*, published in March 1967, Johan talks about the loss of his father, about his love of children and his aversion to the long-haired contemporaries of his who came to blows with the police. 'If you've got so much time on your hands, you must be pretty lazy,' he said.

The trick was to cash in quickly, it seemed. Tomorrow it might all be over. At any rate he no longer had to pay for boots. He was even given money for wearing them, no less unusual in those days than demanding a fee for a biography. He had his fellow player Klaas Nuninga to thank for that privilege. The Ajax 'linkman', in other words its attacking midfielder, acted as a public relations man for the agency Cor du Buy, which promoted the interests of football boot manufacturer Puma in the Netherlands. In late December, Nuninga had put together a provisional contract for his teammate, which Cruyff signed on the bonnet of a car. As well as free boots, he was given free sports bags from that moment on.

A short time later, Cruyff sought direct contact with Cor du Buy, bypassing Nuninga, to ask whether 'there was an arrangement to be made' with Puma. There certainly was. A better contract emerged and it was signed in Baarn by Nel Cruyff-Draaijer and Johan's uncle and guardian Barend Tak. For a period of one year, Cruyff was obliged to play in Pumas and to collaborate on advertisements. Furthermore, his mother and Uncle Barend gave the firm Cor du Buy the exclusive right to market boots and tracksuits with the name 'Cruyff' or 'Cruyffie' on them. In return Johan was paid fifteen hundred guilders plus one guilder and seventy-five cents for each pair of boots sold. It broke new ground on both sides. 'In our view Cruyff was being given a considerable sum,' said Du Buy later. 'Because although we thought Johan was quite a nice guy, who during his visit to our office tried to hide his shyness behind heaps of bravado, we were still wondering whether his character would develop in a positive direction.'

Cruyff took leave of his 'clogs', his reinforced and extra-high boots, to promote Puma. It was typical of Cruyff not to wear the famous three stripes of market leader Adidas. Puma was the rival boot, as it were, a brand that had set itself up in competition with the dominant make, an alternative with an elegant, even slightly artistic decorative 'swoosh' on the side. He got that logo into the picture whenever he could. For the photo on the cover of *Elsevier Weekblad*, which featured endlessly in other media, he crouched at the front, his Pumas in full view.

Shirts with Cruyff's name on them were manufactured, along with other paraphernalia through which the 'enfant terrible', as the newspapers called him, cashed in on his name. The young sporting hero was frequently asked to open shops, too. Since he was bad at saying no and because it was easy to earn a couple of hundred guilders that way, he sometimes ceremonially kicked a ball at the window of a new shop several times a week, or kicked off a charity soccer tournament. Wherever he went in the country, boys would climb into trees in the hope of catching a glimpse of him, while the police closed off the streets as if expecting the Rolling Stones.

On the pitch Cruyff had increasing difficulty with the vigorous man-to-man marking that a phenomenon such as he could only expect. That was obvious again in the quarter-final of the European Cup. Against Dukla Prague in March 1967, Cruyff achieved little in the small amount of space left to him. Only one good opportunity came his way, and he fell short. In the middle of the second half in Prague he only needed to head home a cross from the left wing with a swallow dive right in front of the goal and Ajax would probably have gone on to the semi-finals. But he failed to connect properly with the ball, goalkeeper Ivo Viktor got his fingers to it and it bounced weakly, right on the line. The score was then 0-1, thanks to Swart, and 0-2 would have been the deathblow for Dukla after the 1-1 in Amsterdam. Instead, the confidence of the Czechs revived. They profited from two botched moves by the Ajax defence and won 2-1.

Afterwards Cruyff took a seat at a table with a vase of flowers. As the youngest player he was interviewed by television commentator Herman Kuiphof along with the oldest, canny Dukla technician Josef Masopust. Cruyff looked miserable, because of the defeat but perhaps also because he had one of the headaches he still suffered from, especially after important matches like this. When 36-year-old Masopust complimented him and called him, among other things, 'one of the most dangerous attacking players around', Johan pursed his lips and stared ahead. What use were compliments to him?

Had Johan had a good match? 'Not really,' he said. 'I was marked by two players the whole time. We played a bit more defensively than in the home match, and that way you get less support, but that was generally coped with quite well, I thought.'

Had he often got boxed in? 'That's what I just said,' Cruyff snapped. 'In Amsterdam when I got stuck I could pass the ball on. That was far more difficult this time.'

That's what I just said. Other players would not be so quick to say such a thing to Kuiphof, a courteous, erudite commentator of forty-seven with glasses and curly hair. In his live commentary, the former head of sport at the *Haagsche Courant* had called

Cruyff the 'Ajax wunderkind'. Now, with the cup elimination on his mind, the wunderkind showed less respect for him than Kuiphof did for the wunderkind. Times were changing.

His 'That's what I just said' was a sign of irritation, of course. Opponents were paying more and more attention to him, and there were distractions off the field too. For the second time, he had caused a car accident. In his new car, a light grey Austin Glider with a 1100cc 'heavy four-cylinder' engine, he had driven far too fast along the streets of Amsterdam-Noord on his way to see a friend. It was his second car inside eighteen months; Cruyff clearly had a liking for wheels and for speed. Adjusting to the constraints of circumstance had never been his strongest suit and he seemed to have an almost pathological hatred of traffic lights. Impatient and hasty, Cruyff would defy traffic all his life and this time, in Amsterdam-Noord, a 5-year-old girl ran on to the road from between parked cars, chasing a ball. The reckless Cruyff had not taken account of that possibility and he hit her.

Bystanders rushed over to help the girl, whose name was Eveline, and they recognised Cruyff immediately. Eveline was taken away by ambulance and spent weeks in the OLVG Hospital with a double leg fracture and concussion. 'The plaster came right up over my hip,' she recalls. 'Later my parents told me that Cruyff visited a couple of times. I was given a tea set and some dolls that he'd sent. He didn't offer any compensation; the national health insurance paid for everything. My father and mother never had anything negative to say about him. My family has its origins in the Dutch East Indies. We are unassuming. My parents absolutely didn't want any fuss.'

Interactions with other girls were more enjoyable. The goals Johan scored and the publicity surrounding them had appreciable consequences for his powers of attraction in the nightlife of Amsterdam. He was less and less the pale flappy-eared boy who hid behind his brother Henny's back, no longer the tag-along who, if he went out at night at all, would lean against a pillar drinking a bottle of Coca-Cola while the others danced and got their kicks. His fame gave him self-confidence, which in turn increased the girls' curiosity. One of them was called Nelleke. A friend had asked 18-year-old Nelleke whether she'd like to meet Johan Cruyff. Although she didn't care in the least about football, she immediately said yes. The two were introduced in the Sheherazade night club and she found him to be a sweet young man, not at all a show-off, in fact rather shy. She saw how Cruyff's older teammates acted like fathers to him to some extent and sometimes sent him home if it got too late.

Johan and Nelleke went out a few times and Nelleke could tell that he was thoroughly at ease with her. She was attracted by the fact that, despite his fame, Johan was never pushy and didn't act the macho man. There was an open attitude on both sides. 'It immediately felt safe,' Nelleke remembers. Both were still living at home, so evenings sometimes ended with them lying in his Austin Glider, the seats folded back. There was no other option. 'He tried things first on me,' says Nelleke. 'It came down to some clumsy touching and exploring; in truth we mainly chatted a lot.' Their relationship petered out before it became really serious. They each went out with someone else and lost touch.

Fortunately for Johan, Amsterdam was full of Nellekes. They came in their droves to the dance halls and discotheques of the city centre, where life went on deep into the night. Around the Rembrandtplein and the Leidseplein, one place after another opened its doors and soul music fans tried out their dances to the rhythms of James Brown, Aretha Franklin and Sam & Dave. Whether the clubs were called Extase, Tuf-Tuf, Club '67 or Lucky Star, on the waves of rising prosperity and the craving for entertainment, the pretty girls and the hip boys found each other. Five years after the introduction of what was universally known as 'the pill', everything was possible. Even for Johan. 'Sometimes I went out with a girl for a week,' he said in an interview. 'Sometimes it lasted two weeks, but hardly ever three. We might go dancing, or to the cinema. I didn't fall properly in love. Flitting and gadding about, I made my way from one week to the next as an unattached young man.'

On a couple of occasions Johan's dealings with girls were downright embarrassing. He'd got to know Yvonne, or rather she got to know him, while out dancing. Yvonne hadn't found Johan particularly appealing, he didn't buy her a drink and he couldn't dance, but he attracted a good deal of attention and – 'I might as well be honest' – that was what sparked her interest. They started chatting and a few weeks later Johan picked her up at her house in Osdorp to go to a film together. He wanted to smoke undisturbed, so they took seats in a private box at the Theater Tuschinski. After the film finished they stood outside in the dark next to the richly ornamented front wall, and Johan bluntly made a proposition. 'Shall we go to a hotel next time?'

Yvonne was taken aback. They were both still living at home with their mothers, true, but this was really very unromantic of the famous footballer, a bit arrogant even. 'No,' she said. 'Eventually, perhaps.' Now it was Johan's turn to be insulted. He walked away, leaving Yvonne to make her own way home.

By this point Johan, in the words of one of his girlfriends of the time, was very sexually active. 'In that period all my friends went to bed with him,' she says. 'And they found him interesting mainly because of his fame. I think at the time he was simply oversexed.'

If that's true then Amsterdam's small hotels did well out of him. Taking a girl home was out of the question. He didn't even have a room of his own any longer, because his grandmother was sleeping in it. Known as Granny Kee, 82-year-old Corrie Draaijer-Van Stelten, his mother's mother, was ill and had to be taken into the home. Granny Kee would not be around for much longer. Johan had given her his bedroom as a matter of course. The two had a warm relationship and now he was doing something for her in return. Logical. Family harmony was made complete by brother Henny who, now that Johan was without a room, bought bunk beds with his own money so that Johan could share a room with him.

Despite sleeping in a bunk bed, Johan's self-confidence had increased to the point where he dared to cast meaningful looks at a girl who until recently would have been out of his reach, because practically all the young men had their eyes on her, a red-headed rich girl who wore her skirts so short that it wasn't only adults who took offence. Danny Coster gadded about on the Leidseplein just as Johan did, perhaps even more often, but she generally went out with different boys, cooler boys mostly, tough sons of entrepreneurs, guys who walked into Club '67 fashionably dressed as if they owned the place. They couldn't take their eyes off Danny, who with her dark eye-shadow looked a little like Dusty Springfield. Even if they were not going out with her, the young lads liked to be with her, this Danny from Amsterdam-Zuid who alternated between bouts of shyness and a pithy kind of warm-heartedness.

One day Johan walked into a new discotheque called Can Can and saw her sitting there. 'I'm going to seduce that girl,' he said to a friend.

'You can't do that,' said the friend. 'She's engaged.' That was true. A year earlier Danny had said a provisional 'yes' to Sanny Lampie, son of a family that owned a ladies' fashion house on the Kalverstraat called De Vries & Lampie.

The two were introduced nevertheless and from that moment on Johan and Danny exchanged greetings wherever they happened to see each other, whether in Amsterdam or in the beach resort of Zandvoort aan Zee.

Before long a brief meeting took place between Johan and Sanny Lampie, somewhere on the highway between Amsterdam and Beverwijk. They knew each other from the Nieuwe Hoogstraat, from the time when Johan worked in Harry Blitz's textile wholesaler and Sanny in his father's drapery shop. They parked at the side of the road. 'How's it going with Danny?' Johan asked.

Sanny told him the engagement had just been broken off. He had been spotted in the city centre late at night by Danny's father, Cor Coster, which had signified the end of the relationship. That was how it went: dealing with Danny meant dealing with her father, the brazen Cor Coster, for whom the Amsterdam business world held no secrets.

Sanny's news must have encouraged Johan. On 13 June 1967 he attended the wedding of his friend Piet Keizer. Danny Coster was there; her father, a familiar face on and around the Leidseplein, knew the bride Janny Hoopman's father. At the reception, Johan and Danny got talking. An elderly lady, Piet Keizer's grandmother, came to stand with them. 'Hello, Johan,' she said. 'Is this your girlfriend?'

'Don't you know her,' Johan asked, pretending to be surprised. 'This is Danny, my wife.'

'Oh, no, really?' said Piet's granny.

'Yes, really!'

'I had no idea you were married.'

Danny turned red and didn't know where to put herself. 'Bye, then,' said Danny to Johan and she walked away.

'I'll be seeing you,' Johan grinned at her.

An offensive, a feint, a curving cross that awaited the final strike.

In October 1967, after they'd been circling around each other for a while in Amsterdam and Zandvoort aan Zee, Cruyff walked into the Can Can dance hall with no particular expectations. Before he knew it, Danny, who was dancing with someone, was pushed towards him, as if her dance partner, who turned out to be her brother-in-law, wanted nothing better than to see them get together. They complied. Cruyff, who had a total lack of rhythm, was a hopeless dancer, his teeth were far from perfect (dentist phobia), and in other ways too, as Danny said later, they were an 'impossibly contradictory couple'. Danny in her mini-dress and Johan looking 'terribly old-fashioned' in a 'ridiculous baggy suit', with 'his hair combed backwards in the style of a hundred years ago', seemed to come from two different worlds.

Nevertheless, the glamorous Danny stuck it out on the dance floor for ages with her outlandish partner and later that night Cruyff drove her home in his recently purchased Austin-Healey Sprite – a red litter bin on wheels with rubbish all over the place inside. 'Ash and cigarettes, an empty chips wrapper and football clothes scattered everywhere,' Danny remembered later. 'I sat down half-rigid.' He dropped her on the Herman Heijermansweg, a street in Amsterdam-Zuid lined with newly built mansions and semi-detached houses. He even managed to get her to agree to go to the movies with him the next day. He called out after her through the open car window, 'Make sure you're wearing a skirt at least twenty centimetres longer.'

Danny couldn't believe her ears, but she kept on walking to her front door.

'And you don't need all that make-up as far as I'm concerned either.'

According to the joint biography *Boem*, published in 1975, for which they were both extensively interviewed, Danny spent the next hour trembling with rage in her room. What was the guy thinking? It might be 1–0 to him now, she thought, but tomorrow I'll even the score. I'm not finished with that little guy yet.

But she decided to go shopping with her mother the next day and buy a slightly longer skirt. It was the start of a series of agreements between them. They went out several times and both fell in love, which is not to say they immediately got along. Johan derived a lot of self-confidence from his sporting performances, was her impression, while she was burdened by an 'inferiority complex' because at eighteen she hadn't achieved very much. They continued to argue about each other's appearance. Johan detested Danny's red hair with fake curls and Danny despised his baggy trousers. It was a 'continual trial of strength', of falling behind and catching up, a form of competition their friends say never ceased. Yet they gradually adjusted to each

other. Johan bought more closely fitting trousers, which his
mother thought were like tights, and Danny started to wear her
hair straight and blonde.

Cruyff even went so far as to take his girl out for a meal, quite
something for him. He didn't like treating other people and
he'd made a habit of not accepting drinks, because, as he said
in a long newspaper interview, 'They immediately expect you
to buy a round in return.' He wasn't keen on that. He had to
'slog far too hard' for his money. The frugal market boy found
'laughing and earning money' the best things of all and liked to
live a normal life. In the Weidestraat they thought restaurants
a waste of money – you could eat just as well at home, couldn't
you? On the Herman Heijermansweg, where Danny's wardrobe came mainly from Parisian fashion stores, dining out was
entirely normal. If there was anything Danny found a complete
'disaster', it was that Johan was capable of spoiling a romantic
evening by saying he needed to be home by ten.

Truly disastrous perhaps was the fact that Cruyff was now
caught in the middle, between the girl he was going out with
more and more often and a profession that demanded punctu-
ality. The one time that he gave in to what Danny wanted and
arrived late at a training camp as a result, he was promptly fined
by Michels. It seemed that the closer his relationship with the
blonde entrepreneur's daughter grew, the worse his conflicts
with Ajax became.

CHAPTER EIGHT

Pig-headed, egotistical and contrary

Johan felt important, and he was. He had ended the previous season as the country's top scorer, with 41 goals in 41 official matches. Scoring 33 times in the premier division, he'd dominated the torrent of goals (122, a national record) with which Ajax had won the national championship for the second year running. He'd also been chosen as Footballer of the Year, and his contract with Ajax had been significantly improved and extended. In the members' council the question had arisen of what the board would do if, for example, Milan made an offer of a million guilders for him. That could happen at any time and Cruyff had responded remarkably casually to such speculation. 'Look,' he would say, 'I'm an *Ajacied* through and through, but love of a club only goes so far. Beyond that, your own affairs are going to count.'

The board had decided to tie in key players like Cruyff and Keizer for longer. As a consequence, the striker was going to earn not 15,000 but 35,000 guilders over the coming four years, plus a thousand for every match won and 500 for a draw. He would also get 5,000 guilders if he played at least twenty-five competition matches in one season. With a bit of luck his salary would be more than 60,000 guilders a year from this point on, putting him financially somewhere between an alderman and a mayor. Which did not, incidentally, prevent him from going over to a call box during breaks in training and engaging in business transactions, making appointments about shop openings, appearances in advertisements, or meetings with businessmen who wanted something from him.

His self-image was further improved when the KNVB decided to waive his suspension from the Dutch national team, which had been due to run until November. He was after all 'the most feared striker on the Dutch pitches', said the chairman of the football association, and 'a huge chunk of propaganda' for Ajax and the national game. So, on 13 September 1967, Cruyff was once again allowed to join Oranje, for a match against East Germany. In this European Championship qualifier he shone, according to the papers, and scored a goal of 'consummate class'. After just a few minutes he stopped a deep pass from Henk Groot with his chest, took a few paces forwards and smashed the ball into the top left corner. One–nil, which was where the score stayed. He immediately had plenty to say again, too. Responding to criticism from the East German coach, who thought he could have scored more goals, he said, 'The man's right. I missed several chances. But what does it matter? One's enough, isn't it? He should be glad. If I'd got three in the net it might have cost him his job.'

Through his matches with Ajax, Cruyff became known as the 'animator of the team' and was praised for doing 'astonishingly brilliant things'. During a practice match against Everton, a top team with several England internationals, he contributed two goals in the 3-0 victory, including a 'miraculous backheel shot'. There were compliments on that occasion even from Michels, who told a camera crew on the training pitch that in his view Johan was a 'true centre forward'. 'Always watching for a chance. Dynamic. Agile with the ball. And perhaps most importantly of all,' Michels stressed, 'in the right place at the right time. That's what I find the most typical of him. He keeps getting into dangerous positions.'

'It's all the lad cares about,' Michels also said. 'He plays and doesn't think about anything else.'

All the same, 'think' was the key word in all the problems that emerged around Cruyff that season. He thought and saw more on the pitch than most of the others and behaved accordingly, partly by discussing in interviews the tactics to be deployed, as if he was the coach. He clashed increasingly frequently with the real coach, Michels, who, after their unnecessary elimination by Dukla Prague, had decided to be tougher on his rather unprofessional team. Michels demanded more discipline and tried to lump all his players together in that respect. Johan, for his part, seemed to long for the privileged position he'd so often been given in the past by his father and by his youth trainers. The top scorer felt he understood better than anyone what Michels meant by 'every move at the service of the result' and 'carry out team tactics to perfection', and he wanted recognition for that.

It's no coincidence that Cruyff so often mentioned one occasion, years ago now, when Michels had driven him to the doctor in his own car, early in the morning (Cruyff didn't yet have a driver's licence). Michels was sensible enough to take his talented striker aside occasionally for a tactical tête-à-tête, and if he found Johan secretly smoking in the shower room before a match he usually turned a blind eye. But that was about as far as Michels seemed willing to go. He didn't shrink from scolding his famous pupil as if he was a child, as he had on the day of the last match of the previous season. They had all been sitting in the bus that morning, ready to leave for Rotterdam – all but one. From his usual seat behind the driver, Michels growled, *'Avanti'* – let's go. Despite, or probably because of the fact that he could see Cruyff driving up in his Austin Glider, he wanted to leave right on time. Eleven o'clock was not three minutes past eleven. To Michels everyone was equal, a number, a part of the whole, and windbag Johan must be made to realise it.

The bus slowly moved off. Cruyff raced to the parking spot, got out and ran after the bus with his sports bag. The players' bus turned on to the Middenweg and stopped. The door opened. Cruyff stepped in, panting for breath. Michels said merely, 'Go and sit down.' Everything seemed in order, but in the stadium where they were to play run-of-the-mill Xerxes it became clear that Cruyff would not be allowed on the pitch. He had to sit in his tracksuit on the subs' bench and watch the team win 4-0 without him. 'I thought it was a bit cheap,' recalls his team-mate Theo van Duivenbode. 'Would Michels have done that if something important had been at stake? I don't think so. It was a way of putting Johan in his place, to show who was boss while everyone was watching.'

The complicated situation surrounding Cruyff became obvious in the run-up to the important European Cup match against Real Madrid on 20 September 1967. 'Care-less ball, Jo-han!' Michels shouted during training, a kind of muck-about with two against three. 'Care-less a-gain, not ne-cess-ary.' And a little later, even more sarcastic, 'I want two new boys. Johan and Piet. They played careless balls, so they can go in the middle.'

Michels may have put extra sarcasm into his bass voice because the training session was being recorded by a camera crew. But shortly after this kindergarten treatment, Cruyff explained in front of that same camera crew that in the first round Ajax had been far from outgunned by Real. Eyebrows raised, he offered a know-it-all explanation of why the Spanish team was weaker than a few years before. 'And,' he analysed like a veteran, 'we've got a whole lot better'. His direct opponent, Pedro de Felipe, was 'terribly tough and mean' but not all that strong 'as a player'. 'I've been playing in the first eleven for three years now so it'll be fine, I reckon.' (Johan pulled a face that said: get it?)

In reality Cruyff had been part of the Ajax 1 squad not for three years but only for a year and a half. It was an exaggeration that the recently hired Ajax psychologist put down to Johan's 'insecurity'. The 35-year-old sports fan and child psychologist was clearly fascinated by the interaction between the 20-year-old star and coach Michels, who was almost twenty years older. After the departure of psychologist and graphologist Slikboer, Grunwald was the new person the players could talk to, so that he in turn could advise Michels. Grunwald took their problems and sensitivities seriously and soon had his hands full with Johan Cruyff, to whom he attributed an 'above average sensitivity'.

The psychologist regarded Johan as like the highly gifted child who is allowed to skip a year and therefore 'gets into emotional difficulties'. Johan had always associated with older boys, was Grunwald's analysis, and as a result he was underdeveloped socially. Because of his minimal time at school and his rejection for military service, Cruyff had had little opportunity to learn about solidarity with contemporaries. He had few close friends. And ever since Piet Keizer's wedding he'd been the only member of the team without a wife or fiancée. 'Because of all this,' Grunwald wrote in his report, 'he finds himself rather alone.'

Grunwald meticulously noted all developments in the weeks leading up to the Ajax vs Real Madrid match. As usual, Michels put together a strict programme. On the Sunday morning, three days before the match, the players and their team would meet at eleven-thirty to leave by bus for the training camp in Zeist – from the Olympic Stadium, not the Ajax stadium, where Johan was waiting. 'A 250-guilder fine and a talking-to from Michels, in front of everyone,' Grunwald noted. In Zeist the team was filmed for a documentary. After filming finished, Cruyff had a long chat with the famous director Bert Haanstra. It made him late for dinner and Johan got 'another talking-to' from Michels 'in front of everyone'. On the Wednesday morning, the day of the match that half the Netherlands was looking forward to so eagerly, he overslept. In response to which the coach gave him 'another talking-to'.

That evening in the Olympic Stadium, Ajax drew 1-1 with

Real. The single Dutch goal was scored by Cruyff. 'In the second half I roamed about quite a bit,' he told the press proudly afterwards. 'I thought my place in the forward line wasn't being filled in quickly enough. Nuninga did that properly once, and then he immediately got a great chance.' He also knew what his team would need to do in Madrid. 'There we'll have to play from the defence. I think Keizer and I will be strikers.'

So it was. On 11 October 1967 Ajax played in the imposing Bernabéu Stadium with a reinforced five-man defence and only Cruyff and Keizer in the attacking line-up. Johan came on to the pitch bouncing the ball – but his self-confidence stalled right there momentarily. Along with Keizer he was a 'useless pawn' in the first half, to quote *de Volkskrant*. When Real made it 1-0 fifteen minutes after half-time and Michels reverted to the usual 4-2-4, everything began to run smoothly again. Groot scored the equaliser with a fabulous header into the top corner. From then on Ajax had the best chances, but after ninety minutes it was still 1-1. That was the same score as in Amsterdam, so thirty minutes of extra time were needed. Everyone in Madrid was astounded: Real, because this unknown little club from the Netherlands refused to give up; Ajax, because they saw they were at least as good as the richest and most famous club on earth, possibly even better.

As soon as the whistle blew for the start of extra time, Ajax resumed their resolute play. The team dominated and when after just two minutes Piet Keizer broke out on the left, outplayed a defender in the Spanish penalty area with his familiar grace and then calmly slipped the ball sideways to Cruyff, it had to happen. Yes. It had to. It could. The thousand Ajax supporters rose to their feet. Millions of Dutch people shouted at their television sets as they slid to the edge of their seats. Right next to the penalty spot it was Cruyff's ball to shoot in. No Real player was anywhere near to thwart him: ball past the keeper and that's it.

But Cruyff was circumspect. Since his debacle with Oranje against Czechoslovakia the year before, he had been trying to master his impulses. 'It may sound strange,' he'd said about that occasion, 'but I learnt something from it', namely 'how vulnerable you are' if you let yourself go. Deep down he'd therefore been 'a tiny bit glad' of the long punishment by the KNVB. He had 'needed' it to make him think about his behaviour. 'Otherwise I'd probably have gone off the rails,' he said.

He would control himself better in future, at all times, including when it came to seizing chances. The previous year, for example, he'd often shot without looking where the keeper was standing, he'd told Grunwald recently. From now on he would look more and not act so impulsively.

That was indeed how it seemed in Madrid. Instead of giving the devil in him free rein and intuitively thwacking that extra-time ball from Keizer into the Real goal, Cruyff hesitated. To be on the safe side he first stopped the ball with his favoured right foot and then kicked it without much pace into the body of the approaching goalkeeper Andrés Junquera. On the stands, in living rooms, on the sidelines, people clutched their heads, whether in despair or in delight. The striker that Real coach Miguel Muñoz was eager to bring to Madrid had missed a golden opportunity.

Cruyff was about to clutch his head too, it seemed, but he stopped halfway. There was work to be done. Real were mounting an attack. He might be able to interrupt it. Nothing was yet lost. There were twenty minutes left to play. Even after such a dramatic failure he was intuition itself, the 'total footballer' (even though the term didn't yet exist) who switches instantly from attack to defence and thinks ahead without stopping to lament what might have been.

Ajax continued to attack. But, the way it often goes with great clubs and experienced heroes, Real profited from a moment of disorder in midfield. An Ajax player skidded, the pitch lay open and Spanish striker José Luis Veloso sent the ball unhindered from outside the penalty area past keeper Gert Bals. Ajax tried everything then, but a goal refused to come. An exciting and heroic, even unforgettable match came to an end and Ajax were out.

In the dressing room the journalists saw Cruyff sitting, bent over, on a bench, his ribs bare above his white shorts and his football boots, which he was slamming on to the floor tiles. He uttered words you would rarely catch him using. 'I don't understand it,' he said in between the pounding of his studs. 'I don't understand it.'

The moment of his tragic mistake in Madrid marked the introduction of the verb 'should' in Cruyff's career. Until half past ten on the evening of 11 October 1967 it had always been 'could'. This time he should have scored. Michels, for example, didn't name any names but his message was clear. 'We should have won,' he said. 'Real were outclassed, especially in extra time. We got four chances then. My maxim is: from every three chances you should get one goal.'

'Cruyff's job is to score,' added Henk Groot, the scorer of the one, beautifully headed, goal. 'That's all. He doesn't have to make much of an effort. All that's expected of him is goals. But then you can't go missing chances like that.'

The journalists too reacted sombrely. The bungled chance was 'unforgivable really', wrote *de Volkskrant*, while *De Tijd* said that Cruyff had 'let his team down at an extremely important moment'. 'Three times he missed, in a position that wouldn't normally have been a problem for him at all. So the defeat by Real Madrid will be blamed on him.'

'I feel a bit guilty,' he said to the press afterwards. 'Especially since the others worked so hard for it and then I go and miss at the decisive moment. Because I'd so rarely had the ball, I felt uncertain. Which never happens to me. Normally you just put a ball like that in. This time I hesitated. I never should have stopped that ball. I lost my nerve.' He went even further: 'What a great idiot I am, what a great dimwit. Really guys, I wasn't able to take that ball from Pietje straight away. It was as if I froze, standing there in front of Junquera. Terrible! Terrible! I'd give a thousand guilders to have that chance again.'

In the Dutch league that autumn, too, Cruyff missed more chances than a year earlier. On the list of top scorers, Ove Kindvall, the new goal-getter of frontrunners Feyenoord, was ahead of him. Cruyff was troubled by the pressure, Grunwald concluded in his notes. 'He feels it's partly his fault that Ajax are now playing rather less well and he's scoring fewer goals.' After the miss in Madrid, he was too quick to feel attacked and as a result even more 'nervous and talkative' than usual. 'Yet more shouting at people. He talks to mask his sense of failure.'

During a premier division match he was called to order by captain Gert Bals for swearing at an opponent. He also let fly at his own teammates Swart and Muller, to such an extent that, according to a note by Grunwald, a 'Muller–Cruyff conflict' arose. 'Muller fragile and tearful; Cruyff quite aggressive. Complains that Michels says he's in the wrong.'

As so often happened, the tension made the troublesome prodigy better rather than worse. A few days after a hefty fine from Michels he was in 'excellent form', according to the press, scoring the only goal in a difficult away game. When Piet Keizer was sent off while playing for Oranje, and as a result was banned from five Ajax games, Cruyff expressed solidarity without hesitation. The striker found it so unfair that (along with four other Ajax internationals) he responded by refusing to play for Oranje. He had a view of events rarely found in young players. 'We're professional footballers,' he explained to the press. 'We live from football. Many people higher up in the football association are amateurs. That urgently needs to change. You earn your money at your club, not in the Dutch national team. If you had to live on what you earn there, you'd have a pretty impoverished life as a footballer.'

*

Cruyff's self-confidence was visibly growing. He was now scoring weekly and he often openly defied prevailing conventions. One day he saw women training in the gym at De Meer, the first female referees. One of them told Cruyff she'd love to see the next Ajax match, but she'd been told she couldn't because the tickets were sold out. 'So,' Cruyff said, 'you do a whole lot for football and don't have a ticket, while others do nothing and sit in the main stand.' He went to the boardroom to express his displeasure – and at the next match the women had seats in the stadium.

Furthermore, how could you be forbidden to play with amateurs in your free time? In the autumn of 1967 Cruyff did exactly that whenever he felt like it. Via masseur Salo Muller, a Jewish student association had made contact with him and he'd said yes. Actually, he was only supposed to referee that morning, but after a while the temptation became irresistible and he decided to help the Jewish students, who were 5-0 down, despite the fact that the evening before he'd left the pitch injured after playing in an Ajax friendly. When the game was over he happily posed with the cheerful students next to a wooden crate of Heineken.

Shortly after that, Cruyff was forbidden by Ajax to appear at the opening of a shoe shop in Millingen aan de Rijn. Despite the ban he accepted the invitation and had a particularly enjoyable afternoon in Millingen, near the German border. After the opening, Cruyff stayed for at least an hour and a half, signing autographs and selling Pumas.

Not for the first time, dismay at Ajax about his conduct was mounting. Johan smoked too much (two or three cigarettes immediately after a match, Michels confided to the psychologist, saying, 'He's too young for that'), and according to the coach his behaviour was pig-headed, egotistical and contrary. Michels feared the player's popularity was going to his head. Cruyff always thought he knew better, made comments about everything and could never admit he was wrong. For his part,

Cruyff said he didn't mind doing exercises as long as the reason behind them was explained to him. 'If everyone says it's X, I still want to know why,' he said in an interview.

Cruyff, for whom 'could' had become 'should', seemed increasingly to be taking the initiative, as if he couldn't leave anything to his coach and fellow players. 'I sometimes see things better,' he told psychologist Grunwald. 'I lead the team and I always talk – the others don't open their mouths.' So it was that 'the tiddler' wanted to show how big he was during a crucial match between Ajax and Feyenoord in January 1968. Ajax were in second place in the league, behind by three points, so winning was particularly important. An even thicker fog hung over the Olympic Stadium than during the Ajax vs Liverpool match fourteen months earlier. And since Michels on his bench could barely see how badly his tactics were working out, Cruyff unilaterally changed them. As a result the team worked better and, when Feyenoord's play later gave reason for it, Cruyff restored the old set-up. A superb move by a highly talented player of just twenty-one. The newspapers wrote that after half an hour, when the match was stopped at 1–1 because of the fog, Ajax were clearly dominant.

Afterwards Cruyff proudly told Michels what he had done. According to the notes by Grunwald, the coach growled, 'Okay, good.' Several days later Michels had a very different opinion. During discussion of the match in the dressing room, he asked who had changed the tactics in the Olympic Stadium.

'I did,' said Cruyff.

'Well, dammit,' said Michels. 'Who do you think you are?'

He is also said to have called the centre forward a 'liar' and a 'malingerer', and then added, 'You can bugger off'.

Grunwald wrote that the coach and the precocious striker now had a 'tense relationship'.

Feelings ran so high that Cruyff was suspended briefly for disciplinary reasons. In February he was not allowed to play in a match against MVV. All the same, the sports pages published a good photo of him, showing him in the stands in civvies with Danny next to him, her hair blonde again, wearing a coquettishly askew beret. It was a strange picture, the centre forward staring ahead, supposedly suffering from 'an old back injury' and still with his old-fashioned hairdo including a firm parting, and at his side a pretty, still nameless 'girlfriend' who could easily have been mistaken for a trendy French singer.

It was probably in this period that Michels threatened to suspend him for three matches rather than just one and Cruyff said, okay, but then I want to choose which matches, which of course wasn't possible. At that Cruyff said, okay, but then I'll sit out another three matches too. He then watched the whole affair fizzle out. 'It would have been a fine thing,' he reflected four years later. 'Michels playing the tough coach, who dared to grab naughty Johan Cruyff by the ear and exclude him from the team, and no doubt during the game against little Lutjebroek.'

There could be no clearer indication of his growing self-assurance. He understood that the coach couldn't do without him and that he could therefore get away with a lot. Too much, in the view of some, including Michels himself. Yet Cruyff would carry on in that frame of mind, as if no other option was open to him but to push the boundaries.

CHAPTER NINE

'We're just going to buy two rings'

At home in the Weidestraat, Cruyff was able to spend a little time recovering after the death of Grandma Kee. He'd accepted as a matter of course that he would help to care for his sick grandmother, until she could no longer go on and an end came to her 'long and patiently endured suffering', as the death notice put it in early March 1968. The visitors who came round, the funeral service, the burial in the family grave at the Nieuwe Oosterbegraafplaats: everything had gone well. Cruyff found that very important, he told psychologist Grunwald. Things had to go well. And they would, if everyone did their job, at home and at work, in the team or wherever. You could achieve a great deal then.

They were serious words from a young professional footballer and there may have been a connection between this new-found gravity and the fact that on 25 April he turned twenty-one, which meant he had legally come of age. High time for more solidity in his life. He and Danny had been going out a lot since the autumn. They'd celebrated carnival in the south of the country with Wim and Maja Suurbier (Maja and Danny already knew each other from the dance halls and bars). It was there that the two of them spent the night together for the first time. Now he wanted to make Danny his own, and in her eyes he did it in a rather businesslike, not to say unromantic manner. One overcast spring day he took her to a jeweller's near the Kalverstraat. 'We're just going to buy two rings,' he said, and in no time they were outside again.

Johan looked at the two packets. 'Here,' he said, and he gave her a little box. 'Otherwise I'll have to walk around like an idiot holding both of them.'

Danny – who had rather imagined a candlelit dinner – accepted it from him. She had her ring.

That summer the young couple drove a red Porsche 911 to Paris to celebrate their engagement. Johan and Danny then carried on to the south of France, where their speedy four-wheeler – with its 2.0 litre air-cooled six-cylinder engine and 130 horsepower – regularly broke down, on one occasion on the boulevard in Nice. The engine kept overheating and more than once they killed the time spent waiting for a mechanic by playing cards on the dashboard. Nevertheless, they drove all along the coast of Provence and also visited Italy and Spain.

After a month of bickering (that would never change) and relaxedly lazing about, they returned to the Netherlands. Johan had by then been somewhat remodelled by Danny, which is to say that his hair now covered his prominent ears and he wore a modern shirt. At the same time, Danny had adapted to her new position as the woman behind his success. She had promised him, among other things, that she would no longer work as a model.

Johan was now firmly attached to Danny and therefore to her father. In the small world of the Leidseplein there was little doubt about the influence Cor Coster exerted on the relationship between Johan and Danny. Many people could think of only one reason why image-conscious Danny would go out with unprepossessing Johan. 'She was steered by Coster,' says

Danny's former fiancé Sanny Lampie. 'I'm certain of that. It was all to please her father. It was only later that they actually began to love each other. She didn't give a damn about football, either. I took her to matches a few times and she was bored to death. She always fell for glamour and fame, and through Johan she got them.'

Coster did indeed find it 'marvellous', as Danny would say, to be able to talk with Johan about football. They had long conversations and soon Coster started giving his daughter's boyfriend unsolicited financial advice. Wristwatch dealer Cor was amazed at the small sums for which Johan had agreed to be hired. Cruyff might act smart about his little business arrangements, but what was he left with after one of those shop openings in the provinces? After travel expenses and refreshments had been deducted, very little. He could do better, Coster calculated. From now on Johan must present himself as an entertainer who knew what he was worth. He rose to the challenge. 'I needed to understand that a footballer is a performer,' he said in an interview. 'Just like a Concertgebouw violinist, except that a musician can go on working until he's sixty-five.' In other words, 'The period in which a footballer needs to seize his financial opportunity is short. Anyone who ignores that fact is stupid.'

He was now even more of a soloist, going after his own interests, and he spoke about that with an honesty unusual for those days. The Porsche 911, for instance, had been sold to him for half the usual price, on condition that he could be photographed with it: a highly advantageous deal thought up by his future father-in-law. Cruyff, who was already appearing in the papers remarkably often with his car, now sometimes dropped the name of the German automobile manufacturer into conversations. On television he might suddenly say, 'So I drive a Porsche,' thereby managing to get a plug into coverage by a public broadcaster that carried no commercials. He would then look at the interviewer with a grin, as if he'd just outsmarted him with a smooth bit of evasive action on the pitch.

'Right,' the questioner would say. 'You thought, I'll just drop that in?'

'Yes, logical,' Johan would reply. 'Benefit a little.'

With a similarly pragmatic attitude, Ajax had become national league champions again that May. No Dutch club had managed that since the triple by Sparta in 1910-13. They had fewer goals in their favour but also significantly fewer goals against, a consequence of 'consciously dealing with risk', as Michels put it. The coach had taught his players to improve the way they calculated everything, slowing the game down if they had to. And although Cruyff was again Ajax's top scorer, with twenty-five league goals – eight fewer than in 1967 – he was not the top scorer in the premier division. In that respect he'd fallen behind Ove Kindvall of Feyenoord and the new star of run-of-the-mill Xerxes/DHC, Wim van Hanegem.

Businessman Cruyff took a further step forward on 8 August 1968, when along with his brother Henny he opened a sporting goods store on the Elandsgracht, on the edge of the Jordaan neighbourhood. For years it had been Smit's Leather Goods. The eponymous Jan Smit was the specialist in handmade sports shoes who years before had made Cruyff's 'clogs' with his own hands. The shop was well known to football players all over Amsterdam and it seems Jan Smit liked the idea of selling it to the Cruyff brothers. They agreed that Smit would remain manager for the time being.

Johan had fame, while Henny had a business diploma: it looked like a promising combination. The name Cruyff on the shopfront – and in advertisements – would attract customers, and Henny would win them over with his handsome face and smooth talk. That illustrated the inverted relationship. As a football player Henny had slipped down into amateur teams, but for the past two years he had been managing a small department store on the Kinkerstraat. He knew how to talk big, charm customers and purchase wisely. People acquainted with both brothers said he was even closer to being a 'real Jew' than Johan.

Henny could imagine a future for himself as his famous brother's manager; they complemented each other wonderfully. Together they could earn a fortune. No wonder he felt threatened by the arrival of Danny, daughter of a seasoned wheeler-dealer. On their first meeting in the Weidestraat, he greeted her with a forthright, 'What are you going to do with my brother?'

The opening of the shop on the Elandsgracht was the occasion for countless attractive pictures in the newspapers, which only annoyed the bosses at Ajax. Everyone could see, once again, what Johan had on his mind. Michels felt the full-time professional Cruyff was placing himself 'outside the group' with his commercial sidelines and ought to concentrate more on football. Virtually all the summer's practice games had been played without the striker because of an ankle injury, and what did he do as soon as he was declared fit? Open a shop.

As a punishment he was not deployed in the first league match against Go Ahead. He wasn't even allowed to accompany the team to Deventer, since he had to stay home to play for Ajax 2. Furthermore, he was banned from speaking to journalists. Michels (and not only Michels) felt he opened his mouth too much in public. Footballer of the Year or not, he should know his place.

Michels had decided to be extra tough with his players this season, to ready them for the European Cup. Oddly, Cruyff empathised with him in that. 'Our coach sees everything,' he'd said a week before his suspension. 'There's no point bullshitting. He's the boss and if you give him any lip he'll make you sit out the game.' The article in the *Algemeen Dagblad* included a photo of a smiling Cruyff, hair jauntily covering his forehead, in a trendy rollneck sweater and a nice jacket, with the Munttoren – 'Mint Tower' – in the background. The message: this lad has made it. Beneath his backside was the shiny bonnet of the Porsche 911.

Forbidden to speak, he would need to let his feet do the talking, and he did, perhaps fuelled by resentment, by scoring five times for Ajax 2. The first eleven seemed unable to do without him, losing 2-1 to Go Ahead.

A few weeks later, Cruyff was again dropped from Ajax 1. Despite exhortations from Michels to put more common sense into his game and stop his 'football juggling', which only invited fouls, the striker had persisted in his 'individualism'. In interviews Michels openly denounced Cruyff's 'egotism', saying he could become a real star only if he was prepared to put himself 'at the service of the team'. On the one hand, of course, Ajax were guilty of 'burning out' their 'dribble artist' by having made him play so often in the spring with a swollen ankle, the coach admitted. On the other hand, he really must stop those 'provocative' moves of his. Cruyff refused to listen to advice and was back on the subs' bench after two matches.

In a KNVB Cup match on 14 September 1968 he was allowed to prove himself 'fit' for the crucial game that would follow five days later, against FC Nuremberg. If he failed to do so, Ajax would play the first round of the European Cup against the champions of West Germany without him. It worked. During the match Cruyff jumped into the air in good time when the defenders tried to tackle him and often kept the ball close but only briefly. He played carefully by his standards, almost modestly, and with one goal and one assist he contributed to the 4-0 victory.

So on the Monday he was allowed to go to Nuremberg. But whatever his sports bag may have contained, it was not a pair of Puma boots. Since February he had refused to play in the brand to which he was contractually tied. On further examination he'd discovered that Pumas were inferior in quality, they were hurting his delicate feet, so he wanted to extricate himself from his obligations. Despite various attempts at mediation, he simply played in Adidas boots both for Ajax and Oranje, and almost weekly he ensured the famous three stripes were on show in the sports pages – all free publicity for the German parent company from which Puma had extricated itself after the war as a result of an argument between the Dassler brothers, and of which it had been a passionate rival ever since.

It was not the first and certainly not the last quarrel in Cruyff's life that degenerated into an unfathomable slanging match. There seems never to have been any discussion about having Puma footwear adjusted to suit him. The dispute soon started to look like a power struggle. Cruyff stubbornly refused to pay the fines imposed for breach of contract. When a claim was made on his salary, he applied for an injunction against Puma's agent Cor du Buy and lost. The judge did not agree that, as Cruyff's lawyer claimed, he had 'medical grounds' for playing in Adidas. The claim on his pay was upheld. He had to pay the court costs as well and could expect a substantial fine every time he played in any brand except Puma.

Still, to Cruyff, admitting you were wrong was the same as losing, and losing anything was the same as losing everything. That's what he had thought as a boy and that was what he would always think. Games were being played here, he said to reporters after the verdict. It was a form of words he would often use to place himself on the morally virtuous side of a conflict. He therefore simply continued to play in Adidas boots, although now with the stripes made invisible. Things came to a head in February 1969. Puma and Cruyff agreed on a new contract. Instead of fifteen hundred guilders he would be paid 25,000 guilders a year – more than sixteen times as much. Documents were signed, Puma created a special pair of boots for him to wear and no one heard anything more about 'medical grounds'. Being unreasonable had paid off. Or, you might say, after taking a hard line he was now getting what he was worth.

Cruyff had a lot on his mind once again, including surgery on his ankle, conflict with Michels, tensions surrounding his sports shop and the legal wrangle over his boots. It was as though the Footballer of the Year had to start from scratch to prove himself in the European Cup match against FC Nuremberg. 'I know there's a lot of criticism of my play at the moment,' he said to the press before the away game. 'But I'm afraid I can't do any better.'

The board at Ajax had increased the pressure even further by calling to mind once more, in a newspaper interview, Cruyff's miss in Madrid in October 1967 – as if the young player had failed to comply with a business agreement. When Johan kicked the ball into the arms of the Real keeper in extra time, Ajax had been eliminated as a result, and that, the board calculated, had cost the club at least one sold-out home game: half a million guilders.

Even journalists who were favourably disposed towards him were now expressing their doubts. Maarten de Vos, a young reporter at *De Tijd* who liked to get under a sportsman's skin, wrote, 'His materialist cravings overshadow the primitive longing for sporting success.' Cruyff was 'sometimes more accountant than footballer', De Vos wrote. As a result, it would be wise to keep 'the most talented player in the Netherlands', a man 'whose outfit has become that of a hypermodern twenty-something', on a tight leash.

'Cruyff is now at a crossroads in his career,' noted Wim Jesse in *Het Vrije Volk*. 'Over the coming months it will be "to be or not to be" for him. If Johan surmounts his mental and social depression, he can certainly be once again what he was. If not, then we must fear that one of our greatest talents will never live up to expectations.' Cruyff had been 'very much changed' by all the fame and attention, the newspaper believed. 'As his star rose, Johan's spontaneity was lost. His exuberant bursts of laughter ceased, as did his impulsive, uninhibited play. People are now saying, even those close to him, that it's almost impossible to talk to Johan. You simply feel he's conning you with his eyes open.'

To put it bluntly, 'Will Cruyffie, who hasn't been an integral part of the Ajax team for weeks, ever be his old self again?'

On 18 September 1968, in front of 45,000 spectators in the Städtisches Stadion, FC Nuremberg launched a tremendous offensive. The pace of the game and the fighting spirit of the Germans were overwhelming, and most of the Ajax players had no idea how to respond. It was exactly as Michels had feared. But no matter how intimidating the waves of attack towards goalkeeper Gert Bals were, Cruyff seemed utterly untroubled. On his 'neutrally' blackened boots he ran wherever he needed to, agile and purposeful. He was determined to show that all the doubts were misplaced. That he could live up to his fame. That he was mentally and physically fit for top-class football. He was once more that talented junior on the pitches outside the De Meer stadium, who after a roasting grew bigger, not smaller. As if public criticism by Michels had energised him. As if the derogatory comments by Nuremberg coach Max Merkel – 'Cruyff isn't suited to modern power-football' – were pounding through his head and driving him on.

He wasn't put out by the substitutions (Hulshoff for Pronk, Suurendonk for Nuninga) with which Michels tried to resist the Nuremberg 'steamroller'. The fact that many of his fellow players were desperately getting mixed up together, because they were suddenly having to play with three instead of the usual four forwards, seemed not to bother him. He even kept his cool when Suurbier was unable to hold back German left-winger Georg Volkert, who scored after just six minutes.

The players of 'slave driver' Max Merkel increased the pressure even further. Time and again the Nurembergers appeared in the Ajax penalty area and shot just over or past the goal. Many of the Ajax players panicked and, on the bench, Michels too became nervous (perhaps partly out of discomfort at his own tactical interventions). The crowd chanted, *'Noch ein Tor!'* – another goal!

Cruyff, the often lonely number 9, moved skilfully between his desperate teammates, composed and capable. Despite vicious fouls by his man-marker Ludwig Müller, he cheekily dribbled past his opponents. He stepped neatly over a ball so that Swart had a chance to shoot (and miss). He boldly played himself free and created a chance, only to discover that none of the others had dared to run with him. 'The Amsterdam jack-in-the-box,' wrote *de Volkskrant*, 'sometimes tugged himself loose from his guard with brilliant moves, but he never found a comrade in arms capable of completing his dazzling work.'

As if by a miracle, there was no second German goal before half-time. In the second half the storm in the stadium gradually subsided. Ajax managed to cross the halfway line more and more often and shortly after half past eight came The Moment for Johan Cruyff. There were ten minutes left to play. Out on the left, Keizer had space for a long kick towards the goal. His left foot went to the ball and from the other side of the pitch Cruyff read his friend's body language. That left arm flung outwards, that particular swing of the foot towards the ball; based on years of kickabouts together, Johan knew that the ball wouldn't end up at the near post as everyone expected but at the far post. He set off in that direction and even foresaw that the ball would curl away from the goal somewhere in the penalty area. That too was what happened. Keeper Jürgen Rynio was astonished to see it fly past the near post and veer away from him like a UFO, towards Cruyff, who now needed only a short sprint in order to do the right thing: half fall forwards, arms spread to keep his balance, and head the ball into the gap between the far post and the approaching German goalkeeper. It fitted precisely – 1-1. The Nuremberg defenders looked at each other in despair. Cruyff left the scene. Accounts had been settled. The doom-laden newspaper stories, the comments by Michels, the bragging by Max Merkel: he had proved the whole lot of them wrong. He was embraced by his teammates and must have been relieved that after 'Madrid' there was now a 'Nuremberg', a city where instead of messing up a simple chance he had seized upon an almost impossible one.

It remained 1-1 – in view of the home game two weeks hence a good result. All the more so because the rule of away goals counting double in the case of an overall draw had just been introduced, meaning that 0-0 in Amsterdam would be enough to see Ajax through to the next round. All thanks to Cruyff, who because of hellish pain in his ankle had been unable 'even to kick straight', as he put it afterwards. Perhaps the adrenaline had wiped away all the pain and all the doubt. 'Cruyff not only scored a goal that counted for two,' Michels said after the match, 'he also proved that he is willing and able to sacrifice himself for the team and do his job the way I want him to.'

It is just possible that as he left the pitch Cruyff briefly thought about a twelve-piece china tea service. The previous day he had spontaneously bought the plates and cups in nearby Bayreuth. From the players' hotel in the hilltop village of Pegnitz, the squad had driven to Bayreuth and there Johan had pulled out his normally hermetically sealed wallet. Six hundred guilders he'd paid for the costly porcelain from the Rosenthal company. For Danny. Because in ten weeks they would be married.

Cruyff had played his way right to the top once again. The editors of the popular television programme *Mies en scène* wanted to get to know the lad from Amsterdam better and they invited him to be a guest. So one Friday evening, nine days after his performance in West Germany, it was, Ladies and gentlemen, here is 'the most popular and artistic footballer we have at the moment'. Smiling shyly, he took a seat facing Mies Bouwman. As usual in this part of the programme, called 'In the Chair', they sat close together on an S-shaped seat. The presenter gave him a motherly, even encouraging look. At the end of her talk show, Mies usually put ten questions to politicians, cabaret artists or writers, experienced speakers in middle age with whom it was often hard to get a word in edgeways. Now she was faced with a skinny soccer player in a baggy, pale-coloured suit who was doing his best to hide his nerves. Without complete success.

'Do you feel at ease?' Bouwman asked. 'A bit like before a match?'

'More nervous,' said Cruyff.

'More now than before a match?'

'No, less.'

Nice dodge. He might be having difficulty swallowing, and his tongue was working hard to keep his lips moist, but he was as alert as a street footballer. A light-hearted conversation developed, about this and that. He described his bedroom in the Weidestraat, from the pennants on the wall – 'they're probably still looking for those at Ajax' (laughter) – to the bedside table with the photo of Danny on it. What did he dread most? The crowd at away matches. 'If it doesn't go the way they want,' he said, 'their fanaticism comes to the surface and they yell insults.' 'Do you react to that?' Mies wanted to know. 'No, you just try even harder. At least, three or four years ago someone shouted something at me and I was so angry I kicked the ball in his face.' A smile. 'That was in my fanatical years.'

'Are they over?' Bouwman asked.

'They have to be over, yes,'

'I dare say people go on about that quite a bit with you?'

'Yes, it's one of my weak points.'

The preparations for the upcoming home game against FC Nuremberg were mentioned too and he described the training camp in Hooge Vuursche where they would be going that Monday. After talking about his sleeplessness during the compulsory afternoon nap they arrived at his reading habits.

'What's the last book you read?' asked Bouwman.

Cruyff gave her a mischievous look, as if embarrassed to admit that he didn't read much. Playfully naughty, he said, 'Willard Motley, *Knock on Any Door.*'

'Still on part one?' Bouwman wanted to know.

'No,' he said immediately, as if evading an approaching tackle.

'Part two.' Then with an instinct for bluff he promptly added that part two was 'excellent'.

But he couldn't get around Bouwman that easily. 'Er ... Last year you said the same.'

That was true. In fact, *Knock on Any Door*, a lengthy novel about a boy growing up in the slums of Chicago, was almost a standard answer from Cruyff to any question about what he liked to read. In 1965 he'd mentioned it in a documentary about literature. Two years later *Knock on Any Door* was treated in some detail as his favourite book in his mini-biography. Six months on, an interviewer asked him what he'd read most recently. '*Knock on Any Door*,' Cruyff answered. Four months after that, a weekly magazine asked Dutch celebrities which was the latest book they'd read. Cruyff's answer: *Knock on Any Door* by Willard Motley. He assured the readers of women's magazine *Margriet* that he was 'still too restless' to 'keep burying myself in a book'. Although for the truly 'wonderful' *Knock on Any Door* he was happy to make an exception.

Now it was Mies Bouwman who wanted to know what book he'd most recently absorbed. It seemed that saying honestly there was only one book he really thought was any good – or indeed that he didn't much like reading – was difficult for an ambitious sportsman such as Cruyff. All the more so since he was often annoyed by the cliché of the brainless footballer and didn't want to be known as the man without a diploma. Cruyff knew only one tactic: attack. 'I've also got part three, *Let No Man Write My Epitaph*. I'm just about to start it. For next year.' He laughed contentedly. Bouwman smiled back and left it at that. All the viewers could see that an evasion had been accepted as such. *Let No Man Write My Epitaph* was not part three, although it was a kind of sequel by Motley to the 1947 novel that Cruyff appreciated so much. Like *Knock*, it tells the melodramatic story of a poor street kid who tries in vain to escape the criminal world of Chicago in order to win the woman he loves.

What was it that so appealed to Cruyff in that great tome of an adventure book? Did he feel there were similarities between him and the central character? Fictional Nick Romano started out as his father's favourite, just like Johan was. Nick's father died young, if rather later than Johan's father. Both boys had a problematic time at school and afterwards developed in ways different from the norm, Nick as a criminal, Johan as a foot-baller. They learnt to stick up for themselves in a difficult world. Nick knew an older journalist who gave him good advice. Johan was always looking for support from a father figure after his real father died. But Nick stole and beat people up without any noticeable sense of guilt. He hit passers-by with a lead pipe to rob them; he enticed homosexuals into a tunnel and took their wallets. For almost six hundred pages Nick behaved diabolically, and although there was something good deep within him, his misconduct – theft, deception, even homicide – was ultimately punished with the electric chair.

Might Cruyff have recognised something of Nick's aggres-sion? It is striking that in *Oog in oog met Johan Cruyff* he describes the death penalty as an unjust sanction. After reading *Knock on Any Door* he said, 'Imagine there's a mistake. That's pos-sible, isn't it? Judges are only human. Then it's happened and everything's over.'

Johan seemed to need anger to inspire him to play his best football. This became evident again five days after the television interview. The Ajax vs FC Nuremberg match had only just begun on the evening of Wednesday 2 October 1968 when he received the ball close to the left touchline. Facing him stood central defender Horst Leupold, who had followed him to the left to mark him. Cruyff accelerated and half passed Leupold, stopped, turned round, turned round again so that he was facing the German goal, quickly brought the ball forwards from behind the leg he was standing on and accelerated again. For each of Cruyff's moves, Leupold needed one more step than Johan, which made him look stiff and ridiculous, as if he was desperately trying to hold on to a playground roundabout that Cruyff was spinning faster and faster with humiliating nonchalance.

The belittling of Leupold led only to a corner, but that was of secondary importance. This was what Cruyff called 'putting myself and others in the spotlight'. Everyone could see which of the two was gifted and which was not. Poor Leupold, a substitute, realised as much and behaved accordingly for the remaining eighty-eight minutes. Cruyff was on top of him throughout the match, teasing him and all those around him. Since he had noticed straight away that not one but two opponents were marking him, he went out on to the left wing more than usual, thereby creating space in the centre for the rest of the team. 'We hadn't agreed on that beforehand,' Cruyff said later. 'It goes of its own accord.' His fellow players enjoyed the space he created and put themselves 3-0 ahead. In the final minute it was at last Cruyff's turn. He ran along the right side of the pitch, past several defenders, and kicked the ball without a moment's hesitation from around 17 metres into the far bottom corner: 4-0. Three times he jumped up wheeling his arms in his triumphal march back to his own half. Later that evening he said, 'What a treat.'

According to *De Tijd* he was 'the old Cruyff again'. Nuremberg coach Merkel now thought he was 'tremendous' and the German press described him as '*wunderbar*', the best player on the pitch. His childhood hero Alfredo Di Stéfano, a coach in Argentina and present as a spectator, called him 'very good'. This time Michels told journalists, 'With Johan we're going ahead at full power again. The team can hardly do without him, but' – he added tellingly – 'he only truly flourishes because of the team.'

Whether because of the measures taken by Michels or Cruyff's approaching marriage, there was no sign of any rebelliousness at that time. Although Johan was still sometimes troubled by his ankle injury, he tried to get the most out of his game by roaming. 'I now run everywhere,' he said in an interview. 'No longer just in the attack. I've also become more experienced, as far as it's possible to say that at my age.' He increasingly had to deal with opponents who followed him like a shadow. Benno Huve, whom Cruyff called 'that redhead at FC Twente', was one of them. 'If he dropped back, I simply followed him,' Huve says now. 'That was my job. Marking was still real marking. If he takes a piss, my coach said, then you take a piss too. I could manage that; I had great concentration. Sometimes I wasn't even aware of the score. I was entirely focused on Cruyff.'

By running away from the forward line, Johan forced his opponents to choose between staying where they were and following him. If they followed, they would end up in midfield, where backs felt ill at ease. That happened to Don van Riel of Willem II. He would never forget saying to Cruyff before the match, 'You won't get into the sixteen-metre box today, friend.' In response Cruyff dropped further and further back in Tilburg. 'And I carried on going with him,' Van Riel still remembers. 'Eventually he was right inside his own defence. He coolly sent some passes from the back. It even got to the point where he took a goal kick instead of the keeper. "Yes, that's how we do things at Ajax," Cruyff said to me.'

The alternative for a defender was to stay in place and leave the marking of Cruyff to a midfielder. Telstar defender Frans van Essen usually did that. 'The disadvantage was that he could come at you from midfield, where there was more space, at great speed,' Van Essen says. 'Then you'd simply be outplayed. Kicking was often pointless then, since he'd jump up before you could touch him. He was like quicksilver.'

Johan always demanded hard passes from his midfielders. The faster the ball was travelling, the less chance the defender had to get between it and him. 'If the ball was kicked gently,' marker Jo Toennaer of MVV recalls, 'he could be really furious with his teammates.' That was logical, since soft passes increased the chances of collisions and injuries. If the ball rolled towards him while a defender was standing right behind or next to him, he generally wouldn't take it but instead would tap it straight on to the left or right. 'So you couldn't dash at him and he was always too quick for you,' says Jo Toennaer. 'And I can tell you, I followed him everywhere.'

Because of the strict marking, ingenuity became the watchword: being constantly alert, running away, misleading opponents. Furthermore, he had to save himself a little for the European Cup. Not just Cruyff but all of Ajax was now focusing more on the European competition than on the league. The team therefore dropped to fourth place in the premier division and winning the championship came to seem out of reach. But that didn't matter. The match against Fenerbahçe from Istanbul was coming up. It was in Europe that it had to happen. And it happened. One great remaining obstacle was the mud in Istanbul. Persistent rain had made the grass disappear and the match was actually postponed by a day. The often so nervous, all too human Ajax were dreading the match, but despite endless skidding and despite provocations from Fenerbahçe, they managed to survive the mud wrestling. Partly as a result of some fine moves by Cruyff, the final score was 0-2. 'We've proved we're a first-class team,' Michels said afterwards, proud and relieved.

Ajax in the European Cup quarter-finals and a wedding to come in three days: Cruyff's life was looking pretty good. There were only a few photos of him with a belly dancer to ruffle the surface of the pool of romance. It had been an innocent outing on the Wednesday evening, when the players were free because of the postponement of the match. Come on, they'd thought, we're all going into Istanbul: players, trainers and medics. The famous Kervansaray night club became the scene of hilarity and good cheer. A provocative belly dancer with long black hair had raised the tone a little. 'Go and sit with him,' photographer Bob Friedländer told her. The dancer did so. She nestled up against Johan and put her hand on his forearm, her near-naked breasts practically against the shoulder of his club suit. Everyone laughed. A little later Johan danced on the stage with the glamorous young woman. Everyone laughed even louder, because of course he couldn't dance.

When they had all finished laughing, Cruyff whispered to the photographer, 'You can't use those photos.' Not such a strange thing to say shortly before his marriage to Danny, who had said of herself in an interview, 'I'm jealous, yes, very.'

Friedländer, who was on good terms with many Ajax players and with the Coster family, was prepared not to print the photos, but that would cost Cruyff 150 guilders in compensation – because imagine how much in demand they would have been.

Cruyff refused to pay and so he found himself on the front page of *Het Parool*, being intimate with the Turkish beauty, and on the sports pages again, dancing awkwardly beside a pair of female legs partially clad in tulle. The player seemed to 'be having quite a good time in the company of a Turkish belly dancer', ran the caption. Danny came to the same conclusion. According to Friedländer she got seriously angry and Johan had to go and see her in Amsterdam and explain everything in minute detail.

Cruyff was long used to 'belonging to people' and having everything he got up to recorded in words and pictures. Danny had yet to adjust. She wasn't alone in that. As a reader in Rotterdam wrote in a letter to *Het Vrije Volk*:

So much gets written about Johan Cruyff, but who and what is he, actually? One ordinary footballer, not a demigod. There's a whole team on the pitch, isn't there? What could Cruyffie pull off if there were eight duffers on the pitch? Don't give him so much kudos or he'll soon get too big for his breeches. And is it really appropriate for a man who is engaged to be married to be dancing in Turkey with a half-naked belly dancer? Let the reporters write about the other players for a change.

But there was no stopping it. The reporters increasingly mentioned only one name, that of the national phenomenon who had meanwhile transcended the sports pages, and whose wedding on 2 December 1968 became a great media event. The young couple were received that morning not by an ordinary registry office clerk but by the alderman for sporting affairs. In the spacious council chamber, packed with countless members of the Cruyff and Draaijer families, and a few of the smaller Coster family, the alderman made jokes that the happy couple, Hendrik Johannes Cruyff (twenty-one) and Diana Margaretha Coster (nineteen), were able to laugh at.

Danny looked exquisite in her long white wedding dress, with tulle like a cloud around hair piled high on her head and blonde ringlets. The fabric for the dress, the old French lace and the puffed sleeves, had been provided in exchange for a photo in a shop owned by a Jewish society draper. Johan had taken care of that. Something from the rag trade for Danny; something in a national rag for the fabric merchant. The market never slept if your name was Cruyff.

On this her wedding day, contrary to habit, Danny was forced to playact. The night before she had developed acute appendicitis. A range of injections and 'great dollops of make-up on my face and about fifty curlers in my hair', as she said later, were needed to get her through it all. And it was a long day. In the evening the celebrations continued in the Hilton Hotel, which was crawling with police outside and with journalists and camera crews inside. Half the Amsterdam jet set were there, along with folk singers, and of course the place was packed with members of Johan's family from the Jordaan.

For all Johan knew, this was how you got married. The crush barriers around the town hall were a feature of his job and a day like this was an opportunity to thank everyone who had been important to him for their help. But Danny, having grown up among the nouveau riche of Amsterdam-Zuid, never felt drawn to Johan's 'Jordaanese' milieu. She wasn't at all keen on all those noisy parties with accordion music, and she felt nauseous throughout. Fortunately, later that evening, partly as the result of a brief nap and further injections, she was able to recover a little during a private family dinner for twenty guests in the Doelen Hotel.

After a long and tiring day, they arrived at their new home on the Scholeksterlaan in Vinkeveen, south of Amsterdam. The terraced house, built only three years before, was full of flowers. There were vases of them in the hall and when they went through the saloon doors to the living room there were many more. They walked straight on past the exposed brick wall to the kitchen, with its inviting bar covered in vases of flowers, and when they climbed the wooden stairs there were bouquets to left and right. Flowers adorned the landing all the way to the bedroom doorway, where Johan, still in his dinner jacket, kissed his blonde wife – 'Mrs Cruyff' – and – 'here we go' – carried her over the threshold.

He'd forgotten to do that at the front door, which had caused Danny the umpteenth disappointment of the day. Now he'd made up for it a little.

CHAPTER TEN

Loner in the team

Johan was not very romantic and the home into which he now moved with Danny did not at first sight look particularly romantic either. The terraced house was in Zuiderwaard, a new estate on the western edge of Vinkeveen. With its large windows front and back, and an attic under a sloping tiled roof, it met all the domestic requirements of the 1960s: sound and presentable, with light and space for the whole family. Not a house you would expect of a popular sportsman with the status of a rock star and a red Porsche parked outside. A simple dwelling with a through lounge, it was above all a practical choice. Vinkeveen was just twenty minutes' drive from De Meer. From this inconspicuous house the traditionally minded Johan would go out and earn a living. Meanwhile, Danny, like the other young women in the neighbourhood, would do the housework. On free days they could walk beside the magnificent lakes, which the farming village gave on to like the mouthpiece of a giant horn.

For centuries city people had come to Vinkeveen for peace and quiet, and that was precisely why the Cruyffs settled there. On the first floor were children's bedrooms and in the bathroom was a modern washing machine that Johan had got hold of in his own unique way. In the white goods shop he'd initially been shocked by the prices, but he put a proposal to the manager. 'If you take a photo of me like this, with this machine, you can use it to advertise.' A short time later a new washing machine was delivered to the couple at Scholeksterlaan 41 free of charge. It didn't stop there. Half the house was furnished similarly, at reduced prices. So Cruyff remained a dealmaker and that stood him in good stead, because for the moment they would have to count every cent. He'd even been forced to reach a special arrangement when buying the house. For the first two years he would pay a kind of rent and after that he would lay on the table the full agreed sum: 60,000 guilders.

Danny regarded fashion and design as her hobbies, so the interior was far from ordinary. In the bedroom was a double bed in the form of a huge heart, with a sky-blue bedspread, and behind it dark blue walls with light blue lamps affixed. The ceiling and the floor were lilac. On the ground floor the wall of the open kitchen was covered with moss-green velvet of the kind seen in shop windows. The banisters of the spiral staircase were painted gold and the paving slabs in the garden alternated between flesh pink and blue. In the living room the tone was set by comfortable red leather furniture under a slatted ceiling of American pine, an exposed brick wall and a wall painted olive green.

The rather wild interior seemed to typify their lifestyle. Johan and Danny were not granted much peace. A nice relaxed honeymoon was out of the question, since competitive football went on all winter in those days. Johan even had to play on Boxing Day, and again shortly after New Year's Day. Danny went into hospital to have her appendix removed, but after that she continued to have bouts of stomach pain. And at home, too, people continued to pester them. They couldn't pick up the phone without hearing heavy breathing, insinuations or threats. They were repeatedly buttonholed in the street (which didn't particularly trouble Johan, incidentally) and quite often they discovered on arriving home that washing had been stolen from the line, such was Cruyff mania.

Then there was Sanny Lampie. Danny's former fiancé sometimes turned up in the front garden, calling the Cruyffs all
kinds of names. Johan was soon going to find out what kind of
a woman he'd married, Sanny would shout from the peaceful
Scholeksterlaan. He couldn't stand the fact that Danny had left
him. 'I spoke threateningly towards Johan and that wasn't very
nice of me,' Lampie says, looking back. 'My parents always got
along well with the Costers. We'd all been on holiday to Spain
together. And now this. I couldn't get over it. I was crazy about
Danny. For at least a year I was heartbroken and I simply had to
go there sometimes to frighten them.'

Danny's lack of enthusiasm for her husband's footballing career
was perpetuated by all the carry-on. She found it 'annoying
sometimes that Johan is so famous', and came close to saying
that she was already looking forward to 'the moment when
all this comes to an end'. She daydreamed that 'we could just
live quietly, without any attention. Like everyone else.' Yet she
faithfully attended Ajax home games, sitting alongside the other
players' wives. Although she refused to be compliant to the
extent of modelling herself on them, she did put a lot of effort
into her appearance, and with her hot pants and high boots she
soon emerged as an eye-catching trendsetter. The other women
were sometimes amazed at her aloofness and changeability – on
some occasions she could be quite forthcoming, other times
standoffish. Still, they admired her taste and saw her as the
leading lady of the Ajax stadium.

Like Johan, Danny had not finished her education. Until their
first meeting she, like him, had been a source of some concern
to her family. She was rebellious and capricious, and at the same
time accustomed to luxury and preferential treatment. The
Industrieschool, where girls were taught to cook, sew and iron
among other things, had been a 'disaster'. She'd left at fourteen.
She had then taken a job in her father's company, but that had
ended in a 'mess', she remembered later. Other jobs had come

to nothing. All in all, she was more interested in boys, clothes and going out than in studying.

Since Johan had forbidden her to work as a model, the 19-year-old was now stuck at home, a bit like the average woman that she didn't want to be. With her past of skiing holidays and shopping in Paris, she was far from keen on cooking and cleaning. She advertised for a home help, if only so that she wouldn't be alone so much. She found it hard to make contact with strangers and felt truly comfortable only when Johan was at home. But he went to bed at ten on weekdays and regularly had to go 'camping', as they called it, with Ajax. Danny also had to get used to the fact that, driven by nerves, Johan could let fly at her without warning before important matches.

The newly married couple found it all rather disappointing, yet gradually they did come to feel at home in Vinkeveen. Bickering and 'compulsively' discussing everything 'endlessly' between them, as Johan said later in an interview, they explored independent life by trial and error. For him it was a good sign that Danny didn't care about football. That reinforced his confidence that she cared about him, rather than just about Cruyff the famous sportsman. 'I never knew whether a girl really loved me, or was nice to me, purely because I'm a footballer,' he said. 'With Danny it's different.'

For Danny there was no option but to take over the mothering role from Nel Cruyff-Draaijer. Because whichever way you looked at it, she was the wife of a famous person who had great difficulty organising his own life; who, to quote a later friend, was very good at extraordinary things and very bad at ordinary things. So in an interview she confirmed that she would be at home for him. 'A man like Cruyff demands all your time,' she explained. 'He needs to be well looked after to stay in top condition, and I find that a great job for a woman.'

During the interview the telephone rang. 'Yes, of course,' the reporter heard her say. 'I'll take care of the shirts and shorts.' It turned out that before the first important match of 1969, at

home against Benfica, there was no tracksuit in the sports bag
that Danny had put ready. Cruyff discovered this when he
arrived at the training camp on Monday 10 February to prepare for the European Cup game. The camp was in Huize Den
Treek this time, a country mansion in the woods of Leusden
that had been converted into a hotel. Cruyff was allowed to
wear a tracksuit belonging to Michels, which was too big for
him, and he was wearing it when a snowball fight broke out.
It had snowed heavily that week, which Ajax felt would give
them a good chance against the 'great' Benfica, said to be a mere
shadow of the team that had played in the European Cup final
a year before. They had lost to Manchester United. Moreover,
star player Eusébio was rapidly losing his power and now the
weather gods had boosted the optimism further. More snow was
on its way. Victory was already theirs.

Events proved otherwise. While Eusébio, born in Mozambique,
found conditions in the snow-covered Olympic Stadium to his
liking, Cruyff felt as if he had lead in his boots. Because of his
fragile ankles he was always a little fearful of a hard pitch and
this time he rarely got the ball at the start of the match. He felt
'exhausted even though you haven't done anything yet'. Perhaps
he had concentrated too hard on preparing, he reasoned later,
and had grown nervous as a result. He didn't know exactly how
it happened. During the final offensive by Ajax he missed three
good chances. Ajax lost 3-1.

It was a shocking result and the windbag from Vinkeveen
had to pay for it as if he was the only one who had played
badly. According to de Volkskrant, Cruyff couldn't yet compare
himself to Eusébio. 'We could have got a draw,' Michels said
sarcastically. 'You can't say that Cruyff didn't get any chances.'
The headline in De Tijd read, 'Johan Cruyff adds to miserable
series of misses'. The photo underneath showed the culprit, and
the caption read, 'Cruyff's header misses an open goal'. The
striker had enough talent to be one of the greats of the decade,

the paper wrote, but 'up to now, too little has been seen of it'. Again, there were references to his missed chances against Dukla Prague and Real Madrid in 1967. 'Against Benfica he has added to that rather miserable series. It's as if Cruyff's "brilliance" declines when he's on the pitch with other truly great players, such as Benfica has in Torres, Eusébio or Augusto.'

'How many do I need to set up for him, then?' asked Swart.

'A man like Cruyff can certainly score goals,' said Michels. 'So what do you do about it when he misses three?'

At such moments Cruyff generally carried on in his usual laconic manner towards the outside world, but the criticism hit home. Anyone who knew him well, like his childhood friend Rolf Grootenboer, saw him become agitated. 'Johan would bottle things up,' he says now. 'When he was preoccupied he would make those little sniffing noises, with his hand over his nose. That told me he was nervous and fretting about something.' Insecure and ambitious, Cruyff let the criticism after Ajax vs Benfica sink in. He had no other choice. He would have to work it all out for himself. The others wouldn't understand him and there was no point going to Michels with that kind of problem.

These were the 'enormous demands' that were simply part of his 'trade', as he said in an interview. Cruyff found that 'difficult' and everywhere there were signs of the loneliness that accompanied his efforts to deal with it. Life as a celebrity brought disadvantages, and no one seemed to understand that, the formerly so roguish Jopie believed. 'Out of every hundred people I meet, ninety-nine and a half want something from me,' he said. 'And that's without even talking about money. Hardly anyone comes to give me something.'

With outbursts like that, he sometimes seemed a little too serious for the game he was playing. He rarely made jokes about his direct opponents, for instance, and in the changing room after a match he was often troubled by headaches. 'I can't be truly happy,' he said in an interview. 'I find it impossible

to really let myself go. There are guys who can be so terribly
happy. On the other hand they cry easily too. I've never cried.
Probably repressed.' Naturally he wheeled his arms above his
head after an important goal, but then his gaze turned downwards. If you put your arm round his shoulders after a league
game, he would look at the ground. When kids poured on to
the pitch after the final whistle, he made himself scarce, despite
his love of children.

The footballer who for many people was seen as an even more
extreme version of Dutch fictional rascal Pietje Bell started to
complain of insomnia and of the high expectations everyone
had of him. He had the feeling his success was regarded as
normal and failure as unacceptable. After Ajax vs Benfica that
had been demonstrated yet again. Now he felt tormented. The
performer who had extricated himself from the collective,
partly for the financial benefits that would accrue, was sum-
moning his strength for the return match so that he could prove
himself to everyone.

So it was that in Lisbon on the evening of 19 February there
was no holding him. In the Estádio da Luz he slalomed inimitably, took balls from defenders and produced subtly curving
crosses. Refusing to be disheartened by kicks and gobs of spittle
from Benfica, he grew to become the star of the evening. They
pulled him by his hair, they almost tore his shirt in two, but
there was no stopping the 'virtuoso with the ball', as the newspapers called him afterwards. He set up a goal and scored two
himself. His 'sparkling performance' was 'vibrant' and 'splendid'
and the result, 1-3, a sensation.

Afterwards Michels said to the press, 'This is the best showing
by Ajax since I arrived at the club.'

Okay, but why had the team been so effective? Surely not
just because Michels had spoken to the players in the changing
room at a volume unusual for him, whipping them up? The 3-1
victory was of course to an important extent a result of Cruyff's
unstinting efforts and his ability to shake off his markers, the

sharpness and constant alertness with which he inspired the rest, his issuing of directions, and the extra attention the opposition paid to him, so that fellow forwards like Inge Danielsson were easily able to score, not just now, but throughout the season. Danielsson, a Swede, was a likeable lad, a quick and cool finisher, but without Cruyff's mobility and evasive play he would have achieved little.

If you looked closely you could see all these things. But who was looking closely?

Late in the evening in Lisbon, Cruyff reacted calmly to all the praise. A great weight had been lifted from him, he admitted. He hoped above all that he had now put paid to all the negative comments.

Since both Ajax and Benfica had won 3-1, a deciding match on neutral terrain was required. It took place on 5 March in the Stade de Colombes in Paris. The stadium didn't have floodlights, so the kick-off was at three in the afternoon. The place was packed with 60,000 spectators, half of them Dutch fans who had travelled in carnival mood to the Paris suburb of Colombes by bus, car, train and plane to cheer Ajax on. A phenomenon seen for several years with speed skating – mass trips in traditional costume to the skating stadiums in Scandinavia – now took place on clogs and under red-and-white umbrellas around the lumpy pitch in Colombes, which was generally used for rugby. Every year people had more money and more free time to spend on having a high old time abroad, and the French capital was of course the ideal destination for a 'trek', as it had come to be known.

All the players seemed to be struggling with the hard, cold wind that sunny Wednesday, but above all with nerves – not least Cruyff. He also had to cope with marking that was rigorous even for those days. In the first half he was 'totally blocked', he said later, and he couldn't seem to shake off defender Adolfo Calisto. 'I think I was a bit at odds with myself,' he said honestly.

After ninety minutes of cautious football the score was still 0-0. The game went into extra time and the tension rose. 'He now has to show them a thing or two,' Danny was heard to say from her place in the stands, among the other wives. Sure enough, in the second minute of extra time, Cruyff hit a curving shot with the outside of his left foot. It zipped low, hard and spinning towards the goal. Via the goalkeeper's hands the ball fluttered high and followed a puzzling arc to end in the goal, just under the bar. A strange but crucial goal, the deathblow for Benfica. Danielsson scored another two: 3-0. Victory was theirs. Disbelief took hold of the 30,000 Dutch fans in the old, ramshackle stadium. This was incredible. Ajax had become the first Dutch club to defeat a former winner of the European Cup. Now for the semi-finals.

Two days later there was a review of the match on television and the extent to which Cruyff was now being treated as an individual star was obvious. For a report called 'Cruyff on the Spot' a camera followed him over a period of two hours, as if the other players were irrelevant. Because of the far from thrilling play, and the marking, his brilliant reading of the game barely came into its own, but the twenty-minute report did provide a good insight into the way in which he related to the supporters. After each goal and after the match, the fans ran on to the pitch with their umbrellas, dancing and jumping into the air, among them the Dutch photographers who were so joyful they didn't know whether to do their job or join the celebrations. The older Ajax players let the people have their way and the stewards declined to get agitated, probably assuming the revellers would leave of their own accord. But Cruyff had no patience with pitch invasions; every time it happened he urged the spectators to move off. Even when his teammates walked back to their own half in happy embraces, he tried to impose order. A supporter who flung his arms around him in delight was scolded. After the final whistle, he more or less beat off the fans, as if the jumping and swaying of all those people completely undermined his profession, which he took so seriously. There could be no better way to illustrate his position as a loner in the team.

At the airport in Paris, on arrival in the hotel, on leaving the bus for the stadium: everywhere he had been hemmed in by reporters while the others walked on, calmly chatting. He'd been forced to give his opinion about Benfica, about the grass, his team, his future, and again and again he'd had to pose, smile, be amusing or wise. It was as if he was playing the main role in a film and all the other players were in minor parts. The supporting roles were important too, he said more than once. Sometimes the others had played better than he had, but everyone always wanted to talk to the central character. After victory in Paris, the French referee Roger Machin came up to him with a gift, a reward for him as the best player in the match. 'I didn't want to accept it at first,' Cruyff said. 'After all, you win a match with eleven men. But in the end I took it from him. Because refusing seems an unkind way to treat your hosts.'

The next day the French press called him the 'unforgettable technician' from the Netherlands, a 'fiendish dribbler' and 'absolutely first rate'. He had been 'superior to Eusébio'. As if it was not Ajax but FC Cruyff that had won the match.

It took a local reporter in Vinkeveen to ask him the obvious question without beating about the bush.

'Do you play for yourself or for your team?'

Cruyff sat leaning forward in his armchair on the Scholeksterlaan, contemplative, hair still wet from the shower, and on the other side of the glass coffee table sat Danny in a minidress, her slim legs folded under her: a friendly and hospitable young couple. Cruyff liked philosophical questions and he gave a characteristic answer. 'You play for yourself in a team,' he mused. 'You're an individualist in a team, because self-interest always prevails in my view. It's quite logical too. Which is to say that I play as well as I can for myself. If I score two goals, then I've played well for myself. But the team needs to be there too, because then we win.'

The fact that reporter Dick Piet was a beginner didn't matter.

Always and everywhere Johan could open up to the most diverse range of people, whether famous or poor and unknown. Time and again he was 'activated', as Koos de Boer, his very first interviewer in 1964, put it. Journalists, children staffing the school newspaper, football enthusiasts in the street, fans beside the training pitch, the psychologists at Ajax: everyone asked him questions, and over and over again the Netherlands' most popular footballer shone a light on himself, on his profession or on life in general. Thinking aloud, he arrived at clear visions that he might not have achieved on his own, without the prompts. 'How that lad can talk,' said teammate Sjaak Swart. 'He's as good at that as at football.'

In Vinkeveen, too, Cruyff easily filled the cassette tape. Dick Piet could ask whatever he liked; he always got a response. After a second of silence Cruyff would simply start talking and very often – perhaps to his own amazement – something original would roll out. To the delight of his interviewers, he disliked evasive clichés and tedious preambles. Take the question, 'What are relations like with the board and the coach?' Most professional footballers would have confined themselves to a couple of noncommittal statements, for fear of reprisals by the club leadership, or criticism at the very least. Cruyff was different and he cheerfully improvised. 'I think at this point the boards are too important, or think themselves too important. Most important of all are the players.' The board was made up of unpaid enthusiasts, of nitwits in fact, and he felt they 'didn't value the achievements' of the team. If you took a proper look, then you would see that the players were 'number one', followed by the coach and only then the board. After all, he said, 'we take care of the money that comes in'.

He openly expressed a preference for the English set-up, with full-time managers who could take decisions at a high level and be held responsible afterwards for what they had done. 'With an individual you can discuss things. You can't do that with a board. Your life isn't your own.'

Signed, professional footballer Johan Cruyff, aged twenty-two.

Later in his career he would say that he was good at only two things: football and public relations. He developed continually in both respects. The reporters conveniently, and spontaneously, made sure that what he said got into the papers in a form that was grammatically correct and coherent. 'Everything positive that's written about you counts,' he said. 'Things like that determine your salary.'

For yourself in a team: that was how Cruyff played on 13 April 1969 in the semi-finals of the European Cup. With the stress on 'team'. An hour before the start of the match against Spartak Trnava, an unknown but spectacular team from Czechoslovakia, during the warm-up on a side field at the Olympic Stadium he felt pain in his left calf. He limped to the changing room. Club doctor Rolink examined him and found, as so often, that there was little wrong. In his view, complaints from Cruyff always had more to do with affectation than with the highly strung nature of a prodigy. He regarded the idea that Johan, like many creative footballers, had a relatively low pain threshold as hogwash. 'You're playing,' the doctor said bluntly. And since Johan didn't want to miss this opportunity of his first semi-final, he played. But he wasn't really part of the match that evening. As soon as he set off on a sprint he felt as if his calf was splitting apart. Even so he opened the scoring after less than half an hour. It barely cost him any effort. Spartak goalkeeper Josef Geryk punched a header from Hulshoff back on to the pitch and Johan, alert as ever, tapped the ball into the goal. 'I knew then that I hadn't run for nothing,' he said afterwards.

At half-time he complained again about pain and was prepared to carry on playing only if Dr Rolink put 'a bunch of injections' into his calf. In the second half he was again in pain nevertheless, so he limited himself to the most crucial moves, such as disrupting Spartak as they built an attack. In spite of everything, he did his best in a difficult match that Ajax won, rather luckily, 3–0. But who took the flak? Right. Michels called him 'mediocre' and the newspapers wrote that he had played 'far below his ability'. Even his opponents left the Olympic Stadium disappointed, and the Czechoslovaks found it impossible to believe he was the striker their coach had warned them about.

Cruyff almost felt guilty. Not because he had played poorly – he knew the reason for that – but because the others had played less well than usual as a result of his 'handicap'. The striker had felt fortunate that even with his muscle pain he'd been able to keep 'the little fellow' who was marking him busy so that others had got chances.

Here spoke the talented player who was fully conscious of his significance for his teammates. He was old for his years and youthful at the same time. 'A few years ago, as a little boy, I entered a big, strange world,' he'd told a journalist the day before Ajax vs Spartak. 'You normally need ten years to get to the top, but I was able to do it in two.' Now he was at the top in a domain that found itself 'outside of society', where everything was different. He liked to philosophise about that – only to paint himself as the baby of the team the next moment. 'When we stay overnight somewhere with Ajax,' he said, for example, 'I always sleep in the same room as Gert Bals. The youngest with the oldest.' He needed someone who would 'lead' him, like goalkeeper Bals. 'I've learnt a lot from Gert, talked a lot with him while we were lying in bed. He's had a good influence on me. I was always the youngest, but perhaps the most trouble-some too. Maybe that's why I chose to share a room with Bals.'

Eleven days after the home game against Spartak Trnava came the away game in Czechoslovakia. And again Cruyff complained about muscle pain. And again he played. It was a sunny spring day in Trnava, but aside from that everything was overcast from Ajax's point of view. From the first minute, Spartak unleashed an unprecedented offensive, and on a cramped, lumpy pitch too, the kind of hard surface that made Cruyff fearful. If after fifteen minutes he had passively fallen to the ground in the Slovak penalty area, then the match might have turned out differently. But he didn't. On a long sprint, after passing the 16-metre line, he received a kick to his knee from behind. While falling he attempted a shot. The ball missed and Ajax were not awarded a penalty, because that's how the rules worked in those days: anyone who tried for a goal had forfeited his right.

In a sense Cruyff had been too greedy, too eager to score. Instead of diving, he did the opposite, you might say. He regretted that later. His positive attitude had deprived Ajax of a simple chance to make it 0-1. Spartak raged on. Cruyff lay on the grass and called out to Dr Rolink, who was running towards him. 'I can't shoot.'

Rolink took hold of his knee.

'Ow!' shouted Cruyff.

'Calmly now,' said Rolink resolutely. 'Run through it, lad.' (In a tone of: don't act up.)

So Cruyff limped back on to the pitch. He let the game pass him by and watched his team being trampled by the fiercely attacking Slovaks. He waved his arms, appalled. He was in pain; he couldn't go on. The racehorse always so fearful of long-term injuries had to be substituted.

A little later Spartak made it 1-0, and shortly after half-time 2-0. When Keizer dropped out as well there was no one left with sufficient technical skill and initiative to hold on to the ball at the front. Ajax, the club for the better class of football, could only defend.

As if by a miracle, the goal that would have equalised the two matches did not come. The Czechoslovaks, once again under the yoke of Moscow after the Prague Spring, with rolling tanks and political intimidation, had now been defeated on the pitch as well. Before and at the start of the match, the crowd had chanted the names of several of the silenced politicians. 'Dubček, Svoboda!' was the cry that resounded between the grey apartment blocks. It had been the job of footballing heroes

Karol Dobiaš, Jozef Adamec and all those others to provide a flicker of hope for better times. But they had not succeeded in doing so on this afternoon. The crowd on the terraces could only watch as the players from the free West left the field on the shoulders of the fans who had travelled with them.

Ajax were now the first Dutch club ever to reach the final of the European Cup.

Cruyff was of course happy and relieved, but a sizeable contusion meant he could not play for the time being. It seemed he had not been making an unnecessary fuss.

Fit or not, he was in the Top 40 by the time he got home.

> *We went to watch some boxing by a distant cousin*
> *What a beating that lad got from an opponent who was*
>   *buzzin'*
> *The third round came around and it was fatal for our lad*
> *His gym shoes were left on the mat and he lay in the*
>   *crowd.*

The record was a gig his enterprising father-in-law Cor Coster had arranged for him. Coster had been assuming the role of his manager more and more since his daughter's marriage, and, as a result, Cruyff was positioning himself increasingly as a commercially orientated young man. But the song, 'Oei oei oei (dat was me weer een loei)', still available to be watched on YouTube, was certainly among the more difficult ventures. He would surely never have come up with the idea for the gig himself – quite understandably given his limited musical abilities. The origin of the inauspicious plan therefore lay elsewhere, with a few clever guys in the music business who wanted to see whether Cruyff's popularity could be made to pay on vinyl.

None of those involved would ever forget the recording session in the studio in Hilversum, so badly did Cruyff sing his lyrics, which oddly enough were about boxing. He was utterly unable to hold a tune and had no sense of rhythm. The chorus was not exactly a high point in Dutch musical history either.

Oh, oh, oh, that sure was a blow
As if you got thrown out of your shoes by a tornado
Oh, oh, oh, that sure was a blow
Won't see the like again
That one counts for ten
Lads, what a blow
Oh, oh, oh.

Cruyff usually felt insecure in situations that were new to him and the recording session was no exception. Someone suggested alcohol might help, and after several rum-and-Cokes they got the song about the cousin who took blows inside and outside the ring on to the tape more or less to everyone's satisfaction. The song might perhaps have been suitable for carnival, but that was long past when 'Oh, oh, oh (that sure was a blow)' entered the hit parade at number 24 on 19 April. After a few weeks it was out of the Top 40 for good – without coming anywhere near the real hits of that April: 'Goodbye' by Mary Hopkin and 'Get Back' by The Beatles.

A break in recording gave him a brief chance to talk. He told songwriter Peter Koelewijn that during a match he could make sure his sponsor's advertising board got on TV. He would stand at the touchline near the board, with the ball provocatively under his foot. 'Of course, the opposing defender doesn't like that. He wants to get the ball off me, doesn't manage it, gets grumpy and commits a foul. I fall to the ground, pretend to have been kicked and lie there. Referee rushes up, medic rushes up, everyone rushes up. The cameras too, of course. And that entire performance goes on for minutes, right in front of my sponsor's advert.'

On the day of the European Cup final between Ajax and AC Milan, Coster showed once again how to showcase the Cruyff brand. His son-in-law looked out at the readers of *De Telegraaf* not from any old run-of-the-mill advertisement; the entire back page was cleared for him. Sitting on his sofa in Vinkeveen, the footballer gazed into the lens in a way that inspired confidence. 'In this cosy house belonging to Danny and Johan Cruyff,' the advert said, 'they have KVT carpet, good carpet, in other words.' Everyone understood that Coster was behind it and that the times were changing. Business affairs were expanding their reach. The future belonged to commerce. Displaying yourself on such a grand scale as if no fellow players existed in the whole wide world was morally, or rather amorally, staggering for the Calvinist Dutch. That lack of the slightest modesty – wasn't it going too far? The ultimate soloist spoke to readers through a make of carpet, the only deeper message being that it was okay to want to earn as much money as possible.

All this on the morning of the day on which Cruyff as a team player was expected to give his all for his team, his club, his country.

Here and there the advert prompted cynical commentary among the press, perhaps precisely because in that same paper Danny also appeared, likewise filling a whole page, an amused expression on her beautiful face above a row of Seven-Up bottles. That elegantly piled-up blonde hair, those loose locks, her hands elegantly spread across the bottles: she looked every inch the photo model she'd once wanted to be. Next to her were the words put into her mouth by the advertising agency: 'Nothing besides the taste of real lemons and limes. So refreshing, so pure, so truly American. Seven-Up, rightfully the only one. That's why I promise you, Johan, as your faithful wife, that nothing other than Seven-Up will come into our house. PS: Good luck Wednesday night. I'll keep my fingers crossed. Your loving wife Danny.'

Rinus Michels, always up early, was the first in the players' hotel in Madrid to see the full-page advertisements featuring Johan and Danny. He was standing at the hotel reception desk and thought his own thoughts about them. If you asked Michels, Coster was systematically undermining the harmony in the team by arranging all these highly paid gigs for Johan. Cruyff's father-in-law kept coming up with new initiatives and none of them ever had a positive outcome for the team. In an attempt to limit any possible jealousy among both the players and their wives, Michels tore the pages out of *De Telegraaf* and stuffed them into his inside pocket. He put the newspaper back on the desk and went to have breakfast.

CHAPTER ELEVEN

How Cruyff became a Coster

As was his habit, on the evening of 28 May 1969 Cruyff was the last of the Ajax team to walk on to the pitch at the big, if nowhere near full, Estadio Santiago Bernabéu. To his right were the players of AC Milan, directly in front of him defender Theo van Duivenbode and leading them out Gert Bals, the goalkeeper to whom he would give a tap to the stomach a few seconds later. Cruyff's legs looked supple and at the same time more muscular than in previous seasons, a result of the many training sessions and matches he now had behind him. The 22-year-old professional footballer looked seasoned as he walked to the centre circle bouncing the ball ahead of him. Behind him rockets were shot, wild and fiery, into the sky in anticipation of the most important match of the year, the European Cup final.

But despite the routine, something was missing. Where was his chewing gum? Forgotten. In Amsterdam the same had happened to him before the semi-final against Spartak Trnava. Despite the win it had been an unhappy evening for him, with the injury and the poor play. Once again he was unable to fulfil that fixed element of his ritual, the spitting out of the chewing gum on to the opponents' half. And on this evening in Madrid, he really could do with some extra luck.

The night before the match, Michels had let fly at him again in the hotel, in front of the other players. The coach had loudly denounced interference by Cor Coster. That father-in-law of yours, Michels had more or less said, is wrecking the atmosphere in the team with his criticism of Ajax salaries. It was time for Johan, as a professional player at least, to distance himself from the man. Michels could not comprehend how, shortly before a European Cup final, anyone could be concerned with anything other than 'team business'.

It had been a painful scolding for Johan. He had listened to Michels, shrugged and walked in silence to the hotel lift. He slept badly that night.

Whether because of the missing chewing gum, wild speculation about an imminent departure or the row with his coach, Johan Cruyff was not the man of the match. Gianni Rivera was. The number 10 at AC Milan had a great evening, partly because Michels gambled on prioritising the attack and put up only two midfielders. As a result, it was an easy matter for 25-year-old captain Rivera to create a nightmare for his personal opponent, Ajax midfielder Ton Pronk. Rivera repeatedly withdrew to just in front of his own defence, so that Pronk became almost a forward. As soon as AC Milan started a counterattack, the Ajax midfield lay open and Pronk, with his stiff movements and heavy tread, was passed on all sides. In the space thereby created, Rivera scattered passes to his forwards with great gusto.

For Cruyff the opposite applied. He too was wearing number 10 on his back, the number of the linkman. He'd played in that position several times this season and it suited him, because from a position slightly further back, at a safe distance from the pushing and kicking at the centre of the attack, he could create more opportunities for his accelerations and evasions. But no matter what Cruyff did, switching between midfield and the forward line, it was not a great success that evening in Madrid.

Michels was banking on taking an early lead. In his view AC Milan were a slick counterattacking team that would normally be stronger than Ajax. But if Ajax managed to score quickly,

Milan would have to attack and it would be Ajax that could counterattack. Unfortunately, after seven minutes Milan scored and for the remaining eighty-three minutes Michels' players ran about as if they'd accidentally wandered into an unfamiliar house. As members of the team roamed off course, Cruyff seemed to be concentrating mainly on showing how good he was. A couple of times he dribbled skilfully past one or two defenders, cutting inside and turning as only he could. Great to watch, but fruitless.

The jittery, spindly centre forward of earlier years had clearly become an all-round striker. The Beatles-style hair cultivated by Danny, flapping around his lean face, reinforced the image of the elegant professional footballer. He landed neatly on the front part of his feet, resilient and balanced, the way running trainer Cees Koppelaar had taught him. As far as he needed teaching, that is, since in Koppelaar's view Cruyff was a natural talent when it came to running. His upper body stayed nicely relaxed as he ran and his arms stretched out from their joints, as it were, without dragging a shoulder with them at every move. His relatively long legs and loose wrists did the rest. It was as if a ballet dancer was jumping this way and that in the Bernabéu, a graceful striker who unfortunately, in the company of some rather wooden men, lost hopelessly 4-1.

Of course, Cruyff would never admit that was why he had done it, that he'd quickly realised there was nothing to be gained for Ajax in Madrid and had therefore decided to play for himself alone, wanting above all else for everyone to notice him that evening in the Bernabéu. Yet was it pure coincidence that in interviews of late he had emphatically described himself as a performer once again? That his father-in-law had hinted that after the summer he might go and play for a salary of millions in Mexico?

After the humiliating final in Madrid, Rinus Michels expressed himself diplomatically. He said only that his attacking midfielder had cared 'too little' about his 'defensive role in midfield'. The *Algemeen Handelsblad* was less diplomatic: 'Johan Cruyff gave the impression of playing more for the many scouts in the stands than for his own team on this historic evening for Dutch football.'

'Only once did Cruyff dash powerfully through the Italian defence,' wrote *de Volkskrant*. 'At the edge of the penalty area, however, he was stopped by means of a foul. AC Milan will no doubt always remember Cruyff as a talented player who can nevertheless be tamed.'

So it was. Ajax still hadn't mastered the malicious aspects of top-class football. Saving a situation by surreptitiously giving someone a shove was going too far for many players, let alone kicking a player's legs hard from under them. AC Milan were unburdened by such self-imposed limitations. The Italians simply did what suited them best in the particular circumstances – pushing, time-wasting, kicking – as long as it brought the desired result closer. 'It remains a striking difference that we as attackers ended up on the grass more quickly than their attackers in our half,' said Keizer to journalists afterwards. 'Ajax are still far too nice,' Cruyff claimed. 'Not yet well-drilled and cunning enough.'

Since they had won neither the European Cup nor the national league championship in 1969, Ajax would not be eligible to play in the European competition the following year. That honour went to Feyenoord. For the first time in three years there would be no high-level international football for the Amsterdammers. It was time to build a new team. 'Seems it needs to be tougher,' Michels concluded, not for the first time.

The gentleman players Theo van Duivenbode and Klaas Nuninga would have to go. Bennie Muller and Ton Pronk could stay for a while, but they too, punctilious footballers of the old school, would be out of the picture by the summer of 1969. Newcomer Nico Rijnders and an acquisition of the previous year from Volendam, Gerrie Mühren, would need to introduce more dynamism and pace to the midfield. A similar kind of contribution was expected from the robust home-grown defender Ruud Krol, and in the forward line Inge Danielsson made way for Dick van Dijk from FC Twente.

In Van Dijk, who had scored three times against Ajax the previous autumn, Cruyff would have a sturdier centre forward next to him than Danielsson. He would be able to function even more as a linkman. He had every reason to feel satisfied, you might think, but the opposite was the case. The critical noises about Cruyff's play in the European Cup final had irritated him immensely. He felt 'surrounded by a huge dose of unreasonableness'. After his beautiful and effective play in Lisbon and Paris he'd heard no praise from his teammates (possibly because they felt all the adulation in the press was sufficient), but after the let-down against AC Milan he'd been blamed for everything. That was the feeling he got at any rate, he said, because it was continually 'Johan this and Johan that'.

The criticism made him 'tougher', Cruyff told his Ajax psychologist Dolf Grunwald at the start of his fourth full season. Whether on the stands or in the papers, he was 'not always' valued as he should be and as a result his character had changed 'a lot'. If his performance was understated because the match demanded it, he was described by the media as 'lacklustre'; if he came up with a few good moves in a match in which he played badly he received plaudits. All those comments were merely relative, he had decided. When the psychologist asked him in a questionnaire whether he believed he was popular with the public, his answer, verging on disillusion, was, 'Only when I do something eye-catching.'

Cruyff thought professional football was going 'in the wrong direction'. That was because of the defensive play of recent years, and all the 'kicking and spitting' he had to deal with. Furthermore, there was a fundamental problem: 'People still regard it as a game,' he wrote. His sport was of course far more than a game, he believed; it was a craft that had fallen into the hands of the ignorant. Asked to name a comparable profession, he entered, in block capitals, 'BALLET'. Like a ballet dancer, he lived 'in a vacuum', in parallel with normal society, and he had a 'short' career in prospect.

'How long do you think you'll carry on playing football?' he was asked.

'About five years,' was his reply.

He needed to hurry, because, indeed, there was that recurring question: what was Cruyff going to do after his football career ended? Grunwald presented him with questions about his life and Cruyff's answers spoke volumes. He worried a lot about what he would do in the future and 'often' wondered whether he would 'have enough money'. He imagined a future in 'business', and that was no random choice. He was so eager to talk about business that it seems possible he had more faith in that than in the sport that had brought him so much. All the same, how was he ever going to gain diplomas? Or function in a normal work setting? Danny told a journalist in this period that Johan was easy for others to deal with but hard on himself. He entered 'often' when asked whether he felt tense before exams. When he failed, he wrote, it 'seriously' impeded him. After the words 'Working for a long time on something without getting tired ...' he filled in '... isn't something I'm good at'. That was also clear from a test of his intellectual development. Most of his answers were correct, which resulted in a creditable IQ score of 115, but it was striking that Cruyff completed fully only one of the ten pages of tests. Not because he skipped questions, but because he suddenly stopped. Sometimes halfway through. In a linguistic test about logical thinking he left most of the questions unanswered. In the margin he wrote in block capitals, 'DISCONTINUED BECAUSE OF HEADACHE.'

As if he simply couldn't go any further.

When problems arose he would only 'rarely' look to people at Ajax for help, he noted. And if he did, it usually concerned 'finances'. Whom *did* he consult, then? He wrote in capitals next to that question, 'DEPENDS WHO BENEFITS FROM IT.'

His scepticism, bitterness even perhaps, is difficult to interpret in isolation from Cor Coster's influence on him. The striker now saw himself as an underpaid employee who had been 'had' by the board when he signed his four-year contract in 1967. He deserved to get what he was worth, he felt, echoing what Coster had told him, not what the directors *thought* he was worth. But unfortunately the contract was valid for another two years, so all that could be done in the short term was to put Ajax under pressure. Which Cruyff and his 'manager' did to their heart's content. They spoke openly about offers from abroad, where life was far better from a taxation point of view. In fact, life as a professional footballer in the Netherlands was 'practically impossible' with taxation at 60 per cent, which made Cruyff wonder, 'What else can you do but leave?'

Remarks of that kind were extremely unusual in Dutch sporting circles and Cor Coster often took the blame. He quickly became the nation's most notorious father-in-law. Johan's manager was turning the norms of football upside down in a way that testified to his audacity and shameless bravado. With his suntanned face, white-grey hair and working-class accent, he presented himself as the boisterous whisky-drinking type, regarded as colourful by his friends and 'vulgar' by his enemies. In newspaper interviews the businessman deplored the amateurism of still-young Dutch professional football. A true professional knew how to sell himself, he believed, and his famous son-in-law − 'a commodity' for everyone, 'including Ajax and foreign clubs' − should be 'expensive'.

Deploying Johan's image as 'you know, that nice quick-witted footballer', the maximum price would be demanded from now on. Coster was no longer captivated by his trade in watches, gold and jewellery, so he decided in the spring of 1969 to devote three days a week to his son-in-law's commercial activities. 'I

believed that a person who was so good at playing football, and
who entertained people so pleasantly, should receive princely
remuneration,' Coster told journalists.

Those were the laws of the market, and the 48-year-old Cor
Coster was even more wedded to them than Johan. In childhood Cor had been a street kid, like the fictional character Ciske
de Rat. With little schooling and a lot of bluff and dubious dealings, he had managed to work his way up out of poverty on the
Westelijke Eilanden, close to the Jordaan district of Amsterdam.
His father had abandoned the family when he was young,
leaving his mother – like Johan's – to earn a living as a cleaner.
Coster had been a 'difficult boy', he admitted, 'aggressive above
all', but during the war that attitude had stood him in good
stead. After being sent to work in Germany in 1942, at the age
of twenty-two, he rose to become camp leader there, and later
in Latvia. Such a wartime career had the whiff of collaboration
to some. As an assistant *Lagerführer* you were, after all, as a matter
of course, an *SS-Frontarbeiter*. But no firm proof had ever been
produced of morally incorrect behaviour that went beyond the
ordinary survival urges of a forced labourer, let alone membership of the dreaded *Waffen-SS*. Perhaps the young Coster was
simply tougher, more cunning and more of an opportunist by
nature than most of the other prisoners.

After the liberation of the Netherlands he applied those qualities to his trade in watches. 'You know how that goes,' he said
in an interview. 'A bit of black-market stuff. Selling through
the Waterlooplein flea market. Determined to make a fortune
out of a bit of dry bread. In those times I made a lot of enemies.
Trouble and low ebbs. Problems with the tax people; problems
with customs inspectors.' And with defaulters. 'If I didn't get
cash from my customers quickly enough,' he said, 'I'd go and
see them. If there was no other way, I'd beat them up on their
own doorstep for a hundred guilders.' His love of adventure and
his business instincts made him rich. Along with his wife and
daughters he moved into a newly built mansion on the Herman

Heijermansweg in Amsterdam-Zuid. Locally he was known as
The Smuggler.

This self-made man was explosive enough to settle quarrels
in traffic – or in the football stadium, if someone else was sitting
in his seat – with his fists. Roger Pop, son of Cor's stepdaugh-
ter, had a glint in his eye when he thought back to his fighting
grandpa. 'And he almost always got away with it,' Pop says now.
'Johan got that habit of intimidating others from him, by the
way. Frightening people in order to get what you wanted; that's
what Coster was like. Cruyff too, later.'

Not everyone saw the funny side of what Cor Coster got up
to. Some continued to regard him as a dubious character because
of his wartime past. When his daughter Danny wanted to get
engaged to the Jewish entrepreneur's son Sanny Lampie at the
age of seventeen, Coster felt a need to visit all his Jewish business
relations one by one to assure them the wartime stories doing
the rounds about him were unfounded. But the stories did not
go away. Two years later, on Danny and Johan's wedding day,
some members of the Cruyff family refused to shake Coster's
hand, which was hardly surprising, perhaps, given how Johan's
father and Uncle Dirk had helped Jews during the war. Stories
from the war years regularly blew into Henny and Johan's sports
shop on the Elandsgracht too, along with their older customers.
Henny felt passed over because Johan had chosen Coster to be
his manager. 'Johan and I are going to build an empire,' Henny
had often said. He could forget about that now. Jealousy took
hold of him, although for the time being he kept the stories
about Uncle Cor and the SS to himself.

Whatever you thought of Coster, he knew what could be
bought and sold in the world, and he grew to become Cruyff's
new father figure. 'Cor shielded me nicely,' said Johan later.
With his father-in-law's help he no longer needed to 'be
unpleasant' towards people who wanted something from him.
In the summer of 1969, his father-in-law discovered that comparable stars like George Best and Franz Beckenbauer were

earning far more than Johan. Even the new Ajax striker Dick van Dijk turned out to have a higher basic salary, and nobody would dare to claim that the rather static Van Dijk was as good a player as Cruyff.

An adjustment to the contract to take account of new circumstances seemed no more than logical to Coster and Cruyff. But Van Praag refused to hear of it. A contract was a contract. As for Coster, Van Praag had not a single good word to say about him and regarded his meddling with Johan as 'downright exploitation'. So, when Cruyff announced that he was going to bring Coster along to the negotiations, Van Praag forbade it. Players always came to such talks on their own, and he regarded comparisons with other people's incomes as unseemly.

Shortly after that, Johan nevertheless walked into the boardroom with his father-in-law. It was a matter of recognition, of market value, of a right that needed to be fought for.

'Johan,' said Van Praag. 'Won't you first come here on your own?'

'No, both of us,' said Cruyff. Why should he have to come alone to take on five middle-aged men who knew far more about social insurance and tax arrangements than he did?

'Unacceptable,' was the answer. 'We first want to talk with you without your father-in-law present.'

'Talk among yourselves, then. I'll wait outside, because I'm not coming in here without my father-in-law.'

The irritation mounted, but in the end streetfighter Coster was allowed into the boardroom. Eventually Cruyff achieved the same salary as Van Dijk, 50,000 guilders plus premiums and bonuses. It made Cruyff the first Dutch footballer to engage an official business manager, and it proved a success. Many more would follow.

By this time he was busy opening another new shop. For a year now he'd been part owner with his brother of the sporting goods store on the Elandsgracht and he'd got a taste for business.

That became clear during a 'performance/motivation test' that psychologist Grunwald asked him to fill in. Under 'job/occupation' he wrote not 'professional footballer', as one might expect, but 'director of Shoetique'.

His second directorship was the result of a desire to make Danny happy. His wife had been in a bad way since the spring because of a miscarriage. Their dream family with five children suddenly looked very distant. No matter what the doctor said, she had crying fits and nightmares for weeks and Johan struggled to reassure her. He talked to her for hours late at night. He played Nat King Cole records for her. He tried to distract her with plans to have fun. He proposed city trips and took inspiration from Bobby and Tootje Nees, a couple they knew who had been living with them for months. Bobby and Tootje had needed somewhere to stay while their house was renovated, and the door in Vinkeveen was thrown open to them in the Cruyffian manner. Then the idea for Shoetique presented itself. If Bobby is so happy with his restaurant, Johan thought, and Tootje with her hairdressing salon, maybe Danny would be happy with a shoe shop. She can fill her days with her favourite pastime, fashion, and have a good reason to go outside and see the sun shine.

Danny agreed to it.

In the Kinkerstraat in Amsterdam Oud-West, they found a premises that had previously been a dry-cleaner's. The idea of a hip, exclusive shoe shop for young men appealed to Danny. 'There's a tremendous need for affordable, stylish men's shoes,' she was convinced. 'We'll also sell patent leather shoes in all kinds of colours, because I don't see why a man who wears a lovely red jumper shouldn't be able to put on shoes to match.' That a shop selling 'exclusive' footwear might not be the most suitable business for a working-class district like the Kinkerbuurt was no obstacle, it seemed, or perhaps they just didn't give it much thought.

Johan in particular was 'terribly busy' with it, Danny said

later, even though he didn't know anything about shoes. The shop was simply 'a must' to 'liberate' her from the miscarriage, she openly admitted some years afterwards. Moreover, 'In about seven years from now, when perhaps Johan won't so easily be able to play football, he'll have to do something more than coach the Vinkeveense Boys. By that point he needs to be in a position where he doesn't have to work for a boss, and instead we can fall back on something of his own.'

Danny could see it all before her. It would be a friendly little shop without any of that boring straight seating along the walls for trying on shoes. Instead, it would have attractive chairs scattered about on a Bordeaux-red carpet, a little bar so that anyone could drop in for a cup of coffee or a glass of sherry, walls covered in shop-dressing felt, like at home, only ivory coloured, and a ceiling of brass plates.

The shop was due to open on 3 December 1969, so they needed to buy in stocks of shoes quickly. For the right kind of exclusive footwear you had to be in Italy, Danny knew. It seemed to her a good idea to book a trip from Monday 13 to Wednesday 15 October; Ajax could surely do without Johan at the start of that week.

What complicated matters was that Johan needed to be in Holten, Overijssel, at twelve noon on the Wednesday for the start of a three-day training camp for the Dutch national team. And not just any old training camp. The following week, on Wednesday 22 October, Oranje would be playing Bulgaria in Rotterdam. It was a match they needed to win, if the Netherlands were to have any chance of qualifying for the World Cup in Mexico. All parties had agreed to this early training camp. The KNVB and the clubs – which often argued about freeing up their players – wanted to do all they could to get the Netherlands a place in the competition for the first time since the war. The match against Bulgaria was their last chance for 'Mexico'.

It was all or nothing, as Cruyff of course knew. A year and a half before, he had stressed the importance of the World Cup

qualifying rounds in interviews. He also recognised the importance of extra training. But he often found the organisation at the
KNVB 'pathetic' and didn't take the people who worked there
particularly seriously. The social insurance scheme at Oranje
had been improved as a result of his persistent criticism, but he
believed it was still not good enough. Moreover, the international
match was not due to take place for another week, so it would all
be fine. It was with that conviction that he rang national coach
Georg Kessler. He told him he was going to Italy on a business
trip and would therefore arrive at the training camp in Holten not
on the Wednesday but on the Thursday. He said that for personal
reasons – Danny's wellbeing – the trip could not be postponed
and that on his return he would engage with full commitment.

Unfortunately for Cruyff, the soccer bigwigs had decided
to join forces and tighten the reins. Kessler, an intelligent and
articulate coach at just thirty-seven, son of a Dutch mother and a
German father, wanted to demonstrate his authority – especially
when faced with a player who had taken part in only two of the
five World Cup qualifying matches. 'Your shoes are no concern
of mine,' Kessler said. 'You're a full-time professional. The date
of the training camp was announced well in advance. Just you
make sure you're in Holten on the Wednesday at twelve. If not,
you'll have to face the consequences. I won't be making any
exceptions for you.'

Cruyff hung up and his decision was made. He would, of
course, go to Italy. He wouldn't just be buying shoes, he'd be
giving Danny a relaxing trip on doctor's advice and, who could
say, maybe it would also bring husband and wife even closer.
So on the Monday morning they flew, 'a cosy twosome' as she
put it, by KLM to Milan. They visited shoe factories and shops,
and had intimate meals in restaurants. Danny began to see
how much she meant to Johan. His caring, his patience, their
shop . . . This might be exactly what their relationship needed.
'Why had we been treating each other in such a stupid way?'
she wondered later. 'To take each other down a peg? Had I been

wanting to show Johan that not every girl would fall into his lap like a ripe apple?'

They drove to Florence and Verona, where Danny passed 'wonderful days full of distraction'. 'We had such a good time. We were suddenly completely out of the rut. All the misery and wretchedness slipped off us almost unnoticed. No phone calls for once, no interviews, no bullshit in the newspapers.' As far as she was concerned, the further away from football the better. If a match was cancelled because of snow she might exclaim, 'At last a Sunday without football!' And now, instead of being spoken to in the street by complete strangers – 'That was useless again, hey Johan?' – they were enjoying some leisurely shopping in northern Italy, waking up in a good hotel, breakfasting in bed. They met businesspeople and stored away beautiful impressions.

The hours flew by. 'It was Wednesday morning in no time,' as Danny put it.

They didn't land at Schiphol that Wednesday until ten to nine in the evening. Johan treated the journalists waiting for him there to a 'muddled story' about Italian saints' days, a fully booked plane and thick fog around Milan that meant their trip in a rental car to the airport had taken an unusually long time. Cruyff had to admit that it was feeble of him not to have rung Kessler to inform him of his late arrival. In a transparent attempt to set things straight he said, 'I want to take part. I play 95 per cent for Mr Kessler and only 5 per cent for the Dutch team, precisely because Mr Kessler is trying so tremendously hard to make our trip to Mexico a reality.'

All 'cop-outs' said Ajax chairman Van Praag, who had impressed upon Johan before his departure the importance of arriving on time, as had Michels.

'I'm not going to put him in the team,' said Kessler. 'A young man with an attitude like that has no place in the Dutch national side.'

Cruyff was also fined by Ajax for bringing the club into

disrepute. And although he offered the KNVB, in writing, excuses for his 'careless' behaviour, he could forget both the training camp in Holten and the match against Bulgaria. Even Van Hanegem, a great admirer of Cruyff, thought he had 'misbehaved' and therefore didn't 'fit' in the team. In these hard times especially, with countless players injured, he had let the Dutch team down.

In a full De Kuip, Oranje went on to play 'too blandly for Mexico', as the press put it. Above all, the team lacked 'a great individualist' able to create openings in the Bulgarian defence. Which made sense, since the great individualist was at home in Vinkeveen watching the West Germany vs Scotland international. On his roof in the Scholeksterlaan was a large dish antenna and in the living room a modern TV set. That way, he told the press with a pride bordering on defiance, he would see the match in colour on German TV. Perhaps he secretly watched Oranje from time to time. If so, he would have seen, in black and white, that without him the team created too few chances and could not get beyond 1-1.

The now almost guaranteed failure to qualify for the World Cup was Cruyff's fault, according to the football-loving Dutch. He had made a 'stupid move' and thereby 'committed treason', as even supportive journalist Maarten de Vos wrote. There was more, too, because 'as those close to him know', he had 'changed markedly, especially since his wedding'.

Because of his marriage, Johan seemed increasingly to be becoming a Coster. Other factors became more important than football (Danny's influence) and he felt it was acceptable to mislead the press if it suited him (Cor's influence). Business was what mattered. Cruyff saw the fur coats on the stands and in the Ajax boardroom. He knew personally many of the wheeler-dealers who strutted about De Meer. He also knew many of the actors, writers, directors and folk singers who came to Ajax from the city centre on match days to be seen there. Those cultural figures found his elegant and artistic play stimulating and afterwards they came to talk to him in the modernised and expanded stadium restaurant, to give themselves something to boast about for the rest of the week. Everything at De Meer was increasingly modern. There was now 2.5-metre-tall fencing around the pitch, and there were turnstiles at the entrances, all the result of rising income. The club, the entrepreneurs and the entertainers: everyone was earning money at the expense of people like him. Something needed to be done about it.

From that perspective, the opening of Shoetique in the Kinkerstraat was a personal victory, a reason to look into the cameras outside the shopfront brimming with self-confidence, along with Danny. Entrepreneur Johan posed inside just as patiently while helping a customer to select new shoes, in front of his wife and the stylised 1920s eroticism on the wall. Life was looking good. As 'a cosy twosome' they'd ordered close to a thousand pairs of shoes in Italy, which would surely fly out of the Shoetique. After all, Johan reasoned, 'At every match at least twenty thousand people look at us, at me. All those twenty thousand need a new pair of shoes at least once a year. Let them come and buy those shoes from me.'

There was no lack of publicity, at any rate, and Johan was already dreaming of another five trendy shops. A 'drugstore' sounded interesting to him as well.

One person not so happy with all this was Henny Cruyff. Johan's older brother had been caught totally off guard by the opening of the Shoetique. He deduced from it that his plan for the two of them to go into business together was definitively off the table. Johan was ubiquitous in their sporting goods shop on the Elandsgracht – in the name, in the photos on the wall, and in the stories Henny used in his efforts to impress customers – but his actual person was rarely to be found amid the stacks of boxes of football boots, shirts and leather balls.

Not a day went by without customers looking to the left and right, past Henny, in the hope of catching a glimpse of the great Cruyff behind the counter. In vain. That was painful for Henny, confirmation time and again that his famous little brother had been fully absorbed into the Coster camp.

CHAPTER TWELVE

A rebel?

The more Cruyff rebelled, the more he was seen as a child of his time. In the late 1960s, rebellion was almost obligatory, and with his long hair and his impudence, Johan seemed just like a demonstrating student, or an entertainer in a dispute with big business. Anyone who was young and dissatisfied could easily identify with him. It had been that way for years. 'We editors loved to lash out at the sedate sports barons,' recalls Koos de Boer, a former journalist at daily *De Tijd*. 'I sent my children to an anti-authoritarian school and we stuck up for Johan Cruyff. All taken as read.' In 1966, when anarchistic rebels known as the Provos were shaking up public life in Amsterdam with their playful protests against the bourgeoisie, Cruyff was called a 'footballing Provo'. In light of his pig-headedness and the way he taunted those in authority that was perhaps understandable. He was undeniably a self-conscious baby-boomer who refused to submit to the old structures and tirelessly dedicated himself to change.

But such comparisons did not stand up to careful scrutiny. 'Anti-smoking magician' Robert Jasper Grootveld, a famous Provo who poked fun at society's 'nauseating petit-bourgeois mentality', had no interest in sport. For his part, the much-discussed sportsman, unlike many of his generation, never renounced his bourgeois milieu. It would not be going too far to say that every time Grootveld daubed the word 'cancer' on a cigarette advertisement, Cruyff lit up another one. He was not a leftist and certainly not an anarchist. The shopkeeper's son honoured his parents and challenged those in authority only if they were ignorant and preventing him from getting the salary he wanted.

As far as the rise of youth culture was concerned, Cruyff found 'that whole beat generation' rather 'foolish' and he regarded long hair on boys as 'attention-seeking', even 'disgusting'. He thought the hippies at best 'a nice sight' and he had little appreciation for the homosexuals who had begun openly declaring their sexual orientation. His own hippie-like appearance of the late 1960s can be wholly attributed to his fashion-conscious wife Danny.

Unlike most young men, he had no opinion about the Vietnam War or the American presence in that far-off country. When he thought about the violence in Southeast Asia, he saw first of all orphaned children, helplessly staring into space amid the devastation. As far as he was concerned, we should stop arguing about it and go and help those people. Cruyff preferred practical solutions to political wrangling. In Vinkeveen he voted for Hergroepering '70, a local party whose manifesto had as its main policy the protection of the villagers against ever-encroaching tourism. Its plea for less waterside recreation and better waterways for local people appealed to him more strongly than any number of vague ideals. The call for more democracy might be growing louder in society as a whole, but when journalists in leather jackets came to quantify his level of engagement for the umpteenth time, he held them at bay. 'I'm a footballer. I don't know a damn thing about democratisation. Go and ask an alderman or a member of parliament.' If the reporters persisted in fishing for his opinion they would eventually be told, 'I believe in an achievement-oriented society.'

If you insisted on calling him a rebel, then he was more the liberal than the left-wing sort, perhaps even right wing. It was no accident that it was *De Telegraaf*, regarded as unsavoury by left-wingers, that offered him a weekly column in 1970. The right-leaning morning daily saw in Cruyff someone who would retain readers. His opinions were worth a lot to the paper, namely 20,000 guilders a year, an astonishing fee. Some of the players marking him in premier division matches had to sweat their way through a whole season for that kind of money. Coster had spent weeks negotiating terms for the column and had reached a good deal. Because of course it wasn't very much work. On a Friday afternoon, or after a match, he would speak to reporter Jan de Deugd, who wrote the column for him. Then on Monday morning he would read in the paper what his ghost writer had made of it all.

In this period Cruyff also started to do something unusual. He demanded money for interviews. So many microphones were held under his nose that he started to feel like a 'dairy cow' who 'needed to fill column inches'. He was happy to continue filling those columns on the sports and news pages, that was part of his job, but from now on he would put a price on those other columns, in magazines or in newspaper supplements. Naturally Coster was behind that too, naturally there was an outcry, especially from the left, and naturally Cruyff ignored it. 'When you achieve something, it gives you self-confidence,' he said. 'Then you dare to speak your mind, as well.'

Cruyff's obsession with money was obvious when *De Telegraaf* asked him to describe what it was like to live 'at a level the average citizen will never reach'. A conversation about money seemed to Cruyff to be worth 250 guilders. The reporter agreed. She made her way to the canteen in De Meer, where she met the striker along with Danny. When Mrs Cruyff heard what her husband was going to talk about, she protested fiercely. 'When he decides to stick to the arrangement,' the report goes, 'Danny leaves the Ajax canteen agitated, and in a huff. Cruyff, after a final spoonful of asparagus soup, says, "She'll probably go to her mother, who lives right across from here."'

Without the slightest embarrassment he answered questions about his favourite subject: money. 'I'm crazy about it,' he said. 'Because for me it means a good life, doing whatever you like. My problem is that I'm a footballer. And nothing else. How do I create security for later, for me and for Danny? That's my problem. I'm earning well now. More than most Dutch people of my age. How much? I'm not telling, but don't forget that I live accordingly. At least, as far as I'm able to. Because if you look at it purely as a "life" then I have a rotten time. I simply don't have a chance to enjoy myself. And there's always the worry: how can I retain this standard of living?'

The street kid from red Betondorp, about whom Danny was probably grumbling at that very moment, had become a big spender. 'I eat well from it now, wear expensive clothes and don't have any worries; I live in a nice house, go on holiday for a month every year, and I want to keep things that way. Look, as a footballer you stay at the most luxurious hotels, so what do I do when I'm on holiday? I stay only at the top-class places and order the best of the best. I eat quite a lot and I like it; that costs me a fortune.'

The 'right-wing rebel' might strike out at the most unexpected moment in order to raise his salary a little, and sometimes other people's salaries too. He'd learnt that from his father-in-law. Towards the end of 1969 he recognised a suitable opportunity at the ceremony to crown the Sportsman, Sportswoman and Sports Club of the Year. At first Johan and the other Ajax players acted as if everything was fine. They sat looking relaxed in their club suits with all the other athletes in the De Meerpaal restaurant in Dronten, where the television broadcast was to take place. Then Cruyff and team captain Gert Bals walked up to the director. They told him that the players wanted fifty guilders each. Otherwise they'd be leaving immediately.

The director Bob Bremer, who had a hundred and one things on his mind shortly before the live transmission, was shocked. He would never forget the incident and spoke to hardly anyone about it. 'I thought it was ridiculous,' he said later. 'And wrong in principle. Sportspeople never asked for money for appearances like that. They showed up because it was an honour to be there. Cruyff and Bals took advantage of the situation. I refused to give them the money.'

Bremer, then in his early thirties, quickly wrote a script for the presenter: 'Unfortunately Ajax are unable to be here to accept the prize.' But his superiors made him agree to the payment. The broadcast must not suffer over such a trifle. 'So I paid,' says Bremer. One final attempt to get Ajax chairman Jaap van Praag to intervene failed. 'That's a matter for the players,' Bremer was told. 'I'm not going to get involved.' The television director thought it was outrageous for a nationally famous club chairman like Van Praag to walk away from his responsibilities, but he was powerless in the face of such opportunism – or cowardice. 'All deeply unpleasant,' he said.

The programme was a success. Tennis player Tom Okker and athlete Mia Gommers were delighted to be named Sportsman and Sportswoman of the Year. As they had been a year earlier, Ajax were chosen as the most important team and the players were enormously happy with their fifty-guilder windfall. Johan had fixed it nicely for them once again.

Shortly after that another opportunity arose to bring things to a head and again it involved a popular television programme. On the evening of Saturday 17 January 1970, Cruyff appeared in the new quiz programme *Eén van de acht* (One of the Eight). He already knew presenter Mies Bouwman from *Mies en scène*, having been a guest on the programme eighteen months before. Perhaps that was why he acted with such calm self-assurance. The international sports press had named him the fourth best player in Europe, a respectful distance away from the number one, Gianni Rivera of AC Milan. Several days before the airing of *Eén van de acht*, British journalists, after his sparkling performance in the friendly international between England and the Netherlands, declared him a 'world-class player'.

Bouwman made reference to all that praise and the million guilders the British newspapers said he was worth, if not far more. Did Johan actually think he would ever be able to earn such a sum? Well, Johan thought he would, but not in this little country with its low salaries and high taxes. So he had agreed with Ajax that after the current season ended he could go to play for a foreign club, he said. As long as that foreign club was willing to pay at least a million guilders.

It was then that the name Barcelona was first mentioned publicly. He had always wanted to play for that club, Cruyff said. And according to the latest reports, the Spanish borders might be about to open up to foreign players. He knew the current coach at Barcelona, Vic Buckingham, from his time with Ajax, which was good too. But a transfer to Italy would of course be a little more convenient in light of his ownership of a shoe shop, he thought aloud in front of the camera. (Shoetique wasn't exactly doing a roaring trade.) Everything would be different if Ajax were to offer him a fantastic new contract in the summer. Perhaps then he might stay in the Netherlands.

According to Van Praag none of these assertions was true. 'Johan is just flying kites again,' he told the press. 'He was merely selling himself.' But Johan refused to take that lying down. Shortly before the next league match, in Nijmegen, he looked the chairman straight in the eye. 'I'm no liar, Mr Van Praag,' he said. 'In these circumstances it's better if I don't play.' He refused to get changed. Dr Rolink came to mediate and eventually the striker got what he wanted. After the season was over, he would be allowed to move abroad if he could substantially improve his position by doing so.

The next day the agreement was put in writing, during the training camp in Wassenaar, two days before an away match against Naples in the Inter-Cities Fairs Cup. Such a thing would never have entered into any other player's head at such a moment, Cruyff's all the more so. It was Coster's law put into practice: strike while the opposing party is under pressure.

Coach Michels, fearful that his preparations might be disrupted, was relieved and again the businessman on studs saw confirmation of his opinion that in football, a game lacking in norms, you had to create norms of your own. In reality it all came down to the law of the jungle.

But maybe he wasn't yet ready to play abroad. His performance on 8 April 1970 gave plenty of reason for doubt. He certainly wasn't the strongest player that evening in north London. In the semi-final of the Inter-Cities Fairs Cup, Arsenal proved tough and determined opponents. The English team had decided not to assign just one player to mark Cruyff; wherever he was on the pitch, they would make it impossible for him to play the ball. 'No matter who entered into a duel with him, Cruyff had to be tackled extremely hard,' says former Arsenal player Frank McLintock. 'We took it in turns. And it worked.'

In north London the fixture with Ajax was seen as a clash of cultures, between the inventors of honest football and the frivolous characters who played on the continent, fickle types who turned left and right where real men went straight ahead. The motto was: go for it. 'So we did what we always did when we had clubs from the continent visiting,' McLintock remembers. 'It was the only way to deal with their technical superiority.'

In a packed Highbury Stadium, Cruyff was given 'not a single moment' for his accelerations and evasive manoeuvres, as he admitted afterwards. The Arsenal players worked 'like mad' and whatever he tried, there was always a Brit there to block him. He often dropped back to midfield, probably to avoid the uncompromising central defender McLintock, but there too he immediately felt the hot breath of an opponent on his neck.

Everyone on both sides agreed that Arsenal, in theory, had a simple working team and Ajax a team of high-class players. After Arsenal's 3-0 victory, McLintock said he'd been playing against the best team of the year. Victory had been possible because, when it came down to it, the brilliant Cruyff offered 'little resistance'.

Characteristic of the relationship on the pitch was that, in between tackles, McLintock enjoyed playing the 'wonderfully arrogant' Ajax striker. 'He moved differently, he touched the ball differently, he was in places you didn't expect him,' the former Scottish hothead still recalls. 'And meanwhile it was as if he looked right through you because he was busy with more important things.'

Teammate and forward George Graham had been unable to take his eyes off Cruyff. 'I'd heard stories about him during tournaments on the continent,' he says. 'But at Highbury it was a treat to see him from so close up for the first time. He reminded me of the greatest players I'd ever seen, of Ferenc Puskás, Pelé, and above all of Alfredo Di Stéfano, because for a centre forward he ran around in midfield a lot.'

'Ajax simply had more talent than we did,' remembers forward Charlie George, who with his long hair and creativity was to some extent the Cruyff of Arsenal at the time. 'You could tell that Johan had an amazingly quick brain. We were a young team on the rise, like them, but we added a degree of belligerency and team spirit that they found no way to combat.'

Optimistic as ever, Cruyff predicted that in the return match, a week later in Amsterdam, he and Ajax would create 'our usual seven chances'. It didn't work out that way. In the Olympic Stadium the Gunners held their own without much trouble. The final score was 1-0. Arsenal were through to the final – to the annoyance of Michels, who in London especially had seen his star players Keizer and Cruyff jump over English legs 'like starball fireworks'. In other words they were 'frightened little fawns'. A year earlier he had announced that Ajax belonged right at the top of European football, and now this. The 'psychological anxiety' was 'intolerable'.

Eleven days later there was another setback. On 26 April 1970 Ajax allowed themselves to be pushed aside by Feyenoord 'like little children', as *De Tijd* wrote. De Vos had described Cruyff as being fearful before when facing the sometimes rough play of

Feyenoord, and this Sunday afternoon the game had 'not lived up to his magnificent talent for a moment'. Yet it was Cruyff who brought victory in the premier division closer. First, he reacted nimbly by shooting a ball deflected by keeper Eddy Treijtel into the goal. That bit of attentiveness reduced the 3-1 gap in the second half to 3-2. Then eight minutes before the end of the match he leapt at Treijtel with unusual ferocity, enabling a high cross from Suurbier to flutter into the goal.

Again Michels was angry. Despite the 3-3 draw, Feyenoord were 'a class above' Ajax, he said, and more 'ruthless' too. He was not surprised when Feyenoord played in the final of the European Cup ten days later and won (beating Celtic), after which Michels told *Voetbal International* that the Rotterdammers were 'more truly professional' than Ajax. At least they didn't 'bullshit' so much about their finances. For the umpteenth time, Michels used the words 'mentality' and 'attitude' to describe what was wrong with his players.

So what did the players think? As far as they were concerned enough was enough. The 'inhuman' coach now really should stop his eternal nagging, his stupid sanctions and his condescending remarks in public.

The explosion came on 18 May 1970. Ajax had a chance of winning the league in a home game against SVV, who had already been relegated. Before the match the players were fairly relaxed. Cruyff's stepfather Henk Angel was given a cassette recorder for twenty-five years of loyal service to Ajax. Michels delivered a witty speech to mark the groundsman's anniversary, something he was good at, and the board gave Uncle Henk a gold watch with an inscription, as well as an envelope stuffed with cash.

After that the tension mounted between the trainer and the players on this Whit Monday, to the point where the 8-0 victory (Van Dijk five goals, Cruyff three) was almost an irrelevance, a trifle. It was Michels who lit the fuse by substituting three players (Bals, Mühren and Hulshoff) without giving any reason. As a consequence, the entire squad shut itself in the changing room after the championship match was over. Nobody was allowed in. Trainers and board members could forget the usual champagne and entertaining antics in front of the cameras. Without having run a lap of honour, without throwing flowers into the full stands, the players held a serious meeting. They needed to decide whether or not to go to the champions' reception that evening or to boycott it in protest at Michels' dictatorial behaviour.

The Ajax players occupied the changing room the way students had occupied a university building on the Spui a year before, determined to make those at the top see the error of their ways. Leader of the protest was Piet Keizer, described by psychologist Grunwald as 'chief troublemaker'. Keizer, more so than Cruyff, was a democratically minded footballer who thought on behalf of the group and regarded his fellow players as equals. The solution to the conflict was sought in a vote, with the whole squad taking part. That was how things were done in a modern democracy and in the end eight of the fifteen players indicated they did want to go to the reception in the Hotel Krasnapolsky. So the team went.

It was a bizarre aftermath to the fourth national title in five years under Michels. Despite the team's considerable success – Ajax also won the KNVB Cup – dissatisfaction was dominant. Keizer, who had not been on speaking terms with Michels since an argument in the Arsenal changing room, declared to his teammates that he didn't want to play under him any longer. Cruyff once again dreamed out loud about Barcelona. But the Spanish border was still closed to foreign footballers, and since both Michels and Keizer took up the reins again in July (although still without speaking to each other), much remained the same at Ajax. In an attempt to introduce the sturdiness that was required, 33-year-old goalkeeper Gert Bals was dismissed and the relatively heavy reserve keeper Heinz Stuy took his place. Tempestuous junior Johan Neeskens was acquired from

Heemstede and he quickly secured a place in the squad, which meant Cruyff had a tireless 'sentry' behind him.

However enjoyable victory may have been, for Johan, now aged twenty-three, football had been relegated to second place. In first place was Danny and she was pregnant again. That made him 'a hundred times happier' than glory on a patch of grass measuring 60 by 100 metres.

As he had been after the miscarriage, during Danny's pregnancy he was solicitude itself. It occupied all his attention. Danny was nauseous for months, even needing a drip to rehydrate her after vomiting so much. In between training sessions Johan drove to Vinkeveen to care for her with the patience of a saint and to raise her morale. He fed her when all she felt like doing was going to bed after 'puking' yet again. He would sternly call her to the table: 'Come back, your plate isn't empty yet!'

'Please, Johan . . .'

'Eat!'

After a while Johan was grateful for every day that nothing serious happened to her or the unborn child. Danny suffered haemorrhages and grew weaker and weaker. She kept needing different injections. The situation was so precarious that they decided that, if the pregnancy did end well, they wouldn't name their first child after one of their parents. Their life was not in any way traditional, and the name needn't be either, they decided. So if it was a girl she would not be called Nel or Dien.

For Johan it was an advantage that, as he put it, he didn't have a normal job. If he'd been working nine to five he wouldn't have been able to support Danny so assiduously. A footballer could adjust better to extraordinary circumstances, and on top of that he suffered a groin strain on 6 August in Bruges. You might say – and indeed it was said – that the injury was fortunate from his point of view. It was invisible, hard for anyone to check, and it meant he was able to be with Danny a lot, even after the new season started.

Because of his groin strain, Cruyff missed the first three league matches of 1970-71. In the fourth, on 12 September at home to DWS, he suffered another setback. After fifteen minutes he got around two opponents, perhaps rather recklessly for someone who had just recovered fitness, and unfortunately came upon the third directly in front of him, Frits Soetekouw, his former teammate, who had been dismissed from Ajax three years before and had been nursing great frustration ever since. Soetekouw stuck out his knee, because, he said afterwards, 'What else could I do? That guy is so terribly fast!' Cruyff felt the knee right in his groin. He hobbled off the pitch immediately. 'This is what I've always been afraid of,' he said to the press later that afternoon. 'A persistent injury. It'll cost me at least five weeks.'

The fear of being declared permanently unfit lay remarkably deep. It had happened to at least three well-known footballers recently, and in some cases it had led to endless squabbling with insurance companies. To avoid such a nightmare, it seemed to Cruyff best to avoid taking any risks for the foreseeable future.

Weeks went by and nobody understood what was really going on. His recovery was progressing as slowly as his waxwork at the branch of Madame Tussauds that had recently opened in the Kalverstraat. Was Cruyff playacting, and if so why? Because of Danny or to hasten his departure from Amsterdam? Board members gossiped, fellow players grumbled, journalists accused him of malingering. Club doctor Rolink coolly declared him 'completely recovered'. Despite any pain he might have, Johan would be just fine kicking a ball, Rolink said, but 'he lacks the courage'. The groin injury became a national issue and no one, not even Ajax chairman Van Praag, stuck up for Cruyff. 'How terribly disappointed I am in all those people,' the patient responded in October 1970 in *Het Vrije Volk*. 'For years they worship you, pander to you, and now this. Terrible. Only now do I see who my real friends are. There aren't many of them. I talk about it for hours with Danny. We can't figure it out. Yes,

Danny has cried, I don't mind telling you that. It's too much for her as well. Football is my profession. I have to earn my bread by playing soccer. Don't you think I realise that I have to keep on playing? No club is going to want a Johan Cruyff who's been out of circulation for a long time. You can't rest on your laurels. You can't live on fresh air. I'm not stupid.'

Ajax dragged their heels without their agile and creative troublemaker and fell further and further down the premier division. But Cruyff didn't play. He regarded himself as fragile – five years later he would still be using that word in books and magazines. And for precisely that reason he longed for support from others, from referees, fellow players, board members and doctors. Not so much from the sceptical Rolink but certainly from Salo Muller. The masseur had had a soft spot for Johan ever since the day he saw him as a junior cycling along the Middenweg in shorts in the freezing cold. In the following years he had often taken Jopie under his wing, slipped him chocolate eclairs, given him extra meals because the boy wasn't getting enough to eat at home, where he was probably given too few cuddles as well and needed a bit of extra attention from time to time.

But the masseur wasn't blind to Johan's less desirable qualities. 'If I told him that something didn't amount to much, he often refused to accept that from me. He'd simply persist: no, no, Salo, just feel it! Even when there was nothing wrong. I've had to treat him far more often than anyone else. I've never seen him go out on to the pitch without claiming he felt something that wasn't right. If I asked how he was doing he'd start talking about an elbow, an ankle, a calf, if it came to it something in his neck. "I only worry about you when you don't have anything to complain about," I once said to him.'

Muller saw Johan limping so often that he wondered whether it was a way to put himself centre stage. A cry for attention. Muller therefore merely gave him the benefit of the doubt when the groin injury played up so badly in the autumn of 1970. 'I took a midway position,' the masseur remembers. 'Johan wasn't really faking it, in my view, but that groin was in pretty good condition after a while. There wasn't so very much wrong with it. I told him that, too, but not in public.'

You could hardly call Cruyff a wimp. Throughout his career he would hurt opponents with surreptitious minor fouls. In training sessions he could dish it out quite strongly, and even an ordinary collision with his sharp bones could be unpleasant for the other player. The new goalkeeper Heinz Stuy would always remember how rough he could be. 'During training I tried to catch a high ball,' he remembers. 'But Johan was so cunning, he jumped up and just before he attempted to head the ball he knocked my arm away. Goal. I protested to Michels, but he said, "You need to defend yourself better." I was so angry that when the next high ball came in I knocked Johan to the ground with my elbow. Everybody was shocked. He lay there unconscious for a full minute. Then he came round and said, "Nicely done."'

It was this toughness that Cruyff would deploy in the period that followed. And not to everyone's liking.

CHAPTER THIRTEEN

Everything went smoothly with Number 14

Before 30 October 1970 Cruyff had never shown much interest in shirt numbers. After his debut in 1964 he had played as number 8, later number 9 and sometimes 10. It didn't seem to matter much to him, which was rather strange in a way, since from early childhood he had developed a particular sensitivity to numbers. At the counter in his parents' greengrocer's shop he had taught himself arithmetical tricks and all his life he would have a special relationship with numbers and number series. But an event on that Friday evening in 1970 would later be described as historic. It didn't seem to mean very much at the time: an everyday scene in a changing room in a glorified broom cupboard behind a scruffy wooden door, tucked away deep under the stands of the Olympic Stadium in Amsterdam.

It happened amid players walking back and forth in the changing room at the end of a concrete passageway under strip lights. Ajax midfielder Gerrie Mühren had been playing in the forward line for weeks, as a replacement for the injured – or possibly 'faking' – Cruyff. So he had been wearing Cruyff's usual number 9. Johan was back, for a home game against PSV, so Mühren went to get his own number 6 out of the basket. He couldn't find it. Cruyff saw Gerrie's panicky rummaging and said generously, 'Just keep that 9, I'll take this shirt.'

He picked out the shirt with number 14 on it, which happened to be lying there. It was the number for a reserve player, but that didn't bother him. Especially if it meant he could help someone who had never begrudged him anything. Cruyff appreciated Mühren's modesty and technique, and it had been a difficult season for the midfielder; he'd sat out quite a few matches without complaining.

No one paid any attention to Cruyff as he ran on to the field at eight that evening with that strange number, nor indeed to Mühren with his number 9. They focused on Cruyff's play, which after months of absence was surprisingly good. 'He got past opponents almost unerringly,' wrote *Het Vrije Volk*, even 'inimitably', and as a result he was 'the inspiration' for 'many unpredictable Ajax attacks'. Cruyff's presence seemed to be making his teammates play a good deal better than they had done for weeks. As of old, they profited from his agility, his tactically clever manoeuvres and his ball control.

Cruyff had reason to be satisfied with his return. Ajax won 1-0 against the higher placed PSV and, at least as importantly, he played the entire match without pain. In the bowels of the stadium he contentedly lit a cigarette and decided to hold on to the number.

The same went for Mühren. Johan had helped him to give far greater depth to his game and he'd scored the only goal of the match.

Midfielder Gerrie with the shirt number of the striker and the striker with the number of a reserve: it had brought them luck and should therefore stay that way.

Possibly as a result of his successful comeback, several days later Cruyff again felt strong enough for a fresh surprise attack on the club board. It was prompted by the bonuses for matches won. Because of his groin injury, Cruyff had missed three European Cup matches that season, two against Nëntori Tirana (2-2 and 2-0) and the home tie against FC Basel (3-0). He thought it was unreasonable that he had not received the corresponding bonuses, which added up to more than 7,000 guilders. According to the terms of his contract, he had no right to them, since rewards for wins and draws in the European Cup needed to be paid only to players who took part, but in practice injured players often did receive them, whereas Johan hadn't. After all his threats about going to play abroad and his recurring demands, the board had no desire to pay him bonuses. 'The issue,' Van Praag confided in a journalist, 'is that his father-in-law is playing a game with us. What we're doing now is our response.'

It had become a minor power struggle and so Cruyff picked a strategic moment: the run-up to a European Cup match. On the night before FC Basel vs Ajax, in the players' hotel in Switzerland, he asked for permission to speak to the board. It was granted. In the hotel bar Cruyff said that he now really did want to have that money. He had been a normal part of the squad at the time, he said, before adding threateningly, 'And I would like to see that payment arranged before the match begins tomorrow.'

'We'll have to give it some thought,' Van Praag answered, according to *Boem*. The chairman then added, 'We don't know about that yet.'

'What do you mean,' Cruyff went on, 'we-don't-know-about-that-yet?'

The gloves came off in the hotel bar in Basel and the striker decided to fetch the coach. But so close to a European Cup tie Michels had his mind on other things than the financial wrapping-up of matches already played. He wanted peace and quiet. Concentration. Team spirit. 'Those things aren't my responsibility,' Michels growled and then left. At which point Cruyff exploded. 'I want my bonuses!' he shouted. 'The whole lot of you can drop dead. I'm not talking any longer. It's over.'

Van Praag and treasurer Henk Timman once again referred Johan to his contract. But Cruyff stormed off and rang Danny.

'I'm coming home,' he said. 'I'm not playing. I damn well refuse.'

'Stay calm,' his wife replied. 'If you come back you'll just be piling more problems on top.'

'I refuse.'

'Just listen . . .'

The board was used to this sort of behaviour from Cruyff. It wasn't the first time he'd come up with demands immediately before a match. Sometimes he surprised treasurer Timman by sitting in the canteen of an amateur club Ajax was about to play, pointing outside and saying, 'Those people have come here for me.' Ten per cent of the takings as a bonus didn't seem too much to ask; could he just pick it up now? When Timman refused, Johan would generally call Cor Coster for advice, but he usually backed down, if only because the treasurer would eventually end the discussion with an 'Are you out of your mind?' Timman was often troubled by Johan's impertinence and greed, but the tax expert could never be angry with him for long. Johan's pressure tactics were matched by his candour, his playfulness and the endearing fact that he had once driven to the Timmans' house in Amsterdam-Zuid to introduce Danny to them: 'I've got myself a girl!' The other players never did things like that. Johan was after all a child of the club, a rascal, a top talent who always wanted to occupy a unique position.

In Basel, Van Praag and Timman presented Johan with a choice: play the match or take the first train back to Vinkeveen tomorrow. The striker decided to participate on that fourth of November – and how. That evening in Basel he came up with a performance that garnered admiration far beyond the Netherlands and Switzerland. From the very start in the St Jakob Park he drove his direct opponent round the bend. He went ahead of the team in a sublime 'festival of backheels and passes', as *Het Parool* was to describe it. The high point came

twenty minutes before the final whistle. FC Basel were actually
1-0 up, but that soon changed. After a throw-in by Keizer in
FC Basel's half, the ball reached Vasović. The last man, who
in line with the total football advocated by Michels had moved
into midfield, dribbled for some way towards the Basel goal.
He watched as Cruyff, facing him, suddenly turned round and
sprinted ahead. Vasović immediately sent the ball arcing in his
direction. Number 14 took it and ended up on the right-hand
side of the penalty area along with a Swiss defender. There he
stood still, close to the goal line, his back to the goal and with
two defenders behind him now. An impossible position, you
might think. He proved otherwise. As if it was a training session, he flipped the ball up and with an overhead kick created a
kind of backwards cross. Midfielder Nico Rijnders leapt at the
high ball, got to it just before the keeper and headed it into the
empty goal – 1-1.

Wheeling his arms, Cruyff flew at Rijnders as if he'd scored
himself. He had really, too, since his cross had been a rare combination of bluff and technique, with which he immediately got
even with the Ajax board.

Shortly after that he enabled Neeskens to make it 1-2 from
close to the goal. Ajax were through to the quarter-finals.
'Almost everything I did came off,' Cruyff said later to the press.
'Perhaps out of rage.' That might be true – he'd got a high score
for 'positive fear of failure' in Ajax psychologist Grunwald's
questionnaires. The 1970 tests had indicated that he functioned
exceptionally well in tense or 'unstructured' situations. Under
normal circumstances it was a different story. His 'performance
motivation' was strikingly low for a top sportsman. It seemed as
if he needed something to thrill him, a challenge, a misunderstanding, a conflict, to be able to perform optimally.

After the victory over FC Basel, the Ajax board walked into
the dressing room to congratulate the boys. 'What are you
doing here?' Cruyff asked them. 'You should be upstairs. This
is the players' dressing room.' The striker pushed the gentlemen

towards the door. One board member resisted. 'Out,' Cruyff
said to him. 'Or I'll give you a kick up the arse.'

The way it was recorded later in *Boem*, he used the polite
form of 'you'. In reality he will have used the familiar form.
And Cruyff hadn't finished yet, because now Michels was
standing across from him, shaking hands with each member of
the team. 'I'm not shaking that hand,' Johan said. He ignored
the outstretched hand with a sneer and scornfully threw back at
Michels his words of the previous evening, 'I'm just doing my
job here, nothing more.'

You might say the score was now level: Cruyff vs Board 1-
1. But the attacker was after a win. Everything had come off
in Basel; he needed to strike now. As soon as he got home to
Vinkeveen he wrote an angry letter to the board announcing
his departure. He wouldn't play any more matches for Ajax if
he was discriminated against for one moment longer.

He won. 'The unpaid bonuses were in my next pay packet,'
he confirmed later, to his satisfaction.

Nobody fought so hard for pay rises and bonuses as Cruyff. He
thought it all went without saying, but in fact it was unique.
Take Charlie George, a 1970s striker like Cruyff who played for
Arsenal, with long hair and impressive dribbling skills. 'I was
a rebel too,' says George looking back. 'But it was never about
money. The idea of asking for more than I already had didn't
occur to me. At Arsenal everyone got roughly the same amount,
the older players a bit more than the younger ones. We loved the
club so much that we'd have been willing to play for nothing.
I didn't have an agent and going up to the bosses yourself, well,
you just didn't. Johan did, so he was way ahead of his time.'

Ajax were keeping up with modern trends by having a
players' council in which Cruyff looked after the interests of
the players from that season onwards, along with Hulshoff and
Keizer. On his initiative, Michels was asked whether it wouldn't
be better to fine players who had misbehaved, rather than

suspending them. By putting a fit player on the subs' bench, he argued, you were taking work from him. If you saddled him with a financial penalty he could at least continue to develop as a sportsman. Moreover, the player concerned would feel the pain at a place Johan knew to be sensitive – his wallet.

In his view a club was 'in fact nothing other than a firm that sells football', and from that perspective Ajax had little to gain by stopping a well-known player from playing. Michels couldn't put his ideal team together and the public were denied viewing pleasure. No arguing with that. The council – or rather Cruyff – prevailed. From then on there were no suspensions.

Of course, Cruyff himself benefited from the change of policy. One Monday he had to open a shop, a job on the side, and he missed training as a result. He was fined 500 guilders. 'No problem,' he said to goalkeeper Heinz Stuy, who was laughing at him. 'I got eleven hundred guilders for that opening. So I'm left with six hundred. Easy, right?' The next Sunday he was able to take part as usual and earn his match bonus. 'Johan talked a lot about money,' former reserve keeper Sies Wever remembers. 'But often it worked to the advantage of the rest of us. Because of his initiative I always got the match bonuses for European Cup matches, for example, whether or not I participated.' It was a result of the widely publicised quarrel in Basel. Now that everyone knew what there was to be gained, the board found itself forced to let all the players feed from the European trough.

It seemed as if everything was going smoothly for Cruyff now that he was wearing the number 14. Ajax won match after match, and over the winter months they climbed from sixth place to the top of the premier division. He shone, for the team and for himself. 'I have to make it this season,' he told *Het Parool*. 'My contract is coming to an end. The better I am, the better it will be for the negotiations.'

From late February 1971, when rivals Feyenoord lost, the

team drew ahead. But the high point of the spring, possibly of the entire year, was the Ajax vs Celtic match. In this 10 March quarter-final, everything seemed to fall into place. While a cold wind blew through the Olympic Stadium, from a footballing point of view a fiery match unfolded. Celtic had a renowned team that had won the 1967 European Cup and played in the 1970 final against Feyenoord, but however experienced the Scots may have been, on that raw evening they were taught a lesson in modern football.

The Ajax players rattled their opponents right from the opening whistle. Often the entire team were in the Celtic half and, as soon as a Scot even contemplated breaking out, an Amsterdammer would leap in front of his feet. It might be Cruyff – who as ever did all he could to block counterattacks – but it was just as likely to be a defender such as Suurbier, or last man Vasović. 'We practised that every day,' says midfielder Arie Haan, who was still young then and was sometimes brought on as a substitute. 'We played seven-a-side on half a pitch, and anyone who didn't immediately move up got a roasting from Michels. That applied even more intensively in three-a-side. As soon as you hesitated and weren't completely on top of it, the other side could score. Put under that constant pressure, Johan was happy as a pig in clover.

Again, it became clear how much better a 4-3-3 system suited Cruyff than 4-2-4. Without Dick van Dijk as the second centre forward there was less rivalry in the attack, which benefited the overall harmony. The question of which of the two resulted in more goals fell away. In league matches at home Ajax often played with four attackers, including Van Dijk, and sometimes that grated. 'If Dick had scored a couple of goals, Johan would say to me: "Dickie needs to take it easy for a bit,"' Ajax player Ruud Suurendonk remembers. 'That meant Van Dijk must get fewer balls. Johan said it with a wink, but there was a grain of truth there. Later I heard from other people that Johan would sometimes tell them: not so many balls to Dick.' Before Van

Dijk's arrival, Inge Danielsson sometimes came up against Cruyff's assertiveness, and in Oranje, too, relations with his fellow strikers could not be described as serene.

As the one and only roaming striker, Cruyff brought about an astonishing collaboration with the three midfielders behind him. Without Van Dijk there seemed to be more space left to sprint ahead. Time and again, Mühren, Rijnders or Neeskens would run forward to places Cruyff had just left. If such a move failed, a forceful tackle would follow. Rijnders and Neeskens distinguished themselves from their predecessors by their toughness and, at least as importantly, they felt no envy of Cruyff. They hadn't seen him arrive as a nervous kid, let alone ever called him Flipper. Deliberately avoiding giving him the ball out of annoyance at his chatter, as had sometimes happened in the past, seemed unthinkable. Nor were they so irritated by Johan's habit of not completing one-twos. If he preferred to keep possession of the ball, then surely that was up to him.

Mühren was almost as agile as Cruyff and technically perhaps even better, but you could never accuse him of jealousy. The slim ball-juggling Volendammer would never call Johan 'a link in our Ajax chain', as Sjaak Swart once did. Rather he was *the* link. To him and the other midfielders, Johan was simply the central figure, the intelligent, ubiquitous Number 14 for whom they were happy to make every effort. So there emerged a hierarchy that was sometimes reminiscent of cycling. 'All I want is to be seen as a sober player,' Rijnders told the press. 'A water carrier for team leaders Cruyff and Keizer, that's what I am. I carry out the task Michels sets me. If I succeed one hundred per cent at that, then I'm happy.'

Cruyff repaid such players with beautiful passes and he automatically took the place of any midfielder who moved forward. 'He was a soloist, but in fact he always looked beyond his own role, which is what made him so special. He fully understood that he needed the team if he was to shine,' Haan recalls. 'Later he always said nice things about me.' As he did about the other 'water carriers'. Mühren, for example, could do far more with a ball than he was given a chance to show, but the left-side midfielder played behind Cruyff and Keizer, whose play on the left involved taking many risks (and who didn't like going behind defenders after losing possession). So the Volendammer in midfield couldn't afford to lose a single ball. If he did, he'd be loudly reprimanded. 'We complemented each other even better,' Cruyff said about that later. 'The automatic reactions became even tighter and every player was told exactly what he had to do. That improved the quality of the play. As a collective you quickly got above fifty per cent. That makes it simpler for an individualist to climb to eighty or ninety per cent. As a result of iron discipline.'

Set against the collective of Beatles-like, often graceful footballers, Celtic looked like a stiff team of veterans. Even the famous dribbler Jimmy 'the Flying Flea' Johnstone ran as if he was a good deal older than his twenty-six summers. The Scots barely had time to catch their breath and as soon as they did anything aggressive, against Cruyff for instance, they were faced with a counter-move. Cruyff would later recall with satisfaction moments when Vasović, Suurbier and Neeskens consulted on which of them would get back at the player guilty of kicking him, under the motto: an attack on Johan is an attack on us all. 'We had an expression for that,' Cruyff said. '"He's standing on my shorts." That meant his time would come. It's not supposed to be that way, I know it isn't, but if you don't stick up for yourself, you're screwed.'

In the last half-hour against Celtic there were three goals and Cruyff was involved in all of them. First, he reacted sublimely to a volley from Neeskens along the central axis of the pitch and scored: 1-0. Then he was pushed away just outside the penalty area. That led to a free kick from which Hulshoff made it 2-0. And shortly before the final whistle, after a breakaway on the right, he sent a pass to Keizer who promptly put it in: 3-0. In the second half especially, he'd shown how beautifully he could play. Not so much with spectacular solos – the defensive Scots offered little space for those – but by accelerating at the right moment, at the front, on the side or in midfield, whatever was called for.

Were we seeing a new Cruyff? A German TV commentator called him 'one of the best in the world'. The Scottish international David Hay said he was 'far and away the most dangerous footballer' he'd ever seen. Cruyff had played 'directly' and 'effectively' and thereby set a new standard for the future.

The 3–0 victory meant that Ajax had a good chance of reaching the semi-finals of the European Cup. But you could not have told that from the expressions on the players' faces. Cool, arms at their sides, they left the pitch for the catacombs of the Olympic Stadium. The result was great, of course, but there was no cause for outright jubilation. Acting crazy, performing forward rolls after scoring, climbing the fences: they didn't go in for any of that. Not even at this point. They had done their job, and done it well. 'This Ajax is a homogenous, balanced outfit, in which power and class go hand in hand,' was the judgement of Maarten de Vos the next day in *De Tijd*. He wrote that Ajax had put up a fight with 'hard-as-nails, efficient, agile and modern football'. Michels thought the same. This solidarity, this absence of egotism, this preparedness of the individual to sacrifice himself for the collective: he'd often thought it would never come, that he would never entirely get rid of the players' typically Dutch complacency and their desire to play football for their own enjoyment. Now it had been achieved. 'I venture to say that with this Ajax I have found what I was always looking for,' Michels said. 'We are no longer dependent on our form on the day. This team has grown into a larger unity than the team of one, two or three years ago. It's been a long road, but we've arrived.'

CHAPTER FOURTEEN

'Doctor, I feel so tired'

Cruyff must surely have driven back and forth between Vinkeveen and Amsterdam the spring of 1971 as a contented commuter. Both in the Scholeksterlaan and on the Middenweg everything was sailing along nicely. Ajax were running like a well-oiled machine and after a modest 1-0 defeat in Glasgow against Celtic, the semi-finals of the European Cup awaited. But however good that prospect was, the happiest development in Cruyff's life took place at home. For the past six months he'd been a father.

He had looked forward to the arrival of his firstborn ever since the wedding and on 16 November 1970 the miracle happened. He would never forget the sequence of events in the Boerhaave Clinic in Amsterdam-Zuid: he on edge and Danny terrified, because shortly before the Caesarean section the baby ceased to show any signs of life. The gynaecologist reassured them that just before birth babies often become calm, but Johan remained uneasy nonetheless, and when Danny disappeared into the lift along with the doctor his agitation only got worse. He found it intolerable that he wasn't allowed to be present for the C-section. Along with his mother Nel, Uncle Henk and his parents-in-law, he was expected to wait patiently while everything happened on the floor above. He paced up and down and smoked, until after fifteen minutes he could stand it no longer. He cajoled his mother-in-law Dien Coster into the lift with him.

They secretly went up to the first floor, where they were able to peer into the operating theatre through a kind of peephole in the lift door.

'Jesus, Dien, it's there!' said Johan, according to the biography *Boem*.

'Are you serious?' Dien asked.

'Oh, God, everything's covered in blood!'

'Lift me up, Johan, so I can see.'

Johan hoisted his mother-in-law into the air and now she saw it too, through a bit of glass where the paint had been scraped off: the blood, the white coats, the bright lamps.

Since he was, as he put it himself, 'as bold as brass', Johan opened the lift doors and walked into the forbidden room. He stretched out his arms to the blood-covered baby. 'Just give it to me, sister.'

He wiped his child clean with a towel – who could be better suited to doing that than he was? This felt like something he had to do. All by himself. He'd have liked best to have stood watching the operation from inches away from start to finish, while bombarding the gynaecologist with unsolicited advice. It was too late for that, but wiping his child with a towel made up for a lot.

'Congratulations, Johan, on your daughter,' the doctor said.

From his relaxed look Cruyff could tell that everything was fine, both with the little creature and with Danny.

Johan and Danny called their daughter Chantal. Not a reference to a family member, as had been the practice for generations on both the Cruyff and the Coster side, but a name that suited the far from ordinary life that 23-year-old Johan and 21-year-old Danny were living together. They had recently met a Frenchwoman called Chantal, and so they chose that name.

The next day photographers were allowed into the clinic to

record the family's joy. Even the news team from Dutch state broadcaster NOS was welcome. It filled Johan with pride that the birth of his daughter was regarded as so important. 'Because of my football playing, people like me one way or another. And although I try to protect my private life, more and more bits are breaking off. This is part of that. You're no longer in charge of your own body.'

In the spring of 1971 both their bodies were functioning well, incidentally. Johan had now been playing for six months without injury and Danny's health improved after Chantal's arrival. She was no longer plagued by attacks of stomach ache – the legacy of her miscarriage – and she quickly recovered from the thrombosis initially caused by her pregnancy.

Meanwhile, Johan was emerging as a modern father. He liked bathing 'Chantalletje' and wasn't ashamed to say so. After drying the baby he would put a clean nappy on her, although according to Danny he was all fingers and thumbs. When visitors came round, he might spend a lot of time tending to the baby: 'Hey, gorgeous!' Like true Vinkeveeners they'd got a dog, a miniature poodle called Rocco, and they now each had a car. Danny drove a red Mini and Johan a red Porsche, until the spring of 1971 when it was replaced by a silver-grey Datsun 240Z. Japanese cars were on the up and Cruyff's neighbour in Vinkeveen, Jan Koch, was a Datsun dealer in Amsterdam, so it was easy for him to get a good deal on the six-cylinder model.

Now that she had a Mini, Danny could come and go as she liked, but wherever she may have gone it was no longer to her shoe shop in the Kinkerstraat. She was so happy with Chantal that she no longer cared about Shoetique. Ultimately the shop had been little more than a therapeutic distraction after the miscarriage in 1969. 'I hardly ever saw the shoe shop Johan bought specially for me,' she admitted later. 'I only went there occasionally. Usually I just rang. I didn't want to sit among shoes, I wanted children.'

Responsibility for the shop now lay largely with Johan.

Twice a week he drove in his Datsun to Amsterdam-West to see how everything was going and to stimulate sales. The young couple rarely went out. On Sunday evenings they still regularly joined the other team players and their wives for dinner on the Leidseplein, but Johan lost interest in the gatherings on Monday nights, when it was 'all men together' in the Hoopman Bodega for members of the squad and friendly journalists such as Maarten de Vos. (There were those who suspected Danny had banned him from going.)

On Tuesday evenings the Cruyffs watched the American television series *Peyton Place* and sometimes friends came round. Teammate Dick van Dijk and his wife Wanda, for instance, who also lived in Vinkeveen. Or Bobby and Tootje Nees, who were now living in their own renovated house. They sometimes went to a restaurant, but they were just as happy to stay at home, where Danny was content to talk about anything except football. Johan rather liked that taboo; it helped him to distance himself from the tensions at work. Chattering away, they kept each other in balance. 'Johan felt he needed her grit and determination,' says Bobby Nees. 'Danny always had to adjust to his football agenda, but at home she decided everything, and Johan felt that was just fine.'

Fatherhood had something of a calming influence on him. The rebellious player started to use words like 'adult' and 'well-balanced'. His membership of the players' council had a beneficial effect in that respect as well. 'I became calmer,' he said later about this period. 'I started to play less egotistically and was more able to see other people's point of view.' In his fifth season as a continual member of the squad he got less wound up about all the things that were wrong at Ajax: the ever-critical fans, the gossip about him and his supplementary earnings, the jealousy, the incompetence of the board. He still regarded it as unacceptable to entrust the running of a club to a record salesman and two tax officials, but what could you do? The sorely needed professionalisation of the Ajax leadership was not in prospect, so it was good that Michels took all kinds of tasks upon himself. Despite their differences of opinion, the coach was the only person at Ajax that Johan respected. 'Manager' Michels was at least a man who had mastered his craft; he didn't talk crap.

Yet in April 1971 he came into conflict with Michels again. It happened in Madrid, where Ajax were about to play in the semi-finals of the European Cup against Atlético. In the background the name of another beautiful city was going around: Barcelona. Cruyff's contract with Ajax was due to expire in a few months' time and the Spanish border might be about to open up to foreign soccer players. At home in Vinkeveen, Johan and Danny had been daydreaming about Barcelona for months. The past summer they'd been guided around the city for a day and both had fallen in love with the sun-drenched life of the Mediterranean. Johan had spoken to trainers and players in the Camp Nou stadium and even had himself photographed in the club's purple-and-blue strip. In early April, shortly before Ajax left for Madrid, a Catalan delegation had travelled to Amsterdam to meet Van Praag, avoiding the cameras. As so often, the news leaked out. Under the headline 'Cruyff to move to Spain for good?' several newspapers had claimed it was 'a virtual certainty' that Johan would be transferred to Barcelona for 'a phenomenal sum'.

Cruyff claimed to know nothing, but of course there was speculation, and after arriving in Madrid several days before the match, he posed for press photographers with Danny sitting in his lap, he in a fashionable suit, she wearing a coquettish white hat and white hotpants. A stylish young couple on their way to start a grand and exciting life abroad: that seemed to be the message to the world and during match preparations it was the last thing Michels wanted. He had urged Johan and Coster to make their talks with Barcelona a closely guarded secret. For the umpteenth time, peripheral events threatened to disturb his team's concentration.

Cruyff for his part was annoyed with his trainer. Michels seemed yet again to be adjusting the team to suit the opponent. In a defensive sense, naturally, because that was always the tendency of the fretting coach. Despite the team's excellent form of late, the defence was given a man extra and Cruyff and Keizer were left to sort things out up front. In Michels' view, Atlético were a fair deal better than many people thought, so 0-0 seemed to him a good starting point for the return match in Amsterdam. He sent the team on to the field with that as its aim: no goals against. The strategy produced a match in which Atlético attacked and Ajax countered mainly with a lot of tackles, many of them slide-tackles. Most of what was 'modern' about Ajax consisted of calmly smashing balls away as soon as things got difficult at the back.

Meanwhile, Dutch journalists were wondering what was wrong with Cruyff. They had rarely seen him so passive and careless. Was he tense because of the stories about a departure for Spain and the presence on the stands of Barcelona coach Vic Buckingham, his former trainer at Ajax? Atlético made it 1-0 and what Cruyff then tried to do in response was, according to *Het Vrije Volk*, 'barely worth mentioning'.

Ten minutes before the match ended, something happened that the reporters found almost impossible to take in. Horst Blankenburg was preparing to come on. In itself that was nothing unusual. The German defender, acquired from Munich 1860 the previous winter, had been deployed as a substitute several times recently. What was extraordinary was the name of the player Michels ordered off.

Johan Cruyff.

He walked to the touchline, then just short of the dugout he limped conspicuously for a moment, as if to make his exit easier to bear. But he wasn't injured. He'd been found wanting. That had never happened to him since his debut in November 1964. Cruyff was deeply insulted.

With this substitution, Michels explained later to the press, he wanted to consolidate the 1-0 deficit. Such a minor defeat could be set right in Amsterdam and there didn't seem to be any prospect of an equaliser. Defence was the watchword and big blond Horst was simply better at that than Johan. 'Their right back, Melo, struck me as too dangerous,' the coach said later. 'And Cruyff wasn't stopping him. That wouldn't have been such a bad thing in itself if he'd made up for it by attacking. But I didn't feel that was the case.'

The striker was furious. Had Michels deliberately made him lose face with the Spanish spectators? What kind of power games were being played here? The coach's contract was due to expire the coming summer just like Johan's and Michels too seemed to like the idea of a lucrative adventure in Barcelona. Substituting Cruyff would be the ideal way to show the world how much authority he had. Whatever the truth of that, Arie Haan, reserve player at the time, would never forget what he heard Cruyff say to the coach in the Manzanares Stadium. 'You won't pull that one on me again. Otherwise I'll decide from now on for myself whether to take part or not. We'll see what happens then. Against Feyenoord for instance.'

According to *Het Parool*, after the match Cruyff looked like 'a schoolboy sent out of the class', like a 'scapegoat' for one of Ajax's 'worst ever' European matches. In front of the press, he blamed the coach. 'Michels should know why it was difficult to play out in front. I was often on my own against three men. Normally you keep possession of the ball and wait for players from the second and third line to get forward. But they didn't come this time, because Michels had practically forbidden them to. No risks were to be taken. Logical then that you lose the ball.'

Rumours of a transfer to Barcelona persisted. In the run-up to the home game against Atlético on 28 April 1971 the sports pages were filled with all kinds of unfathomable and contra-dictory reports of negotiations between Ajax and Barcelona. The pledges, threats and denials came thick and fast. As he had two years earlier, before the European Cup final against AC Milan, Coster seemed eager to strike at the moment when Ajax wanted peace and harmony. He declared that Johan would leave for Barcelona once and for all if Ajax failed to react within a week to his proposal for a new contract. Because Cruyff and Barcelona were now 'fully in agreement'.

'I want, as I've said, to stay with Ajax,' Johan declared in his *Telegraaf* column. 'But if you stay at Ajax long enough you find you're selling yourself short. I don't want that. I'm a professional and I have to get whatever there is to be got from it.'

Most important for him was not the size of his salary alone but the length of the contract. He regarded seven years as the minimum for a new Ajax contract. 'I'm twenty-four now,' he said. 'I want a solid position until I'm thirty-one at the very least.' Ajax had offered him a contract for five years. 'That's not enough for me. I'll be twenty-nine and no one will want me then.'

In the end Ajax chairman Van Praag managed to calm everything down a little with a reference to the official procedure. Only after the start of the transfer period on 1 June could a possible departure be discussed. That seemed to help. Ajax carried on winning, managed to eliminate Feyenoord from the KNVB Cup competition and beat Atlético Madrid in Amsterdam 3-0. The day after that match Cruyff was praised for his diligence and his brilliant initiatives. His performance had even started to look mildly heroic after his ear started bleeding heavily as a result of a collision with the goalkeeper and a little later, ghostly pale and slightly dizzy, he played on after initially being taken off the pitch by Salo Muller. The crowd didn't see him so unflinching every week. In the Spanish press Cruyff was described as 'the star of the match' and – particularly advantageous for his international market value – an 'intelligent soccer artist'.

But even an intelligent soccer artist can sometimes benefit from a good conversation. In this period Cruyff went to see a psychiatrist.

'What are you here for?' asked Dr Roelf Zeven.

'That's what I was wondering too,' said Cruyff. 'Michels sent me.'

So there they were, standing either side of the open front door, the most famous sportsman in the Netherlands and a psychiatrist who had been part of the medical team at Ajax for four years. Both laughed at the situation, the psychiatrist said later in an interview. Zeven invited the footballer in.

It was unusual for the doctor to receive Ajax players at his home in Teteringen. But the fact that Michels had made Cruyff drive to this leafy village near Breda suggested the need was pressing. As a father, as a busy moonlighter and a player in talks with Barcelona, Johan had a lot on his plate. Moreover, the European Cup final was coming up, and whatever it took he needed to avoid losing again.

The 'psycho-hygienic counsellor', as Zeven called himself, had a close knowledge of the less well-balanced aspects of Johan's state of mind. At Michels' request he was often present to observe the players, whether in the bus, at meetings to discuss tactics or during matches. Zeven had better relations with the players than psychologist Grunwald, who had joined Ajax along with him in 1967 and had since left. A child psychiatrist with a post at the University of Leiden, Zeven found top-flight sport fascinating. He didn't ask for remuneration, but, in accordance with an old Ajax tradition, Van Praag would occasionally slip an envelope into his breast pocket.

Cruyff talked easily and ceaselessly in Teteringen. 'I didn't need to ask questions much at all,' Zeven said later. 'There were hardly any silent moments.' The psychiatrist and the footballer discussed life and continued their conversation in the spacious back garden. Thirty-nine-year-old Zeven was a sporting type, which helped. He concluded from Cruyff's life story that the death of his father and the money worries of the years that followed had made a lasting impression on him. Money was more than simply a means of buying food and drink, it was something far deeper than that, a 'fundamental and vital necessity'. The death of Manus Cruyff had also given him a permanent 'loss of self-confidence', perhaps even an 'inferiority complex', making him feel an almost compulsive duty to be nice to people of humble origins.

Whatever advice he may have been given by the psychiatrist, Cruyff now needed to show some backbone. The build-up to the European Cup final was not going well. In the Olympic Stadium, Ajax allowed themselves to be pushed aside by an unfettered, hard-playing Feyenoord. Again, there was talk of Cruyff being nervous. The Rotterdammers won the league match 3-1, which put them on course to win the national championship. That made the European final even more important. The aftermath of the Feyenoord game did little to soothe matters. Several players, including Keizer (injured ankle), Rijnders (kick to the chest) and Neeskens (broken nose after a blow from Wim van Hanegem), needed medical attention.

'Ajax will win,' Cruyff insisted in his *Telegraaf* column despite everything. 'Not even an important defeat by Feyenoord can change that.' What AC Milan had been for Ajax two years earlier, in 1969, Ajax would now be for the Greeks, was his analysis, namely the team with the most international experience. 'We're the better team,' Cruyff believed. 'And Panathinaikos need to gear themselves to that.'

True, their Greek opponents, Panathinaikos from Athens, were hardly the most impressive of teams. Yet the night before the final Cruyff slept badly and he wasn't the only one. Quite a few of the players in the Selsdon Park Hotel, a country house to the south of London that resembled a castle, were afraid of losing the European Cup final again.

Goalkeeper Stuy was not nervous. Heinz Stuy, like most goalies, was the calm individual in the group. That was precisely why Cruyff insisted on sharing a room with him in the players' hotels. 'He was always busy smoking and making phone calls,' remembers Stuy, an acquisition from Telstar, a small club close to the massive Hoogovens steelworks in IJmuiden. 'Sometimes, when he lit yet another fag, I would ask him to open a window. But Johan never took a thing like that lying down. "You're from IJmuiden, aren't you?" he'd say. "With Hoogovens nearby you must surely be used to smoke."'

Stuy often had a pile of comic books with him to calm Johan. 'He'd lie there nice and quiet reading *Michel Vaillant*,' Stuy remembers. 'He loved it. I never saw serious books on his bedside table. He just didn't have the patience for them. He preferred to sit there endlessly doing deals from our hotel room. But if I gave him a *Michel Vaillant*, the interminable phone calls would often stop.'

Not in the night before 2 June 1971. No matter how many races cartoon hero Vaillant won in Cruyff's hands, the next morning the striker was far from well rested. So when the bus drove down from the hilly grounds of the Selsdon Park Hotel that afternoon, Cruyff knew who he wanted to sit next to: the man who could be his father figure for a short while, Roelf Zeven.

The psychiatrist later told his son Marius all about it.

'Doc,' said Johan, 'I feel so tired.'

The doctor moved over a little and Johan nestled in beside him, ignoring the sniggers of some of his teammates.

'Just have a nap,' said Zeven, giving him two airline sleep masks.

Cruyff covered his eyes with them, one on top of the other.

Zeven knew he was afraid of being defeated for the second time in a final. 'The 1969 final is over,' he whispered into Johan's ear. 'Now is now. You really aren't going to lose to those Greeks.'

Restoring a player to his quality, is what Zeven called it. And it helped. Cruyff fell asleep with his head on the doctor's shoulder and didn't wake up until an hour later, when the famous white towers of Wembley Stadium came into sight.

A little later Cruyff gave goalkeeper Stuy the usual tap to the stomach on the 'sacred' turf in London. Shortly after that, the ball was in the goal, an early lead thanks to Keizer and Van Dijk. After a classic evasion, Keizer, his ankle injury eased by an injection, produced a curving cross from the left and Van Dijk, who was usually allowed only to play against weaker opponents in De Meer, headed the ball fabulously into the far corner of the goal. One-nil up after five minutes. A brilliant start. But after that there was little to match it and the spectators witnessed nervous play full of miscommunication.

Michels had scrambled the team considerably. Midfielder Neeskens was playing right back because left back Krol had a broken leg and right back Suurbier had taken Krol's place on the left. So there was hardly any of the usual showing by the wing backs. Even more importantly, because Van Dijk was playing alongside Cruyff as a striker, Ajax had only two midfielders, Mühren and Rijnders, and in the first half they were frequently overrun by Panathinaikos. Little came of the reciprocity between Cruyff and the midfielders, which meant the striker was on his own. He made an immense effort. Tried a slalom. Accelerated with the ball at his feet. Turned up on the right and on the left. Ran into midfield to set up an attack. Emerged as the most active player on the pitch. But his efforts produced few chances, and to the extent that he created them for himself, he shot too hastily, kicking the ball into the goalkeeper's hands or high over the Greek goal. Normally he gave 'a ball like that some spin', he explained the next day in his column. But 'in view of what was at stake' he didn't dare risk slicing it and just kept on shooting as powerfully as possible.

At half-time Michels decided to strengthen the midfield. He replaced attacker Swart with midfielder Haan (a substitution for which the right-winger would never forgive him). Then Rijnders proved unable to go on because of shortness of breath and Blankenburg was told to take off his tracksuit. With 4-3-3 it went better. The midfield now held up well but, aside from that, Ajax were more standing their ground than playing football. The team was plagued by injuries and tensions, and showed itself to be truly professional in that it no longer even tried to play good football.

This was what Michels had been going on about for years. If you can't win by playing a beautiful game, then play an ugly one. 'Professional football is something like war,' the coach had said to *Algemeen Dagblad* as recently as March (a quote that would later be distorted into 'football is war'). 'Anyone who behaves too decently is lost.'

At Wembley the boring European Cup final seemed to end like a burning torch slowly toppling into the mud. Until Cruyff put an end to the lethargy as only he could. He had been the most noticeable player of the match; it was no accident that six of the thirteen Greek fouls were against him. Now, just before the game ended, he created a tense moment by briefly doing nothing on the right side of midfield. Van Dijk had passed the ball to him. He stared out over the pitch. Then he ran with the ball at little more than walking pace to the Panathinaikos penalty area, as if the game might as well freeze as far as he was concerned, and everyone stand in their current position for 180 seconds to wait for English referee Jack Taylor's final whistle.

The Greek player facing him shrank back. Then he stepped forward, and at precisely that moment Cruyff swerved inwards, supple, supercilious, as if doing something purely for its own sake. To his left Haan ran into the penalty area and instead of playing the ball to his feet, which seemed the obvious thing, Cruyff launched it straight ahead, between two stupefied Greeks, so that Haan had to run away from the goal to get to it. Haan produced a weak shot, partly because the leg he was standing on slipped, but via the heel of a defender the ball bounced high and flew straight over the keeper into the net.

A strange goal. A strange climax to a strange match.

Even Cruyff wasn't himself for a moment. He immediately dived on top of the prone Haan and grabbed him like a judo player. He'd never celebrated a goal that way before. Then Neeskens, Mühren and Blankenburg ran and skidded towards them and they too threw themselves on top of the goal scorer, who disappeared under a mound of players. Two-nil. It was in the bag.

Referee Taylor blew his whistle. The Ajax players cheered. Cruyff and Van Dijk were carried off the pitch on the shoulders of fans. Eighty-seven thousand spectators watched captain Vasović lift the silver-plated childhood dream, 'the cup with the big ears', and festivities broke out in Amsterdam that would last for twenty-four hours.

Nine years before, Johan had felt it an honour to be of service to Ferenc Puskás during the Real Madrid vs Benfica final in the Olympic Stadium in Amsterdam. Now Panathinaikos coach Puskás said of the 1962 ball boy, 'Cruyff is fifty per cent of the team. Give him to us and we'll win.'

The next day Mr Fifty Per Cent was standing on the lawn of Soestdijk Palace. Sunlight glanced off the white residential and working palace in Baarn as Queen Juliana welcomed the whole Ajax squad, its coaches and other staff with champagne. The 62-year-old monarch raised a toast to the European success of her sporting subjects and everyone was happy, to the point of roguishness. Princess Irene put her 18-month-old son Carlos into the gleaming European Cup to please the photographers – that's the kind of afternoon it was. But there was one player who thought it was time for some serious talk. 'You're stopping as a player, I'm told,' he heard Juliana say to Vasović, the captain who had indeed announced he was ending his career. 'Then no doubt you'll get a pension?'

Pension. The Yugoslav didn't know that word. Cruyff, who knew it better than anyone, took over from him. 'That's precisely our problem,' he explained to the queen. 'We don't get a pension.' He gave her a lecture on the short time in which a footballer had to earn his money and the 'huge progressive taxation' to which they were subject. When he retired from the game at thirty-one, the professional soccer player was really only

nineteen from a social insurance point of view, Cruyff philos-
ophised in the midst of his cheerful teammates.

Juliana had to admit that she had not yet informed herself on
the matter.

The 24-year-old star, who like the other Ajax players was
now in line for a bonus of 25,000 guilders, raised the possibility
that Her Majesty might be able to apply pressure to bring an
end to this unacceptable fiscal injustice. He'd love to come and
talk to her about it sometime.

Out of the corner of his eye he saw Van Praag and Michels
spluttering as they walked away, but he paid no attention. After
all, he had 'never looked up to the high or looked down on
the low', as he put it later. A queen was only human, and there
really was 'something sweet' about the woman. The Queen of
the Netherlands was 'very normal', just like him.

So why not make use of the opportunity?

Alas.

'Mr Cruyff,' Juliana said. 'You'll need to speak to the finance
minister.'

CHAPTER FIFTEEN

The best in the world

The Spanish borders were still closed as things stood, and since Danny and Johan were not considering anywhere other than Barcelona for a foreign adventure, they stayed in the Netherlands. Weeks of nerve-racking negotiations with Ajax followed. The discussions were not always friendly and, as would later become an established habit among agents for sportspeople, Coster furnished reports of interest, real or otherwise, from other clubs. *De Telegraaf* had only just published its scoop – 'Johan Cruyff moving abroad' – when Ajax treasurer Henk Timman arrived for coffee at Coster's house. Within an hour it was settled. On the morning of Sunday 20 June 1971, Ajax and Coster agreed on a seven-year contract, precisely the duration Cruyff had always hoped for. The agreement meant he would be able to bring his professional career to a close in 1978, at the age of thirty-one.

Cruyff was genuinely pleased. Not so much by the annual salary of 95,000 guilders plus bonuses, since in truth he thought that too low, but by a second contract, one that was kept out of the limelight. Although Van Praag lied to journalists that no third party was involved, there undoubtedly was one, and it was crucial to the overall deal. In secret, an agreement had been reached with KBB, owners of, among other things, the famous department store De Bijenkorf. Like Cruyff, KBB chairman

Jack Bons had grown up in Betondorp, and he was one of the many Jewish businessmen who supported Ajax with advice and donations. It was decided that after his Ajax contract expired, the footballer could take a job in PR for KBB subsidiary Perry van der Kar, the sporting goods company where he had been so unhappy at the age of fifteen. He was guaranteed a place on its payroll until he turned sixty-five; the soccer player who so often fretted over his physical fragility, his finances and his future could at last breathe a sigh of relief.

From dogsbody in the storeroom to company standard bearer for an index-linked 60,000 guilders a year: he no longer needed to worry. With a bit of luck, he might even be able to live a life of luxury for ever. He'd recently pointed out in an interview the situation of near-slavery he felt professional footballers were in. Now he was no longer a slave. As a result of his father-in-law's business instincts, he had managed to throw off his chains.

Van Praag had meanwhile said farewell to 'dictator' Rinus Michels. The coach would leave that summer for Barcelona. 'So much had broken down in the personal relationship with Ajax that I couldn't stay any longer,' Michels said in an interview. With his 'tough decisions' he had to 'push myself harder and harder', and in the end resignation was unavoidable. Furthermore, his income increased markedly as a result of the move to Spain, and Cruyff was partly responsible for that. In the spring a member of the board at Barcelona had asked the coveted striker whether he thought Michels was suitable to coach Catalonia's top club. Cruyff had replied with a wholehearted 'yes', which Michels greatly appreciated, and with that their successful and sometimes uneasy father–son relationship came to an end for the time being.

While Michels was at his holiday home, concentrating on a correspondence course in Spanish, his successor was unpacking his bags in Amsterdam. Ştefan Kovács was a relatively unknown Romanian coach who was sufficiently mature and intelligent to know what he needed to do at Ajax: loosen the reins. And no one had more to gain from that than Johan Cruyff.

The former coach of Steaua Bucharest was not a strict father, more a friendly uncle, small in stature and fond of a laugh. He was in his fifties, with grey hair and without either a driver's licence, sarcasm or a taste for strange punishments. He was happy to be tested by the biggest windbag in the squad.

'You're known to have come from the Eastern bloc,' said Cruyff. 'Where you trained an army club. What do you think of our long hair?'

'I'm not interested in your hair,' Kovács replied. 'As far as I'm concerned you can grow it ten or fifteen centimetres longer.'

The polite and eloquent Kovács didn't scold, he conversed. He was genuinely interested in the character behind the footballer. He wanted to treat the players like adults who would take responsibility for their own fitness. 'You know more than I do,' he told them. 'Well,' Haan remembers. 'We said to each other: this isn't going to work.' Training sessions became easier and sloppier. Arriving promptly was no longer a priority, and whereas Michels had sometimes deliberately avoided the shower room because he knew Keizer and Cruyff would be in there secretly smoking away their pre-match nerves (he didn't want to control absolutely everything), Kovács would companionably enjoy a cigarette in there with them.

Kovács' slack regime worked remarkably well. The 1971-72 season was characterised by smart and businesslike, sometimes light-hearted and generally effective play. The Romanian sub-stituted players less often than Michels and didn't feel a need to change tactics when facing strong European opponents. After a few months of adjustment (and injuries), things started rolling and Ajax consistently played with three midfielders and three forwards. As a result, the teamwork between captain Cruyff and his 'water carriers' was outstanding. If one advancing mid-fielder was stopped, then the centre forward who had 'sunk back' could simply pass the ball to another, or to an attacking defender. Plenty of options. 'That makes it a good deal easier for me,' Cruyff said. 'Under Kovács the brakes have been taken off a lot of players, to the benefit of the football.'

The game became more varied and less risk-averse, which worked because the players continually kept an eye on each other. 'Under Kovács we're made to take more joint responsibility,' Johan said. 'We can't any longer blame someone else. We do almost everything by ourselves. That's not to say Kovács is a kind of harlequin and we pull the strings. When it comes down to it, the coach makes the decisions.'

The principles of total football, hammered into them by a dictatorial coach, therefore came to fruition under a trainer who allowed the players more freedom. And the player who had been punished most frequently by Michels now enforced discipline, through both words and gestures. Anyone who neglected his duty, for example by failing to take the place of a teammate who had 'departed', was immediately told as much by co-ordinator Cruyff. 'When we went hunting, as we called it,' midfielder Arie Haan remembers, 'Johan would sprint to their last man, while I took care of Johan's marker and behind me Blankenburg would come in to cover my direct opponent. So everyone shifted at the same time. But if I noticed that Blankenburg had stayed back, I didn't move on either, because then there would be a gap. At which point Johan would start shouting, "Where have you got to?" And I'd shout back that I was facing two men. That went on all through the match. We all knew the principles and solved problems ourselves.'

In other top Dutch clubs too, such as Feyenoord, there was increasing dynamism and switching of positions that year, but nowhere was it done so consistently and ingeniously, and with such attacking force, as at Ajax. The team spread out and huddled up, they increased or reduced the pace according to the balance of power and the score.

For some foreigners the way the Ajax players ran crisscross past each other was sensational. During the second round of the

European Cup in Marseille, for instance, against Olympique on
20 October 1971, the French commentator expressed his amazement that the Ajax defenders seemed to run forward as they saw
fit, without holes appearing in the defence. Words failed him as
he attempted to praise this footballing intelligence. Ajax won
practically every duel and all the while Kovács sat contentedly
watching from under his trilby. The coach enjoyed Cruyff's play
most of all. He thought of a characterisation that would never
have been used by Michels, or indeed by practically any Dutch
coach, for fear the players would pull his leg about it. The ever-
smiling Romanian declared Cruyff to be the 'Michelangelo of
football'.

Things were going well with the artist on studs. His life in
Vinkeveen might be described as almost untroubled. Danny was
expecting again and this time her pregnancy went smoothly.
She was far less afflicted by nausea than when she was pregnant
with Chantal. The only fly in the ointment in this period was
the shoe shop. Despite large advertisements in *De Telegraaf*,
turnover was disappointing. 'It's not going the way I expected,'
Johan admitted. 'I rather overestimated the pulling power of my
name. They're not exactly storming the place.' Giving up was
not in his nature – to back down was to lose – but in the autumn
of 1971 he was forced to conclude that a shop selling exclusive
footwear in a working-class neighbourhood had not been a
good idea. When he thought about what he was earning with
his PR activities, he told Danny, he was 'raving mad' to devote
so many hours to those 'bloody shoes' and the shop paperwork.
After that insight the decision was quickly made, as so often.
And he was smart enough to mention the closing-down sale in
his *Telegraaf* column and to ensure there was an advert right next
to it with the message that everything was going at half price.

It was no less typical of Cruyff that while the closing-down
sale at the shoe shop was still underway he turned up in the
province of Friesland. He seemed too restless for a life without

a new business challenge, so Coster had found an internship for him with a former market trader from Amsterdam who ran a clock and jewellery shop in Leeuwarden. There Johan could acquire the expertise he would need if he were to take over Coster's wholesale business in due course. His stay in Leeuwarden led to little more than a photo in the paper, but it indicated Cruyff's ambition to go into business later, and to achieve more than a job in publicity for Perry van der Kar or his brother Henny's sporting goods shop. He didn't regard himself as suited to a career as a football coach. For that he'd have to study and, as we have seen, studying didn't come easily to him.

What did always come easily was talking. At around the time of his internship in Friesland he was visited at home by no less a figure than Godfried Bomans. His conversation with the popular humorous writer and columnist resulted in a story for the Christmas issue of the weekly *Elsevier* that was a long way from the usual Dutch coverage. 'Johan Cruyff is reminiscent of an angel,' Bomans opened his portrait, 'to the extent that an angel is not subject to gravity. I've often watched him play and been amazed when he simply walked off the pitch with the others at the end rather than rising up and disappearing over the stands towards the horizon. Presumably he holds himself back ... His face too has something angelic about it. He's made up mostly of surprise, but it's the astonishment of someone who has fallen to earth from a cloud and then manages as best he can amid the cumbrous creatures he finds there.'

Admiration for Cruyff had never been expressed so metaphorically. In the rapidly secularising but still Calvinist Netherlands, it was almost improper to put anyone on such a pedestal, least of all a footballer. Perhaps it's no coincidence that Bomans was raised a Catholic. His story 'An Afternoon with Johan Cruyff' reads like a contemporary hagiography, playfully submissive in its choice of words, full of curiosity regarding the central character's 'bodily intelligence'. On reading it, Cruyff said it was 'a very good story', based on 'mutual respect'. As so often, a rapport with a creative spirit from a different sphere of activity did him good. Bomans' sudden death, before Christmas that year, moved him deeply.

There was more praise to come. On 27 December he was named European Footballer of the Year by the magazine *France Football*. His first reaction was to say, 'It's a tremendous honour and I'm surprised to have been chosen. There are so many great footballers in Europe.'

His surprise was not entirely feigned, it would seem. He very rarely boasted. If there was ever a player who spotted the mistakes in matches, it was Cruyff. This combination of modesty and certainty of being right was on show in a television interview with Herman Kuiphof after the *France Football* announcement. They sat at a table in the Ajax restaurant and Cruyff was asked why he thought he had been selected for the prize. Dressed in a fashionably chequered shirt with a massive collar, he sounded hoarse and almost whispered, 'I think because we knocked out Marseille. I played well both times. That made a big impression in France.'

He had played down the honour, as if it was almost a stroke of luck, as if the editors of *France Football* had seen only those two matches against Olympique, in which he had indeed excelled and scored three of the six Ajax goals. While answering each of Kuiphof's questions, he studied the tabletop minutely, like a shy adolescent, before looking directly at the sports commentator at the end of each explanation as if to say: that's how it was and don't let anyone tell you any different.

In his answer to a question about whether his way of playing had changed, he used the word 'you' where another person would say 'I'. He did that increasingly often, as if to neutralise himself. At the same time it gave his experiences a universal charge, and that too might be regarded as a form of modesty. The interviewer was told that he had indeed started doing things differently. 'Because it's no longer feasible to play striker. Receiving the ball at your feet, taking on one or two people,

Johan's primary school football team. He had already mastered keeping possession of the ball (bottom row, second from left).

The baseball player – the perfect game for those who like to fool their opponents by curving the ball.

Johan at twelve, dressed smartly for the primary school photographer.

Johan, Manus and Henny in 1951.

The youngest employee at the sports shop at just fifteen, looking into the photographer's lens with questioning eyes.

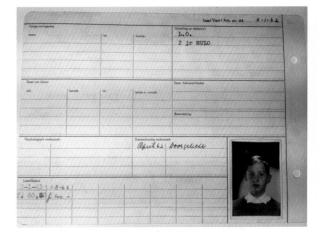

The youngest player in the winning Ajax youth team, Johan (far left) can scarcely believe it.

Fighting for the ball
with Feyenoord's
Rinus Israel in
November 1966.

Johan and Danny in
their sports car,
March 1969.

In a nightclub
in Istanbul with
fellow players and
a belly dancer in
November 1968.

Johan and elder brother Henny in their newly opened sports shop in Amsterdam, August 1968.

In the dugout next to Rinus Michels after leaving the pitch injured against Spartak Trnava, April 1969.

Signing copies of his single *Oei oei oei (dat was me weer een loei)* in 1969. Left, fellow Ajax player Ruud Suurendonk.

1969: As is his style, Johan drops back to the left wing, then stuns defenders with a cross on the outside right foot.

Winning the European Cup in 1973 with Ajax, for the third time in a row.

European Cup holders Ajax pose for a team photo with the trophy in March 1973. Front row left to right, Sjaak Swart, Johnny Rep, coach Stephan Kovacs, trainer Bob Haarms, Ger Kleton, Jan Mulder, Johan and Gerrie Mühren.

Back row, left to right, Arie Haan, Horst Blankenburg, Sies Wever, Wim Suurbier, goalkeeper Heinz Stuy, Piet Keizer, Ruud Krol, Heinz Schilcher, Arnold Mühren, Johan Neeskens and Barry Hulshoff.

Johan and Heinz Stuy at their
training ground at Stadium The
Meer, Amsterdam.

Always a lover of children.
Johan next to his 'brother'
Piet Keizer.

Johan, Henny and Nel, their mother.

The Cruyff family arriving at Barcelona airport in 1973.

Football or ballet? Johan and Ipswich's John Stirk in November 1977.

An icon in the Camp Nou stadium.

making a cross or scoring: it just doesn't work like that any longer. You have to move back a little more. Keep the ball at your feet and then you can have a bit more of an overview.'

That suggested he was both invisible and ubiquitous. Small but very big too, and blessed with insights from which others could benefit. 'To me Johan Cruyff is not only the strongest footballer in Europe but in the world,' wrote Willem van Hanegem in his foreword to a book devoted to Cruyff called *Cupstukken*, which was published after the season ended. 'He would be good enough in any position in a team.'

Before the kick-off for FC The Hague vs Ajax on 2 January 1972, Cruyff was celebrated as European Footballer of the Year. To thunderous applause, the captain of the Hague team Aad Mansveld handed him a bunch of flowers. What happened after that in the Zuiderpark Stadium was like something out of a *Boy's Own Annual*. Decades later the pictures would still be on show, and the more often you saw them, the better they got. Even the prelude was special. Cruyff felt unwell. He'd only just got over a bad dose of flu and in the first half he had a migraine as well. While FC The Hague went on the attack under a grey sky with a powerful easterly wind, he looked almost lost. At half-time, with Ajax 1-0 down, he asked for an aspirin. Eyes shut, he sat in the changing room waiting for the pill to take effect. He was a bit embarrassed at the state he was in: such a reception and then playing a nondescript game; this was no fun. 'I wanted to show there was a reason I'd been chosen,' he said to journalists later.

Perhaps he gave a brief thought to heavily pregnant Danny, who was unable to be there and would give birth within weeks.

Kovács asked his players to increase the pace in the second half. That worked. Within five minutes captain Piet Keizer scored from a long pass by Haan – 1-1. A few minutes after that Cruyff was standing close to the subs' bench. One of his socks had fallen down, so he'd asked masseur Salo Muller to fetch a length of bandage. He was just about to wind it around his sock when defender Krol kicked the ball hard, some newspapers said 'wildly' forwards. The ball blew high towards the FC The Hague half. Cruyff sprang into action immediately. The length of fabric still in his hand, he ran to the spot where the ball would land, some 10 metres beyond the halfway line, close to the left side of the pitch. He had his back to goalkeeper Ton Thie and out of the corner of his eye he saw defender Kees Weimar coming his way. The opposition half was otherwise practically empty. Almost all the FC The Hague players had been drawn into a recent attack.

Instead of getting the high ball under control, as Weimar expected, Cruyff suddenly turned through 180 degrees and put it past the defender with a drop kick. As well as getting a foot to the ball as soon as it landed, he curved it too, by hitting it with the outside of his right foot. The ball flew at hip height through the empty space between him and Thie's goal. He couldn't play the ball along the ground, Cruyff explained afterwards, because 'the pitch is bad here, you can forget about a long dribble'. He ran past Weimar to the ball, which dropped early because of the headwind and was now rolling hesitantly towards the left corner of the penalty area.

Again, Cruyff touched the ball just once, this time with the inside of his right foot, making it curve high towards the goal, seemingly too high. Tall goalkeeper Thie, several metres in front of his goal by now, jumped up desperately and managed to touch the spinning ball, which was being forced downwards by the wind. He failed to prevent it from slipping just under the bar into the goal.

For a moment Cruyff seemed shocked by what he had done. As if he couldn't believe it himself. Then he ran off and leapt into the air wheeling his arms, the length of bandage above his head flapping behind him like a gymnast's ribbon. You'd swear that was why he did it, that he deliberately wheeled and waved so girlishly to make the image of a miraculous goal complete.

But he didn't play football for the beauty of it; he liked the purposeful, the economical, and that applied here too. Twice he'd made contact with the ball, with a short sprint in between. It was highly efficient action. Cruyff had done in five seconds something any other player would have to think about for five minutes first. In a flash of brilliance, he had solved a problem – a high wind-blown ball from his own defence – by taking account of distances and speeds, of the ground conditions and wind strength, and by following his intuition. All of that was clearly visible in a duel between two men on half a football field, magnificent and cruel.

The loser's response was sportsmanlike. Weimar could have stopped Cruyff with a foul. The defender didn't even consider it. 'I play football because I like it,' he said afterwards. 'I happen to get paid for it too, which is a bonus. But I'm a teacher by profession, not a footballer. I actually thought it was beautiful, the way Cruyff did that. And then you're supposed to kick someone's legs from under them?'

There was immediate talk of the 'European goal of the year', even though 1972 was only a few days old. 'Of course you know what you want at a moment like that,' was how Cruyff described his winning goal afterwards (the score remained 1-2). 'That it works, well, you can't always predict that in advance.' He added, as a lover of the game, 'In training sessions I enjoy that as well; against the wind, with spin, those balls fall so beautifully.' Thirteen years later he still counted that goal as among the three most memorable of his career.

At home too, everything continued to go according to plan. Their increased income made it possible for Johan and Danny to buy a plot of land on the edge of Vinkeveen. They wanted to build a bungalow there with a swimming pool and a tennis court. Far more importantly even than that, a few weeks after Cruyff's triumph in The Hague, Danny gave birth to a second daughter. The girl was named Susila, after an Indian woman who had been mentioned in the newspaper shortly before. So, as well as 'Chan', from 26 January 1972 there was 'Suzy' and she too was born by Caesarean section (in the Prinsengracht Hospital in Amsterdam), on a day when Johan was free. The young couple immediately began to long for a third child – they wanted five, ideally. Danny dreamed of a big family (having grown up with only her half-sister Annie, who was five years older) and nothing seemed to matter more to Johan than children. He'd visited an orphanage after his debut for Ajax 1, and he still had the drawing a little Surinamese-Dutch boy had given him there as a memento. Johan regularly made donations to orphanages and he called giving autographs to children 'endless'. No matter how often Danny complained that they never had a moment to themselves, he wouldn't send the youngest of them away. 'It's just that I enjoy it,' he might say from the midst of a swarm of shrieking little boys. Even when they rang his doorbell day after day in the hope of an autograph he still called it 'really nice'. When he had to be photographed with three other professional footballers and a bunch of children for an advertisement – all of them cosy in pyjamas – he was the first to pick up a child and look at the camera, smiling.

Life with two children in Vinkeveen soon found its rhythm and the same went for life in Amsterdam–Oost. In the premier division Ajax notched up victory after victory, and in Europe scores were settled with Arsenal in the quarter-finals without any difficulty. Whereas in 1970 Ajax had been overawed by the tough and fanatical play of the Londoners, it was now the Amsterdammers who made an impression. In a seething Olympic Stadium, which Arsenal forward Charlie George actually described as 'impressively hostile', people sang 'Ajax is world champion' long before that was a realistic prospect. But anyone seeing Cruyff run fluidly past British legs, braking and then accelerating again, knew that the Intercontinental Cup would be theirs eventually. Every time his marker Frank McLintock and his Arsenal teammates rushed at him, Cruyff allowed himself to be pushed forward by their bodychecks like a surfer on a wave. Meanwhile, he nonchalantly kept the ball under control and relinquished it only at a moment of his choosing. The BBC commentator was deeply impressed by the roaming Cruyff and his efficient passes. 'He was always a great individualist, now he's also a great team manager,' the man said. McLintock remarked that the striker was 'far better' than two years before. 'As if he saw everything on the pitch,' he remembers. 'He didn't look at me for a moment, not even at the ball, only at the space around us. He was both explosive and thoughtful. Unpredictable in every respect and delightfully arrogant.'

But in the second half the downside of Cruyff's machismo suddenly surfaced, as if the little devil of Betondorp had risen again. More than forty-five years later, McLintock jumps up from the sofa to demonstrate the trick Cruyff pulled on him in March 1972. An Ajax attack had been beaten off and McLintock was running back to his penalty area with the ball. Cruyff tackled him from behind, which made the Arsenal defender angry. The referee whistled for a foul and everyone got involved. A short-tempered tangle developed. 'I shouted something,' McLintock remembers. 'Not even at Cruyff, but suddenly he hit me in the face. Really, I felt his hand. Hard, too. I was boiling with rage. I wanted to take a swing at him but saw that the ref was close to us. He must have seen Johan hit me, but he didn't do anything.'

Calm was restored and Ajax remained the superior team to the end of the match. Arsenal were beaten only 2-1, but 3-0 would have been a more fitting result. Two weeks later Ajax won 1-0 relatively easily in London. Afterwards Arie Haan dismissed English football as 'simple stuff'. The English thought the same to some degree; compared to this Ajax, with their 'delightfully arrogant' playmaker Cruyff, Arsenal were still living in the Stone Age. McLintock continued to admire Johan despite the punch.

A sense of indomitability took possession of the team and

especially its 'attack leader', as Cruyff was now called. With modern play, which is to say slow or defensive if necessary, 'freezing' the game, Ajax knocked out Portuguese national champions Benfica in the semi-finals. In those matches Cruyff had played rather poorly, but in between he had been on fire in De Kuip in a 5-1 victory over rivals Feyenoord. One moment he was the ordinary boy from Betondorp, the next he said to a referee who called him to order, 'It's *Mr* Cruyff to you.' How did he manage to switch like that? Even journalist Maarten de Vos, who had been close to him for some time, couldn't always fathom it. Thirty-year-old De Vos was no more averse to commerce than the subject of his many analyses and background stories, so he proposed to Cruyff that they should make a documentary about him. The footballer would be able to show the world who he really was. Cruyff agreed. It would be good for uninformed people to see what it took to perform at the highest level, year in, year out.

At first they were thinking of a television documentary. But after the sporting successes of 1972 they decided to think big and make a real feature film. The European Cup final against Inter Milan would be an excellent vehicle for a cinema hit. Cor Coster would take charge of production; De Vos would direct. They regarded the fact that neither had any cinematic experience as irrelevant. The documentary would be made with meagre resources and that didn't matter, since Coster would organise some surreptitious advertising. It would be yet another form of pioneering, a film about a brilliant craftsman on a lonely pinnacle, who was sacrificing a huge amount for his profession. A working-class lad with many thrilling stories to tell.

It seemed a fantastic idea. They set to work in high spirits.

CHAPTER SIXTEEN

Jealousy

Many years later the film *Nummer 14* would gain cult status as a touching, even moving account of the daily life of the legend that was Johan Cruyff. But in 1973 the documentary was accounted a commercial and artistic flop. Even before the premiere on 8 March, it provoked resentment in some people. On the pavement outside the City Theater in Amsterdam that Thursday evening, demonstrators walked around with banners denouncing the 'folly of sport' and suchlike. Cruyff was someone who had 'struck it rich' by 'running after a ball' and was now trying to 'peddle' his popularity to cinema audiences. These were nothing but 'excesses', the demonstrators claimed. A man in his thirties with a moustache and shoulder-length hair declared in front of the television cameras that he would never enter a stadium again as long as 'ridiculous salaries' were being paid to footballers like Cruyff. 'There are people who work with their hands who don't earn a tenth of what he gets,' the man said.

Of course, Amsterdam was the left-wing capital of a country spellbound by a new government with the most left-wing cabinet ever. Under the leadership of socialist Joop den Uyl the aim would be to share out power, knowledge and income. Only a handful of people stood outside the cinema entrance with sandwich boards on the night of the premiere. The demonstration did however make clear that with this documentary Cruyff didn't seem to be achieving entirely what he had in mind. The idea had been that people would see him as a hardworking professional, not as a privileged sportsman with an easy life. Cruyff and the zeitgeist of the 1960s and 70s was an alliance of contradictions.

Afterwards a television crew walked the corridors of the City Theater asking some of the invited guests whether what was going on here amounted to 'a personality cult'. Presenter Mies Bouwman ignored the question and declared with delight that she'd seen 'a fantastic portrait of a footballer'. The reviewers had a rather different opinion. Most of them panned *Nummer 14* for its superficiality. In the ninety-minute documentary the central character had done most of the talking – as a voice-over to footage of matches, at home with Danny and the children, or on a nostalgic visit to Betondorp. To the disappointment of the film critics, what his teammate Keizer and the other Ajax players thought of the striker who floated across the screen so beautifully in slow motion was not mentioned once.

True enough, Keizer, Swart and Suurbier did not speak in the documentary. That was no accident, it seemed. Cruyff presented himself as a soloist, as misunderstood even, as a star who, although not cocky, was more than happy to be filmed driving home after training in his exceptionally beautiful car. Half a century later people would still gape at that vast Citroën SM of his, a revolutionary model that brought together the hydropneumatic suspension of the famous Citroën DS and the speed of a Maserati. It was graceful and aerodynamic, creative and as fast as lightning, just like Cruyff himself. For many viewers – the documentary was shown on television numerous times in the Netherlands and abroad – the film consisted almost entirely of Cruyff chattering away at the wheel of his car as the meadows passed by in the background. The camera showed the spacious interior as if in a television commercial. A footballer could hardly get further away from the working classes.

During the drive from Amsterdam to Vinkeveen he felt like

some music. 'I'll just turn it over,' he said and, sure enough, a cassette tape slid out of the player and then in again, very slowly, so that the camera had enough time to capture a clearly legible brand name: 'Philips'. The film was full of clandestine advertising. As well as Philips, father-in-law Coster had done deals with companies that included Lois and Puma. The latter was an obvious one to include. In April 1972 Cruyff had signed a new 150,000-guilder contract with the sporting goods brand and was obliged to promote it. By walking beside Danny holding, very conspicuously, Puma sports bags, for example. Later Cruyff abruptly turned his bottom to the camera in front of him so that even the partially sighted on the back row could read which brand of jeans he was wearing.

Oddly, his Citroën, with its outstanding front-wheel drive, its avant-garde steering, its six headlights and a licence plate behind glass, was not the result of such a deal. Johan had been driving it for some time because Uncle Cor had made an arrangement that was a forerunner to the lease. But the Citroën SM was of course a showcase on wheels, a 'head-turner'. Hardly anyone could actually drive around in a vehicle worth at least 40,000 guilders. So, while it gave the central character a chance to emphasise his sacrifices and his craftsmanship, many young players saw the documentary primarily as an ostentatious display of success. This was how you lived once you had made it. One of those young men was called Rudi Dil, a half-Surinamese teenager who was a good footballer but had never dreamed of turning professional. It wasn't until he saw Cruyff driving and talking in his supersonic car in the film, accompanied by the music of his choice, that Rudi in Amsterdam decided to go into paid football. All that stuff Cruyff was pontificating about, with his curving shots and so on, was neither here nor there. Rudi Dil took the name of his (absent) father because it better suited a career in sport. He too was going to become important. As Ruud Gullit he signed his first professional contract and the rest is history.

*

Nummer 14 could have been the perfect opportunity to show how brilliantly Cruyff collaborated with his teammates. Because in fact that collaboration was the key to his success. His helpfulness could have come into its own beautifully too. Arie Haan could have described how, as a newcomer, he lived with a foster family in Betondorp and was picked up by the already famous Johan who drove him to away games. Neeskens could have told audiences about the reassuring words Johan whispered to him early in his career. Keizer could have recollected with a smile how he and a good friend who wanted to set up a restaurant had borrowed 5,000 guilders from Cruyff without putting anything down on paper, without any interest being charged and without any agreed payback date: among friends, Johan was a man of trust. Swart will surely have remembered that in his early days Johan would be sent by the older players to Michels' office to test his mood, and was always happy to go.

The squad were full of such tales, but they went unheard in the documentary. Cruyff's fellow players had at best walk-on parts.

Only in the early minutes did they briefly appear in the foreground, as an introduction to the glory to come. First Krol, Neeskens, Haan and Keizer park their sports cars in front of the stadium. Then trainer Kovács cycles – *tring tring!* – on to the De Meer terrain. Everyone has dressed up in club suits and fashionable rollneck sweaters for the occasion, presumably at the request of director Maarten de Vos, because they were only going to a training session, not to do anything official. Then the main character drives up in his silver-metallic Citroën SM with green tinted windows in a way that makes everything that has gone before seem almost ridiculous. Fast, dynamic and gleaming. Nice for a southern European children's film about a superhero and his companions. A bit embarrassing perhaps in a Calvinist country of 'what's sauce for the goose is sauce for the gander'.

As for the highlights of football matches in the film, everyone agreed they were fantastic. You saw Cruyff floating for minutes on end over the outstretched legs of opponents, leaping like a ballet dancer on the grass, landing on the front of his feet like a deer. But those images were misleading. They were taken from the European Cup final against Inter Milan, on 31 May 1972, and from the battle for the Intercontinental Cup against Independiente on 28 September 1972. It was precisely in those matches that he had not been the soloist who bent everything to his will, but far more the leader of a beautifully function-ing team. Both matches had been a triumph of the collective. Indeed, they had probably produced the best football in the world at that moment. Most striking during the European Cup final in Rotterdam had been Ajax's mobile defenders and midfielders. Every single one of them had shown themselves superior to their opponents in Inter Milan. Even centre back Barry Hulshoff, hardly the most supple of the team, had the feared striker Roberto Boninsegna on a leash and occasionally moved up to midfield to deliver passes as a number 10. Everyone ran in between everyone else and there was hardly ever a gap, to the despair of the Italians. With a demonstration of positional play, technique and attacking skill, the 'total footballers' of Ajax, as the experts said, polished off the *catenaccio*. Attacking football seemed to own the future again and Europe heaved a sigh of relief.

Ironically, in the cup final Cruyff had possession of the ball half as often as in an average match up to that point. Even Maarten de Vos wrote in *De Tijd* that Cruyff had 'such a hard time' against Gabriele Oriali 'that he could demonstrate his class only in fits and starts', whereas De Vos in his role as film director had positioned a cameraman close to the touchline to capture Number 14 from up close. Fortunately for De Vos and Coster – and for all of Amsterdam – Cruyff scored both the goals that won Ajax its second European Cup. Shortly after half-time he controlled a high ball – which landed at his feet between the Italian goalkeeper and a defender as the result of a misunderstanding – with awesome ease. The ball plopped obediently down at his feet as if it was deflating and Cruyff firmly slid it into the empty goal. Fifteen minutes before the end of the match he headed the ball hard and high into the net from the midst of a jumble of jumping players.

Both goals were extraordinary enough to bear frequent playback. In the documentary they were packaged between advertisements for the new VCR system from Philips. 'It's a kind of video recorder,' the goal scorer explains as he takes his seat at the dining table in Vinkeveen. 'I can play a bit of it.' With a serious expression he holds up a box of video tapes and a little later, with a bit of a flourish, he presses the buttons on his video recorder. 'It's fantastic fun, this thing.' Inter Milan vs Ajax rolls out and immediately you see Cruyff on the pitch in Rotterdam with the name 'Philips' in huge lettering in the background. Then the Cruyff–Oriali duel. In slow motion you watch the striker and his 19-year-old marker cross the pitch in synchrony as if glued together. Every time Cruyff tries to jump away or leap up, Oriali does something to slow him down or block him. 'Watch this,' says Cruyff. 'You want to do something here and they run right in front of you. Nobody sees that. I'll show you ... Look ... Rewind ... Stop ... Play ...'

The matches for the Intercontinental Cup against Independiente created the same impression, especially the second leg, on 28 September 1972 in Amsterdam. The first leg had taken place three weeks earlier in Buenos Aires and ended 1-1. In the Olympic Stadium Ajax gave the champions of Latin America a pointed lesson in modern football. It was an unequal battle between two teams from different eras, between stagnancy and movement. Sometimes it was downright pathetic; Krol would run up to an Argentine with an attitude of 'here, laddie, your time's up', take the ball from him and make off with it.

In that final, too, Cruyff had been less than dominant, so from the point of view of the film it was just as well he'd been so alert. His splendid passes enabled substitute Johnny Rep to make it 2-0 and 3-0 from two counterattacks. In the film those two splendid assists look like ten, they are shown so often from different angles. Cruyff's fluid moves are likewise repeated many times over and you see him pointing and shouting a lot and thereby, as it were, helping his team to the intercontinental championship. Not a word meanwhile about team discipline, about the ingenious collective pressing, the way the midfielders repeatedly moved forward.

Because of all this, the film fuelled the already growing jealousy among Cruyff's teammates. 'All that eulogising of Johan started to irritate us a bit,' Haan says. 'After a mediocre match in which he'd made two good moves, everyone went on about how brilliant he was. They completely forgot that I'd made good connections in midfield, that I'd held the whole thing together. Of course, he was the best, but you never heard anyone talk about all the other important things that happened on the pitch. Especially not in that film.'

Swart was rarely critical of Cruyff, but after seeing *Nummer 14* the right-winger sneered that he'd never seen Johan train so hard as in that documentary. Mühren even suspected Johan of deliberately moving to the left time and again during the European Cup final because that's where the cameraman was. He was not alone.

'The film follows me, but it's about Ajax as a whole,' Cruyff said on the night of the premiere. It sounded like an attempt at damage limitation.

The film was taken out of circulation after a few weeks. Cinema audiences were no more impressed by it than the reviewers. It nevertheless became a cult hit and the *Nummer 14* concept quickly took root, growing to become a global trademark. The central character profited a good deal more from that than from the film itself. He had hoped it would earn him a fortune and perhaps it did. Forget Citroën, Lois, Puma and Philips: the documentary marked the ultimate triumph of the Cruyff brand.

*

The season in which the film was released, 1972–73, was full of contradictions. The many successes of the thrillingly dominant top-class football played by Ajax, and Cruyff's often wonderful goals and crosses, were offset by much bad feeling and hurt. Several years later Johan would describe it as a 'terrible' period. The season had not started well for him. In the first match, at home against Haarlem, he missed four chances. That produced 'hellish catcalls', according to *De Tijd*. In the second match he scored an own goal. Ahead by 2–0 against FC Amsterdam, he caught the ball with his chest in the Ajax penalty area before, with his back to keeper Stuy, volleying it backwards into the net. A great shot, if you could see the funny side.

In the weeks that followed, the Ajax machinery got itself up and running again as of old, with that glorious victory at home against Independiente as a high point. But in the Dutch league competition disaster struck again three days later. In Breda, Cruyff played as a midfielder. Conscious of his role, he often ran forward, after which players like Keizer deliberately didn't pass him the ball – to torment him, in Haan's view. 'The next time I'm off,' Cruyff shouted after yet another futile sprint. Again the ball didn't reach him promptly enough and despite being 1–0 down he asked to be substituted. World champions Ajax then lost 2–0 to run-of-the-mill NAC.

Resentment crept into the team. In 1972 Ajax had won the league championship, the KNVB Cup, the European Cup and the Intercontinental Cup within the space of four months. 'After the Intercontinental Cup the leadership fell away,' defender Hulshoff said later. 'Everyone started talking and then you could see us all grow apart. We became less accepting of one another. The players confronted each other less and when there were confrontations they were harder, meaner. There was more playing of the man instead of the ball. Personalities became more important, at the expense of the collective. What were we supposed to be striving for? All our aims had already been achieved.'

The core problem, Cruyff believed, was that the supporting

players had started to 'play football' themselves and therefore to neglect their tasks. Water carrier Haan, for example, started to feel he was too good to keep going deep, sometimes for nothing. He wanted to be known as 'champagne carrier' in future. 'On the pitch I tried to clamp down on that by talking and shouting,' Cruyff said later. 'The way we played football, all of us were supposed to be moving. You weren't allowed to run with the ball too long, and some players even thought that getting around the man opposing you was unacceptable.' But his teammates were defiant. Discipline declined. Egos swelled. And when in the autumn of 1972 Cruyff became captain because Keizer no longer wanted that responsibility, the annoyance only increased. Johan may have taken his captaincy too literally. 'It was my job to give instructions and criticism,' he said later. 'In a match I'm a spitfire and I throw out all kinds of things.' His fellow players could sometimes be remarkably sensitive. Substitute Rep believed Cruyff 'talked twice as much' now he was captain. When the team was working well, 'then you didn't give a damn', Rep said. 'You just let him bullshit away. But it felt oppressive if you didn't get a touch of the ball. Some of the lads couldn't stand that. Nor could I.'

What for Cruyff came down to taking responsibility, to helping, seemed to others like nagging. He was never good at knowing when to stop and as captain he wasn't a unifying factor. His pushiness, his individualism and the growing arrogance of others in the team stood in the way. Moreover, in the 1972-73 season he was absent more often than usual, partly because of a lingering injury after a kick to his knee in Buenos Aires. Even when he did play, he was by no means always fit. His authority waned. 'Apart from a few friends,' Cruyff said, 'it was me against the rest.' He often came home 'broken and exhausted' after a day at Ajax. 'I started sleeping badly. I started to fret. I started looking for a way out, and I couldn't find one.'

Illustrative of all this was the issue of Sjaak Swart, which arose in the autumn of 1972. Most members of the team had for some time preferred playing with the fast and high-scoring Johnny Rep on the right wing rather than Swart, who was now thirty-four. But the obstinate popular favourite refused to give up his place, and since coach Kovács lacked the authority to decide the matter, the obvious thing was for skipper Cruyff to make the swap. But the captain let the whole business simmer on for months. True, he had been paying attention for a while to good-humoured Johnny, but that expressed itself mainly in reprimands and disparaging tactics on the pitch – making passes Rep couldn't quite reach, followed by demonstrative gestures of disappointment – which Johnny took to be attempts by Johan to hold him back.

In the end it was former player Henk Groot who, in his role as a member of the commission for paid football, took the 'rotten job' upon himself. He told Swart the bad news. From that moment in early 1973 onwards, the basic forward line was made up of Rep, Cruyff and Keizer. For months afterwards, right into the summer, Groot continued to put the team together (Kovács' wings having been clipped by the board). Cruyff made no attempt to fill the vacuum. 'Johan rarely if ever interfered,' Groot remembers. 'Perhaps because it was a horrible job.' Perhaps also because, as Number 14 says in the film, 'the eyes' of his fellow players turned to him whenever there were setbacks and on the way home afterwards he could feel 'so lonely'.

On 7 March, the day before the premiere of *Nummer 14*, the supposedly strong Bayern Munich, with a team that included Gerd Müller and Franz Beckenbauer, were trounced in Amsterdam 4-0. But anyone watching that first quarter-final closely saw not only that Cruyff scored (with a header just before the final whistle) but that he was making more desperate gestures than normal. As if he felt lost and was calling for help from an island in the forward line. 'Come on!' he seemed to keep shouting. 'Hey!' It was followed each time by that typical Cruyffian look of despair, with shoulders raised high. Often the others didn't come to help him in his efforts to put opponents off their stride. He was on his own.

Meanwhile, he was increasingly referred to as a 'phenomenon'. A biography of him had been published with that word in the title and it celebrated him as 'the Bach of football'. The smiling face of superstar Cruyff on the cover of *Time* magazine didn't make his position any easier. His credit with his fellow players was visibly declining. 'It's as understandable as it is horrifying to be the object of jealousy,' he said of this period two years later. 'You only have to mess up one chance and you get the full broadside.'

The spring of 1973 was full of 'broadsides', and the cause of all the arguments and misunderstandings was an injury to his right knee. The medical staff questioned its seriousness, which led Cruyff to consult foreign doctors, and an endless dispute arose with reproaches and insinuations from both sides. One time he would play (with injections in his knee), the next he would sit out the match, or he might play and drop out limping, some said unnecessarily. The 'umpteenth spat about Johan Cruyff', as the newspapers described it, dragged on for months.

Its climax came with the away game against Bayern. The players were sitting waiting in the bus in front of the De Meer stadium and, however much Van Praag pointed out to him his responsibility as captain, Cruyff did not want to go to Germany. Feverish consultation followed with 'coach' Groot (who had himself been declared unfit because of his knee) and with external specialists, but the captain insisted on putting his own health first. He thought it was more important than giving his teammates moral support in Munich. The players were astonished. 'We just sat there waiting in the bus,' says Haan. 'He surely could have walked over to us to say sorry? To make clear that he'd tried everything but it hadn't worked and to wish us success against Bayern?'

The bus left without captain Cruyff. He got himself treated somewhere in Amsterdam-Zuid by Ajax's former masseur

Salo Muller. The board, the doctors and many of the players now turned against him. Even journalist Maarten de Vos felt that Johan had done 'a foolish thing' that was 'impossible to justify'. But he also pointed to Cruyff's loneliness. There were no psychologists or psychiatrists any longer with whom the players could air their feelings in private. In light of that, the journalist believed, Johan was a victim as well as a perpetrator, a 'hunted animal'.

Bayern Munich vs Ajax was a tough game in which the Amsterdammers, even without Cruyff – and with Haan as a kind of pulled-back striker – managed to limit the damage. Combined with their 4-0 victory of two weeks earlier in Amsterdam, their 2-1 defeat in the quarter-final could do no harm.

On arrival home there were harsh words once more. Cruyff was reproached for isolating himself too much from the group. His refusal to travel to Munich was seen as yet further proof of this. But in the end, after a clear-the-air conversation, the players were prepared to reaffirm their confidence in Cruyff. It meant that, once his knee was functioning properly again after help from outside Ajax, he could return as captain. It was agreed with the club leadership that the players were permitted to seek treatment elsewhere, as long as club doctor Rolink was kept informed: on the face of it a normal state of affairs that was nevertheless not common practice and that 'rebel' Cruyff had secured for them in his own, less than tactful, manner. Swart, Mühren and Blankenburg no longer needed to be secretive about their visits to external specialists, and neither did many players after them.

With their Number 14 back in the team, Ajax won their semi-final of the European Cup against Real Madrid in April 1973. The two victories (2-1 at home and 1-0 away) could easily have been more convincing, so superior were the Amsterdammers, despite the fact that Cruyff was still unable to play at full throttle.

That 1-0 win in Madrid, incidentally, was no exception. In

1973 Ajax became national champions with no fewer than seven 1-0 victories and went on to win the European Cup final in Belgrade that year by beating Juventus 1-0. That was how it went with Ajax at this point. If the opposition wanted to make an open battle of it, Ajax responded appreciatively and beautiful football might result. If not, fine, then the game would be frozen at 1-0 and Ajax would coolly play on until the end of the match.

On 30 May 1973 in the Yugoslav capital, Ajax again froze the game. After Rep made it 1-0 in the fourth minute with a sublime header after a high cross from Blankenburg, leaving Juventus relentlessly on the prowl for a counterattack, Ajax shut up shop. The outcome was a rather boring final. Both teams refused to take any risks. Moreover, Ajax seemed to lack not just the eagerness but the energy to get going. After a long season, the poor discipline under Kovács was taking its toll. Cruyff blamed the weak play on a 'lack of puff' among other things and Hulshoff later admitted that the fitness of most Ajax players left a lot to be desired. 'We couldn't go on,' Haan said too, looking back.

Preparations for the match had been a shambles. Furthermore, news came through that the coming summer would see the Spanish borders open up at last to foreign footballers. That report seemed to occupy the minds of some Ajax players more than opponents Juventus. Cruyff in particular was often mentioned as a player who could expect untold riches in Madrid or Barcelona. Team solidarity evaporated. After the bloodless 1-0 victory, most of the players thought even a lap of honour too much to ask. Only Cruyff and Hulshoff did their duty, carrying the big gleaming cup. 'When we are all old and full of days,' intoned TV commentator Herman Kuiphof, 'we will surely look back with envy. Because it seems an impossibility for things to stay as they are now.'

The Ajax supporters, who had so often turned European trips into a party, returned to Schiphol airport grumbling about the anaemic match.

'Deep down we knew it was over,' says Hulshoff.

CHAPTER SEVENTEEN

Just ring Barcelona

On Monday 9 July 1973 Johan Cruyff arrived at Hotel De Bloemenbeek in De Lutte as if everything was the same as ever. The Spanish borders had been open for a week, but because his contract with Ajax still had five years to run, there was every indication that he would simply continue to play in Amsterdam in the coming season. In the training camp he unpacked his suitcase in the room he would share, as usual, with goalkeeper Heinz Stuy.

De Lutte lay in the lee of the landed properties of the province of Twente and seemed a suitable place for the players to forget the vexations of the previous season. Under the leadership of the new coach George Knobel, who had taken over from Kovács during the summer, the squad could prepare for the next season in peace and quiet. For a week they would train in the daytime on the pitches of SV De Lutte and in the evenings practise against amateur teams from the surrounding region. At a considerable distance from the major conurbations in the west of the country, Ajax would have little trouble from busybodies, and there was good news: Jan Mulder, who had been transferred from Anderlecht the previous year, seemed at last to have overcome his knee injury. The new striker might be able to give fresh impetus to the attack and on Monday evening the early

signs were positive. Mulder and Cruyff, the knee patients who
had grown to like each other over the past year, played smoothly
together in Emmen against fourth division WKE. On the
Tuesday as well everything went like clockwork. With Cruyff
in midfield behind the forward line Rep–Mulder–Keizer, Ajax
beat a Twente team put together for the occasion 6-2.

On the Wednesday there was no match and on Thursday 12
July Piet Keizer unexpectedly made an announcement. After
a game of foot volleyball in the sun, in which he'd made up a
team with Cruyff and Blankenburg, Keizer said he was putting
himself forward for the captaincy again.

Cruyff was flabbergasted. Piet had voluntarily surrendered
the armband and ever since then Johan had found it an honour
to bear the responsibility. Now it turned out that Keizer wanted
it back. A little later the whole squad came together in the
hotel's television room. They decided to vote on it. 'I'm captain,' Cruyff tried. 'And I'm staying captain. So there's no need
for a vote.'

But there was. To many players, Keizer, in the words of Rep,
was the ideal captain. Two years earlier Piet had been chosen
by a large margin. After Michels' departure the appointment of
a captain by the coach was abandoned in favour of democracy.
Only two players had voted for Cruyff then – probably Suurbier
and Neeskens; it was a secret ballot. The circumspect Piet was
popular with the group, he didn't talk as much as the impulsive
Johan and when he did speak he was listened to. The 30-year-
old left-winger felt everyone should earn the same amount and
he wasn't always running in and out to take care of private
business. In contrast to Johan, he passed up most of the entice-
ments of the business world. New players who felt intimidated
by Cruyff's comments were put at ease by Keizer. Pay no attention, he would say. Johan doesn't mean it personally – which
was true. Piet found it easier to put himself in other people's
shoes. Recently he had collected money to give coach Kovács
a leaving present. He'd decided on a Renault, because he knew

the parts would be easy to get hold of in Romania (although Kovács would have to pass his driving test first). 'That's what Piet was like,' says Haan. 'And he didn't complicate matters, like Johan did. He preferred to keep things simple.'

To outsiders Keizer came across as rather eccentric, but the players thought the world of him: he was circumspect, independent and sociable, precisely the qualities that had drawn Cruyff to him in earlier days. For exactly that reason, Piet's message that he wanted to resume his captaincy cut Johan to the quick; it was a sign of distrust after all those years of symbiosis on and off the pitch.

During the 1972–73 season Keizer had decided 'that Johan was too eager to put his personal stamp on the team', as he explained later. The combination of a big mouth on the pitch, wearing the captain's armband and all those commercial activities worked against the team's interests, he felt. Under pressure from his father-in-law, Cruyff had 'sold' himself too much as the figurehead of Ajax. The left-winger seemed to be referring to the *Nummer 14* film.

At the request of the players, the owner of the Hotel De Bloemenbeek brought them sixteen pieces of paper and sixteen pens. Newcomer Pim van Dord declined to vote, so there was a fifteen-man electorate. Cruyff won the support of Gerrie and Arnold Mühren, Neeskens, Suurbier, Mulder and Stuy. But it wasn't enough. Keizer won by eight votes to seven.

Johan froze. There was nothing worse than being dumped by your equals. 'A kind of nervous giggliness prevailed,' Mulder said later. 'Johan sensed that very clearly. He didn't say anything, but you could see: this is wrong. When he was angry, something destructive crept into him. He would be terse. Very terse. He could ignore people and things as if they barely existed. There was no way back, you could feel that.'

The deposed captain stood up and walked out of the recreation room. Mulder, who had been no less surprised than Cruyff by the result, went after him. In the corridor there was a telephone on the wall. Cruyff dialled a number. A little time later he said into the receiver, to his father-in-law, 'Just ring Barcelona.'

Stuy had walked out of the room too and when Johan finished his call, the goalkeeper took him up to their room on the first floor. Cruyff was beside himself. 'In his view the players who had voted for Keizer had made an enormous mistake,' Stuy remembers. Stuy was never able to understand why a vote had been called at all. 'Those were times of democratisation, of course, perhaps it was that.' In an attempt to calm him down, Stuy picked up an orange and laid the segments on a plate. 'Here, Johan,' he said. 'Calmly now. Have another piece.'

That Thursday evening there was a match to be played. Ajax practised against the amateurs of SV Meppen, just over the German border. To the surprise of the handful of Dutch journalists present, Keizer was now the captain. And Cruyff excelled. As so often in his career, having been goaded he produced exquisite football. But after half an hour he walked off the pitch – presumably the demonstration had lasted long enough – and had himself substituted.

After returning to the hotel, Cruyff did little else but make phone calls. 'It went on for hours,' says roommate Stuy. 'At four-thirty in the morning he finally came back to our room. I asked where he'd been. With any of the other players I'd have known, since they'd have been out after the girls, but you didn't often see that with Johan. He told me he'd been ringing about Barcelona.'

FC Barcelona were prepared to do practically anything to acquire Johan's services. Manager (and secretary) Armand Carabén had been in touch with Cruyff for years and with the help of his Dutch wife Marjolijn van der Meer he had brought Rinus Michels to Catalonia two years before. With the Dutch coach as an intermediary, Carabén had first tried to attract striker Gerd Müller of Bayern Munich – Michels feared that along with his brilliance, Johan would bring with him his tendency to engage in conflict – but negotiations with Müller had run aground. So the Barcelona manager was now entirely open to the idea of acquiring the 'expensive' Cruyff, whom he regarded as the best in the world. With him in the forward line, rich Barcelona, who had been performing indifferently for years, would be able to celebrate success again at last, and so help to reinforce Catalan resistance to dictator Franco and the detested Madrid. Now that the military regime in Madrid was on its last legs and the 1962 ban on foreign footballers playing for Spanish clubs had been lifted, it was time for new firepower in the battle for the restoration of old freedoms and self-determination. A great deal of money was available for that firepower of Cruyff's.

In Twente interest from Barcelona drove the parties further apart. Cruyff told the Catalans that his existing Ajax contract was no obstacle; if he encountered opposition he could simply refuse to play. 'Relations had deteriorated to the point that Johan wanted to leave no matter what,' says Haan. 'I believe he was resolutely looking for a reason to be able to go to Barcelona.'

Cruyff thought: They can figure it out. I'll look after myself.

In the next practice match the attack leader, who was clearly stressed out after all the quarrels and the phone calls with Barcelona, got into an argument with the amateurs. He used threatening language with the incredulous referee. He squabbled so loudly with his old mate Keizer that the spectators could understand every word. Meanwhile, Cruyff explained away the arguments as jealousy. He thought the others ungrateful for all he'd done for them. Several team members were now working with his father-in-law as their agent, and Coster had smoothed quite a few paths for his fellow players in the fields of finance and social security. A year earlier all the players and trainers had held out their hands when Coster put 5,000 guilders their way, the result of a clever deal with Esso for a poster featuring the European Cup winners.

*

Cruyff wanted to go to Barcelona whatever. Even when Real Madrid started rattling the backdoor with a vast moneybag, he stuck to his plan. The mores of the market didn't count at that moment. He found his relationship with the Carabén–Van der Meer couple too agreeable to back out now. Lawyer and businessman Armand and his wife (and interpreter) Marjolijn were, as Cruyff put it, 'something in themselves' and they didn't need a sports club to improve their social standing, in contrast to most board members of football clubs that he knew in the Netherlands. He felt drawn to such 'exceptional people'. Moreover, as a small boy Cruyff had followed the club's results with particular interest. The status of the challenger to Real Madrid and the remarkable colour combination of dark blue with garnet (the *blaugrana*) had appealed to him even then.

Since 1970 he had visited the beautiful city on the Mediterranean coast several times, with Danny or with Uncle Cor, which had not always been in the interests of the Dutch team but had strengthened his ties with the Carabéns. As well as the enticement of the climate there was something else, which he often mentioned first in interviews: in Barcelona he could earn more than twice as much as in Amsterdam, and of that top salary he'd have to give up only half as much in percentage terms to the treasury. 'I'd have been willing to crawl there at that point,' he said later.

Now, in 1973, the issue of the captaincy had been added to the mix. According to a *Telegraaf* reporter who was present with Ajax in La Coruña to cover a tournament, his feelings were still running 'very high' on the subject. Negotiations between Van Praag and Carabén would no doubt be successful, Johan believed, so he rang Danny from the players' hotel. 'Honey, we're going to Barcelona.' His roommate Stuy was told matters were all but settled. 'But shortly after that he backtracked again,' Stuy recalls. 'Danny turned out to be pregnant. If he went off to play in Spain, his parents-in-law wouldn't be able to see the baby grow up.'

Both families were in a panic. How could this work, with a third child on the way? Danny's mother Dien Coster had a fainting fit that night from all the turbulence. Cor thought his wife would collapse if she was separated from Danny and the grandchildren, so it didn't take Johan long to decide: no Barcelona. The baby-boomer so often seen as typifying a time of generational conflict stood by his mother-in-law. The family man was not going to abandon the mother of his darling wife. Health and happiness were more important than the heaps of pesetas that lay waiting for him.

For days the coveted striker disappeared into the beautiful Galician port city and when he next appeared before a throng of journalists and fellow players he told them everything had got a bit out of hand. He didn't want to say any more than that. In his *Telegraaf* column he promised to concentrate on Ajax once more. The new coach George Knobel, with whom he had engaged in long conversations, was actually a 'fine man', he believed, a 'craftsman' even.

Knobel was naturally 'delighted'. The coach, a man from the province of Brabant with wavy black hair, rose to higher realms immediately on hearing that compliment. 'It has become clear to me that Cruyff is looking for someone who can offer him protection,' he said to the press. 'He has missed that element over recent years.' An analysis that was probably correct. But the ambitious coach, in reality little more than a messenger boy for the players just like his predecessor Kovács, had spoken too soon. Johan's new father figure was not George Knobel from Roosendaal but 42-year-old Armand Carabén from Barcelona. Carabén had turned up in the Netherlands again because Barcelona, like Ajax, were preparing for the new season. Coach Michels knew his way around and the relatively cool Dutch summer was ideal for getting his players' fitness levels up to standard.

Dien and her pregnant daughter Danny had calmed down by this time. Carabén and Van Praag could resume their negotiations in Amsterdam. Barcelona were willing to have the family fly over at weekends, all year round. So Dien could see the baby once a week. Cruyff was cheerful; that way they could emigrate after all. Chairman Van Praag had moreover reduced the asking price (he'd originally wanted 9 million guilders, an unimaginable sum in those days), and the two clubs reached an agreement on 13 August. Ajax would be paid 3 million guilders and Cruyff could expect the same amount, but spread over three years. A Dutch premier division player had never changed clubs for a fee like that before and no footballer from any country had ever moved to Spain for so much money.

But that was not the end of the soap opera starring Johan Cruyff. Administrative obstacles were put up by Madrid. A trading law turned out to make it impossible for Barcelona to transfer the money to Ajax. The fact that Real Madrid had earlier transferred almost 2 million guilders to Germany to buy midfielder Günter Netzer was apparently irrelevant. In the boardrooms of the Banca Catalana a scheme was devised; for the import of something that could move under its own steam, such as livestock, no legal authorisation was required. Documents and information were shuffled about and so Cruyff, the genius of movement, a *semoviente* according to the paperwork, was able to enter the country as if he were a sheep or a cow. At the same time the transfer money could move across the Spanish border in the opposite direction.

A new episode followed. It was August now, the Dutch transfer window was closed and the KNVB regulations prevented a transfer to Barcelona. There could be no further talk of making an exception.

Cruyff heard the news from a television reporter who was waiting for him in front of his house in Vinkeveen. 'I can't leave in the interim?' the footballer repeated the question as his gaze travelled along the Scholeksterlaan. The pictures betray no emotion – at such moments his tendency to bottle things up was clear to see. Despite all his chatter and practical jokes, he was essentially an introvert. The reporter said again that he couldn't leave. 'I'm a simple-minded person,' was Cruyff's response, and he took his sports bag out of the brand-new, sea-green Citroën SM he had bought to take with him to Spain, his lease car having been returned to the garage. 'But there are two transfer periods. They don't connect up, so one of the two will have to take it or leave it.'

Was there an incorrect use of language here? Or was this a brilliant way of putting it? However that may be, his words testified to a fighting spirit. Not him but the situation would have to give way. 'I've always wanted this,' he said with a straight face. 'I've been working on it for three and a half years. Spain has always been my ideal.'

It was a matter of urgency because in Spain the transfer period would end in just over two weeks, on 31 August. So in the days that followed, Cruyff did two things he was extremely good at: playing football and issuing threats. In an Ajax shirt he produced exquisite goals and crosses effortlessly, it seemed. Both in ordinary practice matches and in the game that marked the departure of Sjaak Swart, as well as in Groningen on the opening day of the season, his play generated jubilant commentary. He himself thought his sparkling performance 'a normal reaction'. He heard voices behind his back saying 'that I can't do it any more. That I can't pull anything off. It's the kind of thing that fires you up.'

With suitable bluff by him and by Coster, Ajax had been massaged, and now it was the turn of the football association. He threatened to take out an injunction because the KNVB didn't have the right to deny him this chance to improve his position. Furthermore, now that Oranje were well on their way to the 1974 World Cup in West Germany (thanks in part to a Cruyff who was motivated at last), would it not be a pity if he passed up the remaining qualifying matches?

He didn't put it like that. He simply kept laying his availability for the Dutch team on the table; that was enough.

The KNVB leadership fell to squabbling, to such an extent that the entire executive committee of the professional football league stepped down. The KNVB offices in Zeist were in crisis. Meanwhile, Cruyff had himself photographed surrounded by prospective teammates, smiling. Barcelona played a friendly in the Netherlands against Sparta and in doing so, according to the press, stuck to an 'outdated' system, but that did nothing to spoil the fun in the Rotterdam changing room, where Michels introduced the players to Cruyff.

Photos of the cheery get-together appeared in the papers. Pressure on the football association increased.

In the days that followed, a solution seemed to be in the offing at the KNVB and it was in that knowledge that Cruyff entered the De Meer stadium on the afternoon of Sunday 19 August for the first Ajax home game of the 1973-74 season. To Number 14 it felt like his last.

The stands were full, unusually for a home game against FC Amsterdam. The huge turnout seemed to stem not just from love of Cruyff but to an important degree from pure curiosity. After all the publicity about his possible departure, nobody wanted to miss what might be his final appearance in their city. It was a show you needed to be at so you could talk about it – a feeling that perhaps characterises the fairly complicated relationship between Cruyff and his home town. He came out through the fence and presented himself in the centre circle without greeting the crowd. Cruyff had heard hissing and whistling and now Ajax was no longer his home. They had raised him here, given him extra meals, helped, listened, admired, instilled discipline, imparted tactics, strung him along, underpaid him, accused him of various things ...

He pepped himself up. He didn't want to leave any other way than to the sound of applause.

Several days earlier he had declined a last-minute offer from Ajax. The conditions were unprecedentedly favourable to him by Dutch standards, but he'd given his word to Barcelona, to

Armand and Marjolijn, and he wanted to stick to it. 'You don't understand,' he said. 'It stopped being about money a long time ago.' By this point Danny was even more fed up than he was. She'd have liked best to stay in Vinkeveen and before long move into their new luxury bungalow, but the anonymous phone calls she'd been getting recently, the torrents of abuse ('rapacious bitch', 'filthy whore'), the death threats, the envelopes of excrement and used toilet paper put through the letterbox had pointed out to her all too powerfully the flipside of the supposedly sober Dutch. She and Johan had also been admonished for giving moral support to dictator Franco by moving to Spain. It seemed as if no one in this little chilly Calvinist country was happy to see the two of them live a great life. 'Danny is completely objective about this kind of thing,' Coster said to a journalist. 'We, as men, sometimes have a tendency to give ground, but Danny is hard as nails in matters like this. She's been pretty brassed off by all the business surrounding Johan at Ajax in recent weeks.'

The whistle blew and it's more than possible that Cruyff was driven by resentment. That was good news for fans of football, because from a resentful Cruyff you could expect the best and most beautiful play.

So it proved once again. Ajax vs FC Amsterdam became a Number 14 show of the kind the spectators in the stadium, where he had once removed stones from the grass, had rarely seen. The often-critical reporter Ben de Graaf wrote the following day in *de Volkskrant*, 'By playing football the way he did yesterday against poor FC Amsterdam, Cruyff embarrasses even his fiercest critics and all those who are tired of the capricious behaviour of the money-maniac. Cruyff easily commanded the match, created the important openings, had a share in four of the six Ajax goals, and distinguished himself from all his pals by the sophistication and speed with which he carried out his solo work. Cruyff was more than ever a class apart.'

Seven minutes before the end of the match he scored: 6-1. On hearing the applause all around him he must have thought: get off the pitch now, leave on a high. He urged coach Knobel to make a substitution. 'I left the pitch,' he said later. 'That was my victory. To my mind it was a dignified departure. I showered, changed. I left the stadium without a word, without shaking anyone's hand.'

Later that Sunday the football association announced a classic Dutch compromise. 'Taking into account the interests of the Dutch national team', the contract between Ajax and Cruyff could be terminated. Nevertheless, the transfer periods must be respected. So an official transfer to Barcelona could not take place until 1 December, at the start of the winter transfer window in the Netherlands. Spain had no transfer period in winter, only in summer, and that would end on 1 September, so Cruyff had to report to his new employer in Barcelona before that date and could play his first match only three months later, after 1 December. It meant that an exception had been made for Cruyff that involved creating a kind of three-month transition period.

Many were amazed – and would continue to be amazed – at the remarkable paths, the sometimes puzzling turns, that Cruyff's career took. He not least of all. Unbelievable, all the difficulties he had already landed himself in. He was just twenty-six years old.

Three days after his departure from De Meer, Cruyff was back. He turned out for Oranje against Iceland. In his column he had promised his readers that he would always be there for the World Cup qualifying rounds – at least, he added with ironic menace, if the national coach still wanted to 'have' him – and so there he was. The Netherlands won 5-0. Cruyff scored twice.

Because of all the uncertainty, there had been little oppor-tunity for Cruyff to prepare for the departure for Spain. But the official reception in Barcelona was already planned for the day after the Netherlands–Iceland game. So, on Thursday 23

August 1973, Johan and Danny, three months pregnant, walked along the pier at Schiphol and stepped on board KL254, hearts racing. Toddlers Chantal and Susila would stay with Grandma and Grandpa Coster until a home had been found in Barcelona. The plan was to live in Spain for three years. After all, in 1976 Chantal would be starting at primary school and her parents would prefer her to have a Dutch education.

Things were to turn out very differently.

CHAPTER EIGHTEEN

And everything grew warm

Nel,
    Sadly, I won't see you. We had to get an earlier plane. I'm leaving money for you. Put the key somewhere on top of the hall cupboard and I'll find it there. Could you make sure no custard, bread and so forth are left, and no washing up! Please.
    Would be good to hear from you!
    All the best, Love, Cruyff family.

Plane? Nel knew nothing about a plane. She'd been helping with the housework in the Cruyff household for about eight months and she hadn't been expecting this. The 17-year-old had reported for duty in the Scholeksterlaan after a fortnight's holiday and was bewildered by the note from Danny in a house with little else in it. She hadn't been told about the move to Spain and, quite apart from that, how was she supposed to contact them? They hadn't left an address or phone number. 'I dropped to the floor and cried,' she remembers. 'Mainly because of the children I'd come to care so much about. I'd been with them day in, day out, I'd felt part of the family. And now they'd all gone.'

Poor teenaged Nel stood for just about all of football-loving Holland. The departure of the Cruyffs caused quite a stir.

Reactions varied from 'good riddance' to anger and distress.
From one day to the next, the country had lost its most famous
sportsman – to a Spain ruled by General Franco. The southern
European country had come closer over recent years, because of
the thousands of Spanish guest workers who had moved to the
Netherlands and because of charter flights to the Costa del Sol,
but a departure for Spain felt like a disappearance. Coverage of
foreign football matches was rarely shown on Dutch television,
for example. Cruyff had gone, vanished.

The couple, in their mid-twenties, twelve hundred kilometres
away, had already been wholly swallowed up by their future.
When they landed at the airport in Barcelona, the reception in
the arrivals hall surpassed all their expectations. Lines of people
waved flags and squirmed their way to the front from all sides
so they wouldn't miss seeing Johan Cruyff and his gorgeous
blonde wife for an instant. It wasn't really anything more than
an informal visit. Johan had to undergo a medical assessment
at FC Barcelona and they needed to find somewhere to live –
which was precisely why the thousands of fans at El Prat airport
made such an impression on them.

   As he stood there it occurred to journalist Rien Robijns that
people should shout out to Johan, 'El Salvador!' The saviour.
It was a nice idea and it added to the atmosphere in his article
for *Het Vrije Volk*. The nickname 'El Salvador' then acquired
a permanent place in the Dutch sporting idiom, as if it was a
concept already fully formed in Barcelona and far beyond. That
does not seem to have been the case, but on that scorching hot
23 August 1973 it felt that way: Johan had come to save the club
and the city, and indeed all of Catalonia.

   A cordon of police helped the young couple to get to a waiting car, so they could drive away from the people who wanted
to give the footballer – unable to play his first official match for
another three months – a big hug. The traffic was gridlocked
in the streets around the Hotel Calderón by the time Johan and

Danny arrived to check in. Once again they had to worm their way through the throng.

Outside the hotel the street was busy for a long time, with people hoping for a glimpse beyond a revolving door, a greeting, possibly even an autograph. Cruyff mania had erupted before he even set foot in Camp Nou. In 1965 the city had experienced nothing like the degree of Beatlemania seen elsewhere in Europe (the Fab Four from Liverpool were received with relative calm), but now Johan and Danny only had to walk along the Ramblas arm in arm to be accosted as if they were pop idols. 'Cruyff's jeans and long hair represented how I wanted to be,' remembers Ramon Besa, now sports editor-in-chief in Barcelona for *El País*. 'They exuded independence, the power to make your own choices instead of doing as you were told. It was exciting to see.'

To Dutch journalists, Cruyff said honestly, 'For me, this is now the time to make money.' But in the eyes of many Catalan nationalists it was more than that. Precisely at this point, with Madrid and the now elderly General Franco starting to allow more room for regional sentiment, it was up to Cruyff, from the freedom of northern Europe, to help accelerate that process. At club level it came down to a desire for 'liberation'. The announcer at Camp Nou was finally allowed to speak to spectators in their own language again, and the club could once more use the letters 'FC' (Fútbol Club) in front of its name instead of the Spanish initials 'CF' (Club de Fútbol). Successes on the pitch would give the Catalans their self-confidence back, and no one seemed to doubt those successes would come. 'Cruyff is a leader,' wrote sports newspaper *Dicen*. 'A man who inspires people to follow him by setting a good example and by instilling both discipline and a willingness to make sacrifices.' Armand Carabén, manager of Barcelona, who came from a Catalan nationalist family, was convinced of that. 'Cruyff will pull the others along with him,' he said. 'He demonstrates that you won't get there with playfulness alone. That's why we bought him.'

*

With the help of Michels' wife Will, Johan and Danny found a third-floor apartment on the Calle de los Caballeros and the whole family moved in a few weeks later. In the chic, uptown Pedralbes district they were hoping to find peace and seclusion. For most of the day the only sounds in its steep streets were those of birds and crickets, and on the ground floor of the apartment complex a concierge would keep any prying eyes at a safe distance. It was a privacy worth the purchase price of 500,000 guilders, a sum that had shocked them at first. Of course, when they walked past the palm trees in the front garden to their Citroën SM, Cruyff could be filmed pushing his younger daughter's pram. Nor was there any reason to keep secret the fact that he started each day by taking Chantal and Susila to the crèche. He was fantastically proud of his fatherhood – as far as that went his attitude changed little. Here too they got along the way babysitter Nel had seen them get along in Vinkeveen: Johan corrected the children and Danny corrected Johan. As in the Netherlands, he said he lived for his family and his sport. After training he liked best to go home and play with the children. Sometimes Catalan journalists were allowed to interview him at home; that way he could satisfy media hunger for human interest stories in a way he was able to control. But aside from that, Cruyff shielded his family life from public view more than before. In Barcelona, where football was experienced far more intensely than in Amsterdam, there was no other option.

Since Cruyff could not officially start playing until 1 December, he and Danny had time to spend on furnishing and decorating their apartment. Organising the household was not easy, but fortunately Will Michels provided them with Eufemia, a Spanish home help who, unlike Danny, was a good cook. Eufemia, soon known to the Cruyffs as Femmie, took a lot of work off Danny's hands, as did family man Johan, despite being all fingers and thumbs. The couple tried to get used to the local climate and customs – 'Mañana seems to take months here,' said Danny – while the players at training sessions got used to Cruyff. Under the leadership of Rinus Michels, that went remarkably smoothly. Although in Amsterdam the trainer and the star footballer had often quarrelled, there was still great mutual respect between them. Cruyff had become more mature over the past two years and, moreover, in Barcelona they would need each other badly. 'You could immediately see they were in touch a lot,' Carles ('Charly') Rexach remembers. 'Michels consulted Johan regularly and Johan clearly had an influence on him.'

Another thing the Catalan players would have to get used to was Johan's commercial streak. Cruyff had only just started to acclimatise when he gathered together several of his fellow players in Camp Nou. They must line up on the pitch so he could dribble around them as if they were living marker cones. A camera team was ready to film the action on behalf of Philips. It was usually impossible to get permission to take photographs in the empty stadium, but for Cruyff different norms applied. He slalomed with the ball between Rexach and several other stars and then said, 'Sorry, guys, just have to do this.' He left his teammates where they were for several minutes, since a rich and impatient businessman was waiting at the side of the pitch. It was agreed that the businessman's son could put on a Barcelona shirt and be photographed next to Johan. He then continued slaloming for a Philips commercial for portable television sets, and thus the new hero took care of two pieces of business simultaneously.

Whereas his sidelines had once been intended to supplement an Ajax salary that he found inadequate, he had now discovered how easy it all was and he cheerfully carried on. The wife of club manager Carabén, Marjolijn van der Meer, effortlessly arranged advertising roles for Johan, including television spots for the Spanish paint brand Bruguer, for which Danny worked too. 'She didn't know anybody here and I spoke Catalan,' says Van der Meer looking back. 'In the period when they had just arrived it was a lot of work.' In Barcelona such commercial activities hardly ever resulted in envy or leftist moralising comments by the media. On the contrary, they contributed to Danny and Johan's image as hip young people who knew what they were after.

Cruyff found his extra-curricular pursuits entirely normal and so the Barcelona players accepted them as part of what it meant to be a modern professional soccer player. They were urged to do likewise. Rexach, with whom Cruyff quickly formed a good relationship, also played in Pumas. He didn't have to do that 'for nothing', Cruyff told him, saying he was earning a couple of hundred thousand a year for wearing them. Just for wearing a specific brand of boot: it set the right-winger thinking, and after him the rest of the team. The Dutchman was happy to teach them the principles of advertising, and how to fight to realise your market value. You can help a person that way, thought Johan. Logical.

Cruyff was to play his first game in Camp Nou on 5 September, a practice match against Cercle Brugge organised specially for him. He was terribly nervous. Cercle was not a high-ranking club, but Cruyff understood well enough that a mediocre performance would be detrimental after all the millions paid to acquire him. He might even be jeered off the pitch. That was probably why he played so well. After fifteen minutes he set up the first goal, a short time later he scored the second after a solo run, and throughout the match he ran about pointing and shouting as if Camp Nou was his living room. He also sprinted forward many times without the ball, to show what moving higher up the pitch meant. The Dutchman, playing as number 9 (his usual '14' was not available to a regular team member), provided a perfect cross from the left with the outside of his right foot, a move that spectators in Amsterdam were familiar with in minute detail but which sent the Catalans into ecstasies. The applause was still audible when the resulting chance was missed by a mile. The crowd found it sensational to watch him in the

flesh as he swerved and turned; that curious mixture of gangli-
ness and purpose – where else could you find anything like it?

Cruyff scored a second time, from a penalty, and so the
match ended 6-0. His good teamwork with another foreigner,
attacking winger Hugo Sotil from Peru, had escaped no one's
attention. The Spanish press applauded Cruyff's smooth action
and his 'sense of organisation'. According to the Madrid sports
newspaper *Marca* his 'good manners' were reminiscent of 'the
style of Alfredo Di Stéfano'. So Barcelona vs Cercle Brugge
had gone precisely according to the scenario agreed beforehand
between Michels and Cercle trainer Han Grijzenhout. The two
knew each other well. Grijzenhout had been Michels' assistant
at Ajax for six years, so as a gesture he had more or less given
Cruyff a clear run for an hour and a half. The Belgian players
had agreed not to ruin the Cruyff show by marking him closely
and the debutant had taken full advantage of that.

'Wow,' said Johan later that evening as he stubbed out a cigarette. 'That heat. And I had to do a bit more than usual. Here
they all just stand still.' If his colleagues wanted to develop a
speed and dynamism comparable to that of Ajax, there was
clearly a long way to go. 'My strongest point – and it's what my
teammates are going to profit from in the future – is tactics,'
Cruyff wrote the following morning in *De Telegraaf*. 'The next
few weeks we're going to be talking a lot about that particular
aspect of top-class football. Tactics are entirely alien to most
Barcelona players.'

Another three practice matches followed and by late October
Cruyff had had enough of token games. To develop teamwork
further he wanted to take part in 'real' duels, so that he could
teach his teammates the ideas of modern football – 'playing
without the ball, choosing positions, running yourself free' –
more quickly. He refused to wait to play in La Liga until 1
December, the start of the premier league transfer period,
and contacted the KNVB to make clear that the agreement
made with such difficulty in August needed to be adjusted.

To emphasise the seriousness of the situation, he reminded the board how indispensable he was. On 18 November Oranje would play the decisive qualifying match against Belgium, was his reasoning, and just imagine if he was insufficiently sharp. The football association would be partly responsible should Oranje fail to qualify for the 1974 World Cup.

The subtle reference to possible outcomes did the trick. On 28 October the Dutch football association allowed him to make his official debut. The starting point was ideal: Barcelona were in fourteenth place in the league, so they could only improve. Furthermore, Cruyff was in exceptional form. After years of playing more often than he felt was good for him, his body had benefited from the extra rest. He was driven, too. Riding the soundwaves of 90,000 spectators, Cruyff led his teammates to a 4-0 victory over Granada. The striker made possible on the pitch what had so often been preached to the team by Michels in training sessions: moving up. He also scored two goals. When the match ended the crowd chanted his name and that evening, over a good glass of Catalan wine, Michels said, 'A 4-0 victory in a league game. I don't think Barcelona has seen that since the Batavians.'

'You can only dream of a first league match like that,' said Cruyff, and it was true. In the matches that followed, his team steadily climbed La Liga: Barcelona vs Athletic Bilbao 2-0, Barcelona vs Sporting Gijón 5-1, Barcelona vs Málaga CF 4-0, Real Oviedo vs Barcelona 1-3. From one week to the next, Barcelona had become twice as good. 'How can you explain a miracle like that?' asked manager Carabén later. 'I think the players felt that with Cruyff they could never lose. Importantly, the fans felt that too. It was as if he'd come from another planet and just fallen to earth for us all.'

The club and the attacking player seemed made for each other. With his optimism and self-awareness, Cruyff believed in winning, whereas at Barcelona fatalism had become a habit. Conversely, he was inspired by the professionalism of the club, the expert services with which it surrounded him, and the cheery helpfulness in the stadium and on the long journeys to away games (which he generally hated). He praised the 'social character' of FC Barcelona and its intense relationship with the many tens of thousands of *socios* (club members). The supporters were faithful and even after a weak game they turned up in their thousands the next time, something he had often missed in his native country.

Camp Nou, the immense and practically unroofed bathtub where the hot wind blew through his hair, set off his appearance more favourably than the small and windy De Meer stadium. He looked great in the *blaugrana*, too, as if the drab-coloured stripes made him even more supple, allowing him to dance over legs stuck out ahead of him more casually than ever. His thighs were so firm now that he didn't look at all fragile to fellow players like Rexach, who shared rooms in the players' hotels with him. 'Johan was stronger than you might think,' he says.

Johan's friendly side came to the surface again, now he could tell that his teammates were happy to see him. 'It was different at Ajax,' he said later. When Danny added that he'd become a different person in Barcelona he answered, 'Well, I was allowed to be.' Everything seemed pleasantly capacious, from the elegant buildings lining the main thoroughfares, the Via Laietana and the Passeig de Gràcia, to the hearts of the people of the city. No one seemed to have a problem with Cruyff's wealth and privilege. He was received hospitably everywhere and hardly ever had to pay for anything. 'The Catalan likes to work hard and earn well, and he loves his family,' he concluded. 'Those are things that appeal to me. Perhaps that's why I've been accepted here so quickly.' He found people in Barcelona 'a lot more cheerful, less cantankerous, less sullen than in the Netherlands'.

Before they left for Spain, the Cruyffs had more than once been told it was unacceptable to go and work in a country run by dictator Franco. 'They say there are more than a hundred countries that don't have a free press,' he would respond. 'So why the continual harping on about Spain when I decide to go there?' All that 'airy-fairy crap' – Cruyff was sick of it.

A few days before the World Cup qualifying match against Belgium on 18 November, Cruyff flew back to the Netherlands. He had more to do there than just play football. He still owned two houses in Vinkeveen and, given that Franco's Spain had a ban on taking pesetas out of the country, paying for them was problematic. So he tried to sell them both, the house on the Scholeksterlaan and the still unfinished luxury bungalow. He didn't make much headway. Cor Coster, who was involved in the sales efforts, thought of a trick. He found a television journalist who was prepared to interview Johan against the background of the bare walls and beams of the bungalow. Cruyff chattered away, about how different playing soccer in Spain was, about how pleasant it was to eat out for free and about high expectations – he'd already received flowers in gratitude for potentially winning the championship.

Suddenly it seemed as if the camera had fallen off its stand. The picture swung down and viewers of *Tros Sport* were abruptly confronted by a huge picture of Cruyff's Puma boots. 'I would venture to bet that was prearranged,' says the journalist involved, Cees van Nieuwenhuizen. 'That's how things went in those days.'

Then the reporter broached the subject he'd come to talk about. 'Here we are at the house being built for you,' he said. 'Is it for sale or for rent, or what's the plan?'

At that very moment, television viewers saw three men pulling upright a huge blue notice board and could not fail to understand what it said, in white letters: 'For Sale. Inquiries to Jorrit de Jong BV, estate agents, surveyors.' There was a telephone number.

For sale, then. 'If I get the right price for it,' said Cruyff. 'Everything is for sale. That's actually fairly logical.'

Unfortunately for the footballer and his father-in-law, the

half-built bungalow did not sell. The cosy family home in the Scholeksterlaan found new owners, however, and the happy couple, Miki and Daan Horstman, would never forget their encounter with Coster. At the notary's office, where the watch dealer acted as Cruyff's authorised representative, he boasted irrepressibly about the wads of pesetas he was carrying weekly in an inside pocket from Barcelona to Schiphol. He claimed the cash was needed to get the builders to finish the bungalow. So Coster proved once again that people in the street where he lived in Amsterdam-Zuid were not entirely mistaken in calling him The Smuggler.

Two days after the television interview by Van Nieuwenhuizen, Cruyff played the qualifying match against Belgium as captain of Oranje. After a nerve-racking duel in the Olympic Stadium, the final score was 0-0, just enough for the Dutch to win the group and travel to the World Cup in West Germany in June 1974. At last, everything seemed to have come right. Shortly before the final whistle a legitimate Belgian goal was disallowed. The Netherlands had qualified for the first time since 1938.

Oranje had got what they were after, Danny's pregnancy was progressing well and on the Spanish pitches too things were going nicely. By December Barça were already occupying top spot in La Liga. According to Cruyff's teammate 'Charly' Rexach, that wasn't merely because they were playing better. 'People everywhere couldn't wait to see Johan,' he says. 'So much attention had been paid to him for months that everybody wanted to watch him. All parties worked together to make a success of the transfer. If an opposition defender fouled Johan, he'd be called to order by his own teammates and sometimes even whistled at by his own supporters. Even the referees gave us the benefit of the doubt – a completely new phenomenon in our experience.'

At the time, Rexach, like many other Catalans, was convinced that Barcelona's poor performances over the past ten years were attributable to 'the authorities'. The feeling was that the Spanish football association wanted Real Madrid, showpiece of the Franco regime, to win the league championship in order to create good international publicity for isolated Spain. So their great rivals FC Barcelona, representatives of the once autonomous Catalonia, had to be thwarted. 'We were hated everywhere,' Rexach remembers. 'The spectators were extremely hostile and, as soon as we got to the top in the league, the referees would start giving penalties to our opponents, you could bet your life on that.'

The last time Barcelona had won the championship was way back in 1960, but now it seemed as if even people in other regions were hoping for something special from Cruyff.

It was Rexach who had shown Cruyff the ropes at his new club and the winger also enabled the newcomer to perform a miracle just before Christmas. It happened in Camp Nou. As is not uncommon in football, the miracle stemmed from a partial failure. In the closing minutes of the first half against Atlético Madrid, with the score at 0-0, Rexach sent a high, curving ball from the right flank (with his left foot) towards the far post. He had to act at great speed to avoid a defender sliding towards him, so the ball had too much momentum and Cruyff, who was somewhere in the left part of the Madrid penalty area, couldn't get to it. Moreover, the ball hit the head of an Atlético player on its way and changed direction slightly. 'The cross was meant to be headed in by Johan, but I saw it go and thought, *No chance*,' Rexach remembers. 'Until he suddenly jumped up.'

Cruyff catapulted himself upwards and forwards, legs wide apart, like a predatory animal attempting to stop its prey from escaping. High in the air, he bounced the ball off the outside of his right foot and into the goal. It all happened in a flash, and because of the sudden deflection he must have changed the position of his body slightly even while he was flying through the air. So alert, so unique – it was a beauty that verged on madness. When he landed, he had his back to the goalkeeper;

because of the twist required during the jump, he'd barely been able to see his own miraculous goal.

The crowd went wild. Camp Nou had never seen such a backheel, no, ankle ball at shoulder height. Neither had he. It seemed like a trick, but in fact – as ever with Cruyff, who didn't like tricks – it was the move that worked best for him in the given circumstances. 'The cross came and I didn't know what to do,' was his sober assessment later. 'I wasn't an especially brilliant header of the ball, so I decided just to jump and turn.'

It had to be so. It could only be so. One–nil to Barcelona. Cruyff ran across the penalty area looking ecstatic as he leapt about, arms wheeling above his head, again and again, evading his delighted teammates – he had to celebrate alone for a moment.

All through the top-level match he was the leader, the feeder who dropped back to midfield to scatter excellent passes around. The final score was 2-1. 'Cruyff has brought a completely new dimension to the team,' Michels said with delight, before adding, as a true Dutchman, 'The other players are in great form at the moment too.' Rexach remembers it that way. 'Before Johan arrived we could all play football,' he says. 'But with him it gained momentum. He gave us fresh hope, which meant we were able to carry on with the innovations Michels had started.' The striker himself said, 'Tactically Michels and I are more or less on the same wavelength. I know what he wants.' Which led to a splendidly Cruyffian conclusion: 'There were some good players around already, but they weren't yet good at thinking. When they started to get good at thinking, it became a good team.'

Over recent years, Spain had not secularised at lightning speed like the Netherlands; people still believed in myths, and the Catalans built on the myth of Johan Cruyff to their heart's content. Even the birth of his third child provided useful material. Danny flew to Amsterdam in early January 1974 to give birth.

After she arrived, a complication arose. She would once again need a Caesarean section and the doctors were planning to deliver the baby on or around 17 February, close to the day on which Barcelona had their most important match of the year, in Madrid, against Real. So Cruyff and Michels, in private, discussed the possibility of having the C-section take place a week earlier. Then Johan could be in Amsterdam for the birth and still play in Madrid against Real. 'Our first place, Johan,' the coach growled. 'Our first place!' The striker nodded.

Danny agreed. The baby would be delivered on Saturday 9 February. The club competition was at a standstill that weekend because of an international by the Spanish national team, and in the days that followed Johan would have plenty of time for his family.

They wanted to give the child a Catalan name. A girl was to be christened Nuria, a boy Jordi. It was a boy. In Amsterdam the child was registered as Johan Jordi Cruyff. But in Franco's Spain the name 'Jordi' was rather complicated.

'Johan Jordi?' the official asked in surprise.

'Yes,' said Cruyff. 'Johan Jordi.'

'Jordi is Jorge, so your son is called Jorge. The name Jordi doesn't exist.'

'Doesn't exist' was officialese for 'is banned'.

'No,' Cruyff said. 'I know perfectly well what I've named my son. Look, sir, here it is, Jordi. And if you don't register him as Johan Jordi, I'm going home. But you need to take note that I've been here to register my son's birth.'

At the town hall he became once more that cocky hotshot who stubbornly insisted on getting his own way. It paid off. 'Eventually I went home and he was registered the way I wanted, as Johan Jordi.'

Cruyff's battle to give his son a Catalan name generated a lot of enthusiasm in Barcelona. It was interpreted as a gesture of solidarity with suppressed Catalan culture, as if political intentions lay behind the choice of the name. In reality Johan's obstinacy at the council offices had more to do with his own autonomy than with that of Catalonia. 'We just thought it was a nice name,' he said to Dutch journalists.

It was not until months later that Danny and Johan realised Sant Jordi was the patron saint of the city of Barcelona, and that the name of the fourth-century dragon-killer consequently had a powerful symbolic significance in the region. 'I'd been here for only five months,' Cruyff explained later. 'I knew hardly anything about the Catalan desire for independence, let alone Catalan as a language.'

As a result, in January, at the start of his column in *El Mundo Deportivo*, he had welcomed his readers in a highly un-Catalan manner with, 'Dear friends. This is the first time I've been able to write anything directly to my many Spanish fans.' After five months of friendship with Barça manager Armand Carabén, who was fiercely anti-Franco and active underground as a Catalan socialist, Cruyff still thought nothing of addressing the fans as 'Spanish'. Johan and Danny clearly weren't preoccupied with the Catalan issue. 'I don't want to get involved in their politics,' Cruyff noted in March 1974 in his *Nieuw Revu* diary. 'I never did that in Holland, either.'

There could be no better illustration of what Johan and Danny were deep down: Dutch people in Spain, or, rather, Amsterdammers in Barcelona. As in Vinkeveen, the family sat down to eat at six and the children went to bed at eight. 'Order, cleanliness and tranquillity' was the motto in the Calle de los Caballeros, as it had been for the Dutch for generations. The Cruyffs assumed they would be moving back to the Netherlands within three years. They took Spanish lessons because the two languages were 'pretty much the same' as far as Cruyff was concerned. 'Although of course I can't say that to the Catalans.'

A week after Jordi's birth, the myth of 'Johan the Catalan' was given a gold-plated frame with curlicues during the Real Madrid vs Barcelona match. On 17 February 1974 he struck.

After half an hour in which at least half his initiatives failed, although he was as diligent as ever, his team stood at 0-1. Then, on that cool evening in Madrid, everything grew warm for Barcelona. Cruyff hoodwinked three opponents in a row on the edge of the penalty area and scored with his left – 0-2. He roamed, built attacks, talked busily to his teammates as soon as there was a break in the game and, meanwhile, he completely outclassed Real's German 'saviour' Günter Netzer. The Spanish television commentator spoke, full of astonishment and admiration, of *el fútbol total*. Cruyff did indeed rather turn the match into a demonstration of total football. As at Ajax, he had a disruptive effect, running to the front and then performing defensive work when he fell back. If he was in the position of a left back, he presented himself at speed as if he was Ruud Krol. He carried out his tasks to the very end without flagging for a moment. His crosses allowed two teammates to score and Barcelona finally walked off the pitch at the Estadio Santiago Bernabéu after an unprecedented 5-0 victory.

The Michels–Cruyff double act had turned the match into a demonstration of modern soccer. Later football fans and journalists would debate exhaustively the question of which of the two was more important to the success. In this first joint Barça year at any rate, it looked like an assist by Michels with a finish by Cruyff. Under 'Mister Mármol' (as the 'hard as marble' coach was called), even lazy *bons vivants* like Rexach learnt what player discipline was. Cruyff profited from that. 'Michels did a lot of the heavy lifting for me,' the striker said after the championship. 'He created a team in which I could develop. It was as if he'd prepared the team for my arrival. I only had to take my place in it.'

Michels explained it like this. 'I can sit on the sidelines bellowing, and discuss tactics in training, but it's a whole different matter when there's someone running about on the pitch giving the players instructions.'

However that may be, to the *socios* Cruyff was the saint who had made it all possible. He'd shown that you could humiliate the standard bearer of Spain's central government in its own home city. On arrival at Barcelona airport, the team was met by weeping fans and until deep into the night the people of the city celebrated the fact that Barça was *més que un club*, more than a football club. It was a way of feeling you were a Catalan.

The cause of it all heard the stories of euphoria only later, incidentally. He spent the night in Madrid so that he could fly to Amsterdam the next day. Johan wanted to be with Danny and the baby as soon as possible, and on the way there he did what you might expect him to do in the absence of his wife and his father-in-law. A Dutch teenager asked if he could sit next to him. Sure, said the star, accommodating as ever. Yes, it would be fine for the boy to ask a few questions on behalf of the school newspaper. 'Congratulations on your son Johan Jordi,' 17-year-old Levie Boektje began. 'How is Danny doing?'

'Thank you,' said Cruyff. 'Danny's doing well.'

'Last night was magnificent, don't you think?' Levie went on, according to his report.

'It was truly tremendous. Everyone on our side was in really good shape. In Madrid it's always difficult. A kind of Ajax vs Feyenoord. And then of course 0-5; they've never seen that before here.'

'The best goal of the five?'

'The fourth, by Juan Carlos, the left midfielder – such a hard, tight shot. Even though it was from such a distance, the goal-keeper didn't stand a chance.'

'Are you going to win the championship?'

'I think so. We're already talking about it. There are a maximum of twenty-four points still to win. If we can get seventeen in the twelve matches left, then we're champions.'

On arrival at Schiphol, Levie went straight to The Hague to write up his article for the newspaper published by the Simon Stevin Comprehensive School. Johan hurried to the Amsterdam hospital where his wife and Jordi were still recovering from the birth. Two days later the family of five flew back to Barcelona, with Jordi lying quietly in a Moses basket. Danny longed for the spacious apartment in Pedralbes. As for Johan, what he was thinking could have been his motto in life: my home is where my wife is.

In Catalonia the mood after Barça's historic 5-0 victory in Madrid was excellent. In fact, all of Spain was impressed, Rexach says. 'From then on they took an even bigger step aside for us.' By March 1974 Barcelona were in top spot in the league with a nine-point lead, and so it remained. The team was running more and more smoothly. 'At the start I gave out instructions far more insistently than I do now,' said Cruyff. 'It's no longer necessary. The other players are really starting to get it.' The team was not yet 'always moving' the way Ajax had shown a team could be, but the manager on the pitch, as teammate Sotil later called him, could see clear improvements.

The Amsterdammer was happy at Barça, but of course you had to avoid acting towards him in a high-handed manner, as a referee in Málaga discovered. He'd blown his whistle for a foul by one of Cruyff's teammates and when Cruyff walked to the spot with the ball, the ref barked at him, 'Put that ball down.'

There was only one possible answer. 'I am, aren't I?'

'When I say put that ball down, then you put the ball down.'

Cruyff, who always had an answer, even in authoritarian countries, said, 'Did you use the familiar form of "you"? Don't they use the polite form of address for players here?'

It earned him a white card, the equivalent of a yellow card. Cruyff had nothing against authority, but if authority challenged him – or acted stupidly in his view – then the anarchist in him stirred. It was that same anarchist who demanded of the home help Femmie that she eat at the table with them. He wanted nothing to do with the local custom of making the staff eat separately in the kitchen. Femmie must simply come and eat with the family. Cruyff didn't like superior behaviour, but he didn't like obsequiousness either.

With another five matches to go before the end of the league season, FC Barcelona became national champions on 7 April 1974 by beating Sporting Gijón 4-2. The gap between Barça and Atlético Madrid was now too big to be closed. Again, Cruyff was the manager on the pitch. Three times he helped a teammate to score, and all through the match he evaded the Gijón defenders. There, on the Bay of Biscay, the prize the team had been longing for over a period of fourteen years was won. 'Even the Gijón crowd cheered us,' Cruyff observed in amazement. When they got back to Barcelona there was a triumphal procession from the airport to the city, everywhere crowds came out, and everywhere they sang not just to the club but to Sant Jordi and the Black Madonna of Montserrat, patron saint of Catalonia – everything was mixed together into a brew of local chauvinism, football and religion that made the Catalans drunk with happiness. And, of course, on the Plaça de Sant Jaume most eyes were turned to 'El Flaco', the Skinny One from the Low Countries who – there was indeed no room for doubt – had saved Barcelona.

On the Plaça de Sant Jaume, the political heart of the city and the region, the *blaugrana* of Barça and the yellow-and-red of Catalonia flew into the air together when Michels and his players showed the championship trophy to the crowd from the balcony of the town hall. 'In those months it was as if people in Barcelona walked the streets with their heads high more than ever before,' says journalist Ramon Besa of *El País*. 'It felt like a turning point in our history.' According to the *New York Times*, which usually paid little attention to sport, Cruyff had 'done more for the spirit of the Catalan people in 90 minutes than many politicians in years of struggle'.

For El Flaco the national title was a course in 'Catalonia for Dummies'. What touched him most, what moved him most, was that the people who came up to him all over the place said not 'Congratulations' but 'Thank you'.

What a contrast, then, with the country of sober Hollanders. Barcelona still had to play three ties to reach the final of the Copa del Generalísimo, as the national knockout competition was known under Franco, but since foreigners were not allowed to take part, Cruyff was able to decamp to Zeist in May. There, at the headquarters of the KNVB, little time was left for the forging of a Dutch team that could avoid looking foolish in the World Cup matches in June. Given the often-lamentable performance of the national eleven, that would not be easy. In March a friendly against Austria had generated a mostly sour reaction. To Cruyff's bewilderment, in a half-full De Kuip in Rotterdam there had been hostile whistling, however hard the team tried. Furthermore, Danny was afraid that Johan's reunion with the national squad, largely drawn from Ajax, might be problematic. Piet Keizer and all those others had been 'not very nice' to him, and now he would have to hang out with them for weeks.

Johan answered her in his usual fashion. 'Don't you worry.'

CHAPTER NINETEEN

A global star

Brimming with self-confidence, Johan Cruyff flew from Barcelona to Amsterdam on the evening of Friday 17 May 1974. The 27-year-old was feeling strong. Travelling with him, Danny, Chantal, Susila and Jordi were all doing well, and with the arrival of a third child their dream of a big family had come a step closer. In less than a month, when he would be going to West Germany and Danny and the children would return to Spain, the pinnacle of his career was in prospect: the 1974 World Cup. 'Not that I'll stop when it's over,' he wrote in his diary in *Nieuwe Revu*. 'But it's the highest possible high point.'

Over the past season he'd had hardly any injury problems, and at FC Barcelona he'd managed to make a lot of the changes he wanted. His fellow players had accepted him, the city adored him and he'd once again been named European Footballer of the Year. Furthermore, and no less importantly, his advertising activities had earned him a fortune in no time. Brands that had linked themselves to the popular player included Philips (100,000 guilders a year), Puma (200,000 guilders), Lois (jeans), Jim (shirts and underwear), Bruguer (paint), Kerzo (lotion) and the El Corte Inglés department store. As in the Netherlands, Cruyff produced a well-paid weekly newspaper column in which he could offer his opinions at will. He had introduced into Spain his system of asking for payment for interviews (to the astonishment of the Spanish press). All told, the money poured in. 'That's logical,' he wrote in his World Cup diary. 'The country is much bigger and you have less trouble with taxation. It's simply a lot more pleasant that way.'

In Catalonia an entire summer house had now been thrown into his lap as well, for which he only had to provide 'a bit of advertising', as he called it. As a celebrity he was expected to help burnish the reputation of a still sparsely populated mountain called the Montanya, a little over 50 kilometres north of Barcelona, as a place for the rich of the city to take up residence.

On the Montanya the Cruyffs had the Carabén–Van der Meer couple as neighbours, since they too sought cooler climes between July and September. In this remote and wooded place, where Rinus and Will Michels had also settled, the children could play 'nice and peacefully', as Cruyff put it in his diary. The bungalows set in spacious gardens offered plenty of opportunities for that. There were stables nearby and for a local benefactor that was reason enough to make the famous Dutchman the gift of a horse. 'I'm not a good rider at all,' Cruyff admitted in his diary, before adding a sportsman's comment: 'At least, not yet.'

Here, not far from the village of Aiguafreda, Danny and the children stayed for the first time while Johan was playing football in West Germany. Marjolijn van der Meer and Will Michels were there too. In the pleasing shade of the cork oaks, with hardly a car to be heard, the women and children would get through the summer just fine.

The men of Oranje gathered in Zeist on Tuesday 21 May at ten past nine in the morning. 'A weird time if you ask me,' said Cruyff in his diary. 'But they were all there. That hasn't always been the case. It immediately shows you the influence of Michels.'

Very much to Cruyff's satisfaction, the Barcelona coach would be in charge of the Dutch national team from the training camp onwards. Because if one thing had been missing at Oranje, it was a boss. The KNVB had for years been unable to speak with one voice. Illustrative of the situation was the presence of not one but two national coaches in Zeist. One of them wasn't taken seriously by the players (František Fadrhonc, for whom Cruyff had a soft spot, incidentally), and the other had a drink problem (Cor van der Hart). The two routinely undermined each other, so it had recently been decided that up to and including the World Cup, Rinus Michels would act as supervisor. With Fadrhonc and Van der Hart as his assistants, Michels urgently needed to bring to an end a long period of chaos and disorientation. He had taken up the gauntlet, despite the fact that he would have to travel back and forth to Spain to coach Barcelona in their battle for the national knockout cup, nowadays called the Copa del Rey. The 46-year-old supervisor was therefore working both ad interim and part-time. Bizarre, but he alone was regarded as capable of handling the massive task ahead.

From a footballing point of view, the colour orange had for years been synonymous with failure. The Netherlands had not qualified for the World Cup since 1938. Even in the early 1970s, when Ajax and Feyenoord were playing the best football in the world, the top players of the two clubs performed barely above average once they put on the orange shirt. The internationals were as lacking in solidarity and ambition as the leadership was in professionalism and authority. Cruyff was among those exasperated by this. He had so little faith in the football association (and in its rewards and guarantees) that since his debut in 1966 he had been absent a number of times and had come into conflict with 'Zeist' on many occasions. In the eight years of his international career, he had been a stable factor for only the past two. In 1972 Cor Coster had reached an agreement with the KNVB about finances and after that Cruyff played in all six of the qualifying matches. He wore the number 14 each time and his captaincy had never been thrown into doubt as it had been at Ajax. Since December 1971 (a friendly international between the Netherlands and Scotland in which he scored after five minutes) he had worn the armband with pride.

His motivation was boosted by the fact that his affairs were in order at Oranje. He had his father-in-law to thank for that. Coster had acted with great speed in early 1974. The Oranje players were initially obliged to let all their World Cup-linked advertising deals go through the KNVB. That was set down in black and white. But when Coster found out that the football association had neglected to extend the collective contract as of 1 January, he immediately visited Philips. The Dutch electronics company quickly came to an agreement with Coster in the deepest secrecy. Around the time of the World Cup, Johan was able to take part in various advertising campaigns for a total fee of 250,000 guilders.

That meant Cruyff was earning several times more than his teammates. It seems firms like Philips found him as an individual far more interesting than the Dutch team as a whole, which often attracted negative publicity. Could the captain help that? He believed he could not. However, you could say that the captain, with his megadeals in his pocket, was able to emerge as a true leader in the run-up to the World Cup. He defended the interests of his fellow players with Cruyffian bluff. The football association had made them a 'ridiculous' financial offer, so what did the captain do? Two days before the trip to West Germany he said the squad would not leave unless the win bonuses were dramatically increased. They were. The football association promised each player a bonus of up to 65,000 guilders, including back pay.

Cruyff had stuck his neck out for the others and now, in Zeist, he presented himself as an extension to Rinus Michels in a positive sense. 'I'm up for it,' he said, without mincing his words. Although he hated the 'unnatural' isolation of a training camp, far from his family, he willingly subjected himself to the tough, almost military-style training programme imposed by the supervisor of the (provisional) squad. Given the pressure of time, it was all or nothing, and Cruyff liked that. Anyone who turned out to be unfit or not up to scratch could clear off right away. 'Michels shuts everyone up,' said the captain combatively. 'Including the officials. The players notice that and it makes an impression.'

Danny needn't have been fearful of friction between Johan and the many Ajax players in the squad. His former teammates had a poor year behind them and were glad to have been called on for the Dutch team at all. After Cruyff's departure Ajax had pretty much collapsed. Without his brilliant passing and his (irritating to some) shouting on the pitch, the team had lost its cohesion, and it seemed no one had the authority, the energy and the iron will to assume his role. In the European Cup the team had been eliminated in the second round by CSKA Sofia, a club that a year before, with Johan, they had beaten easily.

Johan showed no desire to avenge what the Ajax players had done to him a year earlier. In fact, a dominant clique of Amsterdammers soon formed around him. With so little time to put together a decent team, there was no room for lengthy consultation. You were in or you were out, and 'Amsterdam' was clearly in. The former street kids who had managed to hold their own in the Ajax changing room, dominated as it was by merciless jokes, set the tone. They sought each other out and the others, including the mature Feyenoorders Van Hanegem and Israël, joined them. The rest silently adapted. They had no other option.

The battle plan on the pitch had a lot of Amsterdam in it too. Roughly speaking, Oranje was going to play a risky version of Ajax's total football, attacking even more. Cruyff was more than content with that, and his influence as captain grew by the day. After a while it was he who called the shots on the days when Michels was in Barcelona, rather than one of the assistant coaches. The self-assured captain hinted at his preferences and

Michels took more account of them than he was in the habit of doing at Barcelona. Who was Johan talking with or not talking with? To whom did he pass the ball in training matches and who was forced to chase after it? The former brat from Betondorp commanded little tricks like that with the best of them. He used his captaincy almost like a gang boss: anyone who wasn't with him was against him. You did well to stay on his good side.

Partly for lack of time, Cruyff and Michels didn't try very hard to keep the usual Oranje goalkeeper on board. The eccentric stylist Jan van Beveren from PSV seemed reluctant to accept the authority of 'Amsterdam' and was asked to go home. The first keeper was now Jan Jongbloed, a true Amsterdammer who had little experience as an international but was ideally suited to the attacking game that was planned. Cruyff preferred to play with a slightly less competent goalie who 'joined in', who would 'cover' him, than with a brilliant know-it-all. 'For everyone it's a question of what do we do when we have possession and what do we do when we lose possession,' the captain said. 'Everyone needs to take the same line.'

If the choice of Jongbloed was surprising, the choice of defenders was even more so. There, too, Cruyff's hand could be seen. In the attacking game they were aiming to play, and which they practised every day, the defenders would need to have the nerve to go forward in the wake of the forwards and midfielders. The most obvious central defenders – including Barry Hulshoff and Rinus Israël – were injured or in Michels' view insufficiently suited to applying pressure in this collective and risky manner. Shortly before a practice match in Zeist, Cruyff suddenly tossed a shirt to midfielder Arie Haan. Seeing the captain handing out the shirts in the changing rooms at the sports complex was not particularly remarkable, but the words that flew across the room on 30 May in the company of the shirt were.

'Here,' said Cruyff. 'You're playing sweeper.'

'Are you crazy?' said Haan. 'I'm an offensive midfielder. Is this a joke?'

'No,' the captain answered. 'I mean it. We'd rather create two chances than one.'

In other words, let's risk an opposition goal, as long as we score more than they do. At Ajax there had been friction between Cruyff and his 'water carrier' towards the end, but on the pitch they still had a good relationship. 'Haan was capable of playing the ball to me better and slightly more quickly than others,' the captain said later by way of clarification. 'It gave me that extra second to orientate myself.'

Just a week before the start of the World Cup, Haan was joined by another central defender who would surprise Oranje fans: Wim Rijsbergen, the young 'wrecker' at Feyenoord. Thus emerged at the very last minute a rather improvised team that made a hesitant impression at practice matches and therefore seemed unable to count on much support from the Dutch population. Fortunately, Cruyff and his notorious father-in-law, by means of a few threats, had managed to wrest those more than decent win bonuses from the football association, and that gave a welcome boost to the players' morale.

To everyone's surprise, many of the stands turned orange on Saturday 15 June 1974. Spontaneously, without any appeal from organisations or any commercial incentives, thousands of Dutch people had got into their cars or the train and travelled to Hanover for Oranje's first match of the tournament. It gave many of the players goose bumps, and Cruyff was touched by it too. He had been counting on perhaps 3,000 supporters in the Niedersachsen Stadium, not 25,000 – almost half of the crowd of 55,000. Standing to attention between a linesman and goal-keeper Jongbloed, he felt 'extremely tense'. 'I don't know what it is,' he'd noted in his diary. 'I have a pain in my stomach and I'm finding it hard to breathe.' So he swallowed 'all kinds of pills'. As the most expensive soccer player on earth, he would have high expectations to fulfil over the next hour and a half. A flop on this global stage seemed a horrific prospect to him. According to his diary he wanted to make a good impression 'at any price'.

Fortunately, the Orange Army sang the national anthem at the top of their lungs. The captain had 'never yet' experienced anything like it, he said afterwards.

Oranje had the kick-off. Cruyff would be the first to set the ball rolling. He stood at the centre spot. Van Hanegem reported to him, ready to receive the ball. Cruyff looked at the referee and shook his thighs loose. A sign of nerves, of course, since his legs had been loosened up long before on the massage table. The referee seemed about to blow his whistle but he waited a moment. Again, that shaking of the legs, that torso leaning eagerly forward. Then the gesture from the ref: go on then, lad.

Cruyff gave the ball a kick and walked into the Uruguay half.

During the final tournament in West Germany, all the tough training and discussions about tactics seemed to pay off – to the surprise of the fans and the amazement of opponents. It started in this very first match. The Netherlands beat Uruguay 2-0. At half-time a British commentator said it could easily have been 5-0 already. Four days later, Oranje drew 0-0 with Sweden – a 3-0 win would have been a more appropriate score. A Spanish commentator called Cruyff *sensacional*. Four days later the supremacy of the Netherlands over Bulgaria was better expressed on the scoreboard: 4-1. But not optimally. It ought to have been 4-0, given that defender Ruud Krol scored an own goal and Bulgaria created hardly any chances. Oranje came a magnificent first in their group.

In the next round, again in a group of four countries, the formidable Argentina were humiliated 4-0 in the rain of Gelsenkirchen. Four days later Oranje beat East Germany 2-0. Now there was only one group game to go and after that the World Cup final or a battle for third place. Little Holland was certain of a place in the last four – with a team that had never previously played in this configuration.

It was a miracle, and for the first time Cruyff put himself in the global spotlight as precisely that: a miracle of grace and potency.

Oranje drew acclaim from all continents for their 'progressive' total football, in which opponents were hunted like beasts and the hunters ran crisscross past each other. It really did prove possible to go on the attack impetuously and not be caught out by counterattacks, as experts and opponents were forced to admit. (Although the Netherlands also played a remarkably tough, sometimes even vicious game.) Meanwhile, everyone was staring at the man who ran through all those full German stadiums pointing like a traffic policeman, at the long-haired, rather gangly captain who could suddenly flash past with the ball at his feet.

Feeder and finisher, team player and dribbler, fragile and ferocious: for many television viewers Cruyff was a sensation. Where else could you see an attacker who went to pick up the ball from his own defence? He seemed to be reinventing the game. 'Time and again it was a matter of waiting for a creative move by Cruyff,' Michels said later. 'As a coach, too, you could enjoy that.' The high point was perhaps one particular moment against Sweden, a moment of gangly-becomes-flashy in three seconds. Halfway through the first half in Dortmund, Arie Haan – who as sweeper had run on into midfield – sent the ball diagonally to the left wing, where Cruyff was looking for free space. Six metres from the back line he received the lob and quickly got it under control, if with some difficulty. Swedish defender Jan Olsson ran up, but with his left foot Cruyff pulled the ball towards him just in time. There were no other players near, so the battle was between the two of them. Cruyff turned round and moved further from the back line, with Olsson at his heels. He made it look as if he was going to kick the ball to the right across the goal and at precisely the moment the Swede tried to prevent that, Cruyff turned round again, taking the ball with him behind his left leg, towards the back line. For a moment Olsson looked like a blindfolded party guest being turned around for a game of blind man's buff. While the Swede attempted to get his bearings, Cruyff took several steps towards the opposition goal and made a pass with his left foot.

Olsson looked a fool, but that wasn't what Cruyff was after. Even the thrilling beauty of the action was to him incidental at best. 'It wasn't evasion for the sake of evasion,' the striker said later. 'But you had to get past someone, if you wanted to get towards the goal. That's what you did it for.'

Although the cross against Sweden did not produce a chance to score, the move marked the fact that a new world footballer had emerged. The Spanish television commentator thought the evasive manoeuvre '*mágico*' and the BBC showed it for decades in its opening sequence to *Match of the Day*. British journalists gave the 'Cruyff Turn' a place in their sporting history hall of fame and countless 'loners' copied it on streets and in fields for years to come.

But in 1974 the Dutch television commentator reacted to it without getting excited. In his own country people were familiar with that move by Cruyff. Nevertheless, many of his countrymen gaped in admiration at the captain's play. He radiated so much positive energy, he was fresh and robust and seemed best friends with the referees: was this really cocky Johan, the troublemaker? He had gained 2 kilos in Barcelona and it seemed to have given him just that bit of extra weight he needed to steer the whole performance, even during physically demanding duels. His shoulders and chest were still narrow, but his thighs were round and powerful, his crosses with the outside of his right foot flawless.

In the summer of 1974 the world saw Johan Cruyff at his best.

He was enjoying himself, too. Michels had pretty much attuned the team to him. Even the players who were stars in their own clubs (Rob Rensenbrink at Anderlecht, Van Hanegem at Feyenoord) resigned themselves to a modest role for his benefit – and therefore for the benefit of the team. Michels prised that from them with his authority. 'I had so much faith in that man that I thought, whatever he says will work best,' Van Hanegem said later of the supervisor. And with midfielder Haan in the rear, there was now space in midfield for the diligent

Wim Jansen, with whom Cruyff liked to play. He knew the clever 'gap-closer' from the national youth eleven. He called the midfield line-up Jansen–Neeskens–Van Hanegem 'the best' of the team.

All the players had been given their instructions by Michels and the captain saw that they carried them out. The 'Clockwork Orange', as the English press was soon calling them, the '*Arancia Meccania*' that struck the Italians dumb, the '*Naranja Mecánica*' in which the Spanish recognised something of FC Barcelona, started with him, with the centre forward who sprinted away from his place. The others responded to that and then to each other, so that everything started moving and opponents didn't know where to look. Meanwhile, Cruyff set about pointing and shouting as soon as he saw an agreement not being adhered to, or whenever a tactical change was needed in response to a switch by the opposition.

Cruyff worked as part of the machinery and deviated from it as well. That was made obvious by his shirt number and strip. During the World Cup the Oranje players wore numbers that reflected the alphabetical order of their surnames. So Jongbloed (unusually for a goalkeeper) wore number 8 and Suurbier, because of his 'S', number 20. According to that logic Cruyff, as first in the alphabet, should have had a 1 on his shirt and shorts. But that would have looked ludicrous, so he was given number 14, 'my trademark'. Then there were the stripes. Because Oranje were sponsored by Adidas, all the shirts and shorts had three stripes. But Cruyff obstinately refused to advertise the competitor to his own sponsor Puma. So his kit had just two stripes, which meant the staff at the players' hotel had to carry out repair jobs all through the tournament. At the football association this behaviour, perhaps not unjustly, was interpreted as 'KNVB baiting'.

In between matches, Johan gloried in the team's success at the players' hotel where, to his great relief, there was a light-hearted atmosphere. In Waldhotel Krautkrämer, on the edge of a lake in the woods of Hiltrup, 50 kilometres north of Dortmund, a cosy mood quickly developed. Everyone went around together, players and trainers, other hotel guests (mainly businesspeople), advisers, groupies and journalists. The Oranje players tried to ignore as far as possible the road barriers, the rolls of barbed wire and the police (precautions taken in response to the gruesome attack during the Olympic Games in Munich in 1972).

The long-haired Dutch team had become hugely popular in the space of a few weeks, a kind of footballing Rolling Stones, but that didn't seem to lead to showiness. In the lounge, in the dining room, on the balcony with a cup of coffee in the sun, the players sat chatting with anyone who happened along – whenever they weren't fishing on the lake or hanging about by the basement swimming pool. And Cruyff talked more than anyone: because he continued to serve his commercial partners during the tournament; because along with Coster he had to sort out an issue about film rights; because a drinks merchant needed to be confronted for earning money off his back; and above all because journalists from the Netherlands and elsewhere followed him every day like a cloud of mosquitos. The star who eventually wanted a career in public relations said, 'I'm always prepared to do interviews. You reap the rewards yourself. At least I do!'

He was the focus of practically every press conference. A British journalist wrote that he was 'the heart and soul of the team'. The 'Von Karajan unter den Kickern' (Von Karajan among footballers), as a German newspaper called him (being compared with prominent artistic figures always greatly pleased Cruyff), had to answer hundreds of questions, not just immediately after matches but back at the players' hotel. It was one of the reasons why goalkeeper Jongbloed thought him 'awesome', a 'magisterial leader'. Krol used the word 'magnificent' for Johan's performances, and Keizer did too, as did Haan – all three of them players who a year earlier had voted Cruyff out as captain of Ajax.

The press were surprised by the easy manner of 'the new Pelé'. He was informal and quick-witted. *Locker*, as the Germans said: laid-back. The man who had dropped out of school sla-lomed niftily around his grammatical shortcomings. Playful and free, he adapted Dutch words into English and German. And he never blurted anything out; there was always an idea behind it, sometimes even a brainteaser. After the disappointing 0–0 against Sweden, for instance. To the disbelief of the journalists, he showed no sign of distress in Dortmund. He'd played fantas-tically, but his crosses had miraculously failed to lead to goals. 'Playing football and scoring goals are two different things,' he explained. 'They have nothing to do with each other. Anyone who runs about on a football pitch can score a goal, but they can't necessarily play good football. We play excellently, but the scoring has fallen behind.'

The foreign journalists were lost for words. Until that evening in Dortmund they'd believed you played football in order to score. Now they had learnt from this chattering magician that scoring goals was 'something nice that's outside of the football'.

Cruyff felt the admiration and rose to fill the role of ambas-sador. He praised the 'Dutch mentality' of adaptability and trade-offs, and enjoyed being able to present his small mother country in a positive light. 'Outside of football anyone who has anything to do with the Netherlands, whether economically or in any other area, benefits from it,' he said proudly. 'You need to make the most of that.' Everyone joined in the promotion and as a result an experienced Dutch journalist was taught a lesson by several Oranje players that he would never forget. The reporter, Ben de Graaf of *de Volkskrant*, kept writing criti-cally about Oranje's unnecessarily rough play, and that irritated Cruyff no end. It made his stomach churn, he said. So De Graaf, clothes, passport and all, was thrown into the swimming pool at the players' hotel. The journalist found that intimidating – which was of course the intention – and said it was a disgrace. To gang leader Cruyff it was a way of ensuring everyone stuck together. Under the banner of the crucial 'winner's mentality', this example of 'whoever isn't with us is against us' was briefly necessary, he felt.

The De Graaf incident was no more than a note of discord. The symphony in a major key dominated. The captain had complained countless times about the condescending treatment sportspeople had to put up with. He wasn't complaining now. On this international stage he felt no lack of respect; in fact, respect fluttered down on him like confetti. Of course, he was bearing 'immense responsibility' and leadership was 'a very heavy task', but, 'Football has given me so much back that I feel rich, young and gloriously happy.'

However happy he was, it was not easy to be so far from home. Less and less so, in fact. He had already been gone for weeks and was missing Danny and the children. Father's Day on 16 June had passed without presents and kisses, and although a week later the players' wives had come over, for Danny the trip from their Catalan summer house to Hiltrup was a tall order. She'd have preferred to stay on the Montanya – she couldn't abide the idea of having to put in an appearance for one night in the players' hotel, as if she was some kind of bar girl. In the end it had been fun after all, and now, at the end of June, Cruyff had been alone again for a week. He knew Danny found it 'terrible' that he wasn't with her 'all the time'. 'The sooner the Dutch are knocked out,' she'd said to *Algemeen Dagblad* before the World Cup began, 'the more time Johan will have with us.'

Her dependency didn't make things any easier for Cruyff. In Hiltrup, Danny had again declared that it was all going to last 'a really long time'. 'When you're alone with your little problems,' Johan quoted her in his diary, 'it's as if they're bigger and as if time goes more slowly.' So the tournament became more than just a 'burden' for him, he admitted; it actually became 'inhuman'.

The other players were also troubled by homesickness, and they got bored. Despite the availability of German girls, tobacco and drink, life in Hiltrup had become a drag. So, on 30 June, following the 2-0 victory over East Germany, a party was held in the hotel. Perhaps the captain should have intervened at that point. Perhaps, with a reference to the two matches still to come, he should have demanded discipline. He could have talked to Michels about it. After all, Oranje still had to play Brazil and be fit enough after that for either the final or a battle for third place. But Cruyff didn't intervene and neither did Michels. In fact, the captain was the cause of the remarkable, even tragic consequences of that evening in Waldhotel Krautkrämer.

Pop group The Cats from Volendam performed, the *Sekt* – sparkling wine – flowed freely, cigars were smoked, there was larking around. The son of the owner, Hans-Joachim Krautkrämer, took photos of the merrymakers, including Cruyff – who happened to be sitting next to the wife of a local dignitary. The captain was furious. A photo of him with an unknown woman would quickly do the rounds in the media and reach Barcelona. His jealous wife, who hated Johan's long absences, who hated the world of football, would be beside herself. 'He swore at me,' Krautkrämer said later. 'He wanted me to give him the roll of film. I refused. He followed me into the kitchen, but he didn't get the film. There, in the kitchen, my girlfriend mediated. She calmed Cruyff down and told him nothing would be done with the photos.'

Peace was made. Later that evening, when the party was over, Cruyff joined a group that had gathered in Hans-Joachim's room in his parents' hotel, where he lived. Rob Rensenbrink and several other players drank whisky there and smoked cigarettes to the sound of The Bee Gees. Sometimes they had a quick dance with Hans-Joachim's girlfriend, or with one of her friends. Another German joined them who, unfortunately for Johan, was an undercover journalist. After two in the morning the captain felt like a swim. The others liked the idea. Barefoot and with bottles of *Sekt* under their arms, the young people went down the steps into the basement and dived into the swimming pool naked. Little happened other than a bit of flirting, a bit of thrashing about in the water and some time spent sitting on the edge of the pool, but the following day the undercover journalist shouted from the rooftops about what he had seen. He announced that he had sold the story to *Bild*.

Cruyff heard that and was furious once more. The consequences of an article about nude swimming with girls were inevitable, even if there weren't any photos. He saw the journalist walking near the players' hotel and flew at him. 'What have you written?' he asked.

'Only what happened,' the journalist answered. His name was Guido Frick and he'd signed the hotel register as a pasta rep.

'So what did happen?' Cruyff pressed him. The global star stood there gesturing urgently and made clear what the consequences for his family might be. He got so angry that others had to restrain him.

The journalist was thrown out of the hotel. To Cruyff's horror the story was published in *Bild* the next morning, 2 July. The article, headlined '*Cruyff, Sekt, nackte Mädchen und ein kühles Bad*' (Cruyff, champagne, naked girls and a refreshing dip), was passed around the Waldhotel from hand to hand. No mention was made of sexual acts, but the tone was sufficient reason for consultation between Cruyff, Michels and the KNVB. The decision was made to deny everything and attribute it to a 'smear'. That word was used repeatedly in interviews, during a press conference and in columns (although not in Cruyff's diary in *Nieuwe Revu*; the ghost writer had been unable reach him). The German press was said to have made up the story to undermine Dutch morale in case the two countries should meet in the final. Michels described it as a form of 'Cold War'. Most of the Dutch reporters in Hiltrup echoed his words.

On Wednesday 3 July 1974, in the last group game, against Brazil, Cruyff once again gave all he had in him. He converted the fury he could expect from Danny into hyper-football, as it were. He steered and directed with great concentration and

was nimble in duels. Throughout the match, which degenerated into a kind of street fight between heavies, he was the
positive Cruyff one more time. The friend of the referee. The
fire extinguisher. The ideal captain. Brazil in no way resembled
the artistic world champions of 1970. The hero of that earlier
tournament, Pelé, who no longer played internationals, was in
the stands handing out autographs and his 'successor' wanted
nothing but to win. Cruyff was pulled to the ground as if in a
wrestling match, he was stamped on (out of sight of the ref), but
he scrambled to his feet each time and showed his class.

As if it was only natural, the captain was involved in both the
goals with which his team won the match. He set up the first
of them with a pass to Neeskens, who slid towards the ball to
score, and was responsible for the second himself with a brilliant
volley after an intelligent break on the left wing: 2-0. Towards
the end of the battle his immediate opponent, defender Luís
Pereira, was shown the red card after an insane tackle aimed at
Neeskens' legs.

'The Dutch are the most complete team I've ever encountered,' Pereira said afterwards. 'Who has taught the players
that everyone can do everything? I wish that man could come
to Brazil for a bit.' His coach Mário Zagallo believed the
Netherlands was 'way ahead of all other countries'.

The newspaper *Jornal do Brazil* in Rio de Janeiro summed it
all up, as far as the acclaimed captain went: 'We didn't know
much about Cruyff. Now we'll never forget him.'

West Germany also won their last group game (against Poland),
so the final on Sunday 7 July 1974 would be between the Dutch
and the Germans. To say that Oranje prepared thoroughly for
that match would be putting it too strongly. Perhaps the players
had partied too hard in the Waldhotel, because on the evening
after the bash with The Cats there was once again merry drinking
and smoking to the accompaniment of musicians. Furthermore,
there were countless individual 'escapes' to the nightlife of the
Hiltrup district. Michels had allowed the players a remarkable

amount of freedom (to their surprise they saw little of him) and the tactical preparation for the final was inadequate too; 'spy' and assistant coach Cor van der Hart had been sent home because of his alcohol-fuelled aggressive behaviour. There was little fundamental knowledge of the German team, which had changed its approach and grown during the tournament. Moreover, the idea had taken root in Oranje that getting to the final was a tremendous accomplishment in itself. 'We have achieved our goal,' Cruyff said to the press. Not 'almost achieved'. 'After the 2-0 against Brazil, everyone was so relaxed and content that the next match didn't seem to matter,' he claimed later.

Cruyff's body wasn't really helping either. With all the tension and nerves, he was 'run-down', and a stomach bug after the Netherlands vs Sweden game had weakened him too. 'Actually the world championship went on too long. I was used up. I didn't have a spark of energy left in my body.'

Then there was Danny. The news of the naked swim had reached Spain, as Johan had feared, and now he had a lot of explaining to do. Or, rather, a lot of denying. From that moment on he was often on the phone to his wife, and probably also to his in-laws in the Netherlands, from the hotel call box. The players, coaches and other support staff, even a few journalists, watched him in the little phone cell with its white sound-proofing, right across from reception, talking and gesticulating as if he was playing football. They saw the sweat marks under his armpits grow, his hair become tacky. 'Man, just say you weren't there,' goalkeeper Jongbloed told him. 'That's what I did. Then you're off the hook.' As Johnny Rep remembered later, 'Johan stood sweating profusely in that little box.'

It looked very much as though the star of the tournament was concerned mainly with saving his marriage. According to Johan's brother Henny, Danny was threatening to pack her bags. She has always denied that – just as Johan has always denied the 'swimming pool incident'. She claims it was actually impossible to ring Hiltrup from the summer house on the Montanya. Later again she said she wasn't in the summer house but in their apartment in Andorra. In his autobiography Cruyff came up with that one too. 'Danny was in our second home in the mountains near Andorra, in a place that didn't yet have a phone connection, so we couldn't even have contacted each other on the telephone, let alone argued.' He claimed not to have spoken to Danny again until after the final.

In reality Danny and the children stayed on the Montanya, the mountain near Barcelona, throughout the 1974 World Cup. 'Danny was greatly upset,' neighbour and friend Marjolijn van der Meer remembers. 'I tried to reassure her. Come on, I said, of course nothing is true about that whole story. "Yes, it is," she said. "It's easy for you to talk, your husband isn't there." I suggested the Germans had sent those girls after them to make trouble. But she wouldn't listen to that either.'

The bungalows on the Montanya had no telephones, it's true. So Marjolijn zigzagged with Danny in the car down to the village of Aiguafreda, where they could make contact with Hiltrup from a telephone exchange. 'It was pretty old-fashioned,' Van der Meer says. 'With those plugs stuck into boards. We would ask to ring Germany and then have to come back a bit later when contact had been made.'

On the Saturday, the day before the final, Danny – who had originally planned not to attend the tournament at all – travelled to her father's house in Amsterdam-Zuid. From there it was easier to ring the players' hotel. Father and daughter flew the next day to Munich, where the final was to take place that afternoon. When the last battle was over, Cor Coster is said to have walked through the stadium raging and cursing, largely about the 'blinding row' that had taken place between his daughter and his son-in-law. Journalist Frits Barend, who was on good terms with Johan, Danny and Cor, heard him out. 'Coster was terribly pissed off,' Barend remembers.

*

The night before the final, Cruyff slept even more uneasily than usual. He'd often described Danny as his anchor, his compass in life; to lose her would be to lose everything. 'If I didn't have this safety net of peace and happiness, I wouldn't be able to play football the same way,' he said. More than once he expressed his fear of endling up like playboy George Best, lonely and sinking into a pool of glamour, alcohol addiction and rejection. His former drinking buddy, *bon vivant* Wim Suurbier, had just got through a marriage crisis with Danny's friend Maja. Johan always wanted to avoid trouble like that. Already restless by nature, Cruyff sat in his room smoking for hours that night – not disturbing anyone, incidentally, since his 'roommate' Neeskens had long before asked for a room of his own, unable to tolerate Johan's smoking and night-time revels. The team staff had given Cruyff cartons of Camel non-filter.

Despite the sleeping pills he always had with him, and a pillow purchased specially for him, the lack of sleep was obvious from the shadows under his eyes when he ran on to the pitch in Munich's Olympic Stadium on 7 July 1974. He looked as grey as the sky above the stadium's tent-like roof. Cruyff, as he would admit several months after the final, was 'mentally exhausted'. There was little chance he would play well at what ought to have been the pinnacle of his career. 'If it's going well at home, there are fewer problems for you too,' he had noted in his diary back in late May. 'Then you play more easily.' This Sunday the opposite was true.

Another thing that didn't help was that for the first time in the tournament there was no Orange Army. Only a few thousand Dutch people had managed to get tickets for the final. After six 'home games' this would now be an 'away game'.

Cruyff didn't play badly. He hardly ever did. With his insight into the game, technical skill and concentration he always put in a satisfactory performance. In the final against West Germany that was the case once again. He did, however, play badly in comparison with the other six matches in the tournament. As with East Germany, strong man-marking awaited him (then Konrad Weise, now Berti Vogts), and now too Johan lingered in the centre circle after they'd kicked off, as if to say, *Come here if you dare.* Vogts didn't dare. The entire German team waited in its own half, as if petrified, to see what Oranje were going to do, which demonstrated how much the Germans looked up to the thus far indomitable Dutch. Right back Vogts, positioned in the centre to hamper Cruyff, let the feared striker do as he liked, until after forty-five seconds he moved out of the centre circle towards the German goal with the ball at his feet. Vogts ran towards him to block him.

Cruyff accelerated, made a dummy move to the right but turned left. The blond Vogts ran with him. Cruyff slowed, then accelerated again, running into the funnel of opponents where (he said later) he already knew he would be tripped. The foul was attributed to Uli Hoeness. At the 16-metre line he stuck out his leg and Cruyff fell flat on his face in the penalty area. A penalty was awarded after a minute of play.

Neeskens half kicked the ground from 11 metres but scored nonetheless – 1-0.

'What happened after that,' Cruyff wrote in his autobiography, 'was a classic case of pride coming before a fall. As soon as you're past that point of overconfidence, it becomes incredibly difficult to turn it round.'

To the amazement of the Germans, the Dutch stopped pressing. Instead of finishing off a fearful opponent, Oranje passed the ball around at a tantalisingly slow speed. It was the Ajax attitude of 1972-73: slow the game down, let the opposition come to you and then try to break out. Some of the players, such as Van Hanegem, wanted to humiliate the Germans, the way a cat plays with a wounded mouse: the Germans deserved it for 1940-45. After a while the Germans crept out of their positions and that was the moment when Cruyff could have struck. After a counterattack he ran towards the enemy goal along with Rep, and aside from goalkeeper Sepp Maier he had only Beckenbauer ahead of him. In Ajax shirts they had often adroitly outplayed opponents in such situations, against Independiente in the Intercontinental Cup, for example. Not this time. Instead of accelerating, Cruyff passed the ball to Rep, who was running forward to his left. But Rep was right-legged and he kicked the ball too weakly towards Maier with his left.

Cruyff had miscalculated. In a situation that was easy enough to assess, too. Was it fear of failure? Fear of success? Fatigue? Worry? In any case the upbeat Cruyff, the Cruyff of four days before against Brazil, was no longer on display. 'Throughout the match everyone was either a bit too early or a bit too late, never on time,' was his analysis in retrospect. The interaction with Haan hadn't worked well, among other things. The previously so positive captain ran about swearing at his teammates and was suddenly no longer on friendly terms with the referee. On the contrary, he reproached English ref Jack Taylor for giving him too little protection against the severity of Vogts (who years ago had brought him to a standstill during a youth match).

West Germany equalised after twenty-five minutes. Cruyff shook his head dejectedly, even though there were still sixty-five minutes to go. His usual optimism – always looking for opportunities – had gone. He certainly wasn't dominant; he no longer even dominated his own team. The Netherlands, including Cruyff, reacted weakly to a German acceleration from midfield. Müller made it 2-1 just before half-time. Then, a minute after the match restarted following the goal, Cruyff ran towards Rijsbergen in the centre circle. The central defender had been told by Michels to offload the ball as quickly as possible. Rijsbergen had obediently done just that all through the tournament, in accordance with his lowly position in the hierarchy. But now he blatantly ignored the highest in rank and passed the ball to Haan. That looked like a provocation. Nothing was going according to plan.

Even after Vogts had been shown a yellow card, Cruyff kept griping to Taylor and continued doing so after the ref blew the whistle for half-time. He went and stood right in front of Taylor. He talked and gestured that the Englishman should be stricter. He allowed himself to be sent away and then came back. Was warned but carried on talking, ignoring Taylor's exhortations to keep his mouth shut. And so it went on all the way to the catacombs until finally he was given a yellow card, as if that was what he'd been after. As if Cruyff was unable to free himself from destructive mode. A pity for him, because he had now single-handedly nullified his moral advantage over Vogts, who was already on a yellow card and therefore needed to watch out during the duels between them.

After half-time Oranje attacked better than before, partly because the injured Rensenbrink had been replaced by René van de Kerkhof. Cruyff now stayed at the front, but he barely participated. He looked fretful. He showed his class a couple of times. He took a free kick so perfectly that Van Hanegem could have headed the ball in, but missed. Later, standing near the far post, Cruyff headed a ball back brilliantly to Rep. The right-winger got to it a fraction of a second too late and was immediately subjected to a terrific broadside from Cruyff. 'Just sod off, man!' Rep snapped back. Oranje got a few more good chances in which Cruyff was not involved, and so the captain dragged himself to the end of the fateful match.

After the not undeserved victory by West Germany (the team ought to have been awarded a second penalty in the second half and saw a faultless goal disallowed), the life seemed to have drained out of Cruyff. His eyes were deep in their sockets, his hair lay dark and wet on his head. Sombre, but with the determination of a captain, he called his players to him. They still had to go to the VIP box and complete other ceremonial duties. Cruyff congratulated the Germans and received a fraternal slap on the back from Vogts, his conqueror.

Shortly after the final, Michels said that three stars had played in Munich: Cruyff, Beckenbauer and Müller. Of the three his own captain had not been 'mentally in optimal condition'. It seemed an understatement.

In September 1974 Cruyff said in his Cruyffian way about the World Cup, 'I don't think they won. I think we lost.' The Netherlands, after all, had come up with the best play of the lot. The team had set millions dreaming and given the world new hope of a future full of artistic attacking football. That was how respected journalist Brian Glanville saw it too. The British World Cup chronicler called Oranje 'the most attractive and talented of all losers'.

The captain of the losers attributed the blame in part to a lack of experience in the final battle. The team, put together in a very short time, had not had enough basic values to fall back on. As if its ability to improvise had floundered in a sea of tensions. 'I know for sure that if we had played six or seven more matches before the final, had got more experience as a team and had been playing in the same way a year earlier, the final would have gone differently.'

Oranje, and especially its captain, would later be praised far more often than the victorious West German team. Which raises a question: can you win a final by losing it? The tournament would anyhow remain a 'beautiful memory' for Cruyff. 'Sometimes, even when you don't lift the trophy, in the end you're still seen as a winner,' he wrote in his autobiography. 'Wherever I go in the world, people always want to talk about our team in those days. I think we earned more praise and respect during that tournament than most world champions before or since. I'm proud of that.'

For him personally, his astonishing play during the World Cup in West Germany had an even more important effect. He made his name there, as a player, talker, thinker and innovator. 'Although I'd been part of many trophy-winning club sides, it was only after that World Cup that I achieved true stardom,' he wrote. 'Everything I said and thought suddenly mattered. Not just in Holland, but all over the world.'

CHAPTER TWENTY

It was no longer going so well

Sitting there side by side in a Boeing 707, high in the air between Munich and Amsterdam, they were just like any couple in love. Johan and Danny chatted a little, stroked each other, smiled. Everything seemed fine again. On this Monday morning, 8 July 1974, the division of roles between the two seemed unchanged: Danny looked out of the window as soon as the television cameras focused on them and Johan started talking. Reporter Henk Terlingen, who was travelling with them, asked, in a reference to the World Cup final the day before, whether the striker could accept his loss. 'Difficult, difficult,' he admitted. 'So you think it's a pity?' At that point Cruyff immediately added, perhaps for the sake of his wife, whose blonde hair was lit up by the sunshine through the window, 'On the other hand I thank God on bended knee that it's over. It was brutally tough.'

A slight emotional crack in his voice was audible in the word 'tough'. That was undoubtedly attributable not just to the seven matches he'd played for Oranje within a short space of time but to the pressure to perform, to the expectations and the responsibility of being team captain. He'd been away from home too long and of course he'd also been preoccupied by the swimming pool affair and all the commotion that followed from it. But now they were together. He laid his arm affectionately around Danny's shoulders. It was over.

In the Netherlands a tribute to the Oranje players awaited them, and then a reception by Queen Juliana. After that Johan and Danny flew to Barcelona, where preparations for the next football season would start in early August. They spent the few weeks remaining to them on the Montanya. Their summer house, a country retreat a good distance from the nearest town, was the ideal place to forget all the tension of the World Cup and the agitation surrounding it. Cruyff was good at readjusting. The children played in the park-like garden that flowed seamlessly into that of Armand Carabén and Marjolijn van der Meer, and they all sat together at long tables, often joined by Rinus and Will Michels. That summer, Johan and Marianne Neeskens joined them too.

Johan *Segundo*, as Neeskens came to be known, had signed a dream contract at FC Barcelona with the help of Cor Coster. It instantly released the 22-year-old from the sky-high debts he had incurred in a failed venture with a discotheque in Zaandam. Coster had managed to detach Neeskens from Ajax even though he was still under contract, just as he had Johan *Primero* a year earlier. (The termination of contracts was still rare in the 1970s and only later became entirely normal, in part thanks to pioneer Coster.) Along with his 18-year-old wife Marianne Schuphof, Neeskens was hoping for a good life in Barcelona. The recently married couple lived both in the city and on the Montanya close to the Cruyffs; they too had been able to acquire their summer house on very favourable terms.

In early August 1974, when competitive football started up again, the Dutch enclave moved back down to the city. In their spacious apartment in Pedralbes, an area where many diplomats lived, a pleasant way of life developed for the Cruyffs. In the mornings Johan took Susila and Chantal to a private school in the neighbourhood. Jordi, now six months old, stayed at home with Danny and the Spanish help, Femmie. Danny was happier here than in Amsterdam. People in Barcelona didn't shout nasty comments when she walked along the street with Johan; in fact, on the Ramblas she was sometimes handed bunches of flowers; the Catalans made her feel more shy than angry. Johan and Danny enjoyed the people of Barcelona, as well as the balmy climate and their trips to the beach. They were starting to appreciate the local cuisine and no longer needed to carry large quantities of cold meats, peanut butter and other Dutch products back with them from visits to family. Even shrimps found their way on to the table after a while, although Femmie had to fry them in butter rather than olive oil, otherwise the family would spend half their evening on the toilet.

In Barcelona the Cruyffs could generally count on being treated like royalty. They shopped at the department store El Corte Inglés, for which Johan appeared in advertisements. They were welcomed at the door by the management and once they'd finished stocking up on free items, everything would be carried to the car by the staff. For new clothes they went to 'factories', as Johan called them, large wholesale businesses where they could select their wardrobe in the next season's fashions. In restaurants too they rarely needed to pay, although Johan and Danny generally preferred eating at home because it was usually impossible to eat out undisturbed.

'We never pay for anything,' Cruyff said in an interview. 'We get everything for free.' He was proud of that. Despite his increasing wealth he would always be frugal, cadging cigarettes from everyone and getting great deals in shops, whether alone or in combination with Danny. Parking fines – for pavement parking for instance, so convenient – went unpaid and after being caught speeding Johan only had to stick his head out of the window of his Citroën SM to be allowed to drive on. He could forget trying that in the Netherlands.

These were good times, and Johan's work on the pitch could surely only continue to improve, especially since Michels would be his coach again for another year. 'We've spent seven and a half years of our lives together and we understand each other without saying a word,' Cruyff said. 'His vision of football coincides with mine. His ideas are my ideas, both on and off the pitch. It's a wonderful bit of good fortune for me that he's coach at Barcelona. It makes playing soccer easy. On our horizon we can now see the shape of the European Cup.'

But unfortunately for Cruyff, the season did not turn out as planned. However great his private life may have been, on the football pitch things didn't go as they had in the magical 1973-74 season. After his long and tough World Cup, his summer break had been shorter than usual and all year he struggled with fatigue and irritability. During preparations for the new season, in practice matches, he got a yellow card (in Hamburg) and a red card (in Barcelona). Even after that he got embroiled in more conflicts with opponents and referees than in his first year at Barcelona. The shine had gone off the El Flaco phenomenon.

He could no longer expect beneficial treatment from referees and on top of that his 'guard' Neeskens was finding it hard to adjust. Little came of a further step towards the more modern game that Cruyff and Michels had in mind. Moreover, it turned out that far from everyone at FC Barcelona was keen on the arrival of Johan *Segundo*. Because of the ban on having more than two foreigners in a team, the popular left-winger Hugo Sotil now often found himself on the subs' bench. Many people felt the removal of the Peruvian attacker meant that Barcelona had been robbed of much of its creativity and speed. 'With Sotil and me on the wings, Johan could play his famous game,' teammate Charly Rexach recalls. 'That was now ruined. Also, Michels tinkered too much with the composition of the team, at the expense of the cohesion that had won us the championship so convincingly. An incredible shame.'

Fortunately most of the home games were played in a festive mood. In Camp Nou, Cruyff and his teammates often chalked up decisive victories with attacking play that was a delight to watch. 'Almost every home game was a spectacle,' Rexach claims. 'Harsh fouls against Johan and me were punished when we were in our own stadium.' In the second round of the European Cup, Feyenoord visited, and the match became the high point of the season. Cruyff was outstanding on that Tuesday evening in November 1974. He swerved fluidly around his opponents and seemed to do everything with even greater ease than before. He made frequent use of his 'trained' left leg, putting it immediately in the right position in relation to the ball even more than before, which gave him more time to survey the pitch. Barcelona beat Feyenoord 3-0 and three times Rexach scored from a cross by Cruyff. El Flaco kicked two of those crosses with his left foot over a considerable distance. The individualist in him seemed just as eager to make technical progress as 'Jopie' had ever been at Ajax. As if his personal development never stood still.

So again this season Camp Nou enjoyed the footballer who never did anything purely for the beauty of it, but who garnered more admiration for that beauty than he had in the Netherlands. 'The elegance of his moves and the surprises they brought – we couldn't get enough of it,' says writer and Barça fan Ferran Torrent. 'He brought his personality on to the pitch with him. We weren't used to that. It reinforced his aura of autonomy, of self-determination, even when things were going rather less well with the team.'

In away games, however, Cruyff now had to watch out. 'People would throw all kinds of things on to the pitch and the defenders didn't let him go his own way any more,' Rexach remembers. 'In fact, they dealt with him particularly firmly.' In response Cruyff increasingly sought refuge in the relatively safe midfield. Sports reporter Francesc Aguilar of *El Mundo Deportivo* understood why. 'It was almost impossible,' he says. 'Every match was a war. And the referees allowed it. Not many of the games were on television, so people were never really able to see all the things that happened to Cruyff on the pitches in Spain.'

On top of that, all the travelling was starting to take its toll. Few Spanish cities had airports in those days, so a match in, say, Gijón involved a complicated trip with planes, trains and long stopover times. The team was often away from home for two or three days for one game. Cruyff's sleep was even worse in sleeper trains than in hotels. After finally getting home on the Monday, he might immediately have to pack his bags for an international or European Cup match. The family-oriented footballer was 'wrecked' by it, he said.

Cruyff's fatigue and irritation sometimes did his collaboration with his fellow players no good at all. 'He simply despaired at his teammates' play,' journalist Aguilar concluded later. 'They couldn't adjust to the demands of Michels, and often didn't dare to. It was very difficult, almost impossible, to truly transplant total football to Barcelona.'

Yet in December 1974 Cruyff was proclaimed European Footballer of the Year. It was the third time, a record, and it was no doubt down to his stunning performance in West Germany. That form, that all-consuming dedication, that breathtaking all or nothing play, soon seemed to belong to a distant time.

In early January 1975, in Madrid, during a match against Real that Barcelona lost 1–0, Cruyff was called a donkey by the crowd and by the opposition. The Madrid press gave his play a score of zero and called him 'gabby' because of his continual arguments with the referee. In this period Cruyff increasingly gave full vent to his annoyance at the umpiring. He openly denounced the favourable treatment given to Real Madrid by the football association and the referees. Then in February something happened that everyone had been half expecting for some time. El Flaco was sent off. It was the first time in an official match in Spain. As if a malady from his time with the Ajax juniors had reared its head again.

It happened on the evening of Sunday 9 February 1975 in Málaga. Cruyff refused to resign himself to a blunder by referee

José Luis Orrantia Capelastegui, who allowed an offside goal by Málaga. A number of protesting Barcelona players were shown the white card, among them Cruyff, who continued the argument with the ref on his own. He had the right to a say, because at the start of the year he'd been appointed captain, but when he attempted to fetch the linesman – who had flagged for offside – he was shown the red.

It was a typical example of injustice (the television pictures that evening proved him right) and in such situations Johan was explosive, especially when those in authority haughtily stood their ground. Ref Orrantia gestured to him to step back. He didn't. His teammates went over to Michels to ask him what they should do. The coach didn't know either. After eight minutes of chaos and desperation the referee, as a last resort, called in the riot police. Only after they had taken the obstinate Dutchman away could the match resume.

Cruyff walked off the pitch between three men in peaked caps, looking like a mugger. He was clearly upset. He seemed no less ashamed than on that dark Sunday afternoon more than eight years before in the Olympic Stadium in Amsterdam.

Cruyff now had four white cards to his name and was facing suspension from La Liga. Catalan frustrations took hold of him. 'To me it seems best to say nothing about referees,' he wrote in *El Mundo Deportivo.* 'But I don't have to put up with everything. I think it's outrageous that I've been suspended. It seems clear to me that we're being targeted.' The board at Barcelona declared its backing for Cruyff and said the 'campaign' against the club only strengthened 'the sense of solidarity among all the members and supporters'. Cruyff declared war on the Madrid press. 'Perhaps they'll come to regret all the lies they've told about me,' he said. He would grant no more interviews to journalists from the Spanish capital.

His friend and Barcelona manager Carabén, and other Catalan nationalists, believed the long arm of the Franco regime was behind the suspension – and behind practically all the measures that had inconvenienced Barcelona. But Cruyff didn't take that up. In fact, he never did. He refused to get involved in politics. He didn't even feel a sense of euphoria in response to the death of Franco in 1975. When he spoke out against 'Madrid' he meant the football association, not the military regime.

Barcelona eventually got to the semi-finals of the European Cup. That might seem a creditable outcome, but in fact in previous rounds Feyenoord had been the only serious obstacle. In its semi-final over two legs Barcelona had no chance against Leeds United. Cruyff was not impressive in either match. The English played fanatically and allowed him hardly any space for individual creative flourishes. To the disappointment of the British press, in Leeds he showed only occasional signs of his talent. In Barcelona, where his team had to make up for a 2-1 defeat in the first leg, he was unable to put his stamp on the match 'even for a moment' according to *Trouw*. Other Dutch newspapers too passed harsh judgement. *Het Vrije Volk* noted that Cruyff pulled back from the game remarkably often and, on the occasions when he did engage, he lacked 'the speed of action that once made him beyond compare'. *De Telegraaf* even saw him hit an opponent in the face, a player who behaved irritatingly during the awarding of a free kick for Barcelona. Fortunately for the Dutchman, the referee failed to notice.

The final score in Camp Nou was 1-1. That meant Barcelona would not be able to take part in the European Cup the following year, since a national league championship win was out of reach by then too. They were fifteen points behind leaders Real Madrid. The 1974-75 season was little short of a failure. In the Spanish competition Barcelona managed only thirty-seven points, their lowest total since 1970. The highly expensive Dutch enclave had achieved little.

Rinus Michels was asked to leave. His relationship with the club leadership had not been particularly good for a long time, and fans and journalists were grumbling about the increasing influence of the 'Dutch clan', which consisted of Cruyff, Michels, Neeskens and Coster (plus manager Carabén as the husband of Marjolijn van der Meer). So perhaps it was no accident that the new coach was a German. And what a German. Talent-developer Hennes Weisweiler was fifty-five. The board hoped that under the leadership of obsessively professional Weisweiler, Johan would once again become the diligent, quick and flexible striker of the championship year. Under Michels, El Flaco had grown into a kind of midfielder, especially in away games, and that had borne little fruit.

Cruyff immediately had his doubts about Weisweiler, who had made an excellent name for himself as coach of Borussia Mönchengladbach (by winning the 1975 UEFA Cup among other things). As Weisweiler remembers it, Cruyff tried to put the new coach in his place at an early stage by saying, 'You determine the tactics beforehand and I determine the tactics on the pitch.' The German's dumbfounded response was, 'You surely don't believe that yourself.'

Cruyff certainly did believe it. He demonstrated as much straight away, in Greece, against Paok Saloniki in the first round of the UEFA Cup. Weisweiler had told the team to break out with long balls as soon as possible. 'A long ball came,' Rexach remembers. 'But suddenly Johan was standing on the halfway line shouting. He wanted to have the ball there. I did what he asked and passed him the ball, but I was promptly substituted at half-time by Weisweiler. He was furious. "I'm the boss here," he said, "not Cruyff."'

Weisweiler remained allergic to Cruyff's obstinacy and ready wit, and the Dutchman couldn't stand the new coach's authoritarian 'German' behaviour. In Mönchengladbach the trainer had got into arguments with star player Günter Netzer. 'But at the end of a long conversation, Netzer and I could always find common ground,' he said. 'With Cruyff that was impossible.'

It was true. In Barcelona Weisweiler said to him, 'I'm the best coach with the highest diploma.'

'Congratulations,' Cruyff answered. 'I'm the best player.'

The explosion came on 8 February 1976 during an away game against Sevilla. Weisweiler told Cruyff to play at the front again, whereas he preferred to save his legs in midfield. 'I was deployed in midfield behind him,' Rexach recalls. 'But after five minutes Johan came over to me. He wanted to swap, with me as striker and him behind. No, I said. Yes, we're doing it, he said. I let him have his way.' To Weisweiler's annoyance Cruyff barely appeared in the front line after that, which meant Barcelona created few chances. When the captain kicked the ball carelessly to opponent Enrique Lora halfway through the second half and Lora promptly made it 2-0, Weisweiler took him off.

Being substituted was humiliating. It hadn't happened to Cruyff since April 1971 (Atlético Madrid vs Ajax). He told the press that the coach had no understanding of football. 'Weisweiler knows how badly the team is doing and he's looking for a scapegoat,' he said.

The coach believed his captain's play was 'risk-averse and lazy' and he kept on demanding that Cruyff appear in the front line more often, posing a threat. 'He didn't cross the halfway line,' he said, smiling derisively. 'His skirmishes in midfield don't get us anywhere. I've been patient with him long enough. I've had it up to here.'

The next day the two fighting cocks met with president Agustí Montal Costa. No progress was made and Cruyff knew what he had to do. By this time he was familiar with the machinations of the big, complex football club that was Barcelona. He was aware that nobody could bypass the 70,000 club members, and he mobilised that influence through the media and, as ever in a crisis, by playing fantastic football. Weisweiler initially didn't want him to play in Granada, but at the insistence of the team he changed his mind. Sure enough, under Cruyff's leadership – undoubtedly boosted by the conflict – Barcelona at last won an away game (the second that season). The final score was 0-2 and both goals were set up by Cruyff.

Weisweiler didn't stand a chance against his captain, who now called him 'a man without vision' or simply 'the German'. In contrast to Cruyff, the coach simply wanted to be able to do his job, the way he was used to in Germany. It was a tragic miscalculation. More than 25,000 *socios* demonstrated outside the training complex in support of El Flaco. 'Grandpa' Weisweiler, now branded a 'Nazi', must go. Windows were smashed to shouts of 'Hitler! Hitler!'

In the next match Cruyff was once again indomitable. Encouraged by 100,000 spectators in full voice in Camp Nou, he helped to defeat league leaders Atlético Madrid 2-1. He played so well that even Weisweiler said in front of the cameras that he was the 'star' of the match.

The captain's popularity was assured. In late March, when Barcelona lost 1-0 at home to Liverpool in the semi-finals of the UEFA Cup (and were eventually eliminated after a 1-1 draw in the second leg), the blame fell not on the much-loved footballer but on the German coach. The hundreds of cushions thrown on to the pitch did their work. The board gave way under the pressure and called Weisweiler to account. He felt honour-bound to pack his bags. 'With this Cruyff, Barcelona will never win the championship,' he grumbled. 'He plays only for himself.'

The captain was triumphant, and he signed up for another year. He refused even to discuss a longer contract. 'I want to be able to take the honourable way out as soon as I notice that my performance is declining,' he'd said to the Barça board. He didn't want to experience that decline. He needed to be able to dominate, otherwise others would dominate him. You might say he feared his own weakness.

In 1975-76 Barcelona again failed to win the league championship, but with a first-rate Cruyff they beat Real 2-0 in Madrid shortly before the end of the competition. Since the hated rivals had also been beaten six months earlier in Camp Nou, many of the fans were left with a good feeling about the season. All because of El Flaco.

Because of Neeskens, too. The tireless driving force in midfield had become a favourite with the fans. The people had taken into their hearts the hardworking Dutchman with his long hair and sideburns, the club's top scorer with sixteen goals (seven more than Cruyff). He was even named the league's Best Foreign Player of the Year. Despite the arguments between Weisweiler and Cruyff, Neeskens had continued to play his own passionate game, full of enthusiasm and zeal. As if 'on a high', he would say later.

Naturally his business manager Coster immediately began talks with the board of Barça to secure better financial terms for his second protégé, but after a meeting with president Montal, Coster and Neeskens were surprised when none other than Johan Cruyff walked into the boardroom.

'Johan wanted to know what I was going to be earning,' Neeskens said later in his biography. 'I was very disappointed by that. I'd never asked Uncle Cor what Johan was getting.'

Cruyff, who was always eager to assess his position in the market, and as the best player was determined to earn the most, was not told the amount by the president. Nor was he told later by his father-in-law, who like Montal thought it improper to talk about another person's finances.

The friendship between the two 'Johans' was over. Neeskens no longer showed up at Cruyff family parties and at best continued to associate with him as an affable colleague. Sometimes not even that. Shortly after the incident in the boardroom, the captain ran over to him during a match to take the ball from him. That happened fairly often, but this time Neeskens ostentatiously turned away from him and passed the ball to a defender. Cruyff (who, with his new 1.5 million-guilder contract, had stayed well ahead of Neeskens) responded with indignation.

Despite the cooling of their friendship, Johan *Primero* and Johan *Segundo* were on good terms when they went with

Oranje to the final round of the UEFA European Football Championship in Yugoslavia in June 1976. Partly because of their behaviour, in that tournament the Dutch team played one of the most bizarre matches in the country's history.

CHAPTER TWENTY-ONE

More than a footballer

Ever since the World Cup, Cruyff had managed to mould the Dutch team to suit him. During the tournament in West Germany, he'd been the undisputed leader and when 'supervisor' Michels handed the baton to a permanent national coach, Cruyff was able to increase his influence even further. The new coach, George Knobel, was no match for him at all. On the evening before their first international game in September 1974, in Sweden, Cruyff gave the newly appointed Knobel a lecture on total football that was straight and to the point. The coach listened breathlessly, and so it would always remain. All the prospects Knobel held out to the Oranje players during the qualifying rounds for Euro 1976 were contingent. As soon as Johan arrived (late) in the players' hotel, he might alter the choices that had been made concerning selections and systems. His 'We'll see about that' could throw everything into confusion. Players who protested about his special position were pushed into a corner and forced to leave, as happened to the 'grousers' from PSV, Jan van Beveren (again) and Willy van der Kuijlen.

Trainer and former player Hans Kraay Sr expressed it perfectly to *de Volkskrant* in May 1976. 'Working together with Cruyff involves accepting his total personality, or going against him, which means living in a state of war.' Knobel had opted for peace and, lo and behold, in six of the eight qualifying internationals, Johan the Great was there and he led Oranje to the final round in Yugoslavia without a hitch.

The climax of that series of games came during the final qualifying match, on the evening of Saturday 22 May 1976 in Brussels. The Netherlands had already beaten Belgium 5-0 at home, so the initiative was not actually needed; it was a delicious topping, a cherry on the cake. Thirteen minutes before the end, Cruyff ran full tilt after a hard and deep ball thrust through by Krol. To the left of the Belgian penalty area, 5 metres from the back line, he controlled the ball with a single touch and immediately curled it nonchalantly with the inside of his right foot over the hands of keeper Jean-Marie Pfaff into the top right corner. In a fraction of a second he had spotted a gap and, with astonishing ball control, leaving the ground like a ballet dancer as he took the shot, he hit home – 1-2. Oranje were in the running for the European Championship.

With King Johan at the helm, the Netherlands would surely be European champions. Everyone assumed as much. The would-be world champions of 1974 had become more mature, wiser even. The other three participants in the mini-tournament, hosts Yugoslavia, Czechoslovakia and West Germany, needn't be any hindrance. The semi-final was between the Netherlands and Czechoslovakia. Many therefore assumed the Dutch would be playing West Germany on Sunday 20 June in Belgrade. First dispense with the Czechs in Zagreb and then, in Belgrade, take revenge on the 'Krauts' for the lost final in 1974. That was the idea. There were even headlines reading 'Belgrade: revenge for Munich?' Cruyff noted in his column in *De Telegraaf*, 'We do need to be careful we don't think too much about the final.'

But they did. Which was not at all good for their concentration on the evening of Wednesday 16 June in Zagreb, concentration already much disturbed by the announcement that George Knobel was leaving. The national coach had become thoroughly entangled in a quarrel with the football association that Cruyff had provoked. The captain had been trying for months to get his latest business associate Jack van Zanten a job with the KNVB. The football association refused to hear of it − already worried about Cruyff's ever-growing influence − after which Knobel, in his enthusiasm for being in league with Johan the Great, put Van Zanten's portfolio on the table. The refusal to engage Van Zanten remained unchanged, which meant that for Knobel there was no other option but to tender his resignation.

Until a few hours before the match against Czechoslovakia, Cruyff was fully caught up in this conflict. So he had more on his mind that Wednesday afternoon than football alone − and the decor in Zagreb didn't help. The Maksimir Stadium was ugly and unroofed and the rain poured down. Against a background of ponchos and umbrellas, a match developed that was macabre for Oranje, and Cruyff was unable to do much about it. There was none of the 'hunting', the exciting weapon of 1974. On the contrary, the white-clad Czechs routed Oranje, and the Dutch responded with a combination of loose play and vicious fouls. Cruyff lost the ball unusually often, although it has to be said that the other two forwards, Rob Rensenbrink and Johnny Rep, seemed apathetic.

Only after half-time, when the Czechs were already 1-0 up, did Cruyff start to show what he could do. Nevertheless, the Dutch created few chances and needed an own goal by the Czechs to reach 1-1.

Now turn the match, you would think. Just play on. All the more since the Czechs, having received a red card, were down to ten men. But there was too much exasperation with the fanatical opponents and with the authoritarian performance of referee Clive Thomas. Neeskens was sent off after trying to snap Zdeněk Nehoda's leg in half out of frustration. Instead of getting Neeskens to go, Cruyff made it all even worse by saying something to the referee. Something insulting, it would seem, because the ref looked startled for a moment and held out a yellow card. That meant Cruyff would not be allowed to play in the final against Germany the coming Sunday.

In extra time he quarrelled with the referee again and didn't get a free kick when he was brought down. From the counter-attack Czechoslovakia made it 2-1. Then Van Hanegem got so wound up about the denial of the free kick that he delayed the kick-off, standing there complaining about Thomas. Captain Cruyff allowed him to wind everyone up interminably, rather than pushing him away and taking the kick himself. He limited himself to his familiar raised shoulders and gestures of despair. Van Hanegem refused to go over to the ref for a yellow card and was given a red.

Two Dutchmen sent off in the final round, in front of a global television audience – countless of their countrymen watched their screens with embarrassment. Were these really the national heroes of 1974?

It was now nine men against ten on a soaking wet pitch. The match continued and Cruyff was empty. He couldn't deal with it any more; he suddenly seemed years older. The game went from left to right and Cruyff's body looked – almost blasphemous to use this word about him – stiff. He laboured where he was used to whirling. Watching him slide at the ball while his opponent calmly ran on with it: was this really happening? It was really happening and Czechoslovakia made it 3-1.

The day after the debacle he was no longer King Johan on the sports pages. He had 'messed up just as badly' as all the others. He had been part of a 'poor' Dutch team that had made a 'pathetic show' of it. 'The Netherlands' best footballer of all time' had undoubtedly contributed to what was now a 'stupidly and crassly squandered world reputation'. Cruyff had set 'a bad example' by 'protesting more than he played'.

The 'failing captain of Oranje' saw it rather differently. 'As a whole we all played badly,' he said. Even decades later when the national broadcaster NOS put together a reconstruction of the 'let-down' in Zagreb, Johan offered no self-criticism. Not a word about, to take just one example, his lack of sportsmanship and self-control. Perhaps it was difficult if you had, by nature, a hard time admitting mistakes and had become such a great player that no one ever asked you awkward questions.

Despite the European Championship fiasco, in 1976 Cruyff seemed to be accumulating more and more power. In Barcelona it was no different. In the summer he had managed to get rid of one coach (Weisweiler) and have another return (Michels). Once again, he had put his indispensability on the table and threatened to refuse to extend his contract. 'You might say that Barcelona wouldn't have taken me on if Cruyff hadn't been playing there,' Michels admitted in an interview. He allowed the captain to decide for himself whether and when he appeared in the front line – the essence of the conflict with Weisweiler. Michels preferred not to see his best player 'murdered' in away games, as he explained to journalists. 'The degree to which Johan can make improper use of his unique position depends on the coach.'

But it seemed as if the increasing intensity with which he moved his lips must be compensation for something else. He had already let slip once that after 1974 he was 'physically' not what he had been. As if he felt that his peak, now that he was approaching thirty, was already behind him. Because whether by chance or not, on 13 October it wasn't Cruyff who stole the show in De Kuip against Northern Ireland but the alcoholic George Best, even though he hadn't played a serious match for six months. Best dribbled as brilliantly as ever, while Cruyff, according to *de Volkskrant*, lacked the sharpness to play a dominant role. Cruyff did 'provoke' a disturbance (and also scored). The match, a World Cup qualifier, ended 2-2.

In the Spanish league competition Cruyff's discipline was declining as well. In the first half of the 1976-77 season, El Flaco was given four yellow cards within a short period, which meant he was suspended in late December. In January 1977 he added another card for criticising those in charge. Nevertheless, a few weeks later Barcelona were at the top of La Liga. Then a minor drama took place in Camp Nou. In a match full of irritation between Cruyff and referee Ricardo Melero Guaza, the latter made a conspicuous error. He allowed a goal by Málaga to stand even though spectators in the highest tier could see it was handball. Cruyff protested furiously and was given a white card. He spoke the historic words, 'Melero, *hijo de la gran puta*.'

At least, that's what the referee thought he said: son of a bitch. Or even worse: motherfucker. Cruyff was sent off. For a long time he insisted something else had happened, that he had said to a fellow player, 'Manolo, *marca ya*.' 'Manolo, cover your man.' That sounded less than credible and it was indeed nonsense. Thirteen years of denial later, Cruyff finally told the truth about his much-repeated statement. He had indeed said it, he confirmed in an interview, but he hadn't known 'precisely' what *hijo de la gran puta* meant. 'I'd picked it up in training ... Little did I know.'

In fact, as Cruyff indicated at an early stage, it was all about something far more important. Referee Melero came from Madrid and for Cruyff that was yet more evidence that 'this competition has been cleverly devised so that we lose.' Bunglers like Melero were involved in the 'disadvantaging of Barcelona'. By saying so, Cruyff was brandishing the Catalan flag more explicitly than ever before. It was as if he was seeking support from the people, now that his body was weakening, and his bond with the 70,000 *socios* and the millions of Barça fans would need to compensate. After the red card in Camp Nou, supporters ran on to the pitch. They menaced the referee, disturbances broke out, a TV van was set on fire and Cruyff became the martyr of Catalonia.

Just over a week later, his face was on the cover of sports magazine *Don Balón*, attached to the body of Jesus Christ on the cross, complete with a crown of thorns. The accompanying text included the word *Cruycifixión*. The magazine explained that the 'divine' and 'holy' footballer had been nailed to the cross by 'the terrorism of the centralist state'.

The cross for 'JC' was a suspension for three matches. It meant he would miss the tie against Atlético Madrid, which could surely be no coincidence. 'I ask for the help and support of the fans, who mean so much to me,' Cruyff said at a press conference. 'I'm not fighting just for myself but for all Catalans.' The crucified player believed there was a 'smear campaign' against him and that the disciplinary committee had acted 'shamefully' by punishing him. 'I'm a gentleman,' he said. 'On and off the pitch. It's definitely no accident that these referees come from Castile.'

In the three matches played without Cruyff, Barcelona gained just one point. It demonstrated how dependent on him the richest club in Spain – some said the richest in the whole of Europe – was. Barça lost its top position and in the 1976–77 season it once again missed out on the league title.

Barcelona was 'more than a club' and by now Cruyff was being seen as *més que un futbolista*. He was a symbol that hung above everything: the pitch, the club and the press. 'The greatest personality in Catalonia,' some newspapers called him, and he seemed able to mobilise a multitude whenever he chose. His popularity benefited his commercial activities, but he wanted more. In another year he would stop playing football and continue in life as a businessman. He was certain of that, no doubt influenced by his roots in the commercial classes. It was as if he had no choice but to go into business, but in which country? There were only two places where he wanted to live and work, Barcelona and Amsterdam. So he planted seeds in both.

In his native city he had a mentor in the person of Jack van Zanten, the real estate entrepreneur who had so badly wanted to be on the staff of the national team. Cruyff had known him for fifteen years. Van Zanten had been active in Jewish

Dribbling past Daniele Carnevali (before scoring) in the 1974 World Cup quarter-final against Argentina (4-0).

Queen Juliana of the Netherlands receives the Dutch national team at the palace Huis ten Bosch in the Hague after the 1974 FIFA World Cup in which the Netherlands were beaten in the final by West Germany, 2-1.
L-R are Johan, Queen Juliana and trainer Rinus Michels.

Sepp Maier of Bayern Munich and Johan sharing a joke before Johan's farewell match in November 1978.

Johan waves farewell to his Barcelona fans before his final game against former club Ajax in May 1978.

New York Cosmos star Pelé embraces Johan at a press conference announcing two exhibition games with Cosmos in March 1978.

Playing for Los Angeles Aztecs in 1979.

Johan at a photoshoot promoting Treets confectionery on a KLM aeroplane.

Professor Johan the lecturer on football and business at Erasmus University in Rotterdam in 1985.

As Ajax coach (1985-8), looking and shouting.

Sitting in his 'office', on a ball of course, not at a desk piled with boring papers.

Smoking away the stress of coaching Barcelona.

Celebrating after the European Cup final where Barcelona beat Sampdoria 1-0 at Wembley.

Relaxing with Ronald Koeman at the training ground near the Camp Nou.

Coach Cruyff with his pupil and future coach Pep Guardiola.

Like father, like son Jordi.

Perhaps his last time playing football while opening the Cruyff Academy in Groningen in September 2015.

Protegee and mentor: Johan and Dennis Bergkamp before the opening match of the Cruyff Foundation Cup in May 2013.

DE AJ STERKTE JOHAN! NR. 14 K

Support from Ajax fans when his lung cancer diagnosis was revealed in October 2015.

sporting circles since the early 1970s, and in December 1976 he and Cruyff had set up a trading partnership whose main aim was to enable Johan to learn the ropes in the real estate business. Their company bought four commercial properties in Leeuwarden and in June 1977 Cruyff presented himself there for the first time as an entrepreneur. 'I don't want them to say of me later, Cruyff couldn't do anything except play football,' he told journalists. A 'meaningful job' was what he was after, and therefore in this period he wanted to 'learn a lot, now that I can still combine the two'.

One big question remained: whom to trust? In his experience, businesspeople tried to cash in on his fame. 'In my football career I've been cheated and taken for a ride so often,' he said in an interview. 'Every year I have an average of fifty to sixty court cases on the go against people who one way or another have used my name in print in ways that are illegitimate.' His lawyer in Amsterdam, Jan Jonker, was continually working to protect his interests, and starting your own business was a good deal more complicated than protecting the rights to your name and image. What to do if your signature to just about any contract could be worth more than the average annual salary? It was a matter of making choices, of weighing up who was okay and who wasn't. That didn't seem to be his strongest suit. 'Cruyff was brilliant when it came to litigation, to thinking ahead in conflicts,' recalls tax specialist Harrie van Mens, who advised him on financial matters for years. 'But he was a good deal less good at judging character. In fact, Johan needed constant protection.'

His friend Marjolijn van der Meer-Carabén also says that evaluating people with whom he came into contact was 'his great weakness'. 'I often thought: what do you want with those people?' In that light it didn't seem any great advantage that Danny, in Van der Meer's view, continually acted as a 'filter' for Johan. 'If Johan got along well with people,' she says, 'then it was because Danny had approved them.'

Approval was putting it mildly in the case of Michel Georges Basilevitch. Danny was absolutely captivated by the smooth, 1.9-metre-tall Frenchman with Belarussian roots. Basilevitch, several years older than Johan, had wavy black hair and has been described as an 'eerily beautiful chap with flashing teeth'. Danny had found him utterly fascinating ever since their first meeting in 1976. Basilevitch's daughter went to the same private school in Barcelona as Chantal and Susila, and after a while she was invited to birthday parties at the Cruyff home. Michel came with his daughter and his charms won Danny over.

He turned out to have a lot of things Johan lacked. The Frenchman held doors open for Danny and in no time he knew her children's birthdays off by heart. (Johan was capable of forgetting even Danny's birthday.) He smiled engagingly at her and, just as importantly, he knew a lot about fashion. Michel had been a male model at the Parisian fashion house Pierre Cardin. He wore stylish suits and was a good listener; he was chivalrous and occasionally brought flowers with him for Danny, who responded with delight, because she wasn't used to that.

His international connections made him even more exciting. Michel seemed to know the entire jet set. He claimed to have travelled with Mick Jagger on tours by the Rolling Stones. He was acquainted with prominent businesspeople and bankers. He thought big. He took Johan and Danny for trips on his yacht and might unexpectedly treat Danny to a beautiful coat. It was almost impossible to drag the Cruyffs away from Basilevitch. 'You could see that there was more between Danny and Basilevitch than just friendship,' Jan de Deugd, a journalist at *De Telegraaf*, remembers. 'She was clearly in love. She called him the most beautiful man in Barcelona.'

The friendship between Johan and Michel was becoming more intimate too. After the Spanish league season ended, the Cruyff, Basilevitch and Coster couples flew to Brazil. Bobby and Tootje Nees, the faithful friends who had stayed in the house in Vinkeveen five years before, joined them. In early

June, Cruyff was due to appear in demonstration matches in aid of UNICEF. Coster had managed to agree a fee of 300,000 guilders for those appearances, but when on the day of the first match in São Paulo the money still hadn't come in, Cruyff refused to play – on the advice of Coster – until the finances were settled. By pulling out all the stops, the organisation made the payment just in time.

The four couples had a great time in Brazil, although it struck Bobby Nees that Johan and that strange Michel spent a lot of the time talking. He later wondered if that might have been a portent.

After the trip the relationship became so close that the two couples took part in a seance. Johan, Danny, Michel and Sylvie sat around a table and, during the spiritualist tête-à-tête, which was guided by Sylvie Basilevitch, Johan saw his dead father. 'That made a huge impression on Johan,' Nees remembers. Cruyff told him all about it. 'From that moment on he had even more faith in Michel.'

In the summer of 1977, Johan and Basilevitch developed a closer business relationship. The business itself was rather shady. Around 700,000 guilders' worth of pesetas needed to be smuggled out of the country. It may have been black money earned by Cruyff. There was an opportunity to move the cash to France using the transfer of former Ajax player Johnny Rep from Valencia to Bastia on Corsica as cover, because of the fact that Cruyff's 'business manager' Basilevitch had French nationality. 'But I didn't trust that man as far as I could throw him,' journalist Theun de Winter recalls. As a friend of Rep, he saw what was happening. 'Basilevitch had a look that was impossible to read. Very odd. And he was always boasting about being such good friends with Cruyff.'

From the French island the money could fairly easily be deposited in a Swiss account, a move that, according to tax specialist Van Mens, Johan and Uncle Cor soothingly called 'the stroke'. Cruyff and Coster had a profound aversion to paying tax and in that respect alone Spain, and especially Barcelona, was a good place to be.

After the successful transaction, Cruyff allowed Basilevitch to negotiate his new annual contract with FC Barcelona. That had previously been Coster's job, but Coster had distanced himself a little since 1976, when he'd refused to tell Johan what Neeskens was going to be earning. Coster confined himself mainly to arranging advertising deals for Cruyff. Moreover, Johan sometimes wanted to do things without the influence of his dominant father-in-law, who didn't speak a word of a foreign language and focused on ruthless negotiation. Some friends even saw a delayed puberty in the choice of Basilevitch, as if Johan wanted to demonstrate his independence from father figure Coster.

However that may be, the negotiations went just as well with the clever and multilingual Basilevitch, if not better. The Frenchman, a Barça *socio* who was on good terms with a number of members of the board, managed to arrange an excellent contract. Johan's next – and last – season with FC Barcelona would be more lucrative than in the previous years. Cruyff's confidence in Basilevitch continued to grow.

Basilevitch drove around in a Rolls-Royce. His boutique, his international trade in fabrics and his other businesses must be very successful, Johan and Danny decided. They felt increasingly enthusiastic about the idea of making investments with him. It was hardly a surprising decision. They had ventured into footwear and opened their shop Shoetique, and they had come close to going into the clothing business with French fashion designers Jean Cacharel and Daniel Hechter. Now here was world citizen Michel Basilevitch, full of good ideas. At Danny's urging, Johan was now going to go into business on his own behalf, instead of being the 'face' of something – the reason he had decided not to pursue a career in PR. The greatest personality in Catalonia wanted to cash in on his bond with the public in a way that was truly compelling. 'I think Johan liked the challenge of conquering the world in a new way,' is how his friend Van der Meer sums up his ambitions in retrospect. She had her own thoughts on the subject. As far as Marjolijn was concerned, the ever optimistic and helpful Johan was throwing himself 'into the arms of a gold digger'.

'I was climbing higher and higher,' Cruyff said years later. 'It's so intoxicating that you're blinded to things.' He made the most inexplicable move he would ever make. He gave Basilevitch authorisation to engage in financial transactions on his behalf. The 30-year-old footballer, who for at least twelve years had been famously distrustful, who always feared other people would peddle his reputation, put a series of signatures to documents guaranteeing that he personally would underwrite any debts. Those signatures related to a holding company called Grupeco that he and Basilevitch had jointly taken over. It owned several firms: a business that undertook international transactions (some say to channel black money to Switzerland); a nursery for horticulturalists in Saudi Arabia; a real estate company on Ibiza; an exporter of wine and perfume with Johan's face on it; and a company that would film advertisements featuring Cruyff.

Each of the subsidiary companies was given an attractive name (Import-Export Company, Horticulturas Mediterráneas, Nummer 14, Imago Films), but the little that Coster in the Netherlands got to hear of it did not make him at all happy. Cruyff's business mentor Jack van Zanten distanced himself from the project too. If journalists asked, they would be told, 'Johan runs his company without my help.' And, 'That's none of my business.'

The most important of Grupeco's companies was called Ganadera Catalana, which operated a number of pig-breeding farms. One of them alone, in Artesa de Segre, 140 kilometres west of Barcelona, swallowed up almost 1.5 million guilders. It was a lot of money to pay for a business that was almost bankrupt, but if everything went well it would earn them the most. They were now the proud owners of 1,400 sows and 24,000 piglets, and they would produce many more, Michel told his business partner. The pigsties would have to be completely rebuilt, which meant a huge extra investment, but Basilevitch would take care of that, with Cruyff's signatures. Meanwhile, after the summer of 1977, Cruyff would throw himself into FC Barcelona and Oranje again (having agreed with the KNVB that he would play in the qualifying matches for the 1978 World Cup).

It all looked very promising. At least, if you were prepared to believe that someone without any professional expertise to speak of could take on sectors as diverse as plant nurseries, piggeries, wine, perfumes and international finance.

'We're going to buy a private jet,' Cruyff told his friend Bobby Nees.

'You're crazy,' said Bobby, who like Johan had grown up among stallholders and small shopkeepers.

'No, really,' said Cruyff. 'We're thinking big.'

Bobby thought: he's getting swept along. Johan has lost his way.

The bizarre thing is that precisely when Cruyff was starting to imagine great riches, something happened that all wealthy businessmen feared. You only had to turn on the radio or television to hear about kidnappings of rich industrialists in Germany and Italy, and indeed in Spain and Ireland. Whether the kidnappers had political motives or were only after a ransom, in many cases the results were fatal, or traumatic at the very least. Cruyff knew he needed to be on his guard. Back during the 1974 World Cup he'd been given extra security, and in Barcelona a lot of anonymous phone calls and letters had come in with threats against him or his wife and children. Everyone knew he was earning millions.

Yet it wasn't particularly odd that on the evening of Monday 19 September 1977, when the doorbell rang, Danny went to the door of the flat without any misgivings. Or that Johan calmly carried on watching television. On the third floor of their apartment building on the Calle de los Caballeros they felt safe. They were invisible from the street and on the ground floor was a concierge who could stop shady characters.

Right. Could.

CHAPTER TWENTY-TWO

Johan would go into business in a big way

Carlos González was forty-six years old and at his wits' end. In 1977 he spent months travelling through Spain alone in a Volkswagen camper van, with a bag of weed on the passenger seat and a mattress and camping gear in the back. His marriage to a Rotterdam woman was over. He was unemployed. González had a total of six children, four by his ex-wife and two by another woman. For years he had driven back and forth between his home in Rotterdam and Seixo, in the Spanish region of Galicia, and now he was driving around aimlessly in Catalonia. He was a mere shadow of the athletic, handsome young man he had once been.

He didn't belong in this van; he was a man of the sea. He had sailed with the Holland–America Line and could spend ages staring out along the rugged Atlantic coast at Seixo. He was also a football fan and for one reason or another he detested Cruyff. 'That guttersnipe,' he'd said to a couple of friends in early September. 'He's the best player in the world and we're getting nowhere.'

He may have been referring to an injury that had plagued Cruyff for some time. In the summer the Barcelona captain had suffered serious damage to his calf during a practice match in Hamburg. His recovery from surgery was slow and he had missed the early league matches. On Sunday 18 September 1977 he was due to be part of the team again, but had stayed home with the flu. Without him, Barcelona had scored only once in three matches. Since then, Cruyff had played in the UEFA Cup and led FC Barcelona to a 5-1 victory over Steaua Bucharest.

Without the 'guttersnipe' Barcelona couldn't win La Liga; that much will have got through to González's weed-fogged brain. Cruyff had let him down and now this Rotterdam Spaniard was going to teach him a lesson. Because El Flaco was God. What was more, El Flaco had money and he didn't. González had copies of the Spanish sports magazine *Don Balón* with him in his Volkswagen, and according to the magazine Cruyff owed the taxman 3 million guilders. There was a possibility that El Flaco kept a lot of cash at home.

On the evening of Monday 19 September, González parked his van a hundred metres from the Calle de los Caballeros, the sloping avenue in a fashionable suburb of Barcelona, not far from Camp Nou. It was nine o'clock in the evening.

Taking a shotgun with a sawn-off barrel and a penknife, he walked to the apartment building and rang the bell.

The concierge asked what he wanted. González convinced the man that he had come with a package that he needed to deliver to Cruyff in person. He made clear that he spoke Dutch, which reinforced the impression that he was a friend of the family. He was allowed in and took the lift to the third floor.

A blonde woman opened the door. He knew her to be Danny. He also knew that Rinus Michels had a permanent room in Hotel Princesa Sofia, so he was able to come up with a reasonably plausible story about a personal message from the coach. Danny let him in. He immediately pulled out his gun and forced her into the living room, where Cruyff was watching television. Danny, who was naturally terrified, was ordered to lie on the floor. She did so. Johan had to go and stand against the wall. González tied his feet to the sofa.

The Cruyffs later said little about the bizarre events of that Monday evening. González was no doubt thoroughly confused and intending to demand cash that would enable him to get on top of his personal crisis. In any case, he didn't shout at his victims. He was really quite calm. That gave Cruyff courage. He noticed the intruder had a Rotterdam accent, and he did not get the impression he was dealing with an experienced criminal.

'I have rather sensitive feet,' the sportsman said, truthfully enough. 'I had surgery recently. Couldn't you loosen the rope a bit?'

He could. González fiddled with the rope a little and at that moment 6-year-old Chantal came out of her bedroom. The noise had woken her. The intruder panicked when he saw the little girl. Danny, who was not blindfolded, noticed that and took the opportunity to race to the door and shout down the stairs for help. González ran off in confusion, leaving his gun and penknife behind. At the entrance to the apartment building he was overpowered by the concierge and several residents who had been alerted by the shouting.

The police came and took the attacker away in handcuffs.

Friends of Carlos González were astounded that he was capable of such a thing. 'I was under the influence,' he explained later. He was sentenced to seven years in prison for the attack and for the illegal possession of a firearm. He served only a small part of the sentence, since he had no previous convictions.

Cruyff decided it would be sensible to have a permanent security detail. For years he had ignored advice from FC Barcelona on the matter. He simply didn't like that kind of hoo-ha; he'd always tried to live as normal a life as possible. But now he felt that having security men around him had become unavoidable. Furthermore, Danny and the children were still in a state of shock. For the time being nobody went out of the door without a security guard at their side. Partly because of these changed circumstances, Cruyff began to look forward to the end of his career. Another eight months and he would be done with playing football. 'It's enough now,' he said to the press. 'How long have I been at it? This life eats away at you. I sometimes find myself longing for a rest, so I won't be continuing at this level for another year.'

Fortunately, he didn't need to wear the Oranje shirt for much longer. In October 1977 he played his last internationals, in Belfast (1-0 victory over Northern Ireland) and Amsterdam (1-0 victory over Belgium). Because of those wins, Oranje were certain of a place in the World Cup in 1978. Cruyff kept saying that he would not be going to Argentina, so everyone knew that the match against Belgium on 26 October was his last. Yet there was no ceremony in the Olympic Stadium, probably because people secretly hoped he might yet change his mind. Without the captain, or so the public felt, Oranje would be only half as good. That was indeed the way it looked. In February that year Cruyff had set the pace in a much-celebrated friendly against England (2-0 victory at Wembley) and now, against Belgium, even at half his normal strength he was still the 'director', according to the press, 'the master at giving shape and content to the attacking game'. His insight and class were indispensable.

A campaign started up that looked very much like media-agenic desperation. Almost 40,000 people signed a petition entitled 'Pull Cruyff over the line' and famous performers sang songs in their efforts to convince him. But his decision was made. 'I'm not going to explain it,' he told a camera crew in front of his flat in Barcelona, standing beside his car and several postal sacks full of entreaties. 'Because then there will be debates about debates. I really don't want that. I've made my decision and I'm sticking to it.'

The debate would go on as long as he lived. Many football fans, in the Netherlands especially, failed to understand why an ambitious and apparently fit sportsman would sit out the most important tournament on earth. The questions continued to come and Cruyff himself contributed by, as was his habit, coming up with different arguments at different times. The fact is that even during the 1974 World Cup he had announced he didn't want to take part in a final round like that again. 'This is my first and last World Cup tournament,' he said into a Dutch radio microphone. 'In four years from now I'll be thirty-one. That's when I'll stop playing. The outside world doesn't realise how hard life as a professional footballer can be.' In May 1978 he would have fifteen years of professional football to his name, which he regarded as 'more than enough'. There would finally be 'more time to spend with your family'. After all, 'My children are reaching an age when they're becoming aware that their father is always away. I don't want to do that to them. I can't have them asking for me more and more.'

It was perhaps no accident that he spoke those words the day after the notorious swimming pool incident. Knowing that the storm might erupt at any moment, he may have been trying to soothe Danny's fury. Johan's family and friends have frequently made a link between his refusal to go to the World Cup and his wife. The couple denied the connection right from the start, but then, it would be difficult to admit such a thing. It would give Danny, already far from popular, an even worse name in the sporting world. She had never made a secret of the fact that she suffered terribly when Johan was away for weeks at a time. For years she'd been hoping he would soon end his active career. Danny hated the football world and her husband was sensitive to that. 'My wife doesn't interfere at all in this kind of thing,' Cruyff would say in his defence. But Jan de Deugd, reporter at *De Telegraaf* at the time and ghost writer of Cruyff's columns, who often visited the couple, says, 'Imagine Johan had had a wife who said, "You go ahead, Johan. Enjoy yourself. I'll manage just fine for a few weeks." It would have been a very different story, I'm convinced of that.'

Twenty years later, national coach Jan Zwartkruis said on television, 'I'm free to say it now. Cruyff had to promise his wife Danny that he would never be away from home again for so long and would never make himself available for such big tournaments. I respected that, and he helped me by giving his all in the qualifying rounds.' That reading is confirmed by Charly Rexach, Cruyff's teammate at Barça. In his biography *Ara parlo jo*, published in April 2008, Rexach claims it was purely because of Danny that Johan didn't go to the World Cup in 1978. He calls it a 'shame' that a 'strong personality' like Cruyff, with whom he had been close for a long time, let himself be 'hedged in' like that by Danny (and her father).

Rexach's claim received a great deal of attention in the media and it seems Cruyff felt that then, thirty years after the World Cup in question, he needed to put an end to the mystery surrounding his absence in Argentina. 'Charly should know that towards the end of my time as a player here I had enough problems,' he said on Catalan radio. He then introduced a new element, saying that the attack by Carlos González in 1977 and the tight security for his children on their way to school changed his outlook on life radically. 'We wanted to end that and be a bit more sensible. It was the right time to leave football and after what happened I couldn't play in the World Cup.'

In light of what he had said before on the matter, it was hard not to see this as a gesture to his wife, as a way of protecting Danny from the fingers that continued to point in her direction.

In the background to the suspected main reason, the 'Danny' factor, were his diminishing powers. To Joan Patsy, a television reporter and his confidential adviser in Barcelona, he admitted after the 1977 internationals that he did not feel at his best. On no account did he want to enter into decline on the world stage. The targets of his occasionally merciless comments might be able to get back at him. 'I don't want to give those people a time when I start playing less well,' he said. He would then be 'slaughtered, in all kinds of ways'. It didn't bear thinking about. 'It's impossible to imagine a more stressful situation.' Years later he added, 'I knew I would lack sharpness if I carried on. I could only have failed. You know that about yourself.'

Perhaps fear of failure did have a role to play. He called his refusal 'a complex of a whole bunch of factors'. Sometimes he suddenly seemed to have doubts, as if he was struggling with his decision. Or because he needed a bit of extra obfuscation to protect Danny. Or simply because even off the pitch he was always a player first of all, a manipulator who enjoyed wrong-footing people. 'Perhaps I'd feel differently about it if the final round was nearby,' he said in March 1977, for example. 'Somewhere in Europe. But for Argentina you need too much time to prepare. You'll have to be travelling or in training camps for around six weeks. That's an insurmountable obstacle for me.' So first he'd be slaughtered in the final tournament, and on further reflection he would perhaps have liked to take part after all if it hadn't taken up so much time. It looked like a feint.

Despite all the arguments and petitions, Cruyff said 'no' to Oranje and could therefore concentrate fully on Barcelona. He still had to get through the 1977-78 season, his last. It didn't go too badly at all. In between collecting yellow cards, and interruptions because of treatment for injuries, Cruyff led his team in the autumn and winter to numerous victories in La Liga. In Europe, Ipswich Town and Aston Villa were knocked out and sometimes he shone like the old Cruyff. In November he had proved himself a true captain by taking the last penalty of a series against AZ Alkmaar (both legs had ended 1-1). He rarely took penalties, but this one went in, and helped to get Barcelona through to the semi-finals of the UEFA Cup.

Shortly after that he suffered a broken rib as the result of an elbow punch. Partly because of that he started to resent tough opponents again and referees who didn't give him enough support in away games. It was all too much. 'Forty million people live in Spain,' he said. 'They can all afford to spend a week's salary on football. That means they own you, and a point comes when you've had it up to here, with the huge media interest for one thing. Then you need to stop.' Young opponents who thought they could be rude to him were set right. Such as Jorge

Valdano, the Argentine forward with Deportivo Alavés, a club in the Spanish second division that got through to a cup match against Barcelona in February 1978. Alavés were awarded a free kick, but Cruyff held on to the ball for a moment. Valdano said, 'Johan, why don't you keep that ball and give us another one so we can play without you.'

'How old are you?' Cruyff asked.

'Twenty-two,' answered Valdano.

'Then you use the polite form of address when you speak to Johan Cruyff.'

Valdano went on to become a coach and a writer. Decades later, in a column, he wrote that in his entire career he had 'never seen a player steer a match with such authority' as Johan. 'He even talked while he was dribbling and asked for the ball as if it belonged to him.' 'Moreover,' wrote the Argentine (who won the World Cup in 1986 along with Diego Maradona), 'he was even in control of the referees, continually making them feel the power of his talent by talking to them in between everything he did as if they were his employees.'

That talkative attitude ultimately proved fatal to him, and thus to all of FC Barcelona. On 1 April 1978 he allowed himself to be provoked during the Barcelona derby against Espanyol and was given a yellow card, not for the first time in his career, for talking back to the referee. It was his third yellow card in a short period, which meant he was suspended for the next match, an away game against Real Madrid that was crucial for the league title. Was he deliberately riled to help league leaders Real? First that tough play by Espanyol and then a referee who allowed everything before punishing him for protesting: Cruyff believed it was done on purpose. 'I was expecting that card,' he told the Catalan press. 'I wanted to say goodbye this year with a couple of titles for Barcelona, but you can see that someone's trying to prevent that.'

Without Cruyff, Barcelona lost 4–0 to Real Madrid. The championship disappeared from sight and, partly because of lost matches against lesser clubs, it remained out of reach. The captain was not in the best of shape. The recovery period after his calf injury in the summer of 1977 is thought to have been too short. A series of new injuries and strains resulted, so that he barely managed any serious training and, according to Michels, played 'far below his ability'. 'When he has space it goes okay. But if he has to get free of a man who is determinedly marking him, he no longer has that zip.'

That was obvious again in the semi-finals of the UEFA Cup against PSV Eindhoven. The young midfielder Jan Poortvliet pinned him down in the away game. PSV won 3-0 – to the delight of Jan van Beveren and Willy van der Kuijlen, who had been forced out of Oranje in 1975 by Cruyff. The return match in Camp Nou came two weeks later. Cruyff, tormented by the criticism and by the whistling of the crowd in Eindhoven, played 'brilliantly' this time, according to the press. Although he did avail himself of 'un-Dutch' methods, twice deliberately falling in the PSV penalty area (in front of Poortvliet), which won his team two goals from penalties. But after ninety minutes the score was 3-1 and Barcelona were out.

So Cruyff's last season with Barcelona ended in an anticlimax. Again, no La Liga title and no European Cup, and three of the four matches against the great rivals Atlético and Real had been lost. Winning the final of the national knockout tournament, the Copa del Rey, in April was fun, but no more than that. He regarded his five Catalan seasons as the best years of his life, he said, but he will mainly have been referring to the living environment. Actually, only his first year in Barcelona was truly successful. All the same, Cruyff had so often delighted the people in Camp Nou with his brilliant moves, and he so appealed to everyone's imagination, that all the fans hoped he might stay.

Few hoped that Michels would stay. The board and the *socios* would be happy to see him go. Michels was fairly incensed by that. The coach deserved more appreciation for his work, wrote his biographer Bas Barkman in 2011. It stung him that the league title in 1974 was always attributed to his captain. 'They're eternally grateful to Cruyff there,' he said. 'But my role has always been secondary. He became a hero. I didn't.'

Shortly before leaving, Cruyff struck a rather odd final chord. In early May there was a vote for the presidency of FC Barcelona and, to everyone's surprise, Cruyff turned out to have a clear preference, despite his imminent departure. He advised the members to elect Josep Lluís Núñez. That was remarkable in itself, because Núñez hardly seemed his type. He was an uncompromising building contractor who, his critics said, had defaced the beautiful city on the Mediterranean with high-rise apartment and office complexes, right up to the threshold of Gaudí's enchanting Basílica de la Sagrada Família. Núñez was known as a successful property developer, but also as an opportunist whose only notable aspiration was to make Barça bigger and more modern.

Yet Cruyff wanted the small, crafty builder to become the new club president and not his rival Ferran Ariño i Barberà, a progressive figure who was supported by the Catalan nationalist party. Ariño was aiming to democratise the club further and give the *socios* more influence, but he had also occasionally turned against the 'Dutch mafia', saying they had cost FC Barcelona too much money. Moreover, the socialist pharmaceuticals entrepreneur had openly denounced El Flaco's habit of smoking in the changing room. Cruyff's business partner Basilevitch would later say that a secret agreement had been made back in February. Cruyff would support the fabulously rich property developer in the election and in return he would be able to buy an office on the prestigious Passeig de Gracia for half the more than 500,000 guilders it was worth. Núñez announced during his 'Let's open Barça' campaign that he would do all he could to keep the popular-as-ever Dutchman at the club. With that and other promises, Núñez won the club election on 6 May.

One of the first things the new president did was to offer Cruyff the improbably large sum of 3 million guilders net, excluding bonuses, if he was prepared to play in the *blaugrana* for another year. After all, Núñez had promised as much to the voters, possibly knowing Cruyff would turn down the spectacularly generous offer. Which El Flaco did. Shortly after the club election, he and Basilevitch moved into the office they had bought from Núñez for a song – all the result of the 'agreement' with Núñez, as Basilevitch would later call it.

(Under Núñez's leadership FC Barcelona did in fact grow bigger than ever and meet with enormous success. Decades later, after his resignation, Núñez was prosecuted and convicted for bribery and corruption. But by then Cruyff had long become one of the man's many enemies.)

In June 1978 the World Cup took place and of course Cruyff followed it closely – but not in Argentina. He was in London, analysing the matches as a guest of commercial broadcaster ITV. He did the job with great dedication. After criticising Dutch play in the early matches (the team was 'not a unity' and seemed to be playing several systems at once) he engaged with the final as a patriot. Wearing an open-necked white shirt, he was on edge as he watched. It was a tough, exciting match and against hosts Argentina, too. The game was less fluid than in 1974, but Cruyff praised the tactical approach of Oranje coach Ernst Happel. When it was over, Oranje having lost 3-1 after extra time, he was speechless for minutes. 'This is a terrible disappointment for me,' he said. 'All through the second half the Netherlands were simply the far better team. Argentina were nowhere at all. And then in the last minute Rensenbrink missed that chance. It just didn't go their way. Why did the ball have to hit the post at that particular moment?'

In London he sometimes looked wistfully at the screen, as if he'd have preferred to be on the pitch amid the Oranje players. All the same, he said, 'I knew I wouldn't be able to focus the

full hundred per cent of my mind on it. That's why I didn't go.'
It was a reason he hadn't put forward before and so the list of
anti–World Cup arguments grew a little longer.

The argument was valid in so far as Cruyff did indeed have a
lot on his mind. He had after all become an entrepreneur. But
it didn't seem to be bringing him much success. In September
1978 the Spanish weekly *Interviú* carried a story that said he was
sailing in dubious waters. He was rumoured to have huge tax
debts and his business partner Basilevitch had been described
as a conman, a charlatan who was turning Cruyff's fortune to
dust. The affair became big news in Spain. The Dutchman felt
forced to react and on 29 September he gave a press conference
in Madrid. He called all the allegations absurd. He had not lent
out hundreds of millions of pesetas. There was a fiscal problem, he admitted, but that was because of the new policy. Since
Franco's death, football clubs had no longer been able to pay tax
on behalf of their players. The players now had to arrange their
tax affairs for themselves, and he had been negligent in doing so.
As far as his business was concerned, he would continue to make
large investments in Spain, 'because I have a moral obligation
with respect to this country'.

Basilevitch was sitting at the back of the room. He looked
imperturbable. 'I trust him completely,' said Cruyff. 'He is
my friend and confidant.' The former footballer explained the
investments he had already made and said all his businesses were
healthy. Developments in the fields of pigs, wine, real estate,
plant nurseries, perfume and advertising were extremely promising. He and his partner were also about to become world leaders
in *pata negra* (superior cured ham), having started a special project
in the region of Extremadura, in south-western Spain. He knew
nothing of currency smuggling. 'If I didn't have a clean slate I'd
have left Spain a long time ago,' he said, laughing.

'Cruyff has demonstrated that his sharpness and cleverness are
not confined to the sports field,' concluded *El Mundo Deportivo*.
'But many are not completely convinced by his arguments. This

game is going to last a long time yet.' Revelations did indeed keep coming. In business circles in Catalonia his empire was described as a house of cards that would collapse sooner or later. The Grupeco holding company was a 'bloated entity', they believed. It was asking for trouble to base an enterprise on the money of a former footballer and the vision of a former male model. Moreover, there was talk that Basilevitch had been on Interpol's radar for some time. The 'business friend of Cruyff who lives like a marquis' was said to have amassed huge debts with luxury hotels and famous restaurants. As for the Rolls-Royce and the yacht in which he had taken Johan and Danny for jaunts – they weren't even his property, it was claimed.

Cruyff took little notice of the rumours. He even dismissed warnings from his father-in-law Cor Coster. He continued to stand by his friend Michel, the man Danny, his filter, loved 'as if he was my oldest brother', as she said six months later. Basilevitch, the 'most beautiful man in Barcelona', the charmer with his wavy black hair, was always 'so sweet' to the children, and 'so concerned' when she was ill. Danny simply could not imagine that such a person might cheat them. And therefore neither could Johan. The relationship between them had always been clear, he told *Het Parool*. 'I put my money at his disposal and in return I got a share in all kinds of companies that Michel found interesting. He was the adviser and the executive within the holding, and I relied on his information. Basilevitch arranged everything for me because I was never there. That's why I had to give him the right to sign documents on my behalf, for instance.'

Fortunately, Michel 'always has good ideas', so everything would be fine. He repressed any doubts, because, as he said at the time, 'Once I've made a decision I don't go back on it. Not ever, even if it turns out later that it may not have been particularly wise. That's because if I realise I'm wrong, I'm not a person who finds it easy to admit as much. That's just the way I am.'

In October 1978 he did, however, come to the conclusion

that he ought to learn more about the sector in which he had invested so much money. So he travelled to Barneveld, a Dutch village that was home to an international training centre for pig and chicken farmers. The ex-footballer arrived with several people, including the new chairman of Ajax, Ton Harmsen. After the summer Cruyff had systematically eased down his training programme at Ajax and Harmsen was more than willing to give him a helping hand with his business. The group was given a guided tour, and only now did it become clear to the footballing entrepreneur just how much expertise it took to run something as complicated and extensive in scope as a pig-breeding facility successfully. Especially when, as he was, you were planning to produce your own feed. He turned out to have seriously underestimated the whole thing.

Practically at the same time as he made this visit, Cruyff transferred a million dollars (more than 2 million guilders) to an account at the Banco Español de Crédito in Barcelona, with his own signature. The payment went to a company called Ganadera Catalana: the pig-breeding enterprise. 'Monsieur M. Basilevitch' had the right to draw the money out. It came from the Union de Banques Suisses in Bern. A Spanish football magazine published a copy of the bank transfer and naturally Cruyff was not happy about that.

Amid all his business worries he still had to take his leave as a professional footballer. On 27 May 1978 he had said goodbye to Barcelona in a friendly match against Ajax (chairman Jaap van Praag embraced him with tears in his eyes). Now it was time for a farewell in Amsterdam. This time not against but with Ajax. The main organiser was Cruyff's partner in real estate, Jack van Zanten. Football fan Van Zanten had already made his name as a match organiser with the Amsterdam 700 tournaments and again he was thinking big. The 'match of honour' would be shown live on television not just in the Netherlands but in other countries too, as far away as North Africa. Sponsors were found, and the match in the Olympic Stadium would be followed by a glamorous 'night party'. All the takings would go to a good cause. The slogan 'Thanks Johan' prompted huge ticket sales and the publicity was excellent. Everyone seemed to love Johan, the brilliant footballer who had brought the Netherlands success but had also helped to modernise the professional game. 'Cruyff created the fringe benefits in the world of football, so archaic until recently, from which generations after him will benefit,' wrote *NRC Handelsblad*. Despite all that, another newspaper remarked, Johan had remained a man 'free of pretentiousness'.

That was the tone and so everything went like clockwork as the great day approached. Except that, unfortunately, attempts to find a British opponent for Ajax failed. With the Brits you could make a positive evening out of it, full of respect and humour, was the prevailing opinion. The central character would get the attention he deserved. In the end the choice fell on Bayern Munich. Bayern had won the European Cup three times after Ajax (1973-76), making them an appealing opponent. But the team adopted such a fanatical attitude that many would never forget the match on 7 November 1978.

Before it began, all seemed well. As soon as Cruyff walked on to the pitch in an Ajax shirt with the four major prizes he had won pictured on the front (three European Cups and the Intercontinental Cup), a cheer rose up from the crowd in the stadium. He smiled shyly and munched on his chewing gum. At the centre spot he was spoken to by KNVB chairman Wim Meuleman and by Ajax chairman Ton Harmsen. Meuleman announced that Cruyff had been made a *bondsridder*, a knight of the KNVB. Harmsen, with whom Johan had recently visited Barneveld, said into the microphone, 'You're starting a new life as an entrepreneur. I'm convinced that with your personal attributes and your determination you'll succeed.' The central character beamed.

Cor Coster, one of the organisers of the evening, wasn't beaming. He stood in the centre circle amid the powerful men of football, his stout body wrapped in a winter trench coat, staring fixedly ahead. He had warned his son-in-law about Basilevitch and he clearly saw no reason to look happy when Johan's entrepreneurship was mentioned.

Harmsen talked about the office Cruyff would soon be using. After consultation with Danny the decision had been made to give him a colour television set for that room as a gift. There was laughter from the stands; colour television was fairly common by 1978. But the recipient was clearly touched. He looked moved and embraced Harmsen.

Enough talk, time for football. The 60,000 spectators sat down expectantly. Danny, the children and other family members in the VIP box did the same, as did the dignitaries and former teammates who had flown in from distant countries. Bayern goalkeeper Sepp Maier put a Bavarian hat on Cruyff as a joke – that was what you did on occasions like this. It was of course a shame that Gerd Müller made it 0-1 after one minute. Mistake in the Ajax defence. Can happen. Cruyff delivered a few beautiful curving balls and clearly wanted to make the game go with a swing.

But the swing soon died away. The only player left from the Golden Ajax was Ruud Krol and the others (Simon Tahamata, Soren Lerby, Tscheu La Ling) clearly didn't know what to do with their guest player. As ever, Cruyff dropped back, or moved out to the left wing, but nobody dashed to fill the gaps. The game made no sense.

What made it worse was that the Ajax fans started to needle the Germans. Before the match started they had shouted 'Nazis!' and as the game went on there were cheers when opposition players made a mistake or were brought to the ground. It started to irritate Bayern. For the past twenty-four hours the players had felt poorly treated by Ajax. Nobody had come to meet them at Schiphol airport and the hotel turned out to be substandard. Now they were being treated as 'Germans' in the stadium, so they started to behave more like 'Germans' with every passing minute. From then on they ruined the show with classic results-focused football. They covered the gaps and after a while even brought down the party boy with their fouls. So much for 'Thanks Johan'. Bayern withdrew to behind the halfway line and from there mounted razor-sharp counterattacks, especially via Karl-Heinz Rummenigge. The young forward scored three goals. Gerd Müller and Paul Breitner – who had been hung out to dry here in 1973 with a 4-0 defeat – also scored and by the end the board showed an astonishing result: 0-8.

It was one of those evenings when you almost felt sorry for Johan Cruyff, which didn't happen often. He usually managed to prevent it by quarrelling when in adversity or seeking controversy in some other way – as if he didn't want you to like him but to find him either brilliant or irritating. Yet now, in the role of guest of honour, despite the humiliation, he continued to behave in a sportsmanlike manner. At any moment he might make a bewildering turn away from an opponent or a dummy move, or volley the ball towards the goal. He produced those divine kicks with the outside of his right foot, sometimes even the outside of his left, a sign that after his glory years he had continued to work on his technique to expand his range. A refined curving shot with the outside of his weaker foot: a romantic candle on a dark, cold evening.

Of course, in this stadium where he had started sixteen years before as a ball boy, he also saw openings no one else spotted, and all with that natural suppleness of his, as if he made round things that others left right-angled. In the end he had been, in the words of TV commentator Herman Kuiphof, the equal of Pelé and Di Stéfano. Sometimes he still was. He played at a lonely height and that's how he must have felt, lonely. Let down. By his sluggish fellow players; by his humourless opponents; by the far too serious referee who didn't even give him a penalty for the fun of it, as quite often happened in farewell matches.

In that unpleasant state of affairs he kept going for a long time. Until in the second half he too was running on empty and he adjusted to the wretched game Ajax were playing. At one point he even kicked at a German player who had taken the ball off him. Out of petulance people started encouraging Bayern and threw cushions on to the pitch.

Five minutes before the final whistle, the game was interrupted. Time to say goodbye. A feeble 'Jo-han, Jo-han' went around the stands. An attempt to carry him off the pitch shoulder-high failed. Cruyff did not do a lap of honour, even after the match ended. With a bunch of flowers – which he left in the changing room – he disappeared into the bowels of the Olympic Stadium. 'I know him well enough to be sure that at that moment he was boiling inside with anger and disappointment,' wrote his confidant Cees van Nieuwenhuizen the following day in *Het Parool*. But Cruyff gave nothing away. The brooder and optimist preferred to think about the great atmosphere of the days before the match and the successful ticket sales, which had brought in 400,000 guilders for causes including the Emma Children's Hospital and the Handicapped Sports Foundation. 'I don't regret playing this match,' he said to the press afterwards. 'The publicity it brought me over the past few weeks has given me far more pleasure than the match. I'll think about it for a few days and then forget it. It's now definitely all over.'

People in the neighbourhood of his bungalow in Vinkeveen, where he had been living temporarily with his family, had to get used to the idea too. 'Hey, Johan, you've got to be kidding,' one neighbour called out to him from a distance while he was talking to a reporter. 'You can't stop yet!'

'If he knew all the things I've had to do for it,' Cruyff said to the reporter, 'then he'd have shouted that I'm absolutely right.'

Along with Danny he flew back to Barcelona. There his business worries assumed even greater proportions. Rumours of misappropriation continued, yet partners Cruyff and Basilevitch continued to transfer huge sums between Barcelona and Switzerland in November, December and January. In those three months alone almost 4 million guilders moved from one account to the other. 'We were going to get into business in a big way,' Basilevitch boasted to journalists in the spring of 1979. 'We were about to start earning a fortune. I invested all that money for Johan in projects and some projects were already bringing in money.'

The tempestuous entrepreneurs did business with other banks too, and one of those banks made it known in March that the Grupeco holding could no longer honour its obligations. The guarantees given by Basilevitch at the start were said to be unsecured. When the Spanish tax authorities went looking for Cruyff, he came to the conclusion that he was trapped. Basilevitch could still get credit by using his signatures, but meanwhile Johan could no longer pay for anything himself. He asked his father-in-law for help. Coster got on a plane straight away. He looked at the Grupeco accounts and decided to put all the blame on Basilevitch. Not for the first time, he used the press for the purpose. Johan had been taken for a ride, he announced. The Frenchman had robbed and ruined Cruyff and there was now nothing to be done but to clear the decks. 'Unbelievable that an intelligent lad like Johan could be so blind,' Coster said. 'Ever since I stopped being his adviser on investments, everything has gone wrong. I hope I'm mistaken, but I doubt it.'

Cruyff broke off all contact with Basilevitch and dismissed the staff of the holding company. For a while, unusually for him, he was unreachable when it came to the press. The same could not be said of the Frenchman. He hit back in a press conference and in interviews. 'Before I got to know Johan I had two Rolls-Royces, a good business and a nice family,' he said. 'Now that he's disappearing beyond my horizon I have nothing, and my wife has kicked me out because Coster has claimed I had a relationship with Danny Cruyff.' Basilevitch demanded reparations and threatened to make everything about the ex-footballer's financial dealings public. 'I've kept a copy of every letter, every contract, every transfer of money,' he said. 'Perhaps they'll be of use to me now. In contrast to what Coster claims, I certainly am a businessman.' He said he had 'thirty or forty examples of transactions' by Johan and his father-in-law 'that would not stand up to scrutiny'.

The 'shoeboxes of currency' that were systematically smuggled out of Spain, the 'post box companies' under a Panamanian flag that Cruyff and Basilevitch had set up in Switzerland to mislead the tax authorities: as far as he was concerned, nothing needed to remain secret. 'If Coster and Cruyff want war,' he declared, 'then everything will be on the table. It'll earn them ten years in jail, I would reckon.'

The counterattack worked. Coster shut his mouth. Even if it didn't come to a criminal prosecution, he may have feared further revelations. 'Of course, Cor was afraid his own business practices would now be laid out in front of the press,' says Roger Pop, Coster's grandson who later worked for him. 'He was always keeping large sums of money out of the hands of the taxman. It didn't matter to him how. He would simply drive black money over the border in the boot of his car. If necessary he would use caravans for that. They had good places for hiding everything.'

In the words of Harrie van Mens, the tax expert brought in by Coster to sort out the bookkeeping, Cruyff's father-in-law was 'an interesting storyteller, a criminal in fact, but a fun criminal'.

So it seemed to Coster that it would be better to watch what he said to the press. That self-control will not have come easily to him, since according to Pop he was 'red hot' with anger at the time, principally because Danny had been 'won over' by Basilevitch. 'He shouted that he was going to murder the guy. He believed the two of them had had an affair, which was the start of all the trouble. The relationship was Danny's revenge for the swimming pool incident in 1974 and for several other similar situations. That's how it was seen in the family. Because of course Johan wasn't a saint.'

Grupeco was now worth nothing. An estimated 10 million

guilders had evaporated. Most of the money Cruyff had been so frugal with, for which he'd entered into conflicts and suffered real physical pain, had disappeared in a year or less. According to adviser Van Mens, his debts were now worth more than his possessions. Panic surged through the Cruyff household.

Father-in-law Cor had just one piece of advice: immediately start playing football again. Earn money. It doesn't matter where.

CHAPTER TWENTY-THREE

Lifted up by the greatness of America

According to Cor Coster, Michel Basilevitch had persuaded Cruyff to part with millions, but evidence for that has never been produced. There are also serious doubts as to whether the money actually ended up in the pockets of the 'conman', no matter how often that claim has been made since 1979. Journalists who tracked Basilevitch down to the south of France fifteen years after the debacle reported that he gave the impression of being vengeful and frustrated but also 'impoverished'. Furthermore, it is striking that Johan Neeskens, who employed him as an adviser from 1977 onwards, aired a very different opinion. 'Michel never harmed my interests,' he told the press. The Frenchman negotiated a new contract with Barcelona for him and did so 'correctly'. 'I hope he will continue to handle my affairs,' Neeskens said in 1979.

In the early 1980s, Basilevitch popped up as a team manager at Paris Saint-Germain. There the players had no complaints about him, says former AZ and PSG player Kees Kist, who thought him 'reliable'. Later Basilevitch became an agent for professional footballers and in that role – despite his reputation as the man who cheated Cruyff – he won the trust of famous players including Thierry Henry, Alberto Tarantini and Sunday Oliseh. But he did it all without a licence, and for that reason several clubs eventually closed their doors to him. FIFA even warned against him. The last time anyone heard anything from Basilevitch was in 2003, when he claimed that he was going to make an attempt to become president of FC Barcelona. After that he seems to have vanished from the face of the earth.

All in all, Basilevitch's entrepreneurship shows rather more signs of megalomania and incompetence than of wilful theft. 'The truth is that Cruyff and his partner Basilevitch had too little understanding of the subject matter and bought several businesses and companies that were not going concerns and soon proved to be utterly worthless,' Jack van Zanten told the press. 'That can go quickly.'

In May 1979, when they were still licking their financial wounds, Johan and Danny did not believe there had been malicious intent. 'I still don't know whether it would be right to call Michel a conman,' Danny said in an interview with *Het Parool*. 'I see him more as a fantasist.' She still felt 'emotionally attached to Michel'. Johan was not bitter either, and mainly blamed himself. He'd exercised 'far too little control' over what Basilevitch got up to, he said. 'I'd never really been in business, either. My great self-reproach is that I was so profligate in handling my money, or rather, in having it handled.' In retrospect 'much of the information' that Cruyff and his partner had been given was 'not correct, to put it mildly'. All the same, he had 'contributed in part' to the failure himself.

Even if his debts exceeded the value of his property, he did have quite a few nest eggs here and there. And Cruyff would not be Cruyff if he didn't have all sorts of new plans lying ready. In the wine sector, for instance. Spanish wine was still treated with some suspicion in other countries, so what did he do? He got together with some experts to select a few good riojas. His logo was then printed on the label, as a kind of quality mark, consonant with the Cruyffian line of reasoning that went, 'They can't have made a mess of that one, because the label guarantees the quality.' He had high expectations of the wine exports and had already opened a small office in Barcelona where two people were working for him. 'We're going to trade in preserves the same way,' he said. 'Asparagus, strawberries, and Spanish dishes like paella and zarzuela.'

Cruyff was indestructible. He'd viewed the end of his career as a football player as just fine, and now that he had to play again for big money that was fine too. The only thing that wasn't fine was the prospect of playing for the New York Cosmos, and that was the club with which none other than Basilevitch had arranged a 'pre-contract', an option as lucrative as it was unique. At that point, in early 1978, Cruyff had assumed he would never play again, so he was delighted to get a million guilders on condition that, should he ever pull on his boots for a professional game, he would appear for the Cosmos. Now, in the spring of 1979, he wanted to find a way out of that exclusivity agreement. During negotiations in the Rockefeller Center, where Warner Communications, owner of the Cosmos, had its offices, it was made clear to Cruyff and Coster that throughout the season he would have to carry out all kinds of PR activities for Warner if he signed. That didn't appeal to Cruyff at all. His autonomy was worth more to him than the 5 million guilders a year he could earn with the club. 'I want to be able to say yes or no, always,' he told the negotiators. 'Nobody has the exclusive right to Johan Cruyff. This is impossible.'

Furthermore, playing with Franz Beckenbauer and Carlos Alberto Torres, who were already appearing for the Cosmos, didn't appeal to him. There would be little chance to dominate on the pitch. He also thought it a disadvantage that the Cosmos were in a sense 'complete'. The club had a strong team (by the standards of the weak North American competition), a good organisation (even if there was rather too much wild partying) and a lot of supporters. 'The most glamorous team in world football' had won the championship in both the previous two years. There was little credit to be gained.

According to an investigation by film company Warner Bros, more than half a billion of the total of 4 billion people on earth had heard of Johan Cruyff. His fame was unprecedented. He surely didn't need to be in New York to cash in on it.

On the other side of the United States was a smaller club with few supporters that could only grow. It played on real grass, too, rather than plastic, as in New York. The club was called the Los Angeles Aztecs and the trainer was called Rinus Michels. After leaving Barcelona in 1978, Michels had decided to take things a little easier after fourteen busy years at Ajax and Barça, and at the same time to carry on earning a lot of money. On the American West Coast that could be done. But when the early matches of his first season (April–September 1979; soccer was a summer game there) produced mediocre results, Michels managed to get the owners of the Aztecs to invite Cruyff to California. He was bought out of his pre-contract with the Cosmos and on 22 May Johan moved to the West Coast of North America with his family and two Doberman pinschers, a smaller dog and a cat.

They arrived early in the morning at Los Angeles international airport – Danny miserable, because she had no enthusiasm at all for this American adventure, Johan cheerful and laconic. He believed it was all going to work out. They were met by Michael Kinsbergen, son of a friend in Amsterdam. The student gaped at the sight of Johan, Danny, Chantal, Susila and Jordi, their luggage, and the pets that arrived in cages: a slightly chaotic bunch on the threshold of a new life. No one had any idea how long the adventure would last. Immediately on arrival, Cruyff was due to give a press conference. There was no way 'the most expensive sportsman in the history of Southern California', as the American newspapers described him, could get out of that. He posed in the Aztecs' orange-and-blue shirt with the number 14 on his back. Behind him Michels gleamed with pride. Cruyff was then able to go to his hotel, but there would be no time to catch up on sleep.

The Aztecs had a match scheduled for that same day, at home against Rochester Lancers. 'You surely won't be playing yet?' Michael Kinsbergen had asked Cruyff on his arrival, thinking of jetlag and the fact that he hadn't played a competition match for a year. 'Of course I will,' the footballer answered. Kinsbergen's amazement only grew when later that day Johan showed up with a sports bag full of old, battered Pumas. The student offered to buy new footwear for him. No need. 'These are boots too,' said Cruyff.

They drove to the Rose Bowl, the Aztecs' stadium in Pasadena. He signed the contract with the Los Angeles Aztecs and shook hands with his new teammates, who included former Ajax friend Wim Suurbier, Leo van Veen (formerly of FC Utrecht), Huub Smeets (ex-MVV) and Thomas Rongen (previously an amateur with AFC in Amsterdam). An hour later Cruyff, with his old boots and his chewing gum, ran on to the field between two rows of cheerleaders. 'Ladies and gentlemen, please welcome the greatest soccer player in the world . . . Joehen Kroif!' The immense stadium, with room for a crowd of over a hundred thousand, was less than a tenth full. That illustrated how little soccer meant in California. It didn't bother Cruyff. As a bonus on top of his annual salary of 2 million guilders, he would be receiving a percentage of the receipts. 'That pioneering work attracted me,' he said later. 'I never want to find myself thinking, why didn't you ever try this or that?'

The match against the Rochester Lancers began. Despite his jetlag and a lack of match rhythm he scored twice in the first ten minutes, with his right foot from the edge of the penalty area, then with his left. Both times the ball went high into the goal. Leo van Veen scored too and so Los Angeles Aztecs vs Rochester Lancers ended in a 3-0 victory. A lightning debut in old boots.

*

Most of the Aztecs players lived on the coast, in Redondo Beach in an apartment complex owned by the club. There was fun aplenty, with barbecues and drinking sprees. Reason enough for Johan and Danny to seek refuge elsewhere. They settled on Oxford Road, a broad avenue in a fashionable neighbourhood of San Marino with deep front gardens and little traffic. The children would be able to play outside as much as they liked. Although Danny would have preferred to stay in Barcelona – the children had taken root there and her mother lived a few hours' flying time away – her mood slowly improved. She could walk the dogs, people were friendly, and Johan was soon enjoying himself with the Aztecs. Nobody accosted the couple on the street. Life in Los Angeles was a breath of fresh air in every sense.

The soccer wasn't up to much. Compared to traditional American sports like basketball and baseball, both the standard of play and the conditions were laughable. The players active in the North American Soccer League, which was just ten years old, were mostly discarded or third-rate professionals from Europe and South America, and on the often-appalling pitches (lumpy grass, or a thin layer of plastic turf laid on concrete) they made a kind of pantomime out of it. The clubs were little more than hastily purchased squads plus a few trainers and other staff. They rarely had their own ground, so they tended to play in stadiums used for American football, and the announcers spent half their time explaining the rules. When the Aztecs were unable to use the Rose Bowl for training sessions, they had to resort to a park, where the professional footballers sprinted between trees instead of between bollards. It didn't seem the place for a 32-year-old genius like Cruyff, but he was determined to make the most of it. 'I'm an entertainer,' he said.

All the things that had 'wrecked' him in Barcelona – the relentless pressure, the absolute need to win – were almost entirely absent here. Away from that overwrought atmosphere, he could play a relaxed game. 'In America I rediscovered pleasure in my sport,' he said later. Instead of looking down on everything, as many of the other Europeans did, he saw the advantages of a young and open-minded football culture. Cruyff loved to improvise, and here all kinds of innovations were dreamed up to make the game more attractive for spectators. For example, you could be offside only if you were ahead of a mark roughly level with the 16-metre line. A 'boring' draw was impossible, because if necessary there would be 'shoot-outs' to decide the winner, more dynamic than the traditional penalty, with one player starting from the halfway line and taking on the goalkeeper for five seconds. And as in all the big American sports, the season reached a climax in a closing tournament, known as the playoffs.

Cruyff enjoyed the urge to innovate and the childlike high spirits with which the live commentators praised his best moves. 'It was as if he was lifted up by the positivity and greatness of America,' recalls his teammate of the time Thomas Rongen. 'Other famous players, like Gerd Müller, were there only for the money. They played their matches and left. They didn't even learn the language. Johan was far more serious, interested in everything. Whenever there was an away game, he would find out all about the city where they'd be playing and go to see all the sights.'

Although he led his own life, even when he was travelling with the team, Cruyff indulged in practical jokes here too. The Yugoslav, Hungarian, Mexican and Canadian fortune-seekers in the squad weren't used to Dutch 'kidding'. So they had no idea what was going on when they got back from the toilet and sat down on a fork, or discovered a shoe was missing. It also took time to get used to Johan shouting at them during a match, pointing out their mistakes. It was his way of being helpful. He couldn't keep his mouth shut off the pitch either, of course. 'If you started arguing with him about the flight schedule, for example, or the best way to drive to the stadium,' English forward Chris Dangerfield said later, 'then you had to be smart enough not to keep on too long, or you'd never be rid of him.'

Surrounded by profiteers, he even managed to score one of the best goals of his career. It was on 19 August 1979, in the playoffs against the Washington Diplomats. He was passed the ball by a teammate close to the centre spot, crossed the pitch and after a kind of giant slalom past four or five players whacked it into the goal with his left. In the end the Aztecs failed to get into the final of the North American competition, the Soccer Bowl, but for Cruyff the season was reasonably successful. After twenty-seven matches he had fourteen goals and even more assists to his name. He was declared the most valuable player in the competition, and average attendances at the club rose from 9,000 to 15,000 – fewer than the investors had hoped, but still encouraging.

Cruyff signed a new contract with the Aztecs and already knew what to concentrate on next season: structural improvements in North American soccer. There should be real clubs, he believed, each with several senior teams and youth teams, with their own coaches and a flow of top talents into the first eleven. 'I feel really involved with that,' he told the press. 'I've already started to put programmes together, to raise the level of school football, youth training, coaching courses and so on.'

Just one more year of playing and then he would set up a youth training programme in Los Angeles. That was how he saw his immediate future. Here, too, he wanted to be more than a footballer, a man with ideals. So along with Inter Soccer, an agency he'd established a year before with his own money and which was allied to Cor Coster's agency Inter Football in Amsterdam, he organised a tour of Europe after the competition ended. It would be good for the development of the young Americans in the Aztecs squad. And, of course, it would generate publicity for Inter Soccer. With Johan things always cut both ways.

The tour took place mostly in the Netherlands, and there Cruyff declared himself happy to have escaped the 'poisoned

atmosphere' in his native country. 'Here you have your reputation destroyed by so-called critical magazines,' he told the press.
'If you earn more money, simply because you work harder, they
almost want to ban you from getting it.' In America everything
was much more positive, so the US might quickly catch up with
Europe when it came to football. 'In Europe the standard is no
longer rising, whereas in America they're improving by leaps
and bounds.' Development aid worker Cruyff and his Aztecs
squad also played in Paris (PSG) and London (Chelsea). Then
he went on holiday with his family.

But in February 1980 Cruyff discovered that there were
drawbacks to a fully commercial sport. The Los Angeles Aztecs
got a new owner, a Mexican television station, which wanted
to focus on the relatively close Mexican market. That meant
Mexican players were needed, and they would come only if
Cruyff's astronomical salary was scrapped. The 'King of Soccer'
would have to leave, but he wasn't going to be defeated that
easily. He opened talks with the Washington Diplomats, a club
with even fewer spectators than the Aztecs. An agreement was
soon reached. In the spring of 1980 the family and all their pets
exchanged Oxford Road for a far from unpleasant abode on
the East Coast.

In Washington DC, club president Steve Danzansky and
his wife showed Johan and Danny various 'nice neighbourhoods, with beautiful, spacious houses', as Mrs Danzansky put
it later in *Johan Cruyff, De Amerikaanse jaren*. But the Dutch
couple eventually chose 'a far bigger house than I could have
imagined, between the ambassadorial residences and the pala-
tial homes of top politicians'. The house was on Tracy Place,
a leafy avenue lined with mansions, ten minutes' drive from
the White House. One next-door neighbour was Robert
McNamara, chairman of the World Bank and former Secretary
of Defense under President John F. Kennedy. The other was
a prominent Washington lawyer. Both were clearly more the
type you would expect in such a neighbourhood than the lean

sportsman from Europe, with his beautiful blonde wife and his children and pets.

The neighbour across the road, John Damgard, soon grew curious. The 40-year-old assistant to the US vice-president decided to size up the situation. He crossed the street and introduced himself.

Cruyff said his name and after a short silence from Damgard added, 'I'm a soccer player.'

Again, there was no response. Damgard knew players of American football, basketball and baseball, but not the stars of a sport played mainly in schools.

'I'm the third most famous person on earth,' Cruyff went on.

'Oh really?' Damgard raised his eyebrows. 'You're not the president of the United States and you're not Muhammad Ali or the Queen of England. I suspect you're not the Pope either. So how is that possible?'

Cruyff was not a show-off by nature, but sometimes he needed to brag a little. He delivered a short lecture on the popularity of soccer outside the United States, and about the fact that one of the best footballers in history was naturally world-famous. All fairly logical.

'He didn't strike me as modest at all,' says Damgard looking back. 'Extremely self-assured in fact.'

Neighbour McNamara did know a thing or two about soccer. The World Bank chairman gave Johan and Danny a tour of the neighbourhood. He showed them the shops and explained which would be the best school for their children. Cruyff found his help completely normal – he simply never looked up to anyone. 'Always nice when someone gives you that kind of information,' he said soberly to American journalists. 'And McNamara is hugely sports-minded, so he knows exactly what I've come to Washington to do.'

He had come there to play soccer and, as in LA, to do some development work. It would be good, for example, if the Washington Diplomats were to become less dependent on foreigners like himself, he said. There should be a youth training scheme here too, and more Americans should be persuaded to join. He was definitely thinking in part of African Americans. 'A great many of the prominent sportspeople in this country are black,' he said at a press conference. 'Yet there are hardly any black soccer players. I think there's been too little propaganda in certain ordinary neighbourhoods of the cities. I want to change that.'

A worthy ideal, but it was perhaps a little ambitious. In the immediate term he had his hands full with the modernisation of the team. The Diplomats were used to playing like the British, very physically and with lots of long balls, which of course was in conflict with Cruyff's desire for intelligent interplay. Some players thought him a 'first-class cry baby' who talked more than he footballed. The young American Sonny Askew had so many comments flung at him that he lost his temper with Cruyff during a training session. It was a good thing for the cry baby that former Feyenoorder Wim Jansen had come to swell the ranks of the 'Dips', but Johan was in continual disagreement with English trainer Gordon Bradley. 'The coach is an idiot and the players don't know what they're doing,' Cruyff confided in a journalist. 'And they don't fuckin' listen to me.' The players often simply didn't understand him and the club leadership was sometimes driven nuts by his continual criticism, partly because – and this was no new phenomenon – it was unclear whether he would ever stop making new demands. 'It went on and on,' said Diplomats director Andy Dolich later, according to *Johan Cruyff, De Amerikaanse jaren.* 'His running commentary on the leadership and all the other players was a constant.'

Yet Cruyff's own behaviour was subject to criticism too. He was still smoking constantly, everywhere, even in the shower. The Americans couldn't understand it. But as far as his nicotine intake went, Cruyff had his answer ready. 'Smoking makes me feel less stress,' he said. 'And stress is unhealthy, so smoking can't really be bad for me.'

He aroused at least as much astonishment, even irritation, when he refused to attend a club dinner. The meal was meant to be conducive to team-building. Fun, everyone thought, an evening with the ladies, who, in accordance with the theme 'The women behind the men' were to bring their favourite dishes. Cruyff didn't think that sounded fun at all. Danny, who didn't like cooking and hated having to play the 'footballer's wife' no doubt liked it even less. So they stayed away, and when the players and trainers saw each other again the following day, Johan explained his absence the previous evening: 'Danny isn't behind me. She's equal to me. Danny is beside me, never behind me. That's why I couldn't come to the dinner.'

In the matches Cruyff's participation naturally made a huge difference. The Dips made great advances in their play and in Washington he scored a stunning goal after a solo run. Close to the halfway line he started an inimitable zigzag run from the touchline, past several opponents, ending in a diagonal whack with his left foot into the bottom right corner. No one even noticed that all through the match, against the Seattle Sounders on 16 July 1980, he had done almost everything with his left. An injury meant he could barely use his favoured right leg.

It was beautiful, unique even, but it didn't help much. In August the Diplomats were knocked out early in the playoffs, by the Los Angeles Aztecs. His mate Wim Suurbier was still playing with the Aztecs, and according to the press he obstructed Cruyff 'mercilessly'.

Yet Cruyff never tired of talking about his time in Washington. Not because of the more than 2 million guilders he earned there, nor because he was declared Player of the Year, but mainly because he learnt so much off the pitch. He appreciated both 'the energy' of the Diplomats in 'creating a show' and 'their approach to running a business'. Director Dolich, a contemporary he considered 'a crack businessman', ran the Dips as a commercial concern and thought up all kinds of initiatives to attract and amuse the public. 'In Washington I learnt how to promote sport,' he said four years later. 'As far as that's concerned, I was at college there.' He was shown the ropes of marketing and took part in it. He gave weekly soccer lessons on local television, for instance, and allowed endless questioning at press conferences. Partly thanks to his efforts, the average number of spectators in the Robert F. Kennedy Memorial Stadium rose from 11,000 to 19,000.

At least as important was the fact that rich Americans gave a lot of money to good causes. That appealed to Cruyff, and so it was that he came into contact with Eunice Kennedy Shriver, the 59-year-old sister of John F. and Robert F. Kennedy. She asked him if he wanted to be ambassador of the Special Olympics, which she had founded in 1968. He said yes and from that moment on he held football clinics for disabled children as soccer ambassador. He performed that role with such dedication that tears sometimes came to the eyes of the Diplomats' PR man, who would go with him. For the 'King of Soccer' teaching was simply fun; he enjoyed it as much as his pupils. 'Johan understood perfectly well that he was earning a princely salary in America,' Thomas Rongen remembers. 'For precisely that reason he thought it was great to give something back to society.'

He and Danny had thought nothing of taking Rongen into their home, after he was more or less dismissed by Michels for his unprofessional way of life. Rongen could come and play for the Dips. In the Cruyff household he was surprised to see that Johan didn't act the famous footballer but put a lot of energy into family life. He was 'extremely strict with the children and routine came before everything else,' recalls Rongen, who as a 23-year-old was the 'fourth child' of the household. 'School was extremely important to Johan and at six in the evening the whole family sat round the table to eat. I was meant to stay for only a few days, but those people were so easy-going that I was there for four months. It all spoke for itself. Johan took me to his son Jordi's first match and involved me in everything. I've rarely come across such helpful people.'

The neighbours at Tracy Place, a prominent lawyer and his wife, had a son with Down's syndrome, called John-John. Cruyff kicked a ball about with him from time to time in the garden. 'My wife didn't like that much, because sometimes things got knocked over,' Cruyff said later on Dutch television. 'One hot summer's day I was standing in the swimming pool. The boy saw me and jumped at me with all his clothes on. Well, what do you do then? You put your hands under his tummy and do a bit of explaining: look, this is the way to swim. Just as you do with your own children. He'd lost all fear of the water. That's the best moment you can imagine.'

In late August America's 1980 season ended. It was time for the Netherlands again, for packing suitcases and going to the airport. They unpacked in their spacious bungalow in the fields close to Vinkeveen. Soon Cruyff was driving to Ajax several afternoons a week to keep his fitness up to scratch, as he'd done in the autumns of 1978 and 1979. Logical; he'd grown up there. 'Suddenly there was Johan in the changing room,' remembers midfielder Dick Schoenaker. 'He must have made some kind of arrangement with the coach, but for us it was always a surprise when he showed up.'

Less surprising was that Johan came mainly on Thursdays, when practice matches were played and there was no running in the training schedule. During those matches everyone, including Ajax chairman Ton Harmsen, stared in astonishment. The former 'Jopie', now thirty-three, could do everything. Given that both trendsetter Simon Tahamata and leader Ruud Krol had left, Cruyff seemed the ideal person to help the team notch up some points by joining in a few premier division matches. The idea appealed to him. In his view the new generation of footballers lacked any number of technical and tactical skills that were essential in top-level football. But it proved impossible.

He couldn't play as a professional because he was planning to start again in America in the spring and he couldn't play as an amateur because the enrolment period was over.

In November the opportunity arose again. Cruyff had briefly left the US to play a series of matches in the Far East for the Washington Diplomats. During the tour the leadership announced that the Dips had been disbanded. The owners had come to the conclusion that there was no profit to be made from soccer in North America. The plug was pulled, without warning. So, after getting back from Hong Kong, Johan again found himself wandering about on the Middenweg. This time he'd brought teammate Wim Jansen with him. For a fee, Johan and Wim would help the declining Ajax, the club leadership announced. Cruyff would give instructions beforehand, without taking part, while Jansen would supervise their implementation as a player. 'Anyone who doesn't listen will have a problem,' said Johan, American style. 'He'll either be substituted or not deployed in future.'

Cruyff wasn't qualified as a trainer, so he would be engaged as a staff member, as team leader, technical adviser, or whatever you wanted to call it as long as it wasn't an official function. It was a typically Cruyffian way of navigating the KNVB shoals in an attempt to reach his goal of a better team. 'Diplomas, don't make me laugh,' he said in an interview. 'I don't have a coaching diploma and I'll never get one. But I can tell the guys exactly what to do and especially what not to do. How much do the people with diplomas really know about that?'

He thought all the scepticism about 'two captains on one ship' was merely the kind of whingeing the Dutch were so good at. After all, 'Two captains see more than one.'

The other captain, official coach Leo Beenhakker, bravely insisted he thought it was fantastic that Johan would be involved with the team over the coming months. 'I don't see that as a no-confidence motion at all,' he told the press. 'Last year I asked for someone with a footballing background to support me.' Thirty-eight-year-old Beenhakker was what was known as a CIOS trainer, from the Dutch National Sports Training Institute, not having played in the top flight of the game, and as such he was met with distrust by the media.

For Cruyff, of course, the opposite applied. The first Ajax match after his appointment made that clear at once. The events of 30 November 1980 provided the ingredients for a priceless story that was still being told decades later in bars and in newspapers, and the pictures would often be shown to underline Johan's brilliance. It went like this. Ajax were playing at home in De Meer against FC Twente. 'Technical adviser' Cruyff was watching from the stands. Ajax were being outplayed by FC Twente and soon the score stood at 2-3 (people often exaggerated by saying 1-3). Ajax kept on losing the ball while the maestro sat there fretting. Halfway through the second half, Cruyff got up and made his way down. He got to the metal gate, was let through and, his hands in the pockets of his short coat, went to sit next to Beenhakker in the dugout. Cruyff started gesticulating as he spoke to the coach. He shouted and pointed and then, from one moment to the next, the match turned. It was a magical moment in the history of De Meer. Ajax played FC Twente off the pitch and won 5-3.

The reality was rather different. Cruyff had indeed been sitting in the main stand, with 6-year-old Jordi in his lap. Next to him were Danny and Wim Jansen, who was not due to make his debut with Ajax for another week. It's true that the 'team leader' went to the dugout fifteen minutes into the second half. 'I didn't want to sit on the bench next to Leo for that first match,' Cruyff told *Vrij Nederland* four months later. 'But from the stands I saw so many serious errors that I couldn't take it any more. I believed that with a few simple instructions they could win the match. So it was difficult just to sit there.' The odd thing is that it achieved little. Ajax carried on doing what they had been doing, fanatically attacking to make up the deficit. 'I don't believe anything about our play changed when

Johan came and sat in the dugout,' says Ajax midfielder at the time Dick Schoenaker, still a great fan of Cruyff. 'So much gets shouted in a stadium like that. As a player you concentrate on the ball and the opponent. Don't forget that we played a lot of those matches then. We lost 6–3 at home to MVV, but we beat PSV 5–2. It was often all or nothing.' It is possible of course that the mere presence of Cruyff had a positive effect on the players, but Schoenaker doubts that. 'No one paid any attention to him,' he recalls. 'Johan had been training with us for weeks, he got involved with everything, he was simply part of the group. The story that he turned everything round with a few magic words is just not true.'

One of the reserve players in those days, Keje Molenaar, was sitting in the dugout and he calls the influence of Cruyff on that match 'pure mythmaking'. 'Johan used to shout all kinds of things at Beenhakker, in training too. He was thoroughly used to it.'

Even physiotherapist Rob Nolet, also in the dugout at the time, remembers mainly that 'everyone was shouting at once' to encourage the team. 'Complete nonsense to think they suddenly changed their play,' he says now.

Cruyff was said to have told Beenhakker to take Tscheu La Ling off. The team leader was not particularly keen on Ling. He thought the creative and popular right-winger was lazy and slow, so he picked up the sign with Ling's number on it. Time for a substitution. But Beenhakker thought: I'm the coach here. Ling stayed on. Just before half-time Ling had brought the score back to 2–3; he could get around an opponent and might even score again. Ajax continued to attack and scored three goals, one of them again by Ling. The man Cruyff wanted to have taken off was important for the 5–3 victory with his two goals.

But that was not the drift of the coverage on the sports pages the following day. There Cruyff's 'magic wand' was given all the space. As was the photo of a 'conducting' Johan next to a crestfallen Beenhakker – splendid pictures for those who wanted to believe in fairy tales. The 'eye of the master' had 'drugged' the Ajax players, according to *Het Parool*, ensuring the team had 'unsuspected reserves' available that 'were ultimately sufficient for victory'.

Cruyff had undoubtedly seen very clearly from the stands what was lacking. In their determination to attack, the midfielders had left huge gaps that Twente exploited in their counterattacks. The midfielders had pointed this out themselves at half-time. There in the dugout, Cruyff probably wanted to do something about it by having Ling replaced by midfielder Frank Rijkaard. If you looked at it from his 'logical' point of view, that no doubt made sense, but the story does not tell things the way they actually happened. The team leader did not create magic that afternoon, nor indeed to any great extent in the months that followed. Ajax's performance remained erratic and they did not win the championship that year.

What Cruyff did do was to explain how the lads ought to play. During training sessions he talked endlessly about posture when shooting, about arms that needed to be kept closer to the body in tight spaces so that a player could act more quickly, about how to make the pitch bigger and smaller and about situations where you did better to stand still than to run. All true, but there was no end to it. 'I thought, I can't make sense of all this,' says Keje Molenaar, who had joined Ajax from Volendam in 1980. 'He kept shouting at me, "Not at that angle!" After training was over I asked what he meant. With his hands he explained that a player at an angle to the ball can go in fewer directions than when he's in a straight line: the difference between ninety and a hundred and eighty degrees. Very simple, but I'd never thought about it. That's the way it was with Johan time and again. His criticism irritated you, but you learnt a lot from it.'

Cruyff was amazed at the lack of 'organisation and discipline' at Ajax. The team needed to work harder at 'preventing opposition goals'. He found it 'fantastic' to work there as an adviser, but as far as youth training and the will to win went, his club was in a pitiful state. 'I've had to teach the most elementary aspects of professional football to players who think they've reached the top,' he said.

Alongside his work at Ajax, Cruyff was also busy with good causes and commerce. On 16 December 1980 he flew to Spain for a match in Camp Nou in aid of UNICEF. An international team was to play FC Barcelona. Beforehand a young teammate, Michel Platini, had asked him why he so often had problems with referees. 'Oh,' said Cruyff. 'It's blown out of all proportion. They just don't understand me.' Platini was a great admirer and he would never forget those words. Especially since ten minutes into the second half his hero showed what it meant not to be understood by those in authority. Two goals by the international team were disallowed, and at that point Cruyff complained to the referee. When he was given a yellow card for commenting on the umpiring of the match, he grabbed the referee's shirt and said, *'Eres loco'* – 'You're crazy.' Not as bad as *hijo de puta*, but bad enough to get a celebrity who had come to support the UN children's charity sent off the pitch. The old El Flaco, lifelong rogue, disappeared into the catacombs to loud protests from a hundred thousand spectators.

It was Cruyff in a nutshell. In secret he had for years been donating a great deal of money to a charity working to fight childhood cancer, yet he couldn't control himself when someone asserted their authority over him. Not even in a charity football match.

Several weeks later, in January 1981, Cruyff turned up in Dordrecht. There he knew oil baron Nico de Vries as the colourful and immensely rich owner of football club DS'79. At De Vries' request, Cruyff was to play a few demonstration matches in the DS'79 shirt. That is to say, in the outfit of oil company Frisol. Over the top he wore a tracksuit from computer firm Burroughs; it seemed more than one sponsor was needed to pay for him.

So there he stood, a global sporting hero on a snow-covered pitch in black tights, in a nowhere stadium, with various sponsor names on his clothes. Moonlighting. But Cruyff didn't have any objection to appearing for DS'79. There was nothing wrong with earning money, and he had every respect for self-made entrepreneurs like De Vries – after his time in America even more than before. He met his commitments, he posed for the cameras and showed people in Dordrecht enough beautiful moves for them to go home happy. Meanwhile, reports were appearing about debts worth millions, about Spanish banks seizing his properties. Standing still was not an option.

In late February, Cruyff left Ajax. The big money was waiting. Only this time it wasn't in America. After the fiasco of the Diplomats he preferred to look for a challenge elsewhere. The money was in Valencia, a beautiful city on the Mediterranean coast with an interesting old football club called Levante UD, which played in the second division. It was the club where his childhood idol Faas Wilkes had once played, with a *blaugrana* strip like Barça. He had been negotiating a contract since January and now it was signed: Cruyff would play the remaining thirteen league matches for a fee of 30,000 guilders per match, plus half the proceeds from ticket sales. In addition, although this was kept a secret, he would get half ownership of a tennis complex next to the stadium. A sum was immediately deposited in a Swiss bank account as security for the payments, because Levante was in financial trouble. And special arrangements were made regarding advertising income and the brand of sportswear he would use.

It all looked a bit forced, bringing a global phenomenon and a modest football club together, and that was how it turned out. Both for Levante and for Cruyff, the period between March and June 1981 would be a sporting low, even a tragedy.

CHAPTER TWENTY-FOUR

Only Cruyff would dare

Levante UD was a modest club in Valencia with a far from modest president. Generally speaking, few spectators came to the stadium on the north side of the city, and what they got to see there had more to do with hard work than with positional play and tours de force. But in the 1980–81 season Levante were in good form. So good in fact that president Francisco Aznar thought they could get even better. If the pals team of under-paid professionals was capable of reaching the top of the Spanish second division, thought Aznar in January, then with Johan Cruyff it must be possible to make a great leap forward. Perhaps Levante might finally overtake the despised big brother Valencia CF. An upward spiral of better performances, more spectators, richer sponsors, better players: that was Aznar's dream.

At the start of the new year, Levante were still one point behind the second division leaders. It was time to seize the day. President and real estate magnate Aznar decided Cruyff must come as soon as possible. After some financial hocus pocus, he was able to break the great news to the players.

It made them laugh; they thought the president was joking. The holy Johan, the hero of the great Barcelona, coming to their Levante? To their little stadium out among the fields? That was a good one. After it sank in, the players were so thrown by the news that they lost the match that day. And the two matches that followed. 'Dissent broke out in the changing room,' Franciso Fenollosa recalls. He was friendly with the board at the time and later became president himself. 'The older players in particular were afraid all the money would go to Cruyff and their own earnings would decline.'

The fear that the arrival of the Dutch *pesetero* (money-grubber) would make inroads into the club coffers was not completely unfounded. Levante's bookkeeping had an even worse reputation than its performance in Estadi Ciutat de València. The team of friends fragmented and, as if that wasn't enough, coach Pachín began spreading rumours about Cruyff.

New problems were the last thing Cruyff needed. He already had an abundance of them. Quite apart from the permanent pressure to earn money, Danny's physical condition was worrying. As the result of a fall from a horse, she had been suffering for some time from serious problems with her back and neck. Nerves had been trapped and damaged. On top of that she, like Johan, suffered migraine attacks. He was hoping she would recover in the delightful climate of Valencia, a few hours' drive south of Barcelona, where even in January you could enjoy the café terraces and the beach. Then there was the house they would move into, with a covered swimming pool, fitness room and sauna, in the nearby village of L'Eliana, a place of charming villas. Levante had promised Johan VIP treatment, with his own transport and his own sleeping arrangements at away games.

But Cruyff hadn't played a serious match for six months. In his first game, on 1 March 1981, he did little more than shout and point. Unsurprising: he was not in prime condition. He suffered minor injuries. 'During training Johan often sat on a chair with his leg in ice, just watching,' recalls former Levante player Vicente Latorre. 'Of course, the young players in particular stared open-mouthed at his technique, but even that had its drawbacks. Suddenly everyone was trying to kick the ball with the outside of their foot, the way he did. In matches that went horribly wrong.'

The results were mediocre and Levante started dropping down the table.

On Thursday 19 March 1981 Johan strode nervously back and forth across the patio of his country house. Danny was not getting better at all; in fact, she was ill in bed. The 'nerve pains' tormented her so much it made her vomit. The muscles in her arms, legs and mouth spasmed. Two journalists for the Dutch weekly *Panorama* were visiting Cruyff, intending to drive with him to Deportivo Alavés in the Basque Country, where Levante were to play a match the following Sunday. The journalists – reporter André Naber and photographer Hans Heus – wanted to find out more about the question that had for weeks been occupying the minds of all those in the Netherlands who were interested in sport: did Cruyff want to play for the Dutch national team again?

'I'm really sorry to disappoint you,' Johan said, 'but tomorrow I'm taking Danny to the Netherlands. She needs treatment there.'

'By whom?' asked reporter Naber.

'By a magnetiser; he's the only one who helps her at all. We've tried everything. Lumbar punctures. We've had an acupuncturist. Nothing made any difference.'

The journalists offered to assist him. They could go in search of a local practitioner of alternative medicine, they proposed – if only to save their own coverage. They tried several addresses close to Valencia but got nowhere. Johan was desperate. On reflection, Danny was far too ill to travel and he needed to go to Alavés. 'I can take a fair amount of pressure,' he told the journalists, 'but the fact that my wife is lying here racked with pain, that's something I really can't stand.' Yet he couldn't stay with her. 'I'm a footballer,' he said. 'I have to fill stadiums. The club has taken itself to the verge of bankruptcy by buying me.'

A friend of the family came over to care for Danny so that on

Friday 20 March Cruyff could set off for the Basque Country along with the journalists. His heart wasn't in it. 'The narrow face of the footballer is lined,' Naber noted. 'His eyes look dull.'

Cruyff had a lot on his plate. Because of a damaged toe he hadn't trained all week and, meanwhile, the phone had barely stopped ringing. Would he or would he not put on an orange shirt on Wednesday 25 March, after a gap of four years, to play in De Kuip against France? Everyone got involved: his own family, his manager Hans Muller and even the press.

During a stopover at the players' hotel in Zaragoza, where Johan joined the Levante squad, he received even worse news. Danny had been admitted to hospital. The journalists saw him turn white. After hours of feverish calls back and forth, Cruyff managed to get hold of the name and phone number of the hospital. His wife was on IV fluids waiting for a lumbar puncture. That had already been tried, without success, so Cruyff forbade the procedure in what Nader described as 'a long stream of Spanish sentences'. He demanded that Danny be brought back to the house in Valencia to be examined by a different specialist. He now wanted to go there himself, match or no match, but president Aznar succeeded in persuading him to travel on with the squad to Vitoria-Gasteiz, home of Alavés, where they could assess the situation again.

On arrival at the Hotel General Alava in Vitoria, Johan rang Cor Coster, who urgently advised him to stay in the Basque Country so that he could play against Alavés the next day. The sum of 30,000 guilders was at stake, his father-in-law reminded him; he had to fulfil his obligations. And what good would it do Danny if he came and sat by her bed? But Cruyff decided to drive back to Valencia that evening. He had to go to Danny, whether or not it cost him 30,000 guilders. His fellow players would just have to do without him.

He got back into the car belonging to the *Panorama* journalists and spent most of the 600 kilometres to Valencia at the wheel. Meanwhile, he had made his decision about Oranje: he would not play against France. Purely, he confided to Naber – on condition that the journalist did not write it down – because of Danny. Her recurrent migraines and back pains were more important than the World Cup qualifier in Rotterdam. He couldn't deal with the international on top of everything else. 'My family comes first,' he said as they drove through the Spanish night at 160 kilometres an hour. 'It's all I really have.'

The thought of his wife and children in that house and what he would do without them made him visibly emotional. Naber looked at the star footballer from close up in the darkness. The reporter felt his despair, the panic of a husband who was on his way from the place where he really ought to stay to the place where he'd wanted to be all along. Torn, confused, oversupplied with opinions and feelings of guilt. 'I'll never forget that image of Johan at the wheel,' Naber said later. 'He sat there crying.'

Towards morning they arrived in Valencia.

Later that Sunday, Cruyff rang the Oranje coach. His last words were, 'No, Mr Rijvers, I won't do it. No, never again.' He hung up and was overcome by emotion once more. As if he could already see the angry and sarcastic comments in the press, he said to Naber, 'Cruyff will be loathed.' (In these years he increasingly spoke about himself in the third person.) 'I don't think anyone in the Netherlands gets it.'

He was right about that. Nobody understood. It came down to the fact that the national coach Kees Rijvers had been making frantic efforts for some time to get Cruyff back into Oranje. Qualification for the 1982 World Cup had started badly and now Rijvers was hoping to salvage whatever he could by calling on the old stagers. Cruyff had considered making a comeback on 25 March against France, but naturally under certain conditions. It had already led to a great deal of debate with Rijvers about who else would be selected, or not, and with the KNVB about the wearing of Adidas sports clothing. Cruyff had always refused to wear those three stripes on his kit and now he refused again. But the football association had made firm commitments to its sponsor and wouldn't – or couldn't – any longer make an exception.

It resulted in a series of newspaper articles about the wearing of two or three stripes, but in reality, Cruyff confided to Naber, that issue didn't excite him. It was intended only to give the 'too soft' Oranje a sharper edge. He had wanted to rein in the 'idiots' of the football association so that, based on the respect it would win him, he could become the undisputed leader. 'If I'd got my way, I could have dominated the whole thing, and the lads would have looked up to me,' he told Naber. In an atmosphere in which the players 'had to win because otherwise they'd get knifed' he'd have been willing to take them on. A classic piece of Cruyffian thinking: all or nothing. 'I want all the weapons in my hand,' he told Naber. 'If I bend to their will, they'll use those same weapons against me.' Giving in now meant 'always giving in'.

But while that power game was going on, Danny's health problems had arisen. End of story. The door to Oranje was shut.

The Levante players couldn't understand it either. They were disappointed that Johan had dropped out at the last minute in Vitoria. The match in the Basque Country had been lost and now the club president's dream was about to be shattered. Under pressure from Cruyff, Aznar sacked coach Pachín in late March 1981 and replaced him with Joaquim Rifé, a former Barcelona player and a friend of Johan. But he got nowhere too. 'Under Rifé we suddenly had to start playing technical football and swapping positions,' midfielder Vicente Latorre remembers. 'Towards the end of the season like that it was of course pointless. In the second division the games were tough, with a lot of personal duels. Nothing too clever.'

Levante fell to seventh place. But not everything went badly. Among the battlers in *blaugrana*, Cruyff sometimes 'suddenly turned on the light', as one-time Levante president

Fenollosa puts it, rather poetically. A rapid attacker like Manuel Campuzano might be made to seem a top footballer by Cruyff's deep passes. And for Latorre one match against Granada was unforgettable. Johan made the tempo rise and fall, the way an ordinary mortal turns the gas under a saucepan up or down. 'He didn't behave like a star,' says Latorre. 'But he was one, of course. Very sad; if he'd been with us from the start of the season, we'd definitely have won the championship.'

Cor Coster was the only person to achieve a real victory in this period. Cruyff had alerted him to the fact that the most recent payments for the players had not come through. Uncle Cor flew to Valencia and in early May, shortly before the start of one of the last home games of the season, he walked into the boardroom. No one would be allowed to leave until the players had been paid. 'We were already used to a lot from Coster,' says Fenollosa. 'Sometimes he would come in to demand Johan's fee. He'd stuff all the money inside an old newspaper and walk out with it under his arm. But this was a real set-to.' Coster grabbed one board member by the scruff of the neck and pushed him half out of the window to reinforce the message. When that failed to achieve a result, Coster entrenched himself in the first eleven changing room and told the players not to go out on to the pitch until the money came in. At the last moment a telex from a Spanish bank was slid under the changing-room door: the money was on its way; the match could begin. Levante beat Castellón 1-0 that day. But they went on to lose three times in a row and so the team, which had been in second place in January, ended ninth.

Aznar had gambled and lost. The board resigned and the club went bankrupt, partly as a result of its payments to Cruyff. 'Because he sometimes didn't show up, as in Vitoria, Johan got the blame for everything,' says Latorre. 'But only the board was really in the wrong.'

However that may be, Cruyff had never performed so poorly as he did with Levante. Two goals and a few beautiful moves in ten matches represented a meagre harvest. Out of a possible twenty-four points, Levante gained only ten in that period. His presence had been disruptive and partly because of that he said the club could keep his last payment. He didn't insist on getting the land next to the stadium that he had been promised, either. 'After all, there's no money left,' he said to the board.

That act of kindness gave him the right, he believed, to miss the final championship match. It meant he could take part in his former Barcelona teammate Juan Manuel Asensi's last game, on 24 May. During that celebratory match in Camp Nou he suffered a groin injury that required surgery straight away. So now both he and Danny had health problems.

In June Cruyff flew to northern Italy. As a guest player at AC Milan he took part in a commercially organised mini-tournament. He had committed himself to it, for a fee of a quarter of a million guilders, and although he hadn't yet recovered from his groin operation he didn't want to disappoint the people in the San Siro. He did, all the same. Instead of playing two matches he gave up after a single half. He flew back to Amsterdam promising to return shortly to do some PR work, but he didn't keep that promise. The organisation was baffled and said he had merely wanted to line his pockets.

Cruyff's haste to leave Milan was prompted by yet more new developments. In Milan he had been visited by a doctor from Washington. His old Diplomats team, having meanwhile risen from the ashes, was performing badly and its owners were hoping that the 'King of Soccer' was fit enough to come and change that. If he was prepared to start halfway through the American (summer) season, he could earn around 80,000 guilders per match. The doctor examined him and said he felt Cruyff would be able to play again within a few weeks. The contract was signed, the flight to Washington DC booked – and there was one more reason to leave quickly, perhaps the most important of all: in Washington Danny could get the best medical care imaginable.

It was a dramatic period. Johan was more often in a hospital than on a pitch. It meant he missed out on a lot of money, but that didn't matter to him. He loyally accompanied Danny to hospital time and again, and in all kinds of other ways too he devoted himself to her recovery, as if her health problems in Valencia had made him aware once again of what his life was really all about.

Later Danny confided to several friends how much of an impression Johan's devotion made on her. Their relationship, changeable from the start, buffeted by issues like the swimming pool incident in 1974 and the 'affair' with Basilevitch, entered calmer waters during those months in Washington. Under Johan's constant care they grew closer and so emerged from the medical crisis more stable, older and wiser. Which of course is not to say that Johan changed his spots or that Danny ceased regularly putting him in his place. 'Hey, mister superstar,' was soon heard in the Cruyff household again. 'Go and empty that dishwasher.' And superstar Johan – who preferred to get involved in conflicts outside the home than inside it – would obey immediately. At other times too, to the amazement of friends, he would keep slaloming past the quirks of Danny's moods.

Of course, the sporting aspects of Cruyff's stay in Washington suffered in the meantime. 'If you are practically living in a hospital,' he told an American journalist, 'then it's impossible to concentrate fully on football.' After his comeback for the Diplomats on 1 July 1981 he played in only five of the remaining thirteen league matches. Of those five games he played just twice for the full ninety minutes.

So his third American adventure came to an end less successfully than the previous two. There would not be a fourth; the Washington Diplomats were now rolled up for good. The North American professional competition as a whole went downhill and a long time passed before soccer truly took root in the United States, primarily because of the inspiring legacy of Pelé, the Brazilian hero of the New York Cosmos in the years

1975-77. Cruyff, the hireling with ideals, created his own rather smaller legacy, with as its highlight a historically beautiful goal on 16 August in the last official home game played by the Dips. Close to the halfway line he stood with the ball at his feet, his back to the opposition goal. Then he abruptly turned round, surprising three of the Toronto Blizzard players at once. He increased his pace and from about 35 metres lobbed the ball over the keeper's hand. An unprecedented piece of insight, timing and technique. The *Washington Post* called it an almost bizarre distance shot, 'one of the most memorable goals ever seen at the Robert F. Kennedy Stadium'.

In early September 1981 the family settled in Vinkeveen once more. The children, now aged seven, nine and ten, could go to a Dutch school there, as had always been the intention. Cruyff resolved to take things easy for a while. His groin injury was still troubling him and after all the peregrinations of the past six months he was in need of a rest. But a few days later he reported to Ajax as if it was the only natural thing to do and started training again as if he'd never been away. Weeks went by, his groin healed and he felt fit. He started to want to play in the first team again. His football friend Wim Jansen was still there as last man and the young, rather uneven team could do with a second senior.

Months of complex consultations followed. The club was not eager to open up its wallet for a player of thirty-four who might soon be injured again. Events in Valencia, Milan and Washington did not encourage optimism as far as that was concerned. Moreover, in Ajax's opinion he was asking for a lot of money (around a million guilders) and with his meddlesome character he might cause division in the club. Still, Cruyff was a media phenomenon and an unparalleled player.

Ajax dropped to third place in the premier division, five points behind leaders PSV, and the atmosphere in the squad was far from optimal. A leader was needed and eventually a decision was made. Cruyff would be paid a basic salary plus part of the proceeds from the extra tickets that might be sold. It was roughly the same deal as he had struck in Los Angeles and when he first played in Washington.

His hair was shorter, his expression more businesslike. When he smiled his face had the furrows of a man who had experienced worries in life, who knew a lot and was prepared to take risks, who dared to face success or failure right there in the spotlight. That set Cruyff apart from the malaise that had held Dutch professional football in its grip for years. The premier division had sunk into a morass of debt, and the same could in a sense be said of the Netherlands as a whole. The country was weighed down by a persistent economic crisis and the call for collective action could be heard everywhere. The new government of Christian Democrats, left-wing liberals and socialists fought more against itself than against rising unemployment and inflation. But here was Cruyff, the unreligious individual, the go-getter, the entrepreneur who obstinately went on investing. After an absence from European competition football of three and a half years he was back, and how.

As always with Cruyff it cut both ways. He wanted to help 'his' Ajax and at the same time to get some free publicity for his recently launched clothing and shoe brand, Cruyff Sports. It was part of Euro Fashions BV, a company owned by Hans Muller, his new business partner who also carried out the negotiations with Ajax. (Coster remained involved in the background.) Along with Muller, Johan had decided that part of the profits from Cruyff Sports would go towards sports training and youth tournaments.

The player, the businessman and the benefactor in him never let go of each other from then on. They were united during training sessions on the Middenweg, with Johan shouting and correcting ('helping') in a blue tracksuit from Cruyff Sports while the others wore the red of the club sponsor, Le Coq Sportif. His trickily spinning balls, which the younger players in particular had yet to get used to, were delivered from boots decorated with his own logo, a kind of crushed 'C'.

On the afternoon of Sunday 6 December 1981, the moment arrived. Ajax were playing at home against HFC Haarlem. Cruyff had a massage, taped his ankles, smoked a cigarette for his nerves and, tight-faced, walked through the cage that steered him, along with the players of Ajax and Haarlem, the referee and linesmen, to the pitch. He knew that several of the established players (Tscheu La Ling, Søren Lerby) were not keen to have him in the team. He also knew there were sceptics in the crowd who jumped to their feet when, diagonally behind young Haarlem player Ruud Gullit, he ran on to the pitch. Here and there people whistled their disapproval, but one banner read 'Welcome back Johan'. Twenty-three thousand people were sitting in De Meer, roughly double the number budgeted for – he and the club had hit the jackpot. 'It would have irritated me terribly if few people had come,' he said later.

Haarlem started the match better than Ajax, with various attacking moves and several chances at goal. But after twenty minutes it happened. Cruyff took over the ball from a teammate, avoided several tackles before reaching Haarlem's 16-metre line, then lobbed the ball with a velvety little flick of the foot over the keeper into the far corner: 1-0. The stadium erupted with joy and relief, because, sure enough, the old master had shown he was still up to it. Precisely when he needed to, he did it again, effective and enthralling, just like before.

Johan rejoiced the old way too, leaping up with his right arm wheeling, for a moment totally happy in the chilly December air of Amsterdam. His team began to flow and for the rest of the match midfielder Cruyff with his skilful passing created space and depth, precisely what was needed. His most powerful weapon, that ability to see instantly, was of particular importance given his reduced pace. Using all the surfaces of both his feet he could control the strangest of balls, calm and erect, and move them onwards. He could talk to all his teammates while at the same time hoodwinking an opponent. That gave him new opportunities. 'I venture to claim that because of my organisational capacities, because of my insight and also my play, I'm of more value to a team than ever,' he had said earlier that year to *Panorama*. He may have been bluffing, but seeing him now you'd be more inclined to think it was self-knowledge.

Fifteen minutes before the end of the match, he passed a defender with a subtle feint, ran to the back line and curved the ball in an arc in front of the goal. A move of two seconds on a square metre and striker Wim Kieft could easily head it in. Cruyff demonstrated his arsenal of bending passes and backheel kicks. The crowd enjoyed it right to the end. 'Today worked out like I dreamed it would,' he said after the 4–1 victory. 'The fact that you can play both for the team and for the public, yes, I'm very happy with that.' The mission of the entertainer had been accomplished. The newspapers wrote that he had 'seen off' all the doubts, that he had 'silenced' all the critics, that he had 'shone', that he was 'back, in every respect'.

Only one foul was committed against him. Haarlem trainer Hans van Doorneveld had instructed his players above all to make a good match of it. The premier division, having suffered for years from poor play, fan violence and falling gate receipts, could certainly use a boost like this. So Van Doorneveld had not ordered a player to mark Cruyff closely but his former teammate Gerrie Kleton was detailed against him, a technically skilful attacker from the Ajax 2 team of the early 1970s. The two Amsterdammers gave each other plenty of space.

That pretty much set the tone for the rest of the season. His direct opponent in the next league match said, 'Cruyff is of course a crowd-puller and there's no point constantly running after him.' So the man-marker didn't and Ajax won in Nijmegen 3–1. Everyone wanted to see him play with their own eyes; the stadiums were full both in Amsterdam and for away games. So with each fresh Ajax victory he won everyone over a little. Both the treasurers and the lovers of beautiful passes had reason to celebrate, delighted that they'd been able to experience this. The press crowed with pleasure and his opponents showed respect. Anyone who injured the saviour of Dutch football lost a lot of friends. It helped that Cruyff rarely irritated the team he played against. During the game he concentrated more on his fellow players than on the opposition. 'But it wasn't as if the defenders let him do whatever he liked,' says Dick Schoenaker. 'They were sometimes simply too stunned by his timing, by the way he got hold of the ball. And he had become a master at playing the ball past a defender's standing leg, making it look as if the defender was doing nothing, when in fact his leg was planted firmly on the ground. That ease of Johan's was pure quality.'

Because Ajax hadn't lost a competition match since Cruyff's arrival, it looked as if everything was going smoothly. That was not entirely the case. As ever, Number 14 was weaving his spider's web through the team, which had consequences for everyone. Young enthusiasts who supported him on the pitch progressed; players who were accustomed to calling the shots lost confidence, sometimes because Cruyff made them look like idiots. 'He was always talking a lot to other people,' says Kieft. 'To Jesper Olsen, for example, the apple of his eye. Marco van Basten was another favourite, but Johan went on at him so long that one day Marco ended up in tears.' The senior player made his presence felt off the pitch as well. In the early spring an incident took place in the club restaurant that became famous. While playing pool, Johan once again started commenting on everyone. While Ling was concentrating on his shot, Johan kept on and on talking. 'If you don't shut your trap right now,' growled the right-winger, 'I'll ram this cue up your arse.'

Kieft went to stand next to him, thinking: you don't go saying a thing like that.

Ling had said it and, by his own account, had 'no more trouble' from the know-it-all, who was capable even of explaining to other people how they should pour fizzy water from a bottle into a glass. Ling thought him a brilliant footballer but also half-baked – and for his part Cruyff thought Ling was parasitising on the dedication of his fellow players. You could tell from the composition of the team who was on the short end of the stick. The popular Tscheu was far from always picked to play. 'I remember being reserve once because Ling was playing,' Kieft recalls. 'Johan came to me and said, "Next match, you'll be playing again." That turned out to be the case. He could simply force through things like that.' Ling was criticised non-stop during training and when the season was over he went off to join Panathinaikos in Greece.

Kieft, however, in those days an insecure 19-year-old striker, found precisely what he needed in the leadership of Cruyff (and of Johan's buddy Wim Jansen). 'Their presence meant I could play uninhibitedly,' he says. 'Everything was so self-evident to Johan. Nothing he did seemed forced. He didn't shout at you, he simply intervened when something went wrong and showed how to do it better. But he didn't say much to me aside from that. It seems I belonged in the category of players who would never really get to the top. Like Schoenaker.'

Schoenaker was the type of midfielder who moved forward, the kind Cruyff liked to work with: diligent and obedient and never too lazy to run 'thankless metres' when he didn't have possession. 'As soon as Johan called for the ball, I just gave it to him,' he says. 'Because if I persisted with what I wanted to do and the attack went wrong, I'd hear about it immediately. Johan didn't pull any punches. "You're utterly useless," he'd say, and that hit home, I can assure you. If the attack did go well, it was fine by him, because then we'd earn our money. That's just what Johan was like; it was all about earning money.'

Cruyff was playing so well that national coach Rijvers made another attempt to interest him in Oranje. In March 1982 he seemed to have succeeded. Now almost thirty-five, Cruyff had promising conversations with Rijvers. The thought of helping to nurture the young Dutch team appealed to him. Together the two former hotshots would take on bureaucratic 'Zeist'. But the relationship between Cruyff and the national coach quickly cooled because of what had become known as the 'clothing problem'. In his enthusiasm the player had said yes to the coach, but without Rijvers's knowledge he had told the KNVB that he still refused to play in Adidas. Partly because of that, the lines of communication faltered and misunderstandings piled up. Cruyff was selected by Rijvers and turned down the invitation, to the coach's amazement, at which point Rijvers sent him a letter. It had little chance of success. 'I won't answer,' Cruyff told the press. 'I'm not good at writing. I prefer to talk. I don't know what people want. I'm available, but I think people should be able to put themselves in my position and that means I must be able to play in a neutral shirt.'

Now it was Cruyff's turn to be surprised, because the coach sent the letter to the media.

The Oranje book fell shut. The number of international matches played by the best Dutch player of all time remained at a relatively laughable forty-eight.

Cruyff focused fully on Ajax again. And successfully so. On the evening of Saturday 15 May 1982 his team became national champions again. The Olympic Stadium filled up for the match against AZ'67, who stood third in the league. In six months Cruyff had imparted countless footballing insights to the players. He had irritated and delighted them by turns. He had enabled 17-year-old Van Basten to make his debut on 3 April. He had bolstered his own coffers and those of Ajax. And a week before the league championship finale he had signed a new contract, which meant he could continue to play for another year on roughly the same financial terms.

Cruyff the tactician made himself felt again too. Shortly before the match he said to coach Kurt Linder, 'Not Ling, Keje plays.' Right back Keje Molenaar had not had a place in the regular squad for months, but Cruyff felt he must be deployed as a kind of right half to block Hugo Hovenkamp, the eagerly advancing left back for AZ and the Dutch national team, an older player with the air of a street fighter. The players of Ajax and AZ ran on to the pitch. 'Just go past him,' Cruyff said to Molenaar, loudly enough for Hovenkamp to hear. 'That guy's completely useless.' Molenaar was impressed by Cruyff's bluff, by the craftiness that enabled him to bait and intimidate others, as Hovenkamp now saw. 'So that's what I did,' says Molenaar. 'I went past him.' He went past and made a cross that produced a goal. He went past again and scored himself.

Ajax eventually won 3-2 and became league champions. Young fans ran on to the pitch. Cruyff didn't like that, but they reached him before he realised what was happening and lifted him on to their shoulders. He looked uneasy – that he was a 'man of the people' didn't mean he wanted to sit on top of them. But he must have cheered inside. It was his first national title since the win with Barcelona in 1974, eight years before. The lean years of El Flaco seemed over and done with.

The Netherlands started to believe in its national sport again. *De Telegraaf* praised the 'good example' set by Ajax in relation to Cruyff and below its jubilant coverage was an advertisement for Cruyff Sports. Everybody happy.

To the regret of the saviour of the fatherland, 35-year-old Wim Jansen ended his footballing career. At Ajax the new season began with injuries and suspensions. Cruyff was not fit either; because of a knee injury he didn't play his first full match until 11 September 1982. Four days after that, Ajax were to play Celtic in the first round of the European Cup. Cruyff took aspirin to be able to play in Glasgow. A lot was expected of him, but there were also doubts about whether, at thirty-five, he could still cope with European football. 'If Cruyff manages to get us into the semi-finals of the European Cup this year, then he'll have done more than enough,' said an Ajax board member. It sounded like an attempt to provoke him, to mock him even. Despite his hero status, relations with the club had clearly cooled. The board had recently looked almost relieved when Ajax proved able to win without Number 14. It had started to irritate the high-ups at Ajax that Cruyff interfered with everything and might walk in on anyone if something was troubling him. From the board-room – a snake pit as ever – unpleasant rumours were spread about Johan. 'Of course, Ajax wasn't a nice club,' says Kieft. 'I thought the board members were fairly creepy, standoffish, with no charm at all. They were always trying to fob you off, espe-cially if you were a child of the club.'

The Celtic coach increased the tension further in the run-up to the match. He called Cruyff too old for top-level football. But even in his more mature years, scepticism proved to work like a pep pill. Aside from a penalty against him for a foul in his own area (which threw away a 1-0 lead), Cruyff provided the security the young team craved. As a striker with a free role – which the new Ajax coach Aad de Mos was happy to give him – he could be found all over the place. He sent swerving balls and lobs and helped Lerby make it 1-2. Celtic scored again as well, but in the end everyone at Ajax was more than satisfied with the 2-2 draw. The 'great conductor' had 'shown his team the way', the press wrote. It was starting to look very much as if all the arguments against him had given him extra motivation. But he waved away that suggestion. 'All bullshit,' he said. 'Of course, it was an important match for Ajax and for me, but how many times have I experienced that before?'

The return leg came two weeks after that draw. In the Olympic Stadium the clock stood at ten to ten. Another five minutes to go and the score was 1-1. Along with the 2-2 in Glasgow it would be just enough to get Ajax through to the second round of the European Cup on the away goals rule. Cruyff didn't manage to dominate as he had in Scotland, but that didn't matter now; it was the result that counted. The packed stadium was already longing for the next round. Celtic weren't a star team, so Ajax had a chance. To slow the game down, Cruyff, some 20 metres from the Scottish goal, on the right side of the pitch, did nothing for a moment. His right knee was bandaged – careful now. The ball was at his feet and Murdo MacLeod was standing facing him. To his right was Schoenaker, unmarked, running away from him towards the corner flag. A pass to him seemed the obvious thing, but Johan let the clock go on ticking. Then MacLeod stepped forward and, instead of passing the ball to Schoenaker, Cruyff took him on. He lost the ball with the pitch behind him as good as empty. He couldn't afford to lose the ball so he turned away from MacLeod, but was kicked in the ankle. The referee blew the whistle as Cruyff fell to the ground shouting. He couldn't go on and limped off the pitch.

Without their leader Ajax's play became even messier than it already was. Balls were kicked away wildly, marking was neglected. Shortly before the end of the match Celtic took advantage of the freedom on offer: 1-2. Ajax were out.

The next day nobody wrote that Cruyff had incurred his injury completely unnecessarily, that he ought to have simply played the ball to Schoenaker, that with a bit of imagination you could perhaps put the elimination down to a stupid move by the senior player himself. 'I was trying to force a free kick,' he said afterwards. 'I was challenging my opponent.' Before adding, 'That I was kicked off was a result of my attitude.'

Everyone in Amsterdam-Oost had hoped that the good play of the previous season would have a sequel in Europe. That chance had now passed. In the premier division too they were making little headway, as a result of injuries – although the maestro continued tirelessly pointing out to the players that everything, absolutely everything, on the pitch had a meaning, or ought to have. Cruyff himself regularly failed to appear and his play became less capricious. The supporters increasingly stayed at home. On 5 December 1982 only 10,000 came to watch Ajax play Helmond Sport. But the people who took the trouble to climb the steps of De Meer had a great time. It was Sinterklaas, gift-giving day in the Netherlands, and the Dutch had been given the best of presents by Cruyff.

By way of an overture, he made it 1-0 in the nineteenth minute with a header. That was special because, whether or not on account of his migraines, he rarely headed the ball. Two minutes later came the big surprise. After a foul against Lerby by Helmond player Jack Edelbloedt, Ajax were awarded a penalty. To everyone's astonishment, Cruyff, who hardly ever took penalties, came to stand on the spot. He bent down to ensure that the ball was placed on the ground properly and, as he was straightening up, he gave it a fleeting tap to the left, towards Jesper Olsen who was hurrying in his direction. Olsen ran straight ahead with the ball at his right foot. Goalkeeper Otto Versfeld stepped forward dumbfounded and Cruyff, who knew he would get the ball back, hopped with excitement. Despite his three European Cups, his Intercontinental Cup and his European Footballer of the Year awards, he jumped up as happy as a child. They had tried it out several times during training, but taking a penalty as a one-two-three in a match was not without risk.

It went well. Olsen tapped the ball back to him in front of the keeper and the child of thirty-five simply slid it into the empty goal. He coolly walked back to his own half for the kick-off.

'I wanted to give the public something extra for Christmas,' the mastermind joked afterwards. It was appreciated. The newspapers were full of praise for Cruyff and thought it a 'masterly trick' by a 'magician' because 'only Cruyff would dare to do such a thing'. He had anyhow 'shone' that afternoon with 'original passes'. Partly thanks to Helmond Sport, incidentally. Coach Jan Notermans had told his players not to tackle Cruyff too ferociously. 'You can of course always push, get yellow cards and that kind of thing,' Notermans said afterwards. 'But that's of no use to anybody.'

The score (5-0) was pleasing. Ajax took over the top position from PSV and what Cruyff had predicted was exactly what happened: people were talking about it for days. In fact, the pictures of the 'indirect penalty' went all round the world and Cruyff would be reminded of that historic moment for years. Ajax weren't alone in enjoying the fruits of it. Shirt sponsor TDK was happy too; the Japanese manufacturer of video and audio tapes was Ajax's main sponsor that year and it became world famous in no time, partly because of that stunt.

The good cheer with which 1982 ended was followed by a bleak start to 1983. On 9 January just 6,000 people came to watch the KNVB Cup match between Ajax and FC The Hague, despite the fact Cruyff was playing. The sense of dejection was made even worse by the detonation of a fragmentation bomb on the terraces, injuring twenty people, one of them seriously. The bomber turned out to be a supporter of the Centrumpartij, a young anti-immigrant party the growth of which was worrying many Dutch people. The image of supporters fighting with the riot police reinforced the atmosphere of crisis in professional football and far beyond.

Two weeks later, on 22 January, Johan's stepfather Uncle Henk died. The death of Henk Angel hit Cruyff extremely hard. Since the day the Ajax groundsman moved in with his mother in the early 1960s, after Manus died, he had been a great support to Johan and his older brother Henny by his presence alone. Later too, after Henk retired in the early 1970s, Johan had always had a warm relationship with him. 'We will miss his courage, humour and love,' said the death notice. 'I've lost two fathers,' said Johan later on television.

Yet the day after his Uncle Henk died, he played against FC Groningen. He might have done better not to. The match was a true spectacle (5–5), but not least because Cruyff was incapable of bringing order to the chaos. The newspapers, which had heard nothing of his loss, described him as 'not very inspired'. They criticised his 'woeful passes' in what they called 'his weakest match'.

In consultation with coach De Mos he decided to take a couple of weeks off. He flew with his family to the sun of Gran Canaria. There he could come to terms with everything and rest his back and hip, which had been troubling him lately.

All through the remainder of the season, tensions rose as so often before. The players complained about Johan's mid-season holiday. Moreover, his absence had no noticeable effect on the results. 'He wasn't playing so well any longer,' Kieft says. 'And then if you're not there, your authority declines. That's just the way it goes.' With brilliant young players like Van Basten, Olsen and Vanenburg, it seemed Ajax could do just fine without him. Cruyff's instructions were increasingly brushed aside. *Het Parool* wrote that on 6 March 1983 against PSV he was 'ignored' on the pitch, even 'boycotted'. 'The organisation has weakened a bit,' he admitted himself. 'It's not going the way it went last season. The situation was different then.'

That was all too true. Ajax chairman Ton Harmsen made a show of dropping his most expensive player. He stressed Cruyff's frequent absences and described him to journalists as a profiteer. Because of his injuries, Johan was no longer worth his salary. What Harmsen neglected to mention was the death of Uncle Henk and how much it had affected Johan and thrown him off balance. As if that wasn't bad enough, Leo van Veen, the *libero* brought in on Cruyff's recommendation, had proven useless. Johan knew him from the Los Angeles Aztecs and with his famous loyalty – or obstinacy – continued to back him. That damaged Johan's standing. Meanwhile, he kept on bombarding the club leadership with plans for improvements. Those interventions were interpreted as a kind of coup, which the board 'didn't want to hear about'.

Harmsen, described by his friends as committed and trustworthy and by his enemies as boorish, snarled at journalists, 'We took a decision long ago about whether to go on with him or not.'

Cruyff said, 'There's no way I can continue working here.'

There was a way, of course. The former number 14 – number 9 this season – drew energy from the animosity and from that point on he was always fully engaged. Right to the end of the season, Ajax won practically everything. 'Cruyff was Cruyff again,' wrote *Het Parool* in late March. 'He made fools of opponents with brilliant slaloms, sent passes with the accuracy of a billiard player and scored like a grand master.' Sometimes he was forced to play sweeper and even that new role came easily to him.

By early May the national title was theirs again. The much-discussed 'pain in the arse' was photographed in the dressing room, bare-chested and holding a glass of champagne, radiating a kind of childlike relief. Of course, he was asked why he wasn't staying at Ajax. 'I'd like to,' he told the press. 'But at my age the love needs to come from both sides.'

He could forget about that. On 10 May Harmsen told him there was 'no place' for him for the coming season. Cruyff was insulted. He would have liked to end his career at Ajax and failed to understand why he was being stopped from doing so by people who didn't know nearly as much about football as he did. Coach De Mos would have loved to continue with him, as would many of the team, but there were other players who couldn't help grinning when they heard Johan was leaving. 'Some of us were a bit fed up with his overwhelming presence,' Molenaar remembers. He would never forget the giggly mood in the players' bus with Cruyff still standing outside signing autographs. 'But within a short while we changed our tune.'

On Saturday 14 May the theme of the final league match in De Meer was love for the wiry Cruyff and hatred towards the burly dealer in central heating parts, Harmsen. When Ajax vs Fortuna ended (6-5), the chairman, surrounded by bodyguards, had to seek refuge in the boardroom while the cheering for 36-six-year-old Cruyff continued. Johan wiped his eyes and said to the press, 'Leaving is always sad. But it's a great feeling to have all these people behind you. It's not my fault I'm leaving Ajax.'

He would leave for real three days later, when Ajax, already league champions, won the KNVB Cup with a 3-1 victory away against NEC Nijmegen. Cruyff set up the first two goals and closed his career in the white shirt with red bar with, as *de Volkskrant* wrote, 'a magisterial shot in the top corner'.

But Cruyff didn't want to stop. He still felt fit and was full of hard feelings. For weeks there had been speculation about a switch to Feyenoord. On the one hand that seemed unimaginable – the Amsterdam artist in the chequered shirt of the working classes of Rotterdam-Zuid? Still, he was good at arithmetic. Feyenoord had a large stadium with a great potential for 'increased yields', and a team that after several years in the doldrums seemed to have rediscovered the way to the top. Supporters had been coming to De Kuip in larger numbers this season than a year earlier, whereas in Amsterdam-Oost the opposite was the case. So those with any real knowledge of Cruyff were not surprised to see him go over to the rival. He would show the board at Ajax who was stronger. Nobody but him could decide where and when he would stop.

The boy from Betondorp and the board at Feyenoord agreed on a one-year contract. Over the summer Cruyff prepared himself for his last great venture as a player.

CHAPTER TWENTY-FIVE

A magical self-image

In the autumn of 1983 the Dutch economy went into recession. Fifteen thousand unemployed people were added to the card index of the Social Services department every month, the government had a budget deficit of more than 10 per cent, and spending cuts by the centre-right cabinet were harsh and controversial. Under the leadership of Prime Minister Ruud Lubbers, there was renewed encouragement for private initiatives. A conflict between government and unions led to a lengthy strike by public sector workers. Rubbish piled up in the streets, trains and trams reduced their speed and the post was often delivered late. But Johan Cruyff arrived on time. He reported to Rotterdam-Zuid as if it was the most normal thing in the world, and as a true entrepreneur he took risks. On top of his (less than impressive) salary, he would earn four guilders fifty for every ticket sold above the average of 22,000. A bold agreement, since nobody could predict to what extent the footballer, seen as a symbol of the despised capital city of Amsterdam, would be able to fill De Kuip.

So Cruyff put into practice the preaching of Prime Minister Lubbers. The Rotterdam son of entrepreneurs and the Amsterdam son of shopkeepers were both devotees of practical solutions and of setting about things with energy and commitment, of market forces as a remedy for laziness and bureaucracy. 'Football tells you what's going to happen in society,' Cruyff said shortly after his debut with Feyenoord. 'First we saw levelling in football; a bit later we noticed those tendencies in daily life. And what are we seeing now? That the spectators prefer to watch independently operating players again: individualism, and therefore decentralisation.'

In Rotterdam Cruyff did what he always did, bending everything to his will. At the first training session he moved the marker cones and got on his old hobby-horses. In Amsterdam they could repeat it all in their sleep: don't stand in the corners in games of four against two; don't run towards Cruyff during practice matches but away from him; move up on the right if he has the ball on the left of midfield, so that his most powerful weapon, the curving ball kicked with the outside of his right foot, can have maximum effect; don't hold back when moving forward but keep running so that he can put the ball behind the defenders; after losing the ball at the front go after it again immediately; and having got the ball back, those less well-versed in technique in particular were to deliver it straight to Cruyff.

At Feyenoord there were no brilliant players like Marco van Basten, and at the age of thirty-six Cruyff could no longer do everything he used to, physically speaking. His solution was to talk and direct more than ever. 'Nothing was unimportant to him,' said defender Henk Duut later. 'Even the warming up was focused on achieving the optimal result. Before he came we used to take it easy sometimes during practice matches against amateur clubs. Well, not with Johan. "If you get something wrong now," he'd say, "then you're certain to get it wrong in a difficult match." With him around, you could never slacken off. He was always critical, and self-critical too.'

The Amsterdammer remained entirely himself in Rotterdam, but to claim he was loved from the start would be overstating it. The chequered shirt and black shorts didn't flatter his frag-ile-looking body at all. The alternative strip, all yellow, was so hideous that it seemed intended to make fun of the country's best footballer of all time. Some supporters didn't even want to see him in their beloved attire and returned their season tickets for 1983-84 to the Feyenoord office, cut into pieces. In De Kuip there was whistling as soon as the announcer said his name, and after an unsuccessful pass the most fanatical supporters would shout, 'Can't we get rid of that man?' Cruyff, with his chatter and hand flapping, was Amsterdam made flesh, hard to reconcile with the steely hand-in-hand feeling that had characterised life for so long in Rotterdam. Moreover, Feyenoord had a good season behind them, with their uncomplicated and recognisably 'Rotterdam-style' football.

Despite a promising start and ample victories against weak opponents, irritation grew among the players as well. 'Cruyff kept harping on about positional play,' Duut said later. 'He could talk interminably about taking corners. It sometimes drove us crazy, but most of us didn't dare to argue.' Some Feyenoorders were afraid of looking stupid next to the genius and held back during matches, leaving Johan to deal with things. That was not the intention, of course, and partly because of a lack of chemistry the Rotterdammers suffered a humiliating defeat on 18 September 1983. Ajax showed them up in the Olympic Stadium by winning 8-2. *Voetbal International* chose what for Cruyff was the worst possible headline: 'Ton Harmsen Proven Right'. The Ajax chairman did indeed seem vindicated. His young team, with Van Basten, Vanenburg, Olsen and Van 't Schip, had looked more vigorous in the pouring rain in Amsterdam than Feyenoord, where everything revolved around the expensive meddler from Vinkeveen.

Although Feyenoord often won, the crowd got to see few of Cruyff's tours de force. The maestro, as the newspapers continued to call him, quite often chose to pull back from the fray and thereby draw his opponents away from their positions. That gave his fellow players space for initiatives, but only the experts saw that. Sometimes the press thought him 'invisible' and afterwards he would disappear briskly into the catacombs in the knowledge that he had helped his team to victory.

Cruyff didn't seem to take anything to heart. After the mammoth defeat in Amsterdam he told his teammates that whether you lost by 8–2 or by 1–0 made hardly any difference in the long term. Everything would be fine once organisation on the pitch had been optimised. That was the message again after Feyenoord were knocked out of the UEFA Cup by Tottenham Hotspur. Both at home and away, they hadn't stood a chance. In London, Cruyff was so outclassed by Glenn Hoddle that he went over to exchange shirts with the English midfielder afterwards out of respect. And in Rotterdam the misery on 2 November 1983 was further underlined by rioting among supporters and fighting in the stands. All the same, Cruyff carried on unperturbed with his habitual approach: talking and directing. He did his job; it was what he had come to Rotterdam to do and afterwards he drove back in good humour to Vinkeveen. Fortunately, Willem van Hanegem was there to step in if things weren't going smoothly between Johan and the rest. In the background, invisible to the outside world, the former player acted as a kind of trainee assistant coach alongside the (less than influential) coach Thijs Libregts. When Johan yet again made the players dizzy with his lectures, Van Hanegem would often counter it all with a dry remark. That made the others relax and they were now playing better by the week.

So relations remained pleasantly businesslike. In the boardroom Cruyff did not make major issues out of things as he had done so often at Ajax. Internal affairs at Feyenoord didn't exactly enthral him, which saved everyone a lot of disruption. He concentrated on the game and the results, which were what he was there for. The playmaker wearing number 10 passed up club outings, and the players and trainers let him smoke his cigarettes in the bus or in the toilets next to the changing room. Fine, just as long as Feyenoord won the league for the first time since 1974. The role of Cor Coster was illustrative of the relaxed atmosphere. In the boardroom his appearance caused none of the annoyance it had provoked at De Meer; here there were no memories of aggressive business encounters with Coster. In fact, they found him a convivial Amsterdammer, keen on a drink and full of good stories.

In Rotterdam Cruyff did not stress the artistry of the game so much as its effectiveness. 'The organisation off and on the pitch is decisive for me,' he is said to have claimed after the 1983-84 season. The league would be won not by the team with the most beautiful play but by the team that made the fewest mistakes. He had realised long ago that Ajax, with all those fun young players, were making more and more mistakes and 'his' Feyenoord fewer and fewer. That was logical: in Amsterdam his edicts were increasingly forgotten and in Rotterdam they were being drummed into the team every day. 'The nice thing was,' says defender Duut, 'after a while we demanded from each other the maximum Johan asked of us. The norm became higher.'

Even in the television programme he presented that season along with Dieuwertje Blok, *Cruyff & Co*, effectiveness took precedence over fun. The programme had been Cruyff's own idea; he'd done something similar in Washington. He liked to teach and took it seriously. Young people must know that good technique above all served a purpose. Perhaps they thought technique meant doing tricks. Well, Cruyff didn't. 'Shooting with both legs,' he said, for example. 'A footballer must be able to do that. Not because it's so attractive, that's not the point. It's useful.' He went further. 'In recent years it's irritated me that there's such bad play in professional football. It's partly because of a lack of technique.' Patiently, if not always clearly, he explained how to kick curving shots, how to volley and how to receive the ball. Mind you, children mustn't forget that going to school and gaining diplomas was the most important thing of all. In that respect they shouldn't follow his example.

At Feyenoord, too, Cruyff imparted his knowledge of

football incessantly. As a result, the organisation improved, as did the players' 'mental resilience', as the newspapers called it. In December 1983 the team went into the winter break at the top of the league. Even so, Cruyff kept at it. Everything could and should be improved and the way he achieved that would produce one of the most famous anecdotes in Dutch football. The man on the receiving end was Pierre Vermeulen. A skilful left-winger, Vermeulen might to some extent be called the Tscheu La Ling of Feyenoord: adroit and popular but in Cruyff's eyes also lazy and slow. Vermeulen was treated by the leader much as Ling had been. During training sessions Cruyff would kick balls to him slightly too hard and then gesture, 'What do I do with this guy?' When midfielder André Stafleu asked him what the point of those hard balls was, Cruyff mumbled, 'He just needs to listen.'

As well as dribbling round other players and crossing the ball, Vermeulen always had to bear his defensive duties in mind. That was something he was unwilling or unable to do. He was belittled, just like Ling in 1982. Now the crux: the left-winger was injured and Cruyff replaced him with a left back. The reserve defender Stanley Brard was given a chance to support Cruyff in his role as attacking midfielder by being a 'hanging' left-winger. After he'd recovered, Vermeulen was left on the bench – with Johan it was now all or nothing. 'Especially when you get a bit older, you need to have a firm grip on your team,' Cruyff said a short time later in *De Telegraaf.* 'If you want to achieve a top-class performance with a team, you have to put the whole squad up against the wall. There must be no escape route, nobody can get away. Then I've got what I'm after, I can dominate the rest and the game goes the way I want.'

Brard did precisely what Cruyff wanted: 'defend forwards'. The dedication of the student of physical education enabled Cruyff to swerve all over the pitch and kick his sublime curving balls. In case of emergency Brard could rush to his aid. This had consequences for the composition of the rest of the team – sweeper Ruud Gullit started playing on the right wing – but it worked. Further fixed patterns emerged. 'He systematically hammered it in,' said right back Sjaak Troost later. 'It added movement, dynamism. With endless practice we learnt three varieties of attack.' Cruyff's tactical insight, along with the lung capacity of his Feyenoord 'water carriers', became from that moment on a combination that was hard to beat. 'Everyone knew what he was supposed to do,' believed defender Duut, who now became a left half. 'And if there was a problem, Johan would solve it. That gave us a feeling of invincibility.'

The Amsterdammer who had a world reputation as an advocate of attacking play had put Feyenoord back on track with a defensive measure.

The revenge came in February. Feyenoord threw Ajax out of the battle for the KNVB Cup and in the league Cruyff scored one of four goals against the club that had sent him packing in 1983. After scoring he wheeled his arms through De Kuip like in the old days and afterwards it was good to have a smoke knowing the 4-1 victory had, to some extent at least, erased the 8-2 defeat in the Olympic Stadium.

Without truly sparkling, Feyenoord held their place at the top of the premier division. With a 4-4-2 formation, often used at Ajax to spare the ageing player, many matches were 'controlled', even to the extent that Cruyff sometimes deliberately didn't play 'well' (forcefully, with beautiful initiatives) but 'badly' (understated, to give the other players space). It was a matter of what was expedient. As ever there were professional players no better than average who exceeded themselves thanks to him. The most striking among them was André Hoekstra, a diligent but technically limited midfielder who moved up the pitch time and again and received the ball from Cruyff precisely on time, in other words behind the last defender, so that 'Koko' only had to 'scramble' them in. He hit the spot nineteen times. Hoekstra basked in the glow at the side of the grand master and as a result even played for Oranje once, in March 1984, to his own surprise.

On 19 February FC Groningen were the last team to beat Feyenoord – the Visionary of Vinkeveen didn't play. After the 1-0 defeat in Groningen, *Het Vrije Volk* noted that Feyenoord were 'vulnerable' without Cruyff. 'He's the only one who can bring real serenity and he can often produce precisely the ball that creates the goal that saves the match,' wrote the Rotterdam paper. Sure enough, after Groningen there were no more defeats.

Cruyff had his reputation on his side, of course. Many opponents respected him, and if they didn't the referees would protect him. 'Generally speaking, in his last year at Ajax and after that at Feyenoord it held true that as an opponent you'd have a free kick given against you if you either kicked a random Ajax or Feyenoord player to the ground or took the ball off Johan Cruyff,' wrote Nico Scheepmaker with irony. Referee Charles Corver would later admit that he was sometimes 'manipulated' by Cruyff. 'Just look at that; you can't call that football,' he would say to Corver during a match. The ref was sensitive to such remarks. 'He could needle sometimes and then the opponents would start to say to me: that Cruyff can get away with anything. I'd got used to it; maybe I did let him go too far.'

Benefiting from his charisma and driven by ambition, Cruyff led the Rotterdam club to victory both in the league and in the cup. As far as he was concerned it was clear: in 1983 he had won the 'double' with Ajax and now he'd won it with Feyenoord, missing hardly a match. So who had been proven right, Cruyff or Ajax chairman Harmsen?

On 13 May 1984 Cruyff was lifted on to shoulders for the last time in his career – yet again with apparent reluctance – and then it really was over. His active career definitively ended after that final league match with Feyenoord against PEC Zwolle. His hard feelings towards Ajax had paid off. From a financial point of view the season had brought him slightly less than he'd hoped, since secretly he had been banking on more spectators. The bonus for Cruyff was 'only' close to 25,000 guilders per home game, but the mental satisfaction was far greater.

The board of Feyenoord begged him to sign up again. Despite his thirty-seven years, as far as chairman Gerard Kerkum was concerned he could be given carte blanche to do whatever he liked, if only he'd stay. 'But that's not the sort of thing I do,' Cruyff told journalists. 'It seems I'm important to Feyenoord, and if that's what you are, then you need to be fully present.' The season had placed heavy demands on his body. It had taken him longer to recover from each match. 'When I was twenty, it took me two hours; after my last match it took three days,' he said later in an interview. 'Completely worn out. I was still alive, but I wasn't really there. Two days completely out of it, and the third slowly recovering.' He couldn't defy his body any longer. 'All I'm after now,' he said, 'is rest.'

During the tribute on the Coolsingel he looked out across the tens of thousands of jubilant Feyenoord fans from the balcony of Rotterdam town hall, a glass of champagne in one hand, a cigarette in the other. It was enough.

In the Cruyff household his departure was a completely different experience from that of the 'farewell game' in the Olympic Stadium against Bayern Munich in 1978. 'Then I was relieved and thought finally I'd be able to lead a family life with Johan as if we're any other family,' Danny said later to the press. 'Johan was glad it was over too. He was thoroughly fed up with football and I think months went by before he went to watch a match again. Now it's totally different. The first few days after the decision, the whole family was distraught. When on Friday morning he suddenly told me he was stopping I was astounded. I've seen him flourish again this year because of football and because of Feyenoord. After all the blows he's had to absorb in recent years, this season was a breath of fresh air. I don't think people like Gerard Kerkum, Thijs Libregts and all those others at Feyenoord know the half of it, they've meant so much to him. They've let the person Johan Cruyff stand up again and I'm eternally grateful to them for that.'

But Johan wasn't completely finished. He still had to go on a tour of Indonesia and Saudi Arabia. Feyenoord had contractually obliged him to play in those countries. In Saudi Arabia he played a half with the Saudis and was richly rewarded for it. Prince Faisal handed him a twenty-four-carat gold bar with accompanying tea service to the value of 80,000 guilders. The other players were each given 250 guilders. A distinction had to be made.

His successes in the year and a half at Ajax and the season with Feyenoord meant a great deal to Cruyff. He had led both clubs right to the top, single-handedly, mainly by sticking firmly to his ideas and just letting everyone talk. Board members, journalists, spectators, yes, even most of his teammates: what did they know? They couldn't see what he saw in between his moves on the pitch. He had produced an incredible performance by going his own way with his wiry body and especially with his huge football brain. He knew it, and a certain sense of spirituality, which had been there ever since his father's death, now took hold of him. The awareness of his talent sometimes made him lonely, he admitted after the summer of 1984 in an interview with journalist Ischa Meijer. 'Call it aloneness. You could also say that I'm a good craftsman, better than the rest. I was always more advanced.'

He was 'more advanced' and, as Harrie van Mens, his adviser in this stage of his life, described it, he had 'a magical self-image'. 'It's strange that over the past two and a half years I've lost precisely one competition match,' Cruyff said to Meijer. 'Strange. How is it possible? I think about that sometimes.' It must have been his permanent attentiveness. Ever since his years as an Ajax junior he had probably concentrated from start to finish in practically every match – something that was unique in his sport. Given that he had possession of the ball for about five minutes of each match, it was undoubtedly those other eighty-five minutes that had made the difference, those minutes of 'talking, directing, searching while thinking', as he put it. Cruyff believed this must have involved supernatural forces. First that debacle with Basilevitch, then the forced return to the pitch and now all this success. It seemed that 'whoever gave me my gifts thought I hadn't played long enough', he said to Meijer. 'That I'd let too few people benefit from them. It could be that he thought: have one deep fall, then go all over the world.' As a result, Cruyff concluded, 'I was put in a position to calmly start again. It couldn't have been planned better.'

Jopie, the favourite son, had always been watched over by his father, he was convinced of that. 'I believe in my own way,' he said two years after his retirement as a player. 'Perhaps in a strange way, but I do think there's something or someone up there. In my own way I'm in contact with it.' His contact with the dead Manus had transpired during a second seance in Barcelona. The connection was made with a glass and an ouija board. Cruyff asked his father to make his watch stop, as a sign. The next morning the watch was no longer ticking. 'I had the mechanism looked at three times over,' Cruyff said. 'In the end I was tired of it not working and I said out loud to my father, "That's enough now." After that my watch never stopped again.'

He talked about such things with astonishment, but also with complete seriousness. Until shortly before his death he would bring up the subject, because he really did believe his father protected him. And after the death of Uncle Henk in 1983 there were two men watching over him. 'I've lost two fathers,' he said. 'That's a very great disadvantage, but of course I have two watching out for me. And I suspect that if something is wrong, they'll warn me.'

Under the influence of the supernatural, Cruyff's life had been 'mapped out' in advance. There was no other possibility. 'I assume that nothing in this world happens without a reason, but where that comes from and who thinks it all up, I don't know.' This conviction saddled him with a special responsibility for his fellow human beings. 'I have been given many qualities by God,' he said. 'You can't keep that for yourself, you've got to share it.'

Falling, getting up again and climbing to the top had been his 'destiny', he was convinced, and he was now going to 'share' that with others. 'Johan was convinced that different rules applied to him,' says adviser Harrie van Mens. 'In everything he did, his own thinking was central. He relied entirely on the insights he had acquired as a footballer and confidently applied them in other areas.' Van Mens, who assisted Cruyff with his business affairs for years, found it a fascinating experience. The tax expert had never before met someone who had such faith in his own abilities.

Cruyff knew broadly where his future lay: in the world of soccer. That was also the advice given to him by top business-man Anton Dreesmann in September 1984. The director of the Vroom & Dreesmann department store was regarded as an opin-ion leader in the business world in those years and Cruyff had always felt drawn to entrepreneurs. Dreesmann listened to his life story and spoke the prophetic words, 'Stick to what you know.' Later the former footballer said, 'A whole lot of the opportunities offered to me immediately became taboo at that point.'

He certainly knew all about football stadiums, Cruyff felt. So he joined forces with Philips, the building firm Ballast Nedam and a company that made lighting towers. They all wanted to market hypermodern stadiums, known as 'Tradiums', a com-bination of stadium and trade. The concept was based on the Nieuw Galgenwaard stadium in Utrecht, which had opened in 1982: grass, stands, shops and offices in one complex. Johan was to help promote this multifunctional concept abroad. He had no doubts as to whether or not he would succeed. Two billion of the people on earth knew who he was and among them were plenty of government ministers and top businesspeople who were keen to meet him. 'We have so many qualities and capacities available, it's sure to go well,' he told the press. With his fame and charisma he could help to open doors and thereby sell the Tradiums – which commerce would make affordable – even to poorer countries. It was an example of 'sharing'. He regarded his mission as something really big. 'I'm working on making Dutch business life into a single whole,' Johan told Ischa Meijer. 'So that it can act in the outside world as a solid bloc.' He would be 'a kind of captain' for companies, in charge of their 'Holland promotion'. 'I just compare it to the old days, when we had those ships sailing the world's oceans, which were eventually combined into a company and only then became profitable. Something like that is what we're after.'

Little would come of his East India Company ambitions. Cruyff made two or three trips for the consortium and secured not a single order.

'Of course, his self-confidence inclined towards an overestimation of himself,' says Van Mens looking back. 'He really did believe that everything he undertook would be a success.' But in other fields he was anything but standing still. Commercial activities for a washing powder, for example, and the expansion of Cruyff Sports into Spain kept him busy. He'd also linked his name to a line of cosmetics for sports-loving men (massage oil, shampoo, soap, talc, aftershave). In December 1984 he started work as adviser to the sponsor of football club Roda JC. In March the following year he gave a speech at the Erasmus University in Rotterdam with the message that internationally famous sportspeople (such as he) should be deployed more often for purposes of PR. In early May he helped the club MVV to set up a youth training scheme in South Limburg. But his work as an adviser in Maastricht did not last long. The telephone rang. Aad de Mos had been sacked as coach at Ajax.

Although Ajax were on the point of winning the league, the players were dissatisfied with De Mos. Marco van Basten and John van 't Schip among others had already complained to Johan, whose name had been mentioned as a possible new

coach. He would have liked to do it, but he had no coaching
diploma. Naturally Cruyff was not going to take a course and
be lectured by people who understood less about the game than
he did. Earlier in 1985 he had made an attempt to get special
dispensation. The KNVB had been sympathetic and, because
of his services to football, it had come up with all kinds of ideas
for getting him an alternative qualification. It did not consult
with its own national board, however, and the head of training
was almost sacked for his accommodating attitude to Cruyff.
Now, after a lot of phone calls and letters back and forth, it
proved impossible for the country's greatest expert on football
to become a coach *honoris causa*. The conservative board refused
to hear of an honorary doctorate or any other such solution. Led
by lawyers, the board feared setting a precedent and insisted
Cruyff must obey the rules. Not even a shortened course of
training, such as was used by the skating association for former
speed skaters, was on offer. Any aspiring coach, even if he was
a global star, would have to follow the course from beginning
to end. Cruyff refused.

Diploma or no diploma, Cruyff wanted to work at Ajax. Two
years before, he had felt insulted at being dismissed, but the club
was his family, to which he always returned. Ajax was 'the place
where my heart lies', he said later in an interview. But what job
could he do there? The solution was found in the term 'technical director'. It was a job description hardly ever used in those
days, which naturally made it all the more appealing to Cruyff.
In recent years he had in reality been an informal coach at Ajax
and Feyenoord, and that was what he would be again, disguised
as a technical director. Even better, he would now be both the
coach and the boss of all technical matters. Ajax chairman Ton
Harmsen gave him the space to run both the youth training
scheme and the scouting and team selection. Cruyff had insisted
on total control; at the Washington Diplomats he had learnt
how well it could work when all the technical decisions were
made at one and the same desk.

The spies of the coaches' union shook their heads as they watched Cruyff taking part in training on the Middenweg, which was not really permitted under the rules. They saw him open his mouth on the subs' bench, although even that was forbidden. The nitpickers threatened to take action, but the technical director at Ajax simply got on with his work. He took comfort in the fact that there were three fully certified coaches at Ajax: Spitz Kohn, Cor van der Hart and Tonny Bruins Slot. And where was it written that a director couldn't run across the training pitches? That he couldn't kick a ball about with the lads if he felt like it? Moreover, the three men with diplomas led the training sessions, while Cruyff simply took part in positional play and practice games, giving football lessons as he did so. That was the official hierarchy. The fact that his lessons naturally carried more weight than those of the official coaches made no difference at all. 'He could explain it all perfectly well with his mouth,' Ajax player Ronald Koeman is quoted in his biography as saying, 'but far better when he joined in.'

Perhaps this was the best possible role for Cruyff, as the coach who could show what he meant. There were no longer any people of equal rank, no issues of competence; he was the boss and could take all the decisions he wanted. This was 'sharing' at its best. He could convey to others his entire accumulation of experiences and insights and all in his own way, resolute and radical. He would make 'no concessions', he predicted in an interview, 'even if we lose three times in a row'. Everything had to make way for his 'ideal' of a team that entertained the public with brilliant attacking football. The 'ideal picture' that he had in his head included a 'learning process' on the way to perfect football. Cruyff was after roughly the kind of game he had played in the early 1970s, but purer and more graceful. He rarely patted anyone on the back – he'd hardly ever had that kind of encouragement himself. He left conventional teaching to the three coaches with diplomas. 'I don't have a programme,' he said. 'You see people making mistakes in matches and you can build your training sessions around those mistakes.'

Critiquing and showing how it ought to be done were perhaps his greatest strengths. The converse, telling a coherent story, was best left to others. 'At first Johan would try to explain to us how our upcoming opponent played,' remembers defender Sonny Silooy. 'He did that based on the information trainer Tonny Bruins Slot had given him. But Bruins Slot kept having to correct him. We laughed, of course. The next time he'd struggle again. It was beyond him. Then he said to Tonny, "Just you do it." From that moment on the explaining was left to Bruins Slot and he could ask critical questions while we were listening. That suited him far better.'

Delegation turned out to be the solution. Others could decide on medical matters (specialist work) and condition training (which didn't interest him), leaving him free to achieve what he wanted by correcting the players daily.

But because Johan was not good at picking up signals that enough was enough, there was sometimes irritation. 'Many of the lads thought Johan waffled on too much,' said Arnold Mühren later, the midfielder who had played for Ajax in the early 1970s and had now been brought back to inject calm and facilitate consultation. The young left-winger Rob de Wit was driven to despair by all Cruyff's comments. 'Coach, let me go back inside,' De Wit said after Cruyff stopped the game yet again to point out a mistake to him. 'I obviously don't understand.' De Wit wasn't the only one. Ronald Koeman lost his temper. 'I remember a session when Cruyff wouldn't stop going on at me,' he says in his biography. 'It got to a point when I could no longer control myself and yelled, "If you don't shut your damn mouth right now!" The funny thing is that Johan was calmer after that and our relationship got better and better.'

The technical director shouted all kinds of things during games, but none of it was ever meant personally. After the training sessions ended, his emotions poured away down the drain along with the shower water. Tomorrow was another day.

Like Michels, Cruyff kept hammering on about discipline and sometimes thought up the strangest punishments in order to impose his will on the players. After they had made a mess of a game against an amateur team, he sent them to the A10 ring road, which was still under construction. From the place where the exit for Watergraafsmeer was later built, close to De Meer, they had to run a given distance across the loose sand and back. If they didn't do it within a certain time they had to repeat the exercise.

'Van Basten was late,' Silooy remembers. 'So everyone had to run up that sand hill again. Marco was late that time too. So we had to do it again. When we finally all made it back to De Meer on time, Johan shouted, "From now on, listen!"'

Cruyff drilled the players much as Michels had drilled him in the 1960s. All so that the young squad was ready for the demands of top-class football. But there was more going on than that. He wanted not just Ajax but the Netherlands as a whole to benefit from his formidable insight into the game, from his knowledge, his 'magic'. In a double interview with Michels in the football monthly *ELF*, he denounced the inadequate 'mental condition' of the Van Basten generation; young players had grown up with too many compliments and too little street football. That was why Dutch teams were beaten on international pitches when called upon to put up a fight. He wasn't entirely wrong. Despite having plenty of talent, in 1985 Oranje failed to qualify for the final round of any major competition for the third time in a row.

So what Cruyff did was not merely training, he said in *ELF*, it was 'moulding'. Young people spent too much time indoors, their motor systems were not what they used to be. His mission – his 'destiny' – was to make clear to the country everything that was wrong with sport and society. In 1985 only half as many people came to watch professional football as when he was young. Because of contemptible results-oriented football, most league matches were 'unwatchable'. Cruyff sought the solution in a return to the street. Where that was impossible because of increased road traffic, specially laid out pitches were needed (the later Cruyff Courts). A man on a mission, the Ajax trainer entered into talks with the Ministry of Health, Welfare and Culture. 'Cruyff started talking and in his enthusiasm he was almost impossible to interrupt,' one of the civil servants present, Chris Buitelaar, remembers. 'He was convinced of the social and educational importance of sport for children, which received little attention in the ministry at that time. Young people needed to move more, he believed, and the greatest footballing talents must be trained in the clubs by former top players. That would foster success, from which society in turn would benefit. A crystal-clear story, which unfortunately became completely incomprehensible as soon as he tried to put his political vision into words. But the football idea was simple: play attractive football with well-trained players so that people would come to the stadiums again.'

Full of bravura, Cruyff announced the 'gospel of risk', as the newspapers called it. 'It's all about details most people don't see,' he said. 'Only, will the others take it up too? Otherwise you keep working away on your own. If you think beyond that, then you need to get everything lined up. Oranje, Ajax, Feyenoord and PSV. Then you can make a breakthrough.' Players who had grown up with little opposition needed to realise that football – and really this applied to everything – was a 'struggle for life'. They had to 'learn to lose' so they could go on to improve. 'It's certain to pay off in the long term.'

CHAPTER TWENTY-SIX

Super-consistent

On the afternoon of Sunday, 6 October 1985, Cruyff showed that all his stories about 'the football of the future' were sincerely meant, that even if he had been a 'performance guy' he'd always looked further than the results on the day. Ajax had lost 2-1 to archrivals Feyenoord in the Olympic Stadium, but to look at him you'd think his team had won. A television interviewer summed up his performances as a beginner coach: lost at home to PSV, knocked out of the European Cup by FC Porto, lost to FC Groningen and now to Feyenoord. Ajax had in the meantime given several smaller clubs a drubbing, but the question was whether Cruyff had started to doubt himself a little. After nine league matches his team were five points behind leaders PSV and Feyenoord (although they had played one match fewer).

The word 'doubt' bounced off the coach's pale face; his eyes continued to look fixedly at the interviewer. No, he never had any doubts, he responded, although he was naturally aware of criticism from some experts, Michels among others. The 'association co-ordinator', as Michels now was, had called his attacking tactic 'suicide'. The 38-year-old coach pointed out to journalists the mistakes his players had made in August against PSV, which they had not made today in the match against Feyenoord. That was progress. The lads had improved and Ajax had played well that afternoon. They just hadn't made use of their chances. Clear?

'Well, well,' the interviewer went on. 'A satisfied coach who loses.'

'I'm probably out on my own again there,' said Cruyff. 'But I've been out on my own so often.' He seemed to chuckle as he said it.

'Has there been criticism from within the club?'

'I'm carrying on this way and if they're not happy I'll hear about it.' The magical self-image worked like a shield. Nobody could get past it.

'If Johan believed something, there was no way of holding him back,' says John van 't Schip, right-winger at the time, who had a warm relationship with Cruyff. 'After a while I and a couple of other players went to see him. We kept not understanding what he meant. You're going too quickly, we said. Let's take a step back. He wouldn't hear of it. "We're keeping right on," he said. "After a while you'll get it."'

The team had to learn to fold in and out like a concertina, reflecting the pattern of the game. That could happen only if the players were continually in touch with each other and corrected each other. In training matches Cruyff sometimes deliberately went to stand in an awkward place – and he'd stop the game if anyone in his team pointed this out to him. The striker must be the 'first defender' and the goalkeeper the 'first attacker'. Then you were 'master of your own house' and could impose your will on the opponent. Keeper Stanley Menzo had to be able to 'join the play' far outside his own goal, despite the goals against that might result. Sweeper Ronald Koeman, until recently a midfielder, had to run in front of, rather than behind, the other defenders, even though that sometimes led to fatal misunderstandings. When Koeman moved forward, Ajax were often left with just three defenders – risky and exciting. 'In fact, everything turned on kicking the ball at the correct speed to the correct foot of the correct player,' defender Sonny Silooy remembers. 'Each pass had to have an intention behind it.'

That seemed a bit too much to ask and sometimes it was. 'Johan knows everything better, sees everything better, can do everything better,' Van Basten confided to the weekly *Haagse Post* in August 1986. 'He knows everything about football. Theoretically it all makes sense and there's little about it that you can question. But you're dealing with the reality. You have to put his perfect theories into practice and that's extremely difficult.' The 21-year-old goal-getter sighed that Cruyff 'talked the ears off' the players.

Shortly after that, Van Basten was substituted, in a hurtful manner. In the humble De Langeleegte Stadium in Veendam, Cruyff took him off. The celebrated striker, the captain who was supposed to be an extension of the coach and to set a good example, was showing too little commitment, according to Cruyff. And not for the first time. 'I've been talking for months,' the coach justified the substitution. 'Sometimes too much, or so I've read. But there's a limit.' Van Basten was sent to take a shower twenty minutes before the end of the match. When he walked into the changing room, Van 't Schip was already there. The right-winger had been substituted during half-time, to his own amazement, after his cross had enabled Rijkaard to make it 0-1. 'I couldn't understand it,' says Van 't Schip. 'We were playing nicely. And Marco was absolutely furious. "Cruyff's gone mad," he said. "What's this all about? He's taken us both off." Later I understood. It was Johan's way of keeping us on our toes.'

Cruyff was the kind of obstinate coach who could be discontented even when things were going 'nicely'. He subordinated everything to his ideals, and then it didn't matter that his victims, as in the case of Van 't Schip and Van Basten, had visited his home for years as good friends. (He advised both of them; he was tireless in his support when 'Schip' needed surgery for a slipped disc.) For Cruyff the game came before the mere personages, as defender Sonny Silooy discovered on 19 October 1986.

After playing for half an hour, Ajax stood at 1–0 at home against VVV. The Limburg club had no chance, but the Amsterdam coach could still see ways of improving the Ajax game a little. He substituted Peter Boeve for Silooy. Left back Silooy was astonished. Four days earlier he had played for Oranje in a European Championship qualifying match against Hungary and now he wasn't good enough for a game against VVV? They were ahead! 'I walked to the storeroom and smashed everything to pieces,' Silooy remembers. 'I felt the substitution made no sense. I was having a good game.'

After the 4–0 victory, the defender asked Cruyff for an explanation. 'He told me, cool as a cucumber, that the set-up with Boeve, who liked to go forward, would work better because VVV were leaving gaps on that side. He was utterly unaware of what his decision did to me.'

The radical approach of the technical director often produced spellbinding play, but there were no national titles. In this period those consistently went to PSV Eindhoven, who had built a sound, experienced team that included more and more former Ajax players (Lerby, Kieft, Vanenburg and Koeman). Technician and fan favourite Gerald Vanenburg had more or less been branded a circus artist by Cruyff in 1986 and had left. Ronald Koeman had gone with him, dissatisfied with the new income policy (Cruyff had urged the board to reduce the players' salaries and raise winner bonuses – performance-related pay – and Koeman had not been happy about that).

The coach without a diploma brought players to Amsterdam who didn't seem to fit at Ajax (Jan Wouters, Arnold Scholten) and when he decided it was a shame to keep striker John Bosman on the subs' bench, he thought up a system in which Bosman could play behind Van Basten as a 'shadow striker' – an invention taken up at Ajax and countless other clubs for decades afterwards. On 18 March 1987 Cruyff made a truly audacious move. In the quarter-finals of the European Cup Winners' Cup, in which Ajax were participating as winners of the KNVB Cup, he let 17-year-old schoolboy Dennis Bergkamp make his European debut as part of the squad. It looked like a gamble. Many regarded Bergkamp as still far too skinny and too unassuming for the serious work, and hence he often still played in Ajax 2. The home game against the robust Malmö FF, in which a 1-0 away defeat had to be made good, could undoubtedly be classified as serious work.

But Cruyff saw things differently. He had been following Bergkamp for years and had deliberately got him to play different positions in the youth teams to improve his resilience. Attacker Dennis was a bit like 'Jopie' in the old days, a skinny little fellow, with insight, speed and technique. Cruyff's idea was to get the blond schoolboy out on the wing to run past the slow left back Torbjörn Persson. Cruyff convinced Bergkamp that Persson was ancient and couldn't get it together any longer. Dennis was to 'seek out' the Swede (in reality only twenty-seven years old) and get around him. It didn't matter if that failed a few times, Cruyff said; eventually Bergkamp would drive him nuts. With that conviction, Bergkamp ran on to the field, did what was expected of him and created an unforgettable nightmare for poor Persson in De Meer. The morning after the 3-1 victory, the newspapers wrote of a 'brilliant performance' by the new top talent Dennis Bergkamp.

For the first time since 1980, Ajax got to a European semi-final. There they overcame the Spanish mid-tier club Real Zaragoza, and on 13 May 1987 Ajax played in the final of a European championship, the European Cup Winners' Cup, for the first time in fourteen years. None of the players had experienced such a thing. It was a great day, especially for Frank Verlaat, a 19-year-old central defender from Haarlem who had made his debut with Ajax 1 just three days before. Hardly anybody had ever heard of him when he walked into the Olympic Stadium in Athens. He wasn't actually supposed to be there. Another unknown, Desmond Gemert, had been lined up to play a central defensive position because of the team's many injuries and suspensions. 'Keep in mind that you might be playing,' Cruyff had said to Gemert. But just before the team left for Athens the 22-year-old had gone out on the town in Amsterdam and Cruyff found out. 'Johan always found out about everything,' Silooy remembers. Just as Michels had done, on the night before European away games Cruyff sometimes used to sit in a chair in the lobby of the players' hotel to prevent the mainly young players from going out. He had 'escaped' himself several times in his youth, so he didn't trust anyone – just like Michels.

Cruyff's radical response was a 'no' to Gemert and a 'yes' to Verlaat. The inexperienced stopper did a good job in the nervy and unattractive final. One of the few high points in Athens was a goal headed in by Van Basten from a cross by Silooy. Ajax won 1-0. After fourteen years a European cup was finally brought back to Amsterdam. The European Cup Winners' Cup was not the most important of trophies, but the style of play, the many goals and the team's youth appealed to the imagination. 'Cruyff always stuck to his ideas about football,' says Van 't Schip. 'And when the season was over every one of us had to admit that he'd been right all along with those ideas of his. The worst you could say was that communication didn't always go smoothly. All that nagging away about the third man, about triangles on the pitch, the creation of situations of numerical superiority: it was all interconnected. He believed in football, not in systems or plans.'

Twenty days after the final, Cruyff was asked to come to the KNVB offices in Zeist. He was handed a piece of paper – the diploma he'd wanted for two years but for which he'd consistently refused to take courses. Section chairman André van der Louw presented him with his licence as a Professional Football Coach, a diploma as a token of thanks for everything he had meant to Dutch football in general and Ajax in particular. He was a trainer *honoris causa*, admittedly, but it meant that from

1 June 1987 onwards Cruyff was a fully qualified coach for an unlimited period. In January 1986 he had been given special dispensation; now it was official. He might even become the national coach, a suggestion that immediately stirred the enthusiasm of some at the KNVB. The ceremony seemed to move the 40-year-old trainer emotionally, but he recovered himself quickly as always. Before the press and invited guests he said it was 'normal' for them to pay him this honour. 'I see it as an award,' he said. 'But in fact it's fairly normal that this should have happened. I've achieved something.'

Three months later, Cruyff applied a method he almost certainly would not have learnt on a KNVB course. Van Basten had left for AC Milan that summer, which meant that Frank Rijkaard, Ajax's best player from that moment on, would need to show leadership. To Cruyff's way of thinking, that was unavoidable. As the best player at Ajax and Barcelona, he had become a leader, so others must do the same. The fact that Rijkaard had never shown any interest in the role was irrelevant, as was the fact that the 25-year-old midfielder was quieter and more mild-mannered than Van Basten. Rijkaard simply wanted to play football, as a paid hobbyist, but in the 1987-88 season there was no chance of that.

Cruyff insisted that Rijkaard must demand penalties, must be a presence on the pitch, must intervene when concentration lapsed, must 'explode', must act mean if the circumstances called for it, must go on to the pitch with his chest out and shoulders back, and so be the man that others could rely on. But to quote Rijkaard's friend of the time Arnold Mühren, 'That's not what Frank's like.' The introverted Rijkaard, an international for several years already, was systematically laid into by Cruyff and during one training session in late September things boiled over. 'Dammit,' Rijkaard shouted. 'Fuck you with your interminable moaning.' He threw his shirt to the ground, went to the changing room and then drove home.

To Cruyff's amazement, he didn't come back. Before long
the coach had no idea what it had all been about. 'I haven't
argued with him,' he said two months later. 'I never had any
sense there were problems lurking, and he never mentioned
anything either. Suddenly he stopped coming.' Once again he
had failed to realise what an effect his behaviour could have
on others. The game was more important than the players, as
Silooy too had noticed.

Van 't Schip understood what Cruyff meant with his nagging
about leadership. The right-winger had found himself in a similar boat. Seven years before, when Johan was technical adviser
at Ajax, 17-year-old 'Schip' was given a chance to play with the
juniors, known as Young Ajax. Cruyff arranged for him to join
in a match with players of the same age in the A1 junior team.
'You show them,' Johan said. 'You need to be the leader there
now.' When that failed to happen, Cruyff told the youth trainer
he must put in a substitute for John. The next Monday, Van 't
Schip was told, 'You must take responsibility, not just join in.'

Rijkaard's career flourished, incidentally. He became a top
European player and earned a fortune. Devotees of Cruyff said
it was all down to that tough lesson from Johan; the break was
precisely what softie Frankie needed. It might equally well be
argued that Rijkaard was successful despite the endless badger-
ing from Cruyff. As the years went by, the midfielder became
milder in his view of his departure. 'There's no right or wrong,'
he explained. 'There was something I couldn't do then, which
he believed needed speeding up. He put me under pressure.
With some people that works, with others it doesn't.'

However that may be, after Rijkaard's departure Cruyff was
without his best player and of course that didn't do anything
to increase his support among the board. The relationship was
already troubled. In the run-up to the season a childish quarrel
had arisen between Cruyff and the club leadership about tickets
to matches for the players' wives. In September 1987 interaction
with the board became downright vicious, not least because of

the media. During a trip to a European away game, chairman Ton Harmsen had gossiped about Cruyff to Johan Derksen. At least, that was how the *Voetbal International* reporter saw it. Derksen decided to stand up for the 'phenomenon', for the vulnerable loner who didn't realise what the small-minded board members were doing to him. 'It seems that attracted attention,' he says. 'One day Jaap de Groot at *De Telegraaf* put a proposal to me: "You coming to Vinkeveen on Saturday too?" In early October I rang the doorbell of Cruyff's bungalow and found Frits Barend already there.'

The journalists Derksen, De Groot (successor to Jan de Deugd as ghost writer of Cruyff's columns) and Barend had an 'informal conversation' that morning with the coach, according to Derksen. 'Just a bit of a chat about football, Ajax and the club board,' he says. 'But from that moment on the three of us had his private number. We got exclusive interviews with Johan – which others hardly ever did. For the circulation of *Voetbal International* that was extraordinarily beneficial, incidentally. We were able to go to his house and we could ring him day or night. It wasn't said in so many words that we would support him from then on, but that was how it was. I found Cruyff an engaging man, pleasant, far more modest than you would expect based on his worldwide reputation.'

Of course, Cruyff had for years had his own special way of dealing with journalists. 'With Johan it was always a trade-off,' Cees van Nieuwenhuizen remembers. The reporter for *Het Parool* had done little jobs for Cruyff and his father-in-law since the late 1960s and been granted many an exclusive interview or bit of news in return. 'Johan demanded your complete confidence,' says Van Nieuwenhuizen. 'It was black and white with him. He didn't recognise professional distance, he took everything personally. Betray his trust and you were out.'

Van Nieuwenhuizen had experienced that for himself. In 1981 he had published a rather sour story about the year Cruyff was going through – the year of injuries, strange gigs and failure at Levante. 'It was over immediately. From that day on, Johan treated me coldly and I felt there was no point asking him for interviews any longer. I never did after that.'

In a sense Van Nieuwenhuizen could count himself lucky; he might just as easily have received a phone call from Cor Coster and have heard threats in response to that barbed article along the lines of 'I know where you live', as once happened to Poul Annema of *de Volkskrant*. Coster made columnist Frits Abrahams tremble in the late 1970s by saying, 'Now, you better listen good, jerk. I'm not having this. I'm not having Johan get kicked into the shit.' Abrahams' satirical piece in *de Volkskrant* even prompted the message, 'We're coming over to you right now with some heavies and we're going to beat you up good and proper.' The heavies didn't come, but with Coster you could never be sure. In that period Cor used a pistol to get his money out of the broker's office Inter Football, which he had set up. 'Coster knew a lot of criminals,' says David Endt, a one-time employee of Inter Football.

Cruyff himself was not keen on punch-ups – he preferred to see himself as an idealist. In this Ajax period he had again done all he could to help his country move forward, for example by devoting time and energy to the Het Is Weer Fijn Langs De Lijn foundation and other groups campaigning against the increasing football-related violence and vandalism. But he was capable of slamming the door. 'And of course Derksen, Barend and De Groot there in Vinkeveen knew that well enough,' says Van Nieuwenhuizen. 'They were careful not to write anything that might make Johan angry. It would mean the end of their preferential treatment.'

The 'Vinkeveen consultation' in the autumn of 1987 caused a polarisation that worsened relations between Cruyff and the Ajax board even further. In many newspapers there was criticism of Cruyff: the Ajax game had lost its momentum; several reliable players had left and their replacements, brought in on Cruyff's recommendation, were a disappointment time and again. But in *De Telegraaf*, in *Voetbal International* and in *Nieuwe Revu*, for which Barend wrote, it was mainly the club leadership that was given a hard time. As Cruyff always said, the board was not 'on the gravy train for the sake of Ajax' but for itself. The leadership had meanwhile begun to feel anxious about the coach's many demands, whether laid on the table via the media or otherwise. 'They went further and further,' former board member Van Eijden recalls. 'Johan never discussed things, he had a standpoint and that's how it had to be.' Cruyff wanted a contract for two years, to enable him to develop a technical policy for the longer term. He wanted to broaden his powers so that he was better able to work towards his ideal. Conversations took place on the subject, but it was never made official; the faith the board had in him was crumbling too quickly for that. The leadership looked at the poor results of recent times, at the many acquisitions that had failed and the disappearance of star player Rijkaard. They began to wonder whether or not they wanted to go on with Cruyff.

Perhaps he was more a creative person than a boss from whom reasonably predictable behaviour could be expected. He seemed too playful and too wayward. Too original, also. Take what he did on 4 November. Without any qualms, he had 17-year-old schoolboy Bryan Roy play in the second round of the European Cup Winners' Cup. The most dangerous weapon of opponents HSV from Hamburg was Manfred Kaltz. The seasoned 34-year-old right back had managed to dominate the pitch for years as a kind of playmaker in the rear. With his high-impact passes, Kaltz created a threat everywhere and so the obvious thing was to set a defensive type against him. Any normal coach would have done so. Cruyff did the opposite. As so often, he believed in adventure. Young dribbler Roy was to manipulate the experienced Kaltz. The mission: go past him, Bryan, that old man can't do anything any more. Make him run after you, then he won't get a chance to do his thing.'

Left-winger Roy sought out Kaltz, a player twice his age, and got past him several times. According to *Het Parool*, the feared HSV defender Kaltz was 'almost continually left behind'. Ajax won 2-0.

For Cruyff it didn't matter whether he was playing or in charge. Acting quickly and reliably was what mattered. 'Those guys up there,' he said to Van Basten and Van 't Schip in De Meer, pointing to the boardroom, 'are sitting in a supertanker. We're speedboats. The board members take days to make a decision. By the time they've finally made up their minds, the world has moved on.' So he wanted to improve the squad, plagued by injuries, at a great pace and to reform the training staff. Assistant coach Spitz Kohn must go. A1 trainer Cor van der Hart must go. The Swedish defender Peter Larsson must be bought, immediately. For the board it was all going far too fast; they felt a need to rein in the impulsive Cruyff with regard to acquisitions and transfers. In December 1987 Ajax were eight points adrift of leaders PSV, despite having played one match more. Meanwhile, the coach was leaking to 'his' media and the board were doing the same to newspapers that had been unable to secure exclusive interviews with the football genius. In *Voetbal International* Johan Derksen made clear it was the 'gossip-hungry' board that was 'frustrated' and 'merciless', making Cruyff's work impossible with its 'Judas' behaviour, 'underhand dealings' and 'plots'.

In late December the corpulent Harmsen had his nose rubbed in a scornful remark by Cruyff. In front of the television cameras, he was asked to respond to Cruyff's comment, 'The management is really a supervisory board.'

'He'll find out about that all right,' Harmsen growled.

Things reached a climax on the evening of Sunday 3 January 1988. The setting was almost filmic, an establishment in Zandvoort where all those concerned were sitting at a long candlelit table for supper. 'Old Ajax', a team made up of former players, had enjoyed a game of indoor football earlier that evening in Zandvoort. Cruyff had prepared himself for a conversation with two board members, but the entire board turned out to be sitting at the table, apparently to have strength in numbers. The festive mood was soon over. Cruyff demanded an answer to the question of whether the board was prepared to sign a two-year contract with him. In other words, whether the gentlemen's agreement on the matter was still valid. 'All kinds of people got involved with that,' former board member Van Eijden recalls. 'The irritation around the table increased. Johan reproached me for meddling in his affairs and I reproached him for meddling in mine. It escalated.'

A response came that Cruyff regarded as too vague. He refused to settle for it. Losing something meant losing everything. It was bully or get bullied. Yes or no. He tendered his resignation.

Financially speaking he could afford to do that. Barcelona had been pulling at him for months and were prepared to pay him significantly more than the just over 1 million guilders he was getting from Ajax. (An amount that Harmsen had recently leaked, to weaken the position of 'the most expensive coach in Europe'.)

The players unanimously wanted him to stay and they requested an attempt at reconciliation, so on Wednesday 6 January 1988 the issue was placed before the members' council, a kind of small parliament at Ajax. But the council rejected the proposal for reconciliation talks by 27 to 0. The club was in danger of collapsing under the weight of 'for and against Cruyff' and felt a need to close ranks. 'Johan Cruyff is a great football expert,' a spokesperson said to the press. 'But he wanted to do too much management work.' Many people resented the coach for planning to abandon the squad halfway through the season – just four months after he'd reproached Rijkaard for doing the same.

Cruyff grew bitter. He had the feeling that the board had been aiming to get rid of him from the start: in 1973 voted out by his fellow players, in 1983 sent away by Harmsen, and now thwarted by the board and humiliated by the club parliament.

For the third time Cruyff had been belittled by his 'family'. Yet this split, which also affected his almost 14-year-old son Jordi, an Ajax junior, did not tempt him to throw mud. 'I've never hit back,' he explained a year later in *Nieuwe Revu*. 'There's a God for that. He doesn't allow you to go on and on causing people pain. Because Harmsen hurt me; things can never be put right between us. Actually, he's caused me pain twice over, because he's hurt my son too, who enjoyed playing at Ajax. If you go too far, there's a God, I'm convinced of that, which is why I never hit back.'

Fourteen days after he left, the expected phone call came through from Barcelona. Cruyff had all his demands ready, which was sensible, given his recent experiences. As far as he was concerned those demands came first, before the negotiations over his salary. There would be no interference by outsiders. The professional part of the club, to which he would belong, would remain strictly separate from the amateur part. He would be consulted on the composition of the technical and medical staff. He would work directly under the board so that the lines of communication would be short. And he would bring Tonny Bruins Slot with him, the assistant coach who could fill the gaps in his theoretical framework and organisational abilities.

All his demands could be discussed, was the reply. Follow-up appointments were made. It meant that the Cruyffs could prepare to move house again. But despite the fact that the children were at international schools and therefore flexible, they all wanted to stay in Vinkeveen. 'Danny was full of reproaches,' says Frits Barend, who often visited the family. 'She was enormously cross with Johan for having broken with Ajax when the whole family was so happy where it was. Danny started crying about it and before long they were both in tears. Utterly downhearted.'

Shortly after that, in March 1988, a possibility arose that would allow the family to stay in Vinkeveen after all. A plan was thought up that was so innovative and bizarre that when it was announced it was taken for an April Fool's Day joke. With the support of businesspeople, Cruyff would set up a new Dutch professional club, FC Cruyff. The plan was serious and its originator was Hans Muller, the director of Euro Fashions, which included Cruyff Sports. He intended it as a way to help Johan; as leader of FC Cruyff he could stay in the Netherlands and would not have to go through life as a 'football gypsy'. Muller had first raised the idea in January and Johan had promised to think about it. Shortly after that he met Pieter Winsemius, former housing and environment minister for the VVD, the Dutch liberal party, who had referred to Cruyff for years in his speeches as a source of inspiration for the business community. According to Winsemius, what the Netherlands needed in its battle with high unemployment and unfit-for-work figures was 'world class'. With Cruyff's 'credible leadership' as its example, the country could get back on its feet.

Cruyff and the 46-year-old former government minister gave 'inspiring' presentations together and were soon talking about the FC Cruyff idea. To them it seemed a worthwhile venture.

Winsemius wrote a report and sounded out the business community, while Cruyff sounded out the football world. Their eye fell on FC Utrecht: central location, fanatical fans and a modern stadium. Nice and close to Vinkeveen, too. With external capital, taking over the moribund club must be feasible. Johan would be technical director, with Tonny Bruins Slot as his right-hand man, while former Ajax players like Wim Suurbier and Ronald Spelbos would take care of training on the pitch. A neighbouring amateur club would function as a youth wing. A list of potential players was drawn up, including Dennis Bergkamp. Practically all the current players at FC Utrecht would have to go, but if you saw the big picture, you wouldn't worry about that. (Shortly before, Cruyff had fantasised on television about a directorship at Feyenoord. 'But then the whole of the Feyenoord board would have to leave en masse.')

With these firm plans in mind, Cruyff and his adviser Harrie
van Mens flew to see British media tycoon Robert Maxwell.
They landed by helicopter on the roof of Maxwell's office in
central London. The immensely rich Maxwell owned two
football clubs and might want to invest in FC Cruyff. 'Maxwell
was a strapping fellow,' Van Mens recalls. 'A true despot with
a booming voice who could buy whatever he liked. But Johan
wasn't overawed in the slightest. In all the years I provided him
with advice, I never saw him in awe of anyone.'

Maxwell was prepared to put aside a million pounds for FC
Cruyff, and KLM and Heineken were willing to participate to
the tune of several tens of million guilders. Interest in the project was aroused among lawyers and PR experts, and tax expert
Van Mens put down on paper a tax-friendly route via Liberia.
The football club, run as a business, would in time be floated on
the stock market – an exciting prospect, Cruyff agreed.

The enthusiasm knew no bounds. A club set up from top
to bottom according to the ideas of the world-famous genius:
what could be better than that? Cruyff, lacking a diploma of
any sort, was clearly flattered by the admiration of academic
Winsemius, while for his part the rather snooty former minister was endlessly fascinated by Cruyff's self-confidence and
instinctive 'savvy'. 'Johan was super-consistent,' he recalls. 'But
of course he couldn't tell a properly structured story. I could.
We complemented each other nicely.'

The plans attracted a lot of publicity and after a few weeks
the general consensus was that FC Cruyff might be able to give
declining Dutch football a great boost. But the list of players
for FC Cruyff drawn up by mid-April was not good enough
for decent performances, according to Cruyff himself. The
top footballers they longed for had all been contracted for the
coming season by other clubs. And since there was by then an
agreement with Barcelona, Cruyff drew a line through it all
without delay.

The chairman of FC Utrecht, who had of course been heavily

impacted by the whole situation, thought it was a shame Johan hadn't updated him in person on the latest news.

'Cruyff switches attention quickly,' said one of those involved, and so it was. Off to Barcelona.

CHAPTER TWENTY-SEVEN

Playful dictator

Cruyff's move to Barcelona did not exactly go smoothly. For a start, the first meeting had to take place in secret – in suite 407 of the Hôtel Le Richemond on the shores of Lake Geneva. There Cruyff and Joan Gaspart, the vice-president of Barça who was in charge of transfer matters, met on Thursday 31 March 1988. *De Telegraaf* knew about the meeting and had taken up position in the Swiss hotel; the morning newspaper was to report on it in detail two days later. 'Already at that point I could see that Johan was maintaining special links with the press,' says Gaspart. The Spanish media very soon published the great news as well, which did not suit the Catalan board member at all. The interim coach, Luis Aragonés, was trying to make the best of things and, should Cruyff be taken on, his work would no doubt become even more difficult than it already was. Europe's richest football club had been performing poorly for months and was going through turbulent times. 'Johan and I were broadly in agreement and from that moment we got along well,' Gaspart says.

Two weeks later, Cruyff announced in the Netherlands that he was going to Barcelona. But it was easier said than done; in Spain too a coach needed the right qualifications and a Dutch licence would not automatically be recognised there. In essence his diploma was a kind of exemption and the Spanish bureaucrats had great difficulty with that. Given that El Flaco was naturally unwilling to take courses in Catalonia, an adjustment of the paperwork was needed. Several civil servants at the relevant ministry and lawyers at the KNVB put their heads together. A successful performance by Cruyff in Barcelona would be good for the reputation of Dutch football, the association board members believed. Moreover, a good relationship with Cruyff would increase the chances of him one day agreeing to coach Oranje. 'Cruyff's diploma stated that it was awarded on behalf of the minister,' Chris Buitelaar, a civil servant at the time, remembers. 'It was signed by a representative of the state. But the Spanish insisted it must be signed by the minister himself. After a good deal of internal debate, we scrapped the "on behalf of" and left the signature as it was. That made it seem as if the minister had agreed with the content. That was not officially the case, so it wasn't literally true. From the point of view of officialdom, we were skating close to the edge.'

After that bureaucratic feat, Cruyff had the qualifications he needed to start work in Barcelona. But there were still considerable financial problems to be solved. Tax expert Harrie van Mens held lengthy meetings with the Barcelona board about Cruyff's debts, which were still owing as a result of incorrect tax returns in the 1970s. A Spanish bank, which had given Cruyff a huge loan at the time to allow him to pay off his tax debts, was still owed almost a million guilders. There were other creditors lurking from the time of Basilevitch. Cruyff's past of ill-advised business ventures, unpaid bills and repossessions continued to pursue him. 'That business will have to be sorted out first,' Barcelona president Núñez told the press. Meanwhile, just to be sure, he was sounding out three other possible coaches.

Núñez was not left in limbo for long. Van Mens and the Barcelona board worked out a solution together. In May Cruyff's appointment was confirmed, setting the scene for a classic Spanish one-two between Núñez and Cruyff. The president proposed making 47 million guilders available to the new coach to get the erratic team back on the rails, and Cruyff agreed to support him in the spring of 1989 in the presidential elections. Both kept their promises. According to the magazine *Sport*, published in Barcelona, the president and the trainer lived 'in a sporting romance unique to them'. Although not fond of each other personally, both were ambitious and inclined to a similar form of autocratic impetuosity. Now that half the squad and their coach Aragonés had been dismissed by Núñez, Cruyff put himself forward, with the support of the 'Napoleon of the Ramblas', as a decisive leader.

Cruyff always went his own way, and at the annual presentation of the team on 22 July that was immediately obvious. Some 22,000 spectators had come to Camp Nou to watch, more than for many league matches in the past season. The 1987–88 campaign had ended in drama; the board and the players were at odds and Barça had finished sixth, no fewer than twenty-three points behind Real Madrid, coached by Leo Beenhakker. To make known their displeasure at the team's attitude, the crowd whistled at the new captain, José Ramón Alexanko, during the presentation. Cruyff took the microphone from him. 'It's good that you greeted the president's speech with applause,' he said. 'But I don't like the way you're whistling at the person I've appointed as captain of the team. We need your support, not your protests.'

With this and other things he said, he placed himself above the warring parties. He was right; he badly needed the support of the *socios*, the more than 90,000 club members. To add to the atmosphere, after the presentation of the team Cruyff pulled off his tracksuit bottoms and joined in the first training exercises of the season, to the delight of the crowd. He made some passes, delivered a few curving balls and horsed around with the lads. Message: now stop squabbling, we're all going to have fun together.

In view of the malaise in the club, at a press conference Cruyff used the words 'A dictator is needed here.' New players were brought in, Cruyff had youth players move up into the squad and he soon made clear who was in charge in the changing room: not the players, some of whom were still complaining about the board, and certainly not members of the board, who were allowed to come and go wherever they liked from now on with the exception of the changing room. That way Cruyff had the players to himself and could begin to forge a successful team. With his assistants, Tonny Bruins Slot and his former teammate at Barça Charly Rexach, he trained the players in a way all his own. That began immediately, during preparations for the new season at the Papendal sports centre near Arnhem, where Barcelona (as in Michels' time) had come to escape the Spanish summer heat. The players had to 'work, work and work again', but very differently from the way they were accustomed to. 'We had a qualified fitness instructor who was ready each afternoon for a run in the woods,' recalls Barça physiotherapist of the time Jaume Langa. 'We were used to building up our fitness for the season that way. But Johan says, no, we're going to do a *rondo*.'

The *rondo* was no longer a game with which the players entertained themselves, a kind of mucking about in a circle. In Cruyff's training programme it became an important exercise. Playing the ball around the circle improved insight, technique and speed of action – Cruyffian football in a nutshell. 'At first we thought it was strange,' says Langa. 'But Johan built those *rondos* into a serious form of training, with all kinds of variations, so that the players developed an acceptable level of fitness. The bigger *rondos* served as a model for the matches, the idea being: if you keep the ball in the team, you won't have to run after it.'

As he had at Ajax, Cruyff eagerly took part in positional play and in the *rondos*. 'When you play with the team it's easy to see the mistakes,' he said in an interview. 'Anyhow, I can still demonstrate everything better than the players can, and I still see everything far better. That wins their respect. It sounds like boasting, but it's simply a fact. I'm the boss, but at the same time I feel like a player.' At other times he would sit on the ball and watch his assistants Bruins Slot and Rexach work with the lads. 'I'm sitting on my office,' he would joke with people who were watching. As well as a dig at the paperwork he so hated, it was also the truth: for him this was work; everything was in his head and as soon as he saw a player make the same mistake more than once, he explained how to get it right. 'Many players respected him,' says Langa. 'There was a lot of laughter, but *el mister* could make people fearful too. It wasn't nice to be put in your place by him. By Spanish standards he was extremely direct and he always thought one step ahead.'

In the winter months, morning training started not at ten but at ten-thirty; by that time the sun had started to warm the pitch, which improved the atmosphere. And if the players were a man short for a practice game, the equipment manager or one of the medical staff would join in. 'That was a breath of fresh air,' says physiotherapist Langa, who took part in many a *rondo*. 'The coaches before Johan concentrated only on the first eleven; they didn't even pay attention to the reserves. With Johan everyone counted and everything was about playing games.'

Cruyff wanted to be able to enjoy matches as a spectator. 'I'm occasionally jealous of the players,' he said in *Voetbal International*. 'I sit in that dugout, while they're having a nice game of football.' His envy was greatest when his players had no need to take long sprints. If a player had to run far, he was 'stupid' or had been 'asleep'. To Frits Barend and Henk van Dorp he said, 'Every coach talks about moving, about running a lot. I say: don't run so much; football is played with the brain.' He'd always done that himself and thereby avoided a lot of charging about on the pitch. 'As a player Johan detested running,' says Keje Molenaar, who played with him in the early 1980s. 'And of course that had to do with his limited lung capacity – he was an inveterate smoker.' Friend of the house Bobby Nees would never forget how, while he was staying with

Johan in Barcelona, the two of them went jogging. 'I did that twice a week,' says Nees. 'One day Danny says to Johan, "Go for a run with Bob!" So he obediently did so. We put on our training shoes and went out on to the street, which was quite steep. After fifty metres Johan goes, "You must be insane." He stopped right there and then.'

Jaume Langa sums up Cruyff's approach in four words: empathy and enjoyment; clever and demanding. 'When I see mistakes on Sunday,' Johan told *Voetbal International*, 'I train on that point on the Monday. I keep hammering away at it until it goes right.'

In Barcelona as in Amsterdam, that hammering away by Cruyff was not confined to the pitch. He ensured that the basic salaries were reduced and the bonuses increased, so that players were rewarded for their performance. He also put an end to the club's erratic policymaking. Over the past sixteen years Barça had got through twelve coaches; it was almost impossible for a coach to function normally in such a turbulent club. 'They bought players at random and if those didn't work out they'd buy someone else,' Cruyff explained. Opportunism and impatience predominated, with the result that in twenty-five years, rich Barcelona had been national champions only twice, in 1974 (with Cruyff) and in 1985. The team had played attacking football one year and defensively the next, depending on the kind of coach they had, a ridiculous situation in Cruyff's view. As at Ajax, an attacking style of play needed to become part of the club culture. 'The organisation must be geared to that,' he believed. He was going against the international trend of defensive and 'realistic' football, but that didn't bother him in the slightest. Over the long term everyone would see the advantages of attractive play. Cruyff, 'more than a coach', said, 'I've got work to do that goes further than winning the championship.' He called it 'my fight against cultures and structures'.

While Johan tackled the problems of FC Barcelona, Danny focused on their new home. As in Washington and Los Angeles, the family had settled in a neighbourhood of diplomats and other wealthy families. Pedralbes (where they had also lived in the 1970s) was an area with a lot of green space, lime trees and chirping crickets. They spent the first few weeks in Hotel Princesa Sofia, close to Camp Nou, but in the crescent-shaped Paseo de los Tilos they found a beautiful, luxurious house that happened to be empty. It was part of a line of houses with white window frames and shutters, elegant ironwork and underground parking. From the third floor you could see Camp Nou. The schools were not far away, 16-year-old Susila's riding school was practically round the corner and 14-year-old Jordi could, as it were, walk to the training pitch. The daily distances they needed to cover would be shorter than in the Netherlands, so it wasn't long before the Cruyffs bounced back, despite their reluctance to leave their native country again. The climate and the warm-heartedness of the Catalans did the rest.

At home Danny was his 'dictator', at the club that role was his own. 'I think in all those years I constructed two personalities,' Cruyff said. 'One for home and one for the outside world.' He was accommodating towards Danny, but in bringing up his children he was a stickler for rules. His friend Rolf Grootenboer called him 'traditional'. It seemed as if he was determined to prevent his children from being spoilt by all the fame and riches. Any of them who disobeyed would be sent to bed early, or forbidden to go to a party on the coming Saturday. Sweets and sugary drinks were banned and even hearing the word 'drugs' made him furious. If Jordi annoyed his father, he wasn't allowed to play football that weekend. 'If you don't listen now, you won't listen on Sunday,' he said.

Jordi had to earn his pocket money by washing cars, he later told the monthly magazine *Johan*. If he didn't finish his home-work, which was a fairly common occurrence, he could expect a lecture from his father. 'You have qualities, and you could become a footballer,' his father would say then. 'But if you don't have the will to win then you won't even be able to serve at a checkout. You'll be the one who bags the shopping.' Jordi could forget about having a moped. His Catalan friends rode all over the city on theirs from the age of sixteen onwards, but his father forced him to cycle. Even during the summer months he'd cycle up the Montanya,' friend and neighbour Marjolijn van der Meer remembers. 'Jordi hated that, but there was no other option. In matters like that Johan was a strict father.'

So it was nice for the teenagers that Dad was often at the club and Danny was, in her own words, 'very relaxed, very easy'.

The playful dictator sometimes took tough measures at Barça. Anyone who couldn't keep pace with the intelligent attacking football he was after was dropped. Nevertheless, conveying bad news was not his favourite pastime; at Ajax, too, he had always preferred to leave that task to the board. So in Barcelona he left Gary Lineker to his fate for a long time. The English striker, a reliable and popular centre forward over the past two seasons, had the impression that Cruyff wanted rid of him without daring to say so to his face. Lineker was often deployed by Cruyff on the wing, a position that didn't suit him at all, and therefore in 1989 he returned to Britain disappointed. Others were let go as well, including Roberto Fernández and Luis Milla. 'They weren't on my wavelength,' Cruyff said firmly. 'So they weren't on the same wavelength as the club.' The opposite was the case with players taken on at his urging. Twenty-year-old Guillermo Amor, for instance, moved up from the second eleven to the first and could not complain of a lack of support. 'He had faith in me from day one,' the midfielder remembers. 'So for me it was a treat to train and play under Cruyff. He liked simple solutions and he liked attacking; that philosophy gave me something to hold on to.'

New foreign players whose performances were mediocre would be shielded from criticism for weeks by Cruyff. Ronald Koeman was one of those who benefited. With the acquisition of Koeman in 1989, Cruyff was implicitly admitting that three years earlier he had been wrong in his assessment of the sweeper's abilities. He had calmly dispensed with Koeman at Ajax, but now the player was bought from PSV for 12.5 million guilders, an unusually high fee by the standards of the time.

For several months not much was seen of the 'gap-filling' libero, famous for his distance shots in the 1988 European Championship. The crowd hissed at him and the journalists called him the biggest waste of money of all time. But Cruyff obstinately continued to deploy him and after a while Koeman became a mainstay of the team.

The first two seasons of Cruyff's coaching career in Spain were problematic. Criticism was heaped on Barça for its disappointing results. In 1989 and 1990 the team finished second and third in the league, many points behind champions Real Madrid, but Cruyff carried on unperturbed with an approach derived from his own experiences. 'Dying with your ideas,' he would call it later. To his way of thinking it was eat or be eaten. If he gave in and did what other people wanted, he would be 'slaughtered'. Fortunately, in 1989 his team won the (less than prestigious) European Cup Winners' Cup and a year later the Copa del Rey – otherwise the resistance he provoked might have been fatal to him. The reappointed president Josep Lluís Núñez continued to support him and, when journalists confronted Cruyff with the possibility of his sacking, he said, 'If they want me to go, then I'll go. Hup, immediately, tomorrow.'

In the 1990-91 season Barcelona gradually started to play the way Cruyff had always envisaged. As well as Koeman and the Dane Michael Laudrup (who had been sidelined at Juventus), he now had Bulgarian Hristo Stoichkov (formerly of CSKA Sofia) at his disposal. With Laudrup he had intelligence and dribbling in the attack, with Stoichkov the coup de grace. Pep Guardiola had moved up from the top junior team. Guardiola was regarded by many at the club as too slender for the first eleven, but according to Cruyff, Pep 'got it', and his speed of action and technical skills were more important than any lack of weight and running ability. 'Just make sure you only need to defend a small part of the pitch,' Guardiola was told. 'Then you're the best. But if the distances are too great, they'll come at you from all sides and you're the worst. Everything has to do with distances.' Cruyff was proven right, precisely as he had been in 1987 with Dennis Bergkamp. They were both players who, just like him at the start, were not strong and therefore had to be clever.

Barcelona attacked in ways that were varied and risky. The stadium filled because the coach had ensured there would always be something extraordinary to see. When his team had the ball, every one of the players would be moving. 'Ball circulation' continued as long as everyone was fine-tuning the distances between them. Goals poured in and by February Barça were ten points ahead in the Spanish league. 'The players believed in what Johan was saying,' Guillermo Amor remembers. 'Because of the positional play, everyone improved, whether they had the ball or not. It got more enjoyable by the week.' But on 24 February 1991, halfway through a great season, a drama occurred. FC Barcelona were playing away against Real Valladolid when Cruyff suddenly felt unwell. 'I was sitting next to Johan on the bench and I saw him turn pale,' Rexach recalls. 'I asked what was wrong. He told me it was a digestive problem; he'd been having trouble with that recently. No, I said. It's your heart. He thought that was nonsense, but I advised him to go to the doctor as soon as we got back to Barcelona. He didn't bother going to the first appointment. After that he did go, along with Danny.'

That is to say, on 26 February Danny forced him to go. Cruyff had a tendency not to take such symptoms all that seriously. He'd recently had his stomach examined and he sometimes felt queasy for no apparent reason. This Tuesday morning he'd led the training session as usual and in the afternoon he'd gone with Danny to look at their new, future home in the Bonanova district. Then he started sweating profusely again and Danny drove him straight to the hospital.

Tests showed that the arteries around his heart were clogged. He had arteriosclerosis and needed an operation immediately.

Something with his heart: it was what he had always feared. His father Manus had died young, and as he got older Cruyff became increasingly aware that the same could happen to him. Cardiovascular disease was in the family. Manus's parents had died of heart attacks and his brother, Johan's Uncle Dirk, had also had heart problems. This awareness of vulnerability had made Cruyff fanatical about financial security when he was still a player. 'If something happens to me, my family won't have to worry,' he'd said in an interview. 'That's reassuring, because subconsciously you do think about heritability.'

In two months he would turn forty-four, almost the age at which his father had died in 1959. He responded with remarkable equanimity when his doctors delivered the news, but the superstitious Cruyff must surely have been experiencing anxious moments deep inside.

His son Jordi was at a training session when his sister Chantal's boyfriend, Jesús Angoy, came to tell him. 'Something's wrong with your father,' Angoy said, and naturally Jordi, like the rest of the family, was terrified. 'I think my whole family would have gone to pieces if he hadn't survived it,' he said later in the monthly *Johan*. 'If your father dies, you lose something that you never get back. It doesn't bear thinking about.'

However, an urgent operation was complicated by the fact that Cruyff demanded not only that a surgeon he knew would wield the knife but that he must be kept fully informed. 'They had to explain to him in detail exactly what they were going to do,' Rexach remembers. 'That rationality of Johan's in a crisis situation made me shudder.'

For years Cruyff had been almost as fascinated by medical affairs as by football tactics. Even as a young Ajax player he had questioned masseur Salo Muller interminably. He'd dried his newborn children himself, in the early 1980s he'd involved himself with John van 't Schip's back operation and in the

autumn of 1990 he'd argued endlessly about who should carry
out an Achilles tendon operation on Ronald Koeman. He'd
been present at countless operations on his players, 'reassuring
them that, if the trainer was there, everything would be fine',
he said in *My Turn*. 'I had to put on a surgical suit with a little
hat and a mask over my mouth. That relaxed the player.' He
had even taken the opportunity to see brain surgery from close
proximity and so after 'dozens of operations' he believed he had
'a good insight into the subject'.

That insight came in useful now that he was being prepared
for two bypasses. After thinking about it for a bit, Cruyff agreed
that a surgeon he didn't know could carry out the operation, but
it could start only once he understood exactly what was going
to happen. The operation was performed on 27 February and
took almost three hours. People swarmed around the Clínica
Sant Jordi that day. Camera crews wandered about as if the king
was dying. On the pavement outside and in the lobby, those
who knew the patient were asked to report on the situation.
Members of the board, players at Barça, even politicians were
approached for comment. One lane of the Via Augusta was
closed off for the outside broadcast vans that enabled radio and
television stations to send out live reports. On news programmes
the most important item of the day, the ground offensive against
Iraqi forces occupying Kuwait, was regularly interrupted for the
latest on the condition of the FC Barcelona coach.

The huge amount of media attention being paid to his condition had a calming effect on Cruyff before he was put under the
anaesthetic. 'When your heart surgeon knows damned well that
the whole world will be watching, then you know in advance
that the man is going to make a point of doing his best during
the operation,' he said later in his autobiography. 'That was a
great feeling.'

That evening heart surgeon Marius Petit, surrounded by
dozens of cameras and microphones, was able to declare that the
patient had 'been very lucky'. 'He was on the point of having

a serious heart attack,' he said. 'Now it has been limited to the
symptoms of a heart attack.' Just before midnight this good news
briefly drove the other good news, of the liberation of Kuwait,
into second place in the news bulletins. The 'greatest personality in Catalonia', as Cruyff had been called a full fifteen years
earlier, was going to make it.

Within a few days he was his laconic self again. 'From now on
I'll work more with the head than with the heart,' he smiled at
the journalists. But it wasn't long before he was looking to the
supernatural for an explanation for the hardening of his arteries
and his rapid recovery. 'There's no such thing as chance,' he said
at a press conference. 'There's someone who takes care of it all.
A God who knows and sees more than I do. And there comes
a time when you have to surrender it all to Him. Maybe God
or my father had me driven to the hospital that day.' Almost
three years later he told *Vrij Nederland*, 'If God hadn't wanted
me around any longer, if He had said "good riddance", then I
wouldn't be around any more. So it's not something I did. It
was arranged from on high.'

Along with this magical explanation there was a medical
one too. The doctor said that the furring-up of his arteries was
mainly a result of smoking. Cruyff took that signal seriously
and decided to stop at once. His friend Rolf Grootenboer ('He
smoked like crazy; I was sometimes so cross that I'd pluck a
Caballero right out of his mouth') or Danny no longer needed
to point out that it was bad for his health. He gave up trying to
convince them – or himself – that smoking was a good remedy
for stress.

The black-and-white thinker went straight to the opposite
extreme. Giving up nicotine wasn't enough; he wanted to
convey a 'universal moral'. He achieved it with a beautiful,
irresistible television advert, made in collaboration with the
Catalan Ministry of Health. Whereas in the past he had advertised strong drink (Claeryn jenever) and cigarettes (low-tar,

low-nicotine brand Roxy Dual), he now juggled a pack of cigarettes like a football. Against a dark background and dressed
in an unbuttoned trench coat with a suit and tie underneath,
he caught the pack on his chest, tapped it back into the air with
his left instep, then with his right thigh, then the left instep,
the forehead (twice), then again left, right, left, and so it went
on until he gave the pack of 'Tabac' the thwack with his left
foot that it deserved. With each touch there came a thump like
a heartbeat. 'I'm Johan Cruyff,' he said in the voiceover. 'I've
had two addictions in my life, smoking and playing football.
Football has given me everything in life. But smoking almost
took my life away.'

The advert was made in several languages and shown all
round the world. 'It was exactly the type of message I wanted,'
Cruyff said later.

Johan recovered astonishingly quickly and even before the
end of the season he was back in the dugout. Not with a cigarette now, but with a lollipop in his mouth to calm his match
nerves. In May 1991, for the first time in his career, a club
trained by him became national league champions, no fewer
than ten points ahead of the runners-up, Atlético Madrid. The
city and the region celebrated wildly and, after sleeping it off,
the *socios*, and Cruyff himself, realised that now there was just
one great dream to be chased after: winning the European Cup.
Real Madrid had seized the holy grail six times and outside
Spain just about all the top clubs had won the 'cup with the big
ears' at least once. All of Catalonia yearned for it. Two finals
had been lost (in 1961 and in 1986, when the game went to
penalties against Steaua Bucharest), which had only reinforced
the fatalism.

Barcelona always seemed to have had bad luck at the crucial
moment, and precisely for that reason it did the Barça fans
good that the Dutchman with his lollipop stolidly persisted
in working towards his ideal of creating a team that played
attractively and could win the greatest prize of all. In the new

1991-92 season the playful dictator switched to a formation with both Koeman and Guardiola in the centre of the defence, two former midfielders, one of whom often moved up into midfield. All the top teams had tall, tough backs in the centre, but at Barcelona it seemed as if Cruyff flatly denied the need for defence. If everyone positions himself cleverly, his philosophy was, and if the goalkeeper keeps paying attention, then a weakness (few defenders) becomes a strength (lots of players geared to the attack).

The coach announced a theory that hardly any of his European colleagues would have dared to repeat: the advantage of having few defenders in your team is that few people will be able to make those defensive mistakes. Which almost sounded like: the fewer defenders, the fewer goals against.

'Often Cruyff and Rexach sat in the dugout like schoolboys,' recalls equipment manager Chema Corbella. 'They discussed out loud which player they were going to substitute. As if they were playing dice. It seemed as if Johan had a playful solution to every problem.' If 'spy' Bruins Slot was worried about a striker with good heading ability on the opposing team, then Cruyff wouldn't put a tall centre back in the defence but think up ways to prevent the opponent from delivering high crosses. Sometimes the coach made the risks just that bit greater than they already were. When Bruins Slot warned him about the striker of opponent Atlético Madrid, saying the small, quick Manolo was 'impossible to mark', Cruyff said, 'Well, then we won't mark him, will we.' Manolo was left to run free and had no idea what to do now that he couldn't perform his usual trick of turning away from the player marking him. After such displays of nerve and wilfulness, the players started calling their coach 'Dios' among themselves; his ways were as mysterious as those of God himself.

Sometimes Cruyff did precisely the reverse, letting his assistants tell him what to do in the defence. It happened on 6

November 1991 in Kaiserslautern, where Barcelona were on the verge of being eliminated from the European Cup. The Germans had made it 3–0 fifteen minutes before the end of the match, a fatal score in combination with Barça's 2–0 victory two weeks earlier in Camp Nou. 'They were walking all over us,' says Rexach. 'So I proposed we should put a defender in. But for Johan that went against his principles. After all, we needed to score, and quickly too. All the same, I wanted to get a defender in there to win back control of the game.' Rexach got his way. Centre back Miguel Ángel Nadal was sent out (taking the place usually occupied by Guardiola, who was playing in midfield on this occasion) and in the final minute José Mari Bakero scored. Barcelona were through to the next round on the away goals rule.

In public, incidentally, Cruyff attributed the narrow escape in Kaiserslautern not to Nadal (whose nephew Rafael later became a famous tennis player) but to 'God's help'. After the 'help' he had received in Clínica Sant Jordi, the coach with the magical self-image knew for certain that the higher powers were on his side. 'I'm now very hopeful that we can win the European Cup,' Cruyff said.

After a flawless season, on 20 May 1992 Barcelona played in the European final against Sampdoria at Wembley, the London stadium where Cruyff had won his first European Cup in 1971. 'We were all more tense than usual,' says Rexach. 'Including Johan, who always presented himself as if he was cool but was often nervous inside. We adjusted our team to the opponent's strongest point, Sampdoria's striker, Vialli. That was completely against our normal habit.'

Because they feared the Italian striker Gianluca Vialli, Barcelona played with four defenders on this occasion, who often remained well to the rear, and without a central striker. Both teams held back; you could have cut the tension with a knife. It could hardly be said that Cruyff had sent his players out on to the pitch with his later legendary 'go out there and enjoy yourselves'. The coach in his smart suit kept pointing and shouting all kinds of things at his players, with an expression of powerlessness. He continually consulted Rexach – clearly things were not going the way he wanted. The game was as lustreless as the pale orange strip of the Catalan team.

It was 0-0 for a long time. In the second half Vialli missed three great chances. Laudrup hit the post for Barça. Then, in the second half of extra time, it happened. For reasons that remain unclear, Barcelona were given a free kick in the 111th minute. Stoichkov gave the ball a short sideways tap, Bakero stopped it and Koeman smashed it straight through the wall, which had a remarkably large gap, into the goal. The Barcelona players ran in all directions with joy and Cruyff got his foot caught behind the boarding when he tried to run on to the pitch. But strikingly, he did not share their euphoria. He stopped to think. He told Alexanko to take off his tracksuit top; the captain had not had a permanent place in the team for a long time, but with his experience he was 'the boss in the changing room', as Cruyff called it, and as such the midfielder was called upon to create order and calm. The team's organisation was maintained, as was the score of 1-0.

The referee blew his whistle and 1,200 kilometres away a region that longed for recognition struck up a party. Even *el dictador* let himself go for a little while at Wembley. He lifted goal scorer Koeman off the ground and laughed without restraint. Cruyff was embraced by equipment manager Corbella, by physiotherapist Langa and by practically everyone in the Barça camp. But soon he reverted to his familiar shy smile; Cruyff preferred to rejoice inwardly. 'Johan was very pleased, even though he never particularly showed it,' Guardiola said later in *Johan Cruyff in Barcelona*. 'But he was aware of how important that cup was. You could tell by his hugs, by his congratulations. We'd done something historic.'

Cruyff certainly had done something historic. In the previous four years the fans had been surprised by him, they'd been angry at disappointing results, they'd been annoyed by his obstinacy and then, gradually, cheerfulness had got the upper hand. Even more than in his active years at Barcelona (1973-78) he had unintentionally been a comic with his anomalous use of the language. He had playfully invented his own version of Spanish (he never learnt Catalan, to the exasperation of the more extreme chauvinists). Given that for him the start of each sentence was a new adventure, and he had no better idea than his listeners where it would end up, it was not always clear at press conferences exactly what he meant. He talked the way he coached: loosely and by improvising, unhindered by schooling. To make it sound more fluent, he had learnt certain phrases that helped him win time during interviews, such as *en un momento dado*. This literal translation of a phrase frequently used in Dutch, meaning 'at a given moment', was not incorrect Spanish but it was uncommon, so that by 1992 it had been widely known as Cruyffian for some time. '*En un momento dado!*' the delighted crowd shouted at Cruyff during the tribute to the European Cup winners. The Plaça de Sant Jaume was packed with people and Cruyff attempted to speak to them from the balcony of the town hall. It was impossible. The people were yelling, '*En un momento dado!*' Jordi Pujol, the 61-year-old president of Catalonia who was standing next to Cruyff on the balcony, explained to him, 'You need to say *en un momento dado*.'

The coach spoke the legendary words and was rewarded with a storm of cheers and applause that rose past the medieval facades surrounding the square, past the elegant lamp posts in the heart of the old inner city. Cruyff had to laugh now too. Then he recovered his composure. 'We've got the first one,' he said into the microphone. 'The second is on its way.' Again there were cheers. His optimism and self-confidence dropped on to the crowd like manna.

The second prize was indeed coming. Three weeks later the explosion of local chauvinism and religious adoration was repeated when Barcelona, on the last day of the competition, became national champions as well. And not by the normal means but, one might say, by a fluke. League leaders Real Madrid, after taking a 2-0 lead over Tenerife, botched things up and caused their own downfall, losing 3-2. So much good fortune in one month: according to the media Cruyff had 'a flower in his arse' (*una flor en el culo*). But the bringer of joy himself saw it very differently. Because of help from a higher power, a Madrid player had scored an own goal on the Canary Island. 'There must be something that organises and controls everything here a bit,' he told journalists later. 'I've often had a strong feeling that guardian angels have watched over my life.'

A year later, in June 1993, the same scenario played itself out. Real Madrid were just one point ahead of Barcelona on the final day of the league championship and once again the team had to travel to Tenerife. 'Only God can give us the title again,' said Cruyff, because this time too winning their last home game would not in itself be enough for Barça. But once more the Lord was with him. To everyone's amazement, Real lost 2-0. Barcelona had won the Spanish league three times in a row. The flower in El Flaco's arse – or a guardian angel, father Manus and Uncle Henk, or God himself – had granted Cruyff this glory. Logical, he said. The national title was the reward for his attacking tactics, his perseverance, his positive attitude.

There was no end to it: 1994 made clear once again that Cruyff was 'God's little brother', as daily newspaper *El Mundo* called him. Barcelona were yet again one point behind the leaders, Deportivo La Coruña, on the final day of the league competition. In Camp Nou, Barcelona polished off Sevilla with a 5-2 victory. In La Coruña things were also going well. Neither Deportivo nor Valencia (coached by Guus Hiddink) had scored and, if it remained 0-0, Barça would be champions. Then in the last but one minute Deportivo were awarded a penalty. 'That's a miss,' Cruyff knew for certain, a thousand kilometres away. And he was right. The ball went straight into the goalkeeper's hands. The score in La Coruña stayed at 0-0 and Barcelona won the national championship for the fourth time in a row. 'Luck?' Cruyff repeated a reporter's question. 'No, it's not luck. We've scored ninety goals this season, that proves our potential, and that's how you win a championship like this. I've always believed it. Now we're just going to win the Champions League on top.'

There was something to be said for Cruyff's optimism. The coach had meanwhile acquired Romário. With the former PSV goal-getter, Barcelona were even more dangerous this season than before. The little Brazilian had scored thirty competition goals, three of them during a resounding 5-0 victory against Real Madrid in January. But despite Romário, Barcelona stood no chance against AC Milan in the UEFA Champions League final on 18 May 1994. Although the Dutch threesome of Ruud Gullit, Frank Rijkaard (both having moved on) and Marco van Basten (with a long-term injury) no longer played for Milan, Barcelona lost 4-0. Nothing had come of Cruyff's promise to teach the 'defensive' and 'negative' AC Milan a lesson that evening in Athens.

Shortly after that final, the World Cup kicked off in North America. As in 1990, Oranje had qualified. The question that had for months occupied the minds of all Dutch sports fans to the point of exhaustion was whether Cruyff would act as national coach during the tournament. No miracles were expected of the official coach, Dick Advocaat – of the magician from Barcelona all the more. In the role of interim coach, Cruyff might be able to do something unbelievable along with Gullit and co., was the idea. Countless sports pages, columns, background reports, interviews and television discussions were devoted to the umpteenth Cruyff issue. It was an issue that resembled previous issues in so far as it quickly came to seem difficult to comprehend. Whereas on closer inspection it was in fact a fascinating story.

CHAPTER TWENTY-EIGHT

Enjoying and suffering

Like all such issues, 'Cruyff and the 1994 World Cup' had a long history and its starting point may have been February 1985. Rinus Michels, at that point technical coordinator at the KNVB and for four months also coach of Oranje, was lying in the Academic Medical Centre in Amsterdam after a heart attack. He asked Cruyff to come and visit and sounded him out as to whether he'd be prepared to act as stand-in national coach. Cruyff agreed in principle, but, he said, there was of course a problem. He had stopped as a player only six months before and didn't yet have a coaching licence. Michels thought up a solution. If a colleague with a diploma was appointed alongside him, there could surely be no objection. Hans Kraay Sr would serve as a kind of 'team manager' while Johan did the coaching during the time it took Michels to recover from heart surgery.

Cruyff asked for time to consider the proposal; he first had to confer with Danny. Shortly after that he read in the newspaper that not he but Volendam trainer Leo Beenhakker had been appointed as interim national coach. According to journalist Johan Derksen, that 'pissed him off'.

It got worse. In the months that followed, Cruyff made attempts to get a coaching diploma. For someone with so much knowledge and experience of football it must be possible, it seemed to him, to get a qualification on paper without having to take all kinds of courses. He contacted the KNVB and was told something of the sort might be on the cards; he would be given a kind of honorary doctorate, a diploma in return for exceptional performance. But he would first have to put in a written request. Cruyff pointed out, truthfully enough, that he was not a gifted writer, at which point an official at the football association said he would be prepared to help him write it. The petition was submitted, but the board found out and foiled the plan. The leadership feared it would set a precedent. Before they knew it, they'd have Willem van Hanegem and Ruud Krol breathing down their necks and nobody wanted that.

Real damage was done to the relationship between Cruyff and Michels by a rumour that not the KNVB official but Michels himself had helped Cruyff to put together the petition, only to reject it in his capacity as technical coordinator. That would have been a sinister double role for Michels to play. There was no truth in the story – put out by Jaap de Groot, for years the ghost writer of Cruyff's *Telegraaf* column – as the magazine *Hard Gras* demonstrated in 2017. But unfortunately De Groot's version was adopted extensively by the media and once again Cruyff declared himself disappointed in his former coach.

After that, during his time as Ajax coach from July 1985 to January 1988, Cruyff regularly locked horns with Michels and the KNVB. He refused to relinquish players when national coach Beenhakker called on Ajax players too often, as he saw it, for practice matches. He also expressed criticism of the kind of play advocated by the (now recovered) national coach Michels and tried via the media to get his goalkeeper Stanley Menzo into the Dutch team. An interview with international Danny Blind didn't do relations much good either. According to Blind, Cruyff ordered his players to form a united front at Oranje so that he could play the boss (roughly in the way that Cruyff and his teammates had done in the 1970s). The annoyance felt by

'Amsterdam' and 'Zeist' about this and other matters reached considerable heights, culminating in the claim that, in a KNVB meeting, Michels had called his former pupil a 'psychopath'. The manager of the national team denied this ('lie'; 'well-packaged slander'), but the word nevertheless made its way into the newspapers.

Assistant national coach Dick Advocaat now speaks frankly of a 'power struggle' between Cruyff and Michels. The press put in their twopenceworth, the Cruyff camp regularly asserting that without his brilliant Number 14, Michels would never have won anything important. Of course, suggestions like that spurred Michels' ambition and it is no secret that his victory with Oranje in the 1988 European Championship gave him satisfaction. At last, at the age of sixty, he had shown he could be successful without Cruyff. For his part, Johan responded with striking insouciance to Oranje's victory. After all, it had not been won in a Cruyffian manner but with rather defensive tactics.

In 1990 the relationship between Cruyff and Michels reached an all-time low. Oranje qualified for the World Cup, but the coach under whom that happened, Thijs Libregts, was considered too much of a lightweight for the final round in Italy. A lot of tumult and speculation was thereby unleashed about who, in that case, was the 'strong man' who should lead the team. Star players Van Basten, Gullit, Koeman and Rijkaard in particular wanted Cruyff. After a vote by the squad – a typically Dutch affair – Cruyff (meanwhile coach at Barcelona) came out on top with eight of the fifteen votes. The other votes went to Leo Beenhakker (five) and Aad de Mos (two).

An open-and-shut case, you might think: Johan would coach Oranje during the final tournament in June. He was attracted by the prospect in theory; he knew the most important players well and saw great opportunities for a successful World Cup, but unfortunately for Cruyff, Michels was in charge of technical matters at the KNVB in this period and responsible for decision-making. As in 1985, Johan was passed over in favour of Beenhakker. Michels was on good terms with the Rotterdam coach, who was now at Ajax, having won the Spanish national championship three times with Real Madrid. Beenhakker was the 'let's have none of this nonsense' type and more or less ate out of Michels' hand, which could hardly be said of Cruyff. Moreover, the KNVB manager believed he could conclude from technical matters he heard about in conversations with internationals that the squad was not nearly as pro-Cruyff as the vote had suggested. In a board meeting he expressed his preference for Beenhakker.

It meant taking the easy route, opting for the steady and predictable. Beenhakker would respect the boundaries of his job, whereas Cruyff, as Michels impressed upon his fellow board members, was planning to travel to Italy with 'a whole new colony'. That was indeed how it looked. Black-and-white thinker Cruyff wanted to take radical decisions in the months leading up to the World Cup and not limit himself when it came to tactics and deployment. 'Everything, absolutely everything' must be 'placed at the service of the performance', as Cruyff put it to journalists. 'So that includes the accompanying staff.' As interim coach he would appoint his own assistant coaches and medical specialists, 'otherwise it isn't a worthwhile undertaking'. 'I know precisely what my strong points are,' he said. 'For the aspects I don't completely command, I collect people around me.' After his appointment he would be sticking his neck out for Oranje, so he wouldn't be content with any of the staff unless he could rely on them blind. The fact that five or six KNVB employees would be laid off as a result was an irrelevance. 'I'm not interested in people who want to have a "nice time" at the World Cup, or who "deserve" to be there,' he said.

This attitude made Michels ('I know the advantages and disadvantages of Cruyff') all the more wary. 'As a coach and as a trainer I don't think there's anyone better than Cruyff,' he wrote later in his book *Het WK 1990 van Rinus Michels*. But 'because he wants to control and run too many other things, quite a lot

of tension is created. You can't have that with a one-off task ...
He wants to work only with faithful followers, who'll do whatever he says. Vassals, of a kind. That's fine, but it's absolutely
not going to work at the KNVB. It's asking for problems.' At
a board meeting in Zeist, Michels made a passionate appeal for
Beenhakker as interim coach. The association announced that
it had chosen the Rotterdammer.

The Cruyff following in the squad reacted with indignation. Van Basten in particular hit out against Michels and in
an interview called his behaviour 'low'. Michels had played
'tricks' and 'little games'. Emotions were running high once
again. Beenhakker, who because of all the commotion had
requested time to think, considered declining the honour. 'Leo,'
said Michels when they were in a car together on the way to a
premier division match in De Kuip, 'if you don't do it, I'll have
to go on my knees to Barcelona. For God's sake don't do that
to me.' The 47-year-old Beenhakker caved in to the man he
submissively continued to call 'Mr Michels'.

Under Beenhakker's leadership, Oranje left for Italy the
favourites. But the heroes of the 1988 European Championship
prepared themselves in an atmosphere of annoyance and division and were eliminated in the second round by the eventual
world champions West Germany. Years into the next century,
pro-Cruyff journalists would continue to attribute Michels'
attitude to envy. The coach was afraid his former star player
would outshine him as the national coach of world champions.
Something else that may have played a part in the background
was the fact that Will Michels had a powerful influence on her
husband and she was said to be less than keen on Cruyff. It is
equally likely, however, that technical board member Michels
simply wanted to prevent the unbounded and headstrong Cruyff
from moving on to his turf and causing 'no end of carry-on'.

Whether Oranje would have performed better under Cruyff
than under Beenhakker we will never know. What is certain is that with the all-or-nothing coach from Barcelona,

Oranje's contribution to the tournament would have been more spectacular.

In January 1991 Cruyff made clear once again how resolutely he would have set to work if Michels had asked him to do the job. 'I'd first have wanted to have a talk with the players,' he told *Nieuwe Revu*. 'I'd have said, there's only one way we can go. I'm coming only if you, like me, assume we're going to win. So now it's backs to the wall and a knife to the throat. If I hadn't managed to get beyond that point, I wouldn't have done it.' His approach was 'the only way', he believed. 'A dead straight road without concessions to anyone.'

'It's no accident that the truly great players wanted me. If I'd worked it out with the players, I'd have sorted the rest out too. The rest, from boardroom to press, is artificial. If you need a commotion, you create a commotion, so to speak.'

Despite the hazards of the past few years and despite this harsh language, the KNVB remained receptive to the idea of Cruyff as national coach. So as early as January 1992 a verbal agreement was made for the 1994 World Cup. Assistant coach Dick Advocaat, now promoted to the position of national coach, would take care of the qualification, then Cruyff would be in charge of the final round in North America. But to the despair of the football association, the Barcelona coach left the contract unsigned. In the background a conflict over sponsorship obligations was raging. As always, Cruyff had his own sponsor, and although at first he said he wouldn't be too insistent about wearing his own logo, in retrospect it was clear that the company behind Cruyff Sports harboured great ambitions. That was fairly understandable; Cruyff on the world stage would undoubtedly attract huge media attention. But at a later stage Oranje sponsor Lotto was, like him, less flexible than at the start. The outcome was a great deal of irritation and confusion. Cruyff only became truly angry when it turned out that the KNVB had sold the television rights not to Dorna, the company to which he was connected and that was owned by his Catalan friend and media magnate Jaume Roures, but to the German UFA. He decided to break off contact with the KNVB.

The relevant department of the KNVB had a new board by this point and its chairman, Jos Staatsen, wanted to achieve something great. He would try once again to do business with Cruyff. Staatsen was regarded as a skilful and egotistical business adviser, who as a senior civil servant and mayor of Groningen had built up a good deal of consultation experience. Full of fresh courage, the 50-year-old chairman of the board flew to Barcelona on 26 November 1993. The Dutch team had qualified for the final round of the World Cup nine days earlier, so it was time for action. The business analyst and the coach had a cordial conversation, although it was striking that on his return to the Netherlands, Staatsen said he was hopeful the contract could be signed before the draw for the World Cup on 19 December, whereas Cruyff coolly stated, 'There's no hurry. The World Cup isn't till June.'

Staatsen was in a hurry. In his four-man board Cruyff was no longer spoken of in such positive terms; communication with Barcelona was far too laborious, some felt. If the coach really wanted the job, he must make that clear by signing.

Four days before the deadline of 19 December 1993, Cruyff, who had always said the finances were of secondary importance to him, dispatched his adviser and lawyer Harrie van Mens to meet with the KNVB. Van Mens said that his client wanted to receive 10 per cent of the advertising profits the association would make during the World Cup. He also demanded a guarantee of a basic salary and bonuses adding up to 350,000 guilders in total. Moreover, there must be a contract for the use of Cruyff's name, fame and likeness. 'Of course, Johan knew that the demand of ten per cent would be practically unacceptable to the KNVB for a start,' Van Mens said later.

The football association contemplated ending the negotiations. A trainer who wanted to coach the national team for a maximum of two months (mid–May to mid–July 1994), yet who wanted to go about in his own branded clothes, who wanted to earn twice as much as the players and to bring his own staff with him, so that many of the KNVB staff would be sitting at home unemployed: it was going too far. Yet chairman Staatsen tried to make a success of it, if only for fear that the pro-Cruyff press would crucify him otherwise. 'If you don't agree to reasonable proposals, you'll have a lot to explain to Dutch football fans,' Cruyff's adviser Van Mens had already let slip to him.

A complicating factor was that Staatsen kept having difficulty contacting Cruyff. It certainly wasn't easy. The family had a secret phone number and the man of the house rarely picked up the phone. In despair, Staatsen even approached Jan Peter Wever, Dutch consul general in Barcelona, who had lived opposite Johan and Danny and was on friendly terms with them. 'One day Staatsen rang,' Wever remembers. 'He asked if I'd like to help him get in touch with Johan. I rang Cruyff and gave him Staatsen's phone number, but I don't think he was particularly interested.'

Eventually Staatsen somehow managed to get through to the Cruyff household by phone himself. As he told it later, he got a 'housemaid' on the line who had no idea where her boss was. Perhaps he was playing golf with friends. Cruyff said later that in that turbulent December of 1993 he'd had no time for Staatsen. 'At times like that you saw that Johan felt a profound contempt for the people at the KNVB,' says Van Mens. 'I believe he deliberately made himself unreachable.'

On Friday 17 December Staatsen sent a fax to Barcelona, reaching out his hand one last time. The handwritten message consisted of a brief summary of the conditions, followed by the statement that if Cruyff did not reply before the draw on 19 December, everything was off the table. No response came. Of course no response came. Anyone who had ever visited the family could have predicted that. In the basement at Carrer de

Margenat 86, the city mansion where Johan, Danny and the children had lived since 1991, there was a fax machine, but Johan had no idea how the thing worked. As well as being all fingers and thumbs, Johan was completely at sea when it came to modern technology. Furthermore, if Cruyff had read the fax, he'd have had to send a reply. That was far from simple too. He'd have needed the help of a member of the family, and he already knew what his wife and children thought about this Oranje undertaking. A year earlier, in an interview with two *Voetbal International* journalists in a Barcelona restaurant, the subject had briefly come up and Danny had sneered, interrupting the conversation, 'And why is it so essential for you to go to America, Cruyff?'

To friends it was a clear signal when Danny addressed him as 'Cruyff'. The man who when touring with Barcelona all over the world was more likely to be recognised on the street than his star players could be put in his place for a moment by that 'Cruyff'. 'When I first visited them, I thought they were arguing,' recalls journalist Johan Derksen. 'A whole lot of noise and shouting. Then Danny let fly at him. "Hey, Cruyff, you're making crumbs!" Or, "Hey, Cruyff, just clear up that mess." He didn't seem to hear most of it. Johan had learnt to live with it, and he could look at you askance as if to say: do *you* get it?'

Derksen is certain that Danny did anything but encourage Cruyff to be interim coach for Oranje. 'She hated it when Johan was away for long periods. "Then he's there with those men in a hotel and I'm sitting here," Danny said to me. She always found it hard to be alone. "Whenever there's a creaking sound upstairs in the house I go stiff with fear in my chair." Danny won't have forbidden him to go in so many words, but he certainly took account of what she wanted.'

Van Mens confirms this. 'It was clear to me that Danny didn't much like the thought of Johan doing it. Partly because of his health.'

The children were if anything even less keen about the

America venture, especially after Cruyff's coronary artery surgery in February 1991. 'I wouldn't even let him be national coach,' Jordi said later in the monthly magazine *Johan*. 'I'd break off with him. I'd say, "If you don't have any respect for your family, for your own health, then I don't want to see you any more." I'd really hold it against him. I don't think my mother would accept it either. People forget that he was at death's door.' It would therefore seem that Cruyff at first enthusiastically said 'yes' to the KNVB, without thinking through all the consequences. The prospect of a short, intense collaboration with Gullit and co. appealed to him, and he thought of himself as a 'tournament coach'. According to Van Mens, he also saw his availability during the World Cup as a way of helping his country. Until at a later stage he realised how 'ridiculously low' the fee the association had in mind for him was and asked lawyer Van Mens to negotiate. 'Johan's view was: if the association earns a lot from my work, I want a share,' says Van Mens. 'By making that demand he knew that either he'd make a lot of money or he wouldn't go to America, which, because of the situation at home, wouldn't be a bad outcome either. He'd be fine either way.'

Cruyff left Staatsen's fax unanswered and went to a showroom that day with his daughter Susila to buy a car. He may have glanced at the message, then thought the ultimatum wasn't so very urgent. 'Well, must. There's never any "must" about what I do,' he said to *Vrij Nederland* in early January 1994. 'There's no such thing as must. I must do only what I want to do.' When the whole world wanted something from you every day, then you decided for yourself when to ring someone back. So he treated the KNVB, whose operations were often muddleheaded, the way he treated most other people. If they wanted him so badly, they'd keep trying. Anyhow, an agreement in January seemed to him early enough.

When it suited him the world star was 'a master at evasion', as his former consultant on advertising Henk Koenders puts it. In the words of Frits Barend, Cruyff liked 'hoodwinking, mystification'. Johan Derksen prefers to call it the 'twisted personality' of famous footballers – 'They never ring back' – and Henny Cruyff said in 1993 that his younger brother lived in a 'utopian sphere' with all those yes-men around him.

Perhaps the KNVB ought to have handled Cruyff the way Koenders did. The advertising man flew to Barcelona on spec if he wanted contact with him. On arrival at the Hotel Princesa Sofia he would report that he was available and simply wait until the most famous Dutchman in the world breezed in. 'Sometimes I'd be sitting there until late in the evening,' Koenders recalls. 'But he always turned up eventually. That's the way it is with performers at that level; it won't have been any different with Mick Jagger. Cruyff didn't think or act the way ordinary people do, he was an artist, and the KNVB could never bring itself to approach him that way.'

In that supposedly busy December, Frits Barend, Johan Derksen and Jaap de Groot had no difficulty at all reaching Johan. But the trio of journalist friends had certain privileges. Since the so-called Vinkeveen consultation in 1987 they had acted pretty much as Cruyff's shield bearers in the media. 'I sometimes helped Johan with positive articles when he was having a hard time,' Barend confirms now. Derksen calls himself, in retrospect, Cruyff's 'errand boy'. The journalists were important in helping to cut opponents down to size in an emergency. That happened to Staatsen too. Shortly after the whole affair ended he was described by Derksen in an article as 'a disaster for Dutch football'.

In any case, the ultimatum expired and the deal did not go through. According to Derksen, Cruyff was astounded. He believes Johan was extremely eager to do it and had even had himself declared medically fit. During conversations about the World Cup, Johan enthusiastically moved bottles around on the table to indicate how he would set to work tactically.

In late December 1993 a special edition of the television

programme *Barend & Van Dorp* was broadcast from Barcelona. The whole issue, puzzling as it was to outsiders, was examined again with guests including Johan Cruyff, Piet Keizer and Marco van Basten. Abstruse details and hazy forms of words flew across the table, until Van Basten started to put his mentor and friend Johan on the spot with questions about his precise motives. Cruyff then held forth about, among other things, the wearing of sponsor logos and negotiations over his salary, which had run aground with a gap of 75,000 guilders. At that point Van Basten said what half the nation was thinking. 'It's crazy that you keep talking about money. Surely that's not what it's all about?' In Las Vegas the striker had spoken to Staatsen, who struck him then as 'very credible'. 'The past week he's been ringing Cruyff daily,' Van Basten said on air. 'I think Johan could and should have reacted at some point.'

The next day *Het Parool* called this 'the one time in the conversation that the ever-domineering Cruyff failed to come up with an answer'. But a week later his magical self-image had been restored. 'I can't be touched any longer,' Cruyff said to Barend and Van Dorp in the weekly *Vrij Nederland*. 'Only by a few people, a very few people. The problem is that you can't take it seriously. How can you take people seriously when they say things that don't make any kind of sense? What's it all about, other than the question, how big are we going to let Cruyff get?'

All his life he would regard the fact that he did not coach Oranje for the 1990 and 1994 World Cups as 'the only real failure' in his career. 'I patched things up with Michels,' he writes in *My Turn*, 'but it still leaves a sour taste that I wasn't able to do something very special.'

The contribution of Oranje to the tournament in the United States was not particularly special, as it turned out. The team was eliminated in the quarter-finals by Brazil. The first Brazilian goal was scored by one of the few people close to Cruyff who'd had a great summer in 1994, Barça player Romário de Souza

Faria. Twenty-eight-year-old Romário wasn't just part of the winning Brazilian team. He scored five goals during the tournament and was awarded the Golden Ball as the best player of the World Cup. The other happy man that summer was Hristo Stoichkov. The Barça attacker from Bulgaria surprisingly reached the semi-finals and was joint top scorer with six goals. The problem for Cruyff was that the two star attacking players returned to Barcelona after the summer holiday with heads the size of melons. Romário, moreover, came back a month late. The striker seemed to have lost his enthusiasm; he ignored Cruyff's orders and remained several kilos too heavy. The coach, who had put up with a lot from Romário the previous season, failed to bring him to heel and in January 1995 let him leave for FC Flamengo in Brazil.

Cruyff had such a massive run-in with Stoichkov that season that the Bulgarian announced on Spanish radio in March 1995, 'Either he goes or I do.'

The third brilliant attacker in Barcelona's successful team, Danish dribbler Michael Laudrup, had already left after disagreements with Cruyff. Newcomer Gheorghe Hagi was injured, which forced the coach to let a 20-year-old attacker from the Barcelona youth team make his debut, his son Jordi. On 4 September Jordi was brought on in the second half against Sporting Gijón. He wore number 14. A week later he played a full match in front of a crowd of 90,000 in Camp Nou against Racing Santander, and scored. 'Jordi played a more than decent game,' said Cruyff Sr proudly. 'At times he showed real class.'

Jordi was a quick, two-footed attacking midfielder, a diligent and fairly good winger, but brilliant he wasn't. He didn't resemble his father either by his haircut or by the way he moved. Although he was not in the team from start to finish every week, and sometimes had to go back to playing in the second eleven, some of his fellow players had their doubts about his presence in the squad. Jordi sensed that, naturally. 'It isn't easy to be the coach's son,' he said eight years later in *Johan*. 'People see the clubs listed next to my name and think: he rolled in there nicely. That's not how it was. It was difficult for my father, too.'

Listed next to Jordi's name were Ajax (youth) and Barcelona, but in Camp Nou even assistant coach Charly Rexach thought it wouldn't be sensible to put him in the first eleven. Furthermore, Cruyff had also included the mediocre goalkeeper Jesús Mariano Angoy in the squad, husband of his daughter Chantal. (Chantal and Jesús had been married in May 1992 and vice-president Joan Gaspart was a witness at the wedding.) So now he was training both his son and his son-in-law in Barcelona's first-team squad. With Angoy among them there were suddenly three keepers, whereas in previous years Cruyff had thought two sufficient. Moreover, according to Rexach he often put his son-in-law into the team when there were 'fat bonuses' to be won.

This caused astonishment among the other players and annoyance among the board. But Angoy himself claims it wasn't a problem. 'We kept work and private life strictly separate,' he says. Father-in-law Johan treated him purely 'professionally' and 'never' talked about team matters at home. The former keeper does admit that family relationships influenced 'the entourage'. Rexach is certain they did. 'The family is best kept out of the changing room,' he says. 'Otherwise the atmosphere among the players is no longer safe. The lads have to be able to speak freely about the coach among themselves. I always heard a lot from the captain, so I could sometimes rein Johan in a little, if he'd gone too far with a punishment for instance. That was over now. The mood among the players deteriorated as a result.'

After the end of the 1993–94 season, Rexach had proposed that Cruyff should appoint someone else as head coach, who could then make the necessary changes. 'But Johan thought he could manage it himself,' Rexach said later. 'And I think he wanted to continue supporting his son.' That may be true. Jordi had not been particularly easy in recent years. 'I was an idiot,' he said later, looking back. 'Often sent out of the class.'

'The sacred flame ignited only when I realised how much

pressure there was on me, how great the expectations were. I was the son of Johan Cruyff; I had to be a promise.'

Cruyff had always put his family first and for the coach, who was helpful by nature, it was naturally important to see Jordi succeed. His son could carry on the Cruyff name after he had taken his leave of professional sport. Yet he no doubt took care not to give the boy preferential treatment; in fact, Rexach believes he sometimes tended towards the opposite direction. 'One day Johan was angry with Jordi for playing poorly,' says the then assistant coach, who also associated with the Cruyffs in their private lives. 'Jordi said he had trouble with his knee, but Johan didn't think that was any excuse. "What d'you mean?" he said. "In my day I played with a broken leg." Jordi slunk away and I felt sorry for him. I said, "Flaco, you can't treat the lad like that. You grew up on the street. This is a different generation. You need to take that into account."'

Jordi himself would later call it 'a crazy time' when he was 'son of the coach'. He had consciously 'not got involved' in the dressing room, but he did notice that nobody complained about his father 'when I was around', which sometimes made him feel 'uncomfortable'.

Apart from the lack of a safe refuge in the changing room, the atmosphere at Barcelona was also suffering as a result of disappointing performances on the pitch. In early November 1994 the team triumphed with a resounding 4-0 victory over Manchester United in the Champions League, but such revivals of top form were scarce. In January 1995 Barça were given a thrashing in Madrid by Real (5-0) and in February by Atlético (in the Copa del Rey tournament, 4-1). In May, having finished fourth in the premier league, Barcelona failed to win any other prizes that season. The foreign players brought in on Cruyff's recommendation failed to perform (Gheorghe Hagi, Robert Prosinečki, Gheorghe Popescu, Meho Kodro) – although the young Portuguese Luís Figo did turn out to be an excellent choice. The outstanding goalkeeper who had to leave, Andoni Zubizarreta, was replaced by Carles Busquets, a goalie with 'good feet', which Cruyff liked, but unfortunately not with good hands. Despite various blunders, Busquets was deployed time and again.

Naturally, in the wake of this mediocre season there was a good deal of criticism of Cruyff's work, but no indication it kept him awake at night. 'There was no sign of panic,' his son-in-law Angoy recalls. 'Even when there were rumblings in the club, he was stable. His whole attitude was, losing doesn't matter as long as you show you're progressing. Stand by the style, and the accomplishments will come by themselves. And when the style flourished, it made him visibly happy.'

'After a lost match Danny was often worried,' says friend of the family Rolf Grootenboer. 'We all dreaded what the papers would say the next day. "Nonsense, love," would be Johan's laconic reaction. "So don't read the paper, okay? Then it won't bother you. Next week we'll win again." After setbacks Johan would ignore the newspaper coverage. He found it easy to put things into perspective.' Ronald Koeman noticed that too. 'I always found that so smart of Johan. He shut the door and it all fell away.'

With his superiors, too, Cruyff maintained a certain imperturbability and he achieved that by avoiding them. To quote his publicity adviser Koenders, he was 'not a man who liked confrontation', so conflicts fairly often became 'simmering affairs'. His relationship with the board at Barcelona had not been good for quite a while and his solution was to speak only to vice-president Gaspart. At least Gaspart didn't let him down, unlike *el presidente* Núñez, who openly objected to the 'privileges' Jordi enjoyed, among other things. His 'spy' Rexach kept him informed of the latest developments in the boardroom. Moreover, as in the Netherlands, several important sports journalists were always prepared to stick up for him, including commentator Joan Patsy.

All this meant that Cruyff could live the Catalan life he had come to love. The setting was his huge city mansion, with seven bathrooms and nine bedrooms, and when he went out he enjoyed his favourite restaurants, such as La Venta at the foot of Tibidabo, a hill close to his home in the fashionable Bonanova district. He liked best to be served cannelloni with pheasant and black truffles there, and he invariably started eating without waiting for the others. There was always the stress of having to perform, which he did of course feel inside, but he became more self-indulgent than ever before, despite warnings from his doctors than he must think of his cholesterol level. 'Johan indulged himself quite a bit,' former consul general Joan Peter Wever remembers, having shared many a meal with the Cruyffs. 'He took big helpings, with lots of calories, lots of eggs too. He didn't look to me like a healthy eater.'

It seems Cruyff had adopted the lifestyle and habits of the Catalan elite. If he wasn't invited to have a lavish dinner some-where then he would ask friends to come to his place for a meal, and he in no way resembled the penny-pincher of the old days. 'As far as that was concerned, the whole family was spoilt, of course,' says Harrie van Mens. 'It had become an expensive household.'

When he was travelling with Barça he ate and drank well too. Wine at the table was entirely normal and the coaches enjoyed having one or more glasses poured for them. Although Cruyff was not a heavy drinker, he had his preferences, partly because of his experience as a wine exporter. *Johan Cruyff in Barcelona* includes a description of how 'a large number of crates of Marqués de Arienzo, a rather good rioja' travelled with him when the squad went to Drenthe to prepare for the new season. From 1989 onwards the players had trained in villages like Odoorn and Roden and everything there was taken care of, down to the last detail, by Jan Wardenburg.

The 51-year-old Wardenburg, already known to Cruyff from when Ajax alighted there in the early 1980s, ensured the trainers and players wanted for nothing during their ten-day summer stay in Drenthe. 'If the footballers had to play a match in the evening, they drank wine with their lunch, even beer,' Wardenburg remembers. 'When I asked whether that was a good idea, Johan said, "Yes, sure, it's their own responsibility. I'm not going to check on them." Johan wanted nothing but his own rioja. "Remember, old man," he'd say. "That and nothing else!" He was mad keen on meat products too. One time we were cycling together behind the players during a cross-country run. Johan found it far too dull. "This is a bore, Jan," he said. "We're going back. Just get a bacon roll ready for me." So of course that's what I did.'

If a player had forgotten his toothpaste, Wardenburg would buy some. If anybody had a headache, he'd fetch an aspirin. Born in Valthermond, and a creditable referee for the amateurs, Wardenburg was an organiser who arranged practice matches against amateur clubs every year. He also arranged the considerable payments that were made to persuade FC Barcelona to come and Johan then made sure the players weren't forgotten. At Ajax, too, the coach had always been vigilant in ensuring the club leadership wasn't alone in profiting from well-attended matches at home and abroad.

Cruyff and the obliging Jan Wardenburg got along well. The round-bellied blond man from Drenthe and the skinny Amsterdammer trusted each other implicitly. In the middle of winter, on 13 January, the head coach always rang him from Barcelona. 'Happy birthday!' he'd say. 'How did you know?' Wardenburg would ask. 'The usual way,' was the answer. 'Your name's here on the birthday calendar.'

'In the evenings at the hotel bar he would always invite me to come and sit with him,' says Wardenburg. 'We'd talk about all kinds of things. It struck me that he could never, ever admit someone else was right. Not even his assistant coaches. He never gave an inch. *Your head's in a box*, I thought. Nothing gets in. Even though his ideas about anything other than football weren't very well thought through. Still, otherwise those were unforgettable evenings with him. One day I said, "I'm just an ordinary working man's son. That I'm able to experience this! I never got past elementary school." "That's exactly what I like about you," he said. "Just act normal." His assistants sometimes looked down on me, but Johan never did. I loved that.'

El mister, as the players called their famous coach, was always given a room on the ground floor with a door that opened on to a courtyard. The door stayed unlocked, so that he could receive visitors who were able to leave at the moment of their, or more specifically her, choosing. Sometimes one good-looking visitor in particular would come over from Spain for four days and he succeeded in keeping her hidden from everyone. The visitor would stay in the room all that time to avoid being noticed. *El mister* also sometimes rented two Mercedes from J. Van Dijk & Dochters of Rotterdam, as he did when Ronald Koeman needed to go to some ceremony or other. The head coach drove off at the same time as Koeman in the other Mercedes, but to a completely different destination, able thereby to do so discreetly.

If the head coach said after dinner that he would be 'ill' that evening, then for the few in the know it was clear that he didn't want to be disturbed and would miss morning training. Those in the know 'belonged', as *el mister* put it. Which meant: keep your mouth shut. Jan Wardenburg would always remember a former ballerina, and he wasn't the only one; Johan Derksen can still picture her many years later. 'He received her a number of times,' says the journalist, looking back. 'Until the woman suddenly started seeing a footballer. She gave me a note and told me to give it to Johan. In it she asked why he didn't want to see her any longer. It bothered me. But still, I gave the note to Johan. "So now you know," he said. I nodded. "Well, it's like this," he said. "I have one principle. Going to bed with the girlfriend of a fellow footballer is something you just don't do." Suddenly he turned out to have principles.'

According to Derksen, Cruyff was 'crazy about women'. 'You

might not think it to look at him, but he was. He would stand at the hotel bar flirting with women while their husbands were standing right next to them. Later I came upon him in a brothel somewhere near Assen. I'd seen his car outside and walked in for a moment. He was sitting right there at the bar. "What are you doing here?" he said. I said, "No, what are *you* doing here?"'

Derksen's point is simply that the quiet and unpretentious province of Drenthe was not the only reason why Barça travelled to the northern Netherlands in the Cruyff years.

Discretion was sometimes guarded rather more noisily. One evening Cruyff was sitting on the terrace in front of Hotel De Oringer Marke in Odoorn having a drink with some amateur footballers and their girlfriends. A Spanish journalist walked past unexpectedly while the coach had his hand on the shoulder of one of the girlfriends. All entirely innocent, but it seems the Spaniard made a remark, because Cruyff stood up and went after the journalist. 'Look, guys, Johan's furious,' chuckled assistant coach Tonny Bruins Slot. The head trainer was indeed in a rage; he was talking tough and it looked very much as if he was making all kinds of threats about what he would do if the journalist wrote about what he'd just seen.

The incident is reminiscent of 1974 and Cruyff's anger when the son of the owner of the Hotel Krautkrämer photographed him with an unknown woman. That was the start of the swimming pool incident. It seems Cruyff did not want to call down that kind of trouble upon himself again.

Although in the early 1970s, according to former Ajax players Ruud Suurendonk and Wim de Wit, Cruyff sometimes climbed down the drainpipe of a players' hotel, he seems to have lived it up mainly in this Barça period. Because in Spain too there were secret meetings, with a certain Carla, for instance. An Amsterdam woman who lived in Benidorm, she had rejected his advances when she was younger because he was such an unprepossessing – and still unknown – little man, but now she felt very differently about him. After an away game against

Hércules CF in Alicante, a meeting was arranged in the coastal resort and it became extremely amicable. In the hotel they shared memories of the cosy 1960s, of the kale with sausage that Johan had come round to eat at her house, of the bowling nights on the Rembrandtplein and of a dance hall called Robinson in Landsmeer. In those days Cruyff had been unable to get a girlfriend, whereas now, as he told Carla, 'the women walk behind me when I go to the toilet'. After a night in the hotel, they concluded their lives could have been very different if blonde Carla had found him attractive on that long-ago evening. They agreed to meet again, but nothing came of it.

On countless occasions El Flaco was depicted as a family man, which indeed he was, apart from encounters of this sort. He was one of the very few of his generation of top footballers to stay with his wife, even if he was not always very romantic towards her. 'He doesn't so much as look at me,' Danny once sighed to her friend Grootenboer. 'He looks more at other women.' And Rob Cohen, a close acquaintance of Cor Coster, was told by Danny, 'Those footballers are all adulterers.'

After the summer of 1995, Barcelona did not return to Drenthe. Cruyff's decisions were coming up against more and more criticism. 'Johan had risen so high that he was God in people's eyes and all he thought about was winning,' says Rexach. 'But now that things weren't going his way, it was as if he wrecked everything from the inside out. His behaviour became destructive.' The more the members of the board spoke badly of him to the press, the more obstinate he became, it seemed. A whole series of young players made their debut in the first eleven and of course that did not always go smoothly. Cruyff confessed that during a game in December tears had come to his eyes as he watched. So 'pathetic' he called it.

Meanwhile, he continued to derive great pleasure when young players did well. 'Training young people is great, far better than paying a couple of million guilders for a player

from another club,' he said to *de Volkskrant*. Which was why
he actually found this group 'nicer to work with' than the last.
'I see a young guy like De la Peña break through. And then
I think back to the eleven-year-old boy and his parents, and
the conversations I had with them.' Discovering young talents,
teaching little Bergkamps and Guardiolas the ins and outs of
the trade: there was nothing to beat it. If you asked him what
was wrong with a club, he was sure to start telling you about its
youth training. Even in April 1996 he said he 'knew nothing'
about coaching, only about 'football'.

On 20 April 1996 father and son had a moment in Camp Nou
that was truly moving. In the twenty-fifth minute Jordi scored
a beautiful goal against Atlético Madrid. Jubilant, he skirted his
teammates and ran to the touchline, radiant, his blond hair flying.
There Cruyff briefly held his son and then immediately began
giving the players tactical instructions, because although Barcelona
had equalised, 1-1, they definitely needed to start playing better.

Unfortunately, they didn't. This league match too was
lost, 3-1.

Barcelona won no prizes that season. The final of the Copa
del Rey was lost to Atlético Madrid, and in the semi-finals
of the UEFA Cup Cruyff's team were eliminated by Bayern
Munich. Two matches before the end of the league season it
was clear that Barcelona would not be national champions this
year either. Two years without a trophy. At a rich and ambitious
club like Barça that meant you could expect a visit.

On Saturday 18 May 1996, towards ten in the morning,
shortly before training began, Joan Gaspart came to have a
word with his good friend Johan, who knew what it would
be about. At that point Gaspart, who for a long time had been
his confidential adviser on the board, suddenly wasn't a friend
any longer. During the conversation Johan called him a Judas.
Gaspart delivered the message that all football coaches on earth
factor in from their very first day at a club. It hurt this coach,
with his magical self-image, deep in his soul.

CHAPTER TWENTY-NINE

Man of God and of humankind

Joan Gaspart was Cruyff's last ally on the club board

Gaspart had been vice-president of Barça since 1978 and, in contrast to president Josep Lluís Núñez, he was not known for his opportunism and assertiveness. In fact, he was distinguished mainly by his boundless love of the club, one of the reasons why Cruyff liked him so much. Born in Barcelona, the vice-president was a hardworking enthusiast, who after victory in the 1992 European Cup in London jumped into the River Thames for joy. Gaspart was the only member of the board with whom Johan would go out for a meal. The Cruyffs and the Gasparts had even once eaten Christmas dinner together.

In the last turbulent season, when many of Cruyff's admirers made common cause with Núñez in the press, Gaspart had applied all his diplomatic talents to preventing a premature dismissal of his friend. It had not been easy. Cruyff regularly missed training sessions, his interaction with members of the squad left much to be desired and, meanwhile, he said denigrating things to the media about a board he regarded as incompetent.

Gaspart had even allowed himself to be ridiculed for Cruyff's sake. As a preamble to a contract for the 1996–97 season, the coach was to be forced to sign a list of ten behavioural rules. As he had at Ajax in 1987, Cruyff interfered all over the place and, like Ton Harmsen, Núñez wanted to curb that tendency. The rules were intended to force Johan into a certain degree of compliance. Cruyff had signed the paper and a relieved Gaspart had taken it with him to the board meeting, only to be made to look a fool. Cruyff had not given the document his usual signature but instead signed it 'Jordi'. So the contract was put away in a drawer unsigned.

Gaspart, the 51-year-old businessman who four years earlier had been a witness at Chantal's wedding, went to the coaches' changing room on the morning of Saturday 18 May 1996. He saw Johan sitting there and said he could explain it.

Cruyff knew perfectly well what 'it' was. 'It' had been in all the papers that morning. A delegation of board members from Barça had met in secret with Bobby Robson, the English coach who was to replace Cruyff next season. Like practically everything in the snake pit that was FC Barcelona, the news had leaked out. *'A la calle!!'* was the headline in sports newspaper *Marca*, across a picture of Cruyff, eyes cast down. On the street!! Everyone already knew. He was going to be sacked.

'Hello, Johan,' said Gaspart.

'Good morning,' Cruyff answered, refusing the outstretched hand. 'Why do you want to shake my hand, Judas?'

At such moments the pupil at the Protestant Groen van Prinsterer School surfaced in Johan. In Barcelona the coach had for years been compared to the other 'JC' and sometimes called 'The Prophet', so he had cause enough to make reference to the Garden of Gethsemane.

'Man, Johan,' Gaspart pleaded. 'Don't say such things. It's a difficult time for me.'

'I know you have to do your job, but why doesn't that dwarf come here, that boss of yours?' (Núñez was small in stature and when Cruyff hated someone he would refuse to use their name. In later interviews he continued to say 'him' or 'that man' when he meant Núñez.)

'I wanted to speak to him as a friend,' Gaspart says, looking back. 'I'd gone to such lengths for him, and so often played the diplomat between him and Núñez by giving them messages in a watered-down form, that I now felt a need to share with Johan how uncomfortable I felt. That meeting with Robson needed to take place in secret; given the complexity of our club there was no other option. I found it painful for Johan that it was already in the newspapers.'

There in the trainers' room Cruyff flung all kinds of reproaches at Gaspart. He felt betrayed. 'Gaspart kept trying to apologise to him for the way things had gone,' assistant coach Rexach remembers. 'But Johan was livid. He was deeply offended.' According to Gaspart the conversation got 'totally out of hand'. 'The things we said to each other got worse and worse,' he recalls. 'There came a point when Johan stood up and threw his chair to the ground. Then he said something I won't repeat, but it was so bad that I had no choice but to send him away.'

Shortly after the incident, Gaspart was more open about it. 'God will punish the lot of you for this, the way God punished you before,' was what he claimed Cruyff had said. That was surely a blow below the belt, since by saying 'punished you before' the white-hot coach was referring to a tragedy that was common knowledge within Barça, namely the death of a grandchild of Núñez. Even in a book published with the approval of the Johan Cruyff Foundation, *Wie is Johan Cruyff?*, this reading is confirmed. 'I couldn't accept those words,' Gaspart says now. 'It's tragic, very sad; we were beside ourselves.'

The raging and cursing in the coaches' room was overheard in the players' changing room. 'And then Angoy turned up to get involved too,' says Rexach. Angoy refuses to divulge exactly what he said to Gaspart that memorable morning in Camp Nou, but the reserve goalkeeper and then son-in-law of Cruyff admits that he told the vice-president that it was shameful to do something like that to the most successful coach in the club's history, and that Núñez ought to have dealt with it himself. But clearly he put the message in terms that do not bear repeating.

The shouting went on for a long time, well after the point when the training session ought to have started. Cruyff left. Rexach and the other assistant, former captain Alexanko, decided to lead the training themselves.

Johan was waylaid by a camera crew that afternoon. He was walking his long-haired collie near his house, wearing cotton trousers and a light short-sleeved shirt. Naturally he wasn't in the mood for an interview, but he didn't bark at the reporter to bugger off. He very rarely if ever did that. Near the wall of the hospital, at the end of the street where he lived, he looked straight into the camera from behind his Ray-Bans. He said that he had already made it known that he wouldn't be commenting. But he did comment, summarily. No, said Cruyff, he didn't know he was going to be sacked. He looked around him a bit and reassured his dog, which was whining. The reporter asked what he would think if he was indeed sacked. Cruyff seemed for a moment to think nothing and see nothing and he made that familiar gesture of his with his hand to his nose, as if Barça had fallen behind and he needed to think of a way to recover. Then he answered, frowning, his whole body moving restlessly, 'Then I'll see,' and he walked on, past the yellow stuccoed walls, his dog next to him, one hand in his pocket and the other swinging energetically forwards and back.

The next day, when Barça were due to play a home game against Celta de Vigo in the evening, Jordi said he refused to go on the pitch, as a protest. After the clash with Gaspart, Cruyff Jr had been reluctant to train, out of solidarity with his father. 'I rang Johan then,' Rexach remembers. 'I said, you're God, but Jordi is a footballer; he simply has to come. If you don't want him to join us, I won't let him play.'

Jordi turned up in Camp Nou, got changed and played out-standingly. He seemed more motivated than ever. There was no longer any justification for the old criticism from his father that he lacked the doggedness of the postwar generation. During the match the *socios* clearly sided with Cruyff, the man who had not only been coach at Barcelona for longer than anyone and had won eleven trophies with his team but had also provided them with unforgettably beautiful football. Tens of thousands of white handkerchiefs were waved in support of El Flaco. In the VIP seats Núñez was booed and Gaspart had to be led to safety by the police.

Barça recovered from 0-2 down to 2-2 and managed in the end to win 3-2. The dream scenario. Jordi had been in good form for weeks and a month earlier he'd made his debut with Oranje. Five minutes before the end of the match he left the pitch, so that the crowd could demonstrate in favour of his father. Cheers and shouts of 'Krewieff, Krewieff!' filled the stadium. 'I saw that as a tribute to my father,' Jordi said later. 'It was very emotional.'

Relations with Núñez and Gaspart never recovered. 'For three years they've been trying to wear me down, every single day,' Cruyff told journalists. 'But the board here is hopeless, I have no respect at all for these people. One of them strikes up a tune and the rest dance along.'

At the press conference after the Barcelona vs Celta de Vigo match, the president took a seat at the microphone. Núñez, who had received the support of Cruyff at the elections in both 1978 and 1988, said that the sacked coach had insulted 'the dead', that he had picked up a chair and threatened people with it and that it was therefore impossible to work with him any longer. 'He got rid of players like Laudrup, Stoichkov and Romário so that his son could play,' Núñez claimed. 'He made his son-in-law a reserve goalkeeper. He's turned his changing room in the stadium into an office for his business affairs. He sells himself to the press, he accepts payments from political parties.' According to Núñez, Cruyff, who was earning around 5 million guilders a year, was 'hardly ever' at the club, partly because he was too busy 'selling apartments' in Andorra. 'Cruyff has deceived me, he has deceived the supporters. This is the end of him.'

Four months later, in September 1996, Cruyff and Núñez saw each other in court. Cruyff demanded 1.2 million guilders in unpaid fees plus his basic salary for the 1996-97 season. He lost, but ultimately he did get around a third of the amount he was demanding. More important than the money was the timing, he said later. As a result of his sacking he'd been unable to take his leave of the supporters, and he knew that a good proportion of them were behind him. 'Personally, it causes me a lot of pain,' he said. 'Because of how it was done, and above all the moment at which it was done.'

He had to wait almost three years for his revenge. On 10 March 1999 he finally got to say goodbye to Camp Nou, packed as it was that evening for a match in honour of the Barça team of 1992. That team had become known as the Dream Team, a reference to the American professional basketball players who stole the show that year during the Olympic Games in Barcelona. Because of his feud with Cruyff, Núñez had all but refused to co-operate on the tribute. The organisers had to work out for themselves how to get hold of shirts and they were not allowed to put any club emblems on them. The players who were still in the Barça team, among them Josep Guardiola and Carles Busquets, were not permitted to play in the Dream Team. But that wasn't going to spoil the fun.

In the orange strip of the European Cup winners of 1992, the members of the Dream Team were called to the centre spot one by one. Cruyff was the last on to the pitch. There was cheering as well as applause. Banners had been hung on the fences in front of the stands reading 'Welcome to the home of Cruyff' and 'Cruyff we love you'. On his way to the centre circle he was handed a microphone. He was nervous. He hadn't prepared for this. With the microphone to his mouth, he waited until people stopped chanting 'Joe-han, Joe-han'. He looked smart in a dark blue suit with a chequered shirt and a tie. Then he spoke words appropriate to his attire, but with razor blades sewn inside. 'Only God knows how long we've had to wait for this fantastic moment.'

'We', that meant him and the hundred thousand people all around him. Johan, the 51-year-old lad from Betondorp, who had known for so long that he was the property of the people, who had only wanted to entertain them with real football, with quality and adventure, this 'Joe-han' forged a bond on the spot with the higher powers in which he believed. And as always with Cruyff, you were either in or out. The people in Camp Nou were in. Núñez and Gaspart on the VIP stands were out – and they knew it.

That evening he walked to the centre spot and the players of the Dream Team formed a circle. There they stood, as if in a *rondo*, the game that had become a form of training under Cruyff, symbolic of the belief that you mustn't run but think, that technique and ingenuity were more important than strength. Many of the spectators had tears in their eyes, as did some of the players. Endlessly that 'Joe-han, Joe-han' surged over him. His confidant, television commentator Joan Patsy, later admitted to having broken down at that point.

The worrier on the centre spot was struggling. He swallowed and seemed to be losing the battle with his emotions. He said nothing, was unable to do anything for a moment, then quickly ran his hand over his nose and a little later over the back of his head, over the scalp that was starting to show a little through his hair.

Bumps goose. It gave everyone bumps goose, and the next day many of the newspapers would say as much. It was one of the many incorrect Spanish terms used by Cruyff that had gone on to lead a life of its own, according to *Johan Cruyff in Barcelona*. After one of the Dream Team's best ever matches, a 4-1 victory over Dynamo Kiev in September 1993, the coach had entertained journalists by saying 'goose bumps' in Spanish but forgetting that the Spanish used the words the other way around. Instead of *piel de gallina*, his team had given him *gallina de piel* and everyone had found that amusing. And so, on 10 March 1999 half of Catalonia got 'bumps goose', a special kind of emotion at the sight and sound of the inimitable improviser Johan Cruyff.

During the homage in Camp Nou he sat in the dugout with Rexach again, which was saying something. Rexach had been 'out' ever since 1996. To Cruyff's astonishment the assistant coach had not stood by him after he was sacked and had been persuaded to set to work for Barcelona again in the new season. Cruyff couldn't accept that. You were for him or against him, and if you were for him then you didn't collaborate with people who were against him. That was logical, and so the door had slammed shut. Charly, his former teammate, roommate and companion, his ally for years in the battle for intelligent football and against the board, was pushed away. No matter what Rexach had tried since then – phoning, phoning again, writing letters, driving to the Montanya and ringing the bell – he had not been able to speak to Johan. 'One time I stood at their front door and phoned them,' Rexach recalls. '"Johan isn't here," Danny said on the phone. "Yes he is," I said. "His car's here." "Okay," Danny said then, "but you're not welcome here any more." For me that was a sign she had a big influence. Which turned out to be true. Years later, when I ran into Johan, he was always friendly towards me. We even went out for a meal. But never again with our wives.'

In 1999 Cruyff was living a completely different life from the one he'd been used to between his debut in 1964 and his sacking in 1996. He'd rejected all offers from football clubs. Life without match planning and quarrels with board members suited him 'excellently', as he said to Barend and Van Dorp in April 1997. 'In fact, it suits me far too well. The chances of me starting to do anything are getting smaller and smaller.' The likelihood that

he would take a job as coach anywhere declined even further
in November 1997. He had heart problems again. Now aged
fifty, he felt unwell and went to the hospital attached to the
Vrije Universiteit, not far from the Waldeck Pyrmontlaan in
Amsterdam-Zuid, where he and Danny now had a pied-à-terre.
(They had sold the bungalow in Vinkeveen in 1991.) Cruyff
spent two weeks in the coronary care unit there. A disorder of
the blood flow to his heart muscle had caused 'unstable angina
pectoris', which was accompanied by a narrowing of the coronary artery. The medication turned out to work well, so there
was no need for surgery. According to a spokesperson for the
hospital, his condition had been 'no great cause for concern',
but it was clear that he would be wise to take things easy. It was
unthinkable for him to accept a job as a soccer coach anywhere.
Chantal, Susila and Jordi were twenty-seven, twenty-five and
twenty-three, so there were now four adults to call Cruyff to
order if he did anything silly. According to friends of the family
like Henk Koenders, they were the only four people who told
him the unvarnished truth.

When asked what was the most enjoyable part of his career,
Cruyff said to Barend and Van Dorp in 1997, 'Of course you
had the most fun at Ajax between the ages of twelve and seventeen. That was the best time of all, naturally. Perhaps because
it wasn't a big deal. Perhaps because you were still helped by
everyone then.' Before he turned seventeen. Before his debut
in the premier division. Before all the trouble started. Before
the expectations of the outside world put him under pressure.
Before the arguments began, the tensions, the injuries, the
misunderstandings, the disappointments, the problems at home
because he was so often away.

Cruyff's answer underlined once again how little pleasure
he'd had in his career. His confession at twenty – 'I can't be
really happy' – seemed to apply to the entire life of the professional footballer and coach. Not to the training sessions and

the larking about, nor to playing pool and cards with the lads, but to the matches. Of course, his worldwide fame gave him satisfaction and, with a lollipop in his mouth, he had enjoyed the free-playing Dream Team. But on balance his working life had been tough and life in retirement made him happier. 'I'm not cut out to be a coach,' he had said in an interview back in 1974. 'I don't have the right mentality for it. You get back into those nervous states. Which is exactly what I want rid of.'

Well, he'd been rid of them since 1996 and he threw himself with his characteristic restlessness into good causes and into airing his footballing insights in columns and on television. Charity was something Cruyff had always been attracted to. The seed had been sown in the help that he, his brother and his mother had once received from so many people. In a television programme called *De wandeling* he later said, 'I find helping a normal thing. If I can ever help someone, then I will.' In his early twenties he had started visiting orphanages and he continued to do so. In his years in America he had seen what famous sportspeople and sports clubs did for good causes and discovered his talent for relating to children with learning difficulties.

Now, unimpeded by responsibilities as a coach, he could give his social conscience free rein with the Johan Cruyff Foundation, which was set up in the spring of 1997, shrewdly riding on the publicity surrounding his fiftieth birthday on 25 April. In 1999 the Johan Cruyff Academy was launched, again with good timing, since in the final year of the twentieth century there were countless events, such as the Oranje of the Century, a team made up of the eleven best players of the past one hundred years, in which he was of course asked to take part. Another thing that helped was that an international jury had chosen him as 'European Footballer of the Century'. Franz Beckenbauer came second and Argentinian-Spaniard Alfredo Di Stéfano third. Through the foundation he supported sports projects for children, including disabled children, and with the academy – and the Cruyff College for higher vocational education – he helped sportspeople do what he had never been able to do, namely to engage intensively in sport by following a course that took account of their need to be available for training sessions and matches.

So the retired Cruyff remained active, if not every day. He helped with networking, with generating publicity, with attracting the interest of sponsors. He was involved in new initiatives, which others went on to develop in more detail. After all, as he later said in the book *Wie is Johan Cruyff?* on the subject of running organisations, 'I haven't a clue about that, because whichever way you look at it, I've had only an elementary education ... I do a very specific job of bringing ideas, people and companies together.' During theoretical conversations about legislation and permits he would lose interest, but if the talk turned to Cruyff Courts and what kind of football games you could play on them, he would revive and speak at length.

'In the early years of the foundation you could really see that a weight had fallen off Johan's shoulders,' says his former ghost writer Jan de Deugd. 'He radiated happiness once he was relieved of all the match tensions. He enjoyed his role as patron.' Adviser Henk Koenders saw that Cruyff derived energy from his interaction with children with disabilities. 'He brightened visibly when he put his arm around one of those children,' Koenders remembers. 'He didn't feel superior to children with Down's syndrome, he just wanted to help, as if helping was in his DNA.' Cruyff felt a special connection with sportspeople at the academy too. 'As ever, swimmers and athletes had to do a huge amount of tough training and devote everything to their sport,' says Wim de Wit, the former Ajax player who had set up the academy at Cruyff's request. 'Now he wanted to help them to use their experience of top-level sport as a basis for becoming sports managers or marketers, for example.' In other words, this way there would be modern, well-educated club board members able to push out of the saddle incompetent leaders like Jaap van Praag, Ton Harmsen and Josep Lluís Núñez.

If there was one thing the benefactor found satisfying, he would say in *De wandeling*, then it was the piles of diplomas he had to sign, having given his name to the academy. His lack of qualifications had always bothered him. It was no accident that the first line of his autobiography was, 'I'm not a person with college degrees.' Now he had the authority to make such documents official by signing them. 'I'm extremely proud of that,' he said. 'So I sit there on my own at the desk smiling. I know it's ridiculous, but that's how it is. I sit there signing two thousand diplomas. I must be out of my mind. I could use a stamp, but I don't. I just really enjoy it.'

His educational courses grew at a tremendous rate and, according to his friend Rolf Grootenboer, Cruyff was more proud of these successes than of his sporting triumphs. His national championships (ten as a player, four as coach), his European Cups (three as a player, three as coach), his national cups (seven as a player, three as coach), his Intercontinental Cup and three European Footballer of the Year awards counted for little when set beside proof that he had succeeded as a philanthropist. 'He actually enjoyed himself most from that moment on,' says Grootenboer, looking back. 'He was more relaxed; the success did him good.'

Cruyff summed up his new lifestyle by saying, 'All things come my way by themselves. And through those things I come upon new things.' Via an acquaintance at the KNVB, for instance, he got in touch with a network of health centres that aimed to get people in business life moving again. They clicked, and Cruyff became an ambassador for De Gezonde Zaak, as it was called. That way he could convey 'practically oriented ideas about health' to the organisation, where he made the impression of being a 'warm, intelligent and extremely committed man with a vision about health and convalescence', as founder Geert-Jan van der Sangen put it. He was also on the network's advisory board, 'with a whole lot of professors', which Van der Sangen says he found 'terrific'. At another juncture, Dennis Gebbink, an amateur footballer well known in Amsterdam, crossed his path. Gebbink couldn't find a place where his son, who had congenital brain damage, could join in organised football. There would be a place for him once he turned sixteen, but the younger boys had to rent a space somewhere if they wanted to play. 'Johan was shattered to hear that,' Cruyff's friend Grootenboer remembers. 'He found that kind of thing unacceptable. He rang the mayor of Amsterdam, who took his call immediately, and it was all arranged in no time.' It led to the creation of a sports club called Only Friends, where children with disabilities could play sports together, with financial support from the Cruyff Foundation.

The opportunity to respond to footballing events was also important to Cruyff. After an absence of several years he went back to writing *Telegraaf* columns (again with ghost writer Jaap de Groot) and from 1994 onwards he produced spoken columns for Filmnet, a commercial pay-TV channel. A reporter would interview him in Barcelona, and then his answers would be cut-and-pasted into 'columns'. Filmnet, which also broadcast matches live, was trying to attract more viewers, so it had plenty of money to spare. 'He was paid two hundred and fifty thousand guilders a year for it,' reporter Sierd de Vos, who did most of the interviewing, remembers. 'Cruyff was still coach at Barcelona then, and he was very aware of the influence his opinions could have. Sometimes he watched what he said, because he knew the newspapers would pick up on it immediately.'

In 1996 he began the serious work of analysis during live broadcasts of important matches. It was something he did exclusively for the NOS, saying the Dutch public service broadcaster best fitted the social engagement that he wanted to propagate. He would usually fly to Amsterdam on the Monday and have meetings with the Dutch branch of his foundation and visit his mother. On the Tuesday or Wednesday he would report to the studio in Hilversum, along with Rolf Grootenboer and Rolf's brother Frans. Before a Champions League match, at half-time and afterwards he would answer questions from Mart Smeets, Jack van Gelder or Tom Egbers, and right from his very first appearance (Juventus vs Manchester United on 11 September) he struck a different note from that of his years as player and trainer, more positive and cheerful.

Despite critical tones when he pointed out mediocre ball technique or poor positioning on the pitch – 'Lemme just put it like this' – he was above all a champion of the better class of football. With virtually no preparation, he served up his ideas to viewers. Much of his criticism had to do with his hobby-horses: technique and tactics. Just as he had sometimes sat with his back to his players when they ran round and round the pitch at training camps in Odoorn, so on television he didn't look at the players' ability to run but at their timing and their chosen positions. Once again, it was all about cleverness and stupidity. 'Getting to where you need to be at the right moment is a quality in football,' he claimed. 'If you're not there, you're too early or too late.'

Experts, players and other interested parties who talked to him regularly could usually follow what Cruyff was saying, but the average viewer tended to become lost in his digressions. He would often start a sentence the way he dribbled on the pitch, without any idea of where he might end up but full of confidence in a good outcome. Sometimes his reasoning lacked internal logic. 'Then you can on the one hand say it's not good what Oranje did, but on the other hand, it's the first match, you tried to make the second and control the match.' Thinking aloud, he would take viewers with him on an adventure in his outpouring of words, and even if you didn't understand much of it, or if it made no sense, his commentary could still be amusing. To the question of whether it mattered that a match would take place on Friday the thirteenth, he said, 'You mustn't ever be superstitious. It brings bad luck.'

Of his use of language he once said, 'It seems that from time to time I don't put things very well, but in general everyone understands me.' Unfortunately, that was not completely true.

Sometimes he admitted frankly to his interviewer backstage at the studio that he'd said whatever came into his head to fill the time. But Smeets, Egbers or Van Gelder never sighed and said what people at home were often thinking: 'What on earth do you mean?' The only one who ever said that was Danny. Johan Derksen remembers how, when he got home after an appearance on Spanish television, she might call out to the pundit from her chaise longue, 'Well, Cruyff, no way to make head or tail of that, as usual.' Or his wife might ask him what he had said during a television interview and he would answer, 'I haven't the foggiest.'

Books soon came on to the market with Cruyff's sayings, wise and unfathomable by turns, and some of those books became bestsellers. Because whatever you thought of his use of language, its originality and the almost total absence of obfuscating sporting clichés meant it was never boring. Fragments of profundity often lurked in his assertions, as in the famous 'every disadvantage has its advantage', which he deployed in various versions ('every problem has its advantage'; 'every advantage has its disadvantage'). Or in the fascinating paradox (because he truly believed it), 'Coincidence is logical.'

So the man without a diploma made an impression with complex theories and with deeper truths that other people didn't dwell upon, but they were interpreted in his own way, full of radical stances that admitted no doubt. 'I actually never make mistakes,' he said. 'Because I have enormous difficulty being wrong.' On maintaining a lead at the end of a match he said, 'In the period when you breathe in, you naturally have to keep control. Drawing breath without control is impossible.' And, 'The clock is ticking. There are two minutes left to play. Either we have the ball, or we give nothing away. Not them with the ball and not covering them.'

Without wasting words, Cruyff said how things stood. As when on a hot afternoon Oranje midfielder Wesley Sneijder did something completely wrong, according to Cruyff. 'He gets twenty metres from the goal about four times. In this heat he ought to have shot four times. Either the ball gets stopped, or it rolls in by accident, or it goes over and then you can get back easily. With a shot you insert rest breaks and do something dangerous. And from the stands aggression comes into the game. That makes you happy, the opponent afraid. You get a whole different atmosphere right through the stadium, turning the thing on its head. Not unimportant.' No other football analyst in the world would think up reasoning like that, let alone express it that way. Whereas in fact there's little to object to in any of it.

Often he came out with the ordinary linguistic errors of working-class Amsterdam or slips of the tongue (a poor defence was 'geitenkaas', goat's cheese, instead of 'gatenkaas', Swiss cheese) and sometimes his statements of the blindingly obvious were accepted as special purely because he had said them. 'If we have the ball, they can't score.' Sometimes they might sound funny, which was not to say he had meant them to be funny. Usually, he hadn't. On one television programme he was asked whether he deliberately expressed himself so unconventionally. Cruyff gave a spontaneous answer, with a hint of apology in his eyes. 'No, it's just that I think quicker than I speak, so I'm often already past it and I still have to say it.'

His subjective approach, though, was detrimental to the credibility of his television analysis and his columns. It mattered rather a lot whether he personally liked the players and trainers he was evaluating. In Cruyff's columns in *El Periódico* (later in *La Vanguardia*), Barça coach Louis van Gaal (1997-2000 and 2002-2003) could bank on very few compliments, even when the team's play gave every reason for them. In 1995 Cruyff had if possible even less praise for the UEFA Champions League victory of Van Gaal's Ajax than for Michels' success with Oranje in 1988. At such moments the urge to compete seemed to win out effortlessly over reality and collegiality. 'When in 1996 I told Rinus Michels that I was going to leave

Ajax, he said, "I hope you're not going to Barcelona,"' Van Gaal remembers. 'I asked what he meant and he said, "Cruyff won't much like it if you bring them success. He regards Barcelona as his city." Sure enough, he was right. I had an awful lot of trouble from him.'

Cruyff and Van Gaal hadn't been on speaking terms since 1989. In the autumn of that year Van Gaal had needed an internship as part of his coaching course and had chosen Barcelona, where Cruyff was coach at the time. So the 38-year-old Louis was an intern with Johan, who was four years older. Both had grown up in Amsterdam-Oost, twenty minutes' walk from each other. Both had been trained as strikers by Ajax under the influence of Michels. Both were fervent adherents of attacking, enterprising football. 'Of course I wanted to go to Barcelona,' says Van Gaal. 'Impossible to think of a better club.' All went well, until Danny invited the intern for Christmas dinner. Shortly before they sat down to the meal the telephone rang and Van Gaal received terrible news. His sister Riet had died. He immediately left for the Netherlands to be with his family. In all the haste and emotion of the moment, he apparently forgot to thank the Cruyffs for their hospitality. Although Cruyff always denied he had any objection to that, his attitude suggests otherwise.

Just as Michels had feared, Cruyff showed no joy at all at Van Gaal's arrival in 1997. Even before coming to Barça, the new coach said there was 'much to be done' at his new club. Which did not exactly sound like a way of reaching out to his famous predecessor. 'That comment was not meant as a criticism of Cruyff,' Van Gaal says now. 'It just struck me that there was little structure, that little in the way of a vision had been drawn up. There wasn't even a players' lounge; the wives and girlfriends had to wait for the players in the car park under the stadium. I also helped to introduce a proper youth complex, because that wasn't there either.'

Cruyff and Van Gaal would never speak again. And there

was another person from Amsterdam-Oost with whom Cruyff would sever ties, his very own brother Henny. That rift had to do with jealousy, with rivalry and perhaps with obsession. Naturally it went very deep on both sides.

CHAPTER THIRTY

Probably immortal

So there he sat, the experienced and well-travelled journalist Mark Blaisse, in Johan Cruyff's living room. The agreement was that he would interview the former Barcelona coach about everything with the exception of football. It had been Danny's idea. One day she had found herself with Blaisse in the lift of their apartment block on the Waldeck Pyrmontlaan in Amsterdam-Zuid. On that occasion, in May 1993, she had asked, 'You're that writer, aren't you?' At which point Blaisse received a proposal. Would he like to write a book with her husband about non-soccer subjects? Because Johan knew a lot about them, she said, and no one ever asked him.

Mark, a downstairs neighbour and an expert on politics and economics, said 'yes', so now he was sitting on a sofa in the 170-square-metre apartment close to the Vondelpark looking at someone who didn't at all feel like working on the book. 'Cruyff was clearly doing it because Danny said he had to,' Blaisse remembers. 'Perhaps he was reluctant partly because he soon noticed that he was coming up against his own limitations.'

Eight times Blaisse came round and each time Danny ended the conversation after an hour and a quarter because 'Johan will be tired now'. The interviews were fairly disastrous. The talk often drifted on to the subject of football, which was Cruyff's frame of reference for everything. He divided even the people close to him into 'defenders' and 'attackers'. Danny, for example, was a defender, as was his father-in-law. 'I sometimes just want to go for it,' said attacker Cruyff. 'And then you need a defender who says, "Hey, psss! wait a sec."' His advisers were defenders, too, they 'had his back'.

He also revealed his obsession with traffic lights. He'd been fighting them all his life. A red light meant he had lost. Cruyff regarded it as a matter of concentration. So others had to see it that way too. 'I asked a player, how many traffic lights did you have for and against you on the way here? The lad had no idea. So I said, "Then you weren't paying attention." I always know. When I drive away from here, I know which lights I'll have for or against me. Everything is a game to me. The traffic light is my opponent; that way you never get bored, because there are traffic lights everywhere.'

In the end Blaisse decided not to write the book, but not because of any lack of candour on the part of his central character. Cruyff honestly said that he suffered from vertigo. And that he was mad about puzzles. (Sudoku in particular, because of his numbers mania, but he didn't say that.)

When the conversation came round to modern technology, about which Cruyff knew nothing, it naturally turned back to football. In 1993 there was talk of electronic aids in football stadiums. Cruyff said that struck him as a bad idea. 'You take away everything that is football,' he says on one of Blaisse's cassette tapes. 'We surely can't say, "Hey, wait, we're just going to play that back and see if he was offside." That just won't work with football. In other sports you can do it. And you'd get less alert referees, too. You have to improve the training, then you'll get better referees.'

In the interviews he also explained one of his most famous sayings: 'Italians can't win against you, but you can lose to them.' He substantiated it as follows: 'If we play ten finals against Italians, we'll lose seven of them. Those Italians don't play to have a good match, they play to win the match. And why do the Italians win? Not because they're better, but because you make more mistakes. We want to score a good goal. The Italians just want to score a goal. We simply make too many mistakes.'

Despite Cruyff's 'limitations', after his active career he was much in demand among businesses as a speaker. So it was that in the late 1990s a tremendous proposal landed on his plate – an invitation to be keynote speaker in front of three hundred people during an IBM lunch in the south of France. For 50,000 guilders Cruyff was persuaded to do it. 'What are you going to talk about?' asked Herman Arendse, then a computer expert and manager of youth teams at Ajax, who had booked him on behalf of IBM. 'No idea,' said Cruyff. A short time later, after he arrived in the south of France, Arendse again asked him about the subject of his speech. 'I'll see,' the maestro stalled.

That made the IBM staff nervous; they were used to announcing the subject of a speech in advance. 'Johan stepped on to the stage without having prepared anything at all,' Arendse remembers. 'He was handed the microphone and he stood there talking for an hour. Afterwards no one could say what it had been about, but the whole room had listened open-mouthed. I was slapped on the back from all sides by people grateful to me for having brought them that wonderful Cruyff.'

Years later the keynote speaker agreed to an interview in front of a room full of bank staff, for a fee of 6,000 euros. 'What is good advice?' he was asked. 'Advice that's followed,' he answered. The audience thought that was brilliant, according to someone who was there. The bank, just like IBM, was more than happy to make the payment to the Johan Cruyff Foundation.

With performances like that, Cruyff continued to earn money for his foundation, income that from August 1998 was bolstered in a special and original way. It all came about, like so much else, because of his father-in-law. The scheme revolved around the

Johan Cruyff Welfare Foundation, as his charitable organisation was still called in those years, which entered into an agreement with a children's charity. Together the two foundations would benefit from a lottery that specialised in good causes. Cruyff would act as ambassador for both the Sponsor Loterij and a children's charity called Terre des Hommes. Cruyff was pioneering again, and he was great at it. Both organisations were based in Amsterdam and he helped to bring them greater fame and popularity than they had been banking on. The turnover of the Sponsor Loterij quadrupled within a couple of years.

In return, those running the children's charity helped him to professionalise his own foundation. And the arrangement benefited him personally too. For the use of his name and image he received an annual fee from the lottery of between 210,000 and 420,000 euros per year (excluding VAT), depending on its success. Moreover, Coster had made a secret agreement with the director of Terre des Hommes. Cruyff could put 10 per cent of the lottery's takings into his own company as payment for 'consultancy activities'. If all went well this fee might bring him another half a million euros a year.

Behold the umpteenth cunning trick by the Cruyff–Coster duo. The organisation that brought in the money, the Sponsor Loterij, could not be allowed to find out about the arrangement. The secret deal meant that the successful ambassador need have no money worries for the time being. In early 1998 a Spanish judge had granted him only a small proportion of his claim for damages from FC Barcelona. Something needed to be done, and this was it.

It might be said that by this means Cruyff pocketed some of the money intended for his foundation – with the knowledge, incidentally, of its board members. Or you might say that he deployed his fame and charisma for something that would greatly benefit all those involved.

However satisfied Cruyff may have been about all this, what he enjoyed most was the opportunity to be in direct contact with the 'damaged' children. As in 2000, for example, during a visit to an aid project in India, when he subjected himself to local traditions (a dot of red paint on his forehead), when he sat on the floor amid the poor and traumatised children in his Johan Cruyff Education Centre, when he played football with them there on a dusty pitch and didn't act as if he was their superior in any way. Those present saw the extent to which the patron was then truly one with the children, 'humble and real', as they put it. Cruyff glowed when he saw all the positive things that were happening in his name, miles away from the vainglorious and egotistical directors of professional football, and Danny glowed with him. The benefactor and his wife were in paradise.

After the term of these contracts ended in 2003, the secret came to light. Understandably, the directors of the Sponsor Loterij felt cheated. But their anger was focused mainly on the man who had thought up the scheme, the director of the children's charity. The relationship between the lottery and Johan continued, and how. As a 'regular beneficiary', his foundation received at least 1.5 million euros annually from it and from 2010 onwards also from the far bigger Postcode Loterij. That enabled it to finance, among other things, its now famous Cruyff Courts. For his part, Cruyff helped the Postcode Loterij to make new contacts in the Netherlands and far beyond. And if asked to sign a hundred and fifty footballs, the best Dutch soccer player of all time never said no.

His secret payments came to an end in 2003, and the fee for his ambassadorship of the lotteries was reduced in stages to around 350,000 euros per year. But Cruyff was not going to worry about that. He had meanwhile turned out to be a tremendous marketing device for big international sponsors, who approached him with contracts for millions. BMW and Hyundai, for instance, brought him financial security in spades. Which was nice, because it meant he could go on paying for his huge city mansion in Barcelona, his luxury apartment in Amsterdam-Zuid, his skiing trips and his annual holiday in the sun at Hotel Prince Maurice on the island of Mauritius in the Indian Ocean.

Henny Cruyff, however, was disturbed by his brother's ever-increasing popularity. Two years older than Johan, Henny was still the owner of a sports shop. He had tried various ways of cashing in on his surname and on his relationship with his brother. Nothing had come of his early plan to be Johan's business manager because of the arrival of Uncle Cor, and now his jealousy was growing by the day. Henny, who had once had to look after his little brother, who had been cleverer and more articulate and had got his diplomas, could never accept that Johan had been subsumed by the Costers. 'Meanwhile, Henny kept trying to earn money from Johan's reputation with FC Barcelona trips,' says Hans Loonstein, who was a friend of Henny's for years. 'Of course, those trips to Barcelona were made more attractive by the suggestion they might include a meeting with Johan. But Johan often didn't feel like complying. It got to be a bit pathetic.'

It became even more pathetic when Johan and Danny came home one day to find a group of strangers in their living room. They were customers of Henny's who had been tempted to book a trip to Barcelona by the prospect of a visit to the home of the star. 'Naturally they were all politely requested to leave at once,' remembers Bobby Nees, who was a friend of both brothers. 'Johan and Danny always did all they could to preserve their privacy.'

Such incidents became more frequent and when Henny consistently failed to pay back money his brother had lent him, the door was shut. 'Johan had helped Henny in various ways and shown him a lot of patience,' says Nees. 'But there was a moment when it came to an end, and for Johan there was no way back from such moments.' Cruyff avoided his brother as far as possible and missed more family gatherings than before. (To the relief of Danny, who after all those years still didn't like the sort of conviviality typical of the Jordaan.) Even when his mother had a birthday, he preferred to visit at a time of his choosing – which for Henny was further reason to announce that Johan was neglecting his elderly mother.

According to other family members, the celebrity didn't really neglect her. It was simply a fact that he was in Barcelona most of the time and when in the Netherlands he often had a very full schedule. But there were certainly obstacles. Danny's attitude cannot have been encouraging. Former Ajax player Wim de Wit, who had helped to set up the Johan Cruyff Academy, remembers picking Johan up from Schiphol one time. 'He asked if we could briefly call on his mother,' De Wit remembers. 'So off to Betondorp. It was as if he was going there secretly. It made me a bit sad.' When Hans Loonstein visited Nel Cruyff-Draaijer along with his friend Henny, he could tell that she found her sons' estrangement from each other 'dreadful'. 'She never wanted to go to Barcelona, although Johan offered to pay for everything. She wasn't attracted by all that classy stuff. She preferred to stay in her little apartment in Betondorp.'

To Danny's distress, Henny started a smear campaign against her father. He gave interviews in which he said that during the war Cor Coster had worn an SS uniform in an Eastern European concentration camp. In 2006 Henny even launched a website to enable people who knew more about the case to email or ring him. It all reached such a pitch that the Dutch Institute for War, Holocaust and Genocide Studies (NIOD) was asked to investigate. The NIOD concluded that Cor Coster had no case to answer. He had been put to work in Latvia without becoming a member of the *Waffen-SS*.

Bitterness caused a split in the family. A year after Henny's call for evidence about Coster, Nel died at the age of ninety. Between Christmas and New Year's Eve 2007, Nel Cruyff-Draaijer was cremated, and at what was now known as the De Nieuwe Ooster cemetery the family drama was visible as if in a film. On one side of the aisle sat the Henny camp, on the other side the Johan camp, which included Henny's daughter Estelle with her then husband Ruud Gullit. She had broken with her father. 'Johan and Henny didn't exchange a word that day,' Loonstein remembers. 'Even during the condolences they stood some distance apart. At one point they ended up in the same small group of people. Johan spoke to me and simply ignored Henny's look. That's how it remained.'

Nel Cruyff-Draaijer's urn was given a place on Manus Cruyff's gravestone, behind the fence along the Middenweg where Manus, after his death, had been able to 'hear' the cheers of the Ajax fans. Although not since 1996, incidentally, when the De Meer stadium was demolished and replaced by flats and family homes.

Henny's resentment became an obsession. Whereas Johan kept popping up in the media as an expert, as the funny man horsing around with disabled children at a foundation open day, as an idealist opening one Cruyff Court after another, Henny, who had at one time owned at least four sports shops, watched his empire shrink to just the shop on the Elandsgracht that he and his brother had started many years before. At home Henny put together an archive for a book he was going to write that would unmask his celebrated brother and Uncle Cor. He plastered the walls with photos of Johan, scoffing at them in front of visitors. 'It was total madness,' says Loonstein, who experienced it from close up. 'Fortunately, the book was never completed.' The 'brother of' became ill and then, assailed by dementia, fell silent in a nursing home.

Johan's world was becoming smaller in a sense too. His mother was no longer around, he'd erased brother Henny from his memory and in November 2008 his father-in-law died at the age of eighty-eight. After a lifetime of deals, humour, intimidation and a staggering amount of whisky, it was all over for Coster, alias Uncle Cor. That same year the love between Cruyff and his football son Marco van Basten ended too. On the recommendation of the Almighty from Barcelona, the KNVB had appointed Van Basten as national coach in 2004, with John van 't Schip as his assistant. Not that the 39-year-old Marco and 40-year-old 'Schip' had much experience as coaches, but that had not been a problem. They 'got it' and in Johan's eyes that was enough. After four years at Oranje, Cruyff then arranged for the duo to start at Ajax after the summer of 2008.

Ahead of taking up their posts, Van Basten and Van 't Schip entered into talks with Cruyff in early 2008. Ajax had been going through a rough patch for some time. The first eleven were performing poorly and the leadership was under fire. Johan advised his former pupils to take a firm stance. 'He wanted to sack just about everybody in youth training,' Van 't Schip remembers. 'We thought that was going too far. Did I really have to sack someone I'd had a good working relationship with during my time as Ajax youth trainer, from 1997 to 2001?'

Van 't Schip and coach-to-be Van Basten told Cruyff that, after the summer, they first wanted to see who was doing a good job at Ajax and who wasn't, and only then take measures if necessary. Cruyff withdrew immediately. If you didn't act on his advice, there was no point advising you, was how he saw it.

In August 2009 Cruyff stopped analysing matches for NOS television. After thirteen years he'd had enough of the negativity he detected in some of its programmes. He didn't find items like 'The elbow of the week' clever or funny; they made him angry. 'You don't often see me smile,' he said on the subject in an interview. 'Because often I have to talk about football. For me, football is serious.' When Cruyff noticed that the NOS was doing 'nothing' with his comments and things were actually going 'from bad to worse' he ended his collaboration. 'Johan didn't understand that programmes had their own editors and the NOS management could exercise only limited influence over them,' says adviser Henk Koenders. 'That was typical of Cruyff. Nothing with him was ever relative. He didn't know what that meant, which probably had to do with his limited schooling. But also with his creativity. That's how it works with all great minds.'

A year later, Cruyff said goodbye to FC Barcelona as well. For seven years he had been on good terms with president Joan Laporta, who had won the election in 2003 with his support. Laporta and Cruyff had moved against Núñez together in the late 1990s and become friends. The lawyer and the former coach often had lunch together and Cruyff would ride his hobby-horses with enthusiasm: Laporta must appoint former Barça players to important posts, optimise youth training, ensure attacking football. 'Those were great conversations,' Laporta smiles. 'Johan thought it was important that we entertained the people in Camp Nou with technically excellent football. Then the results would follow of their own accord. I implemented a lot of his advice, too. I appointed our former player Txiki Begiristain as technical director and on Johan's recommendation we took on Frank Rijkaard as coach. That was a great success. Rijkaard used to have lunch with Johan too.'

But however pleasant it may have been in Fermí Puig, the restaurant on the Carrer de Balmes that specialised in traditional Catalan food, after lunch each went his own way. No firm agreements were made, Cruyff did not take a job within Barça. 'He didn't aspire to that and we didn't mind,' says Laporta. 'In our conversations we stuck to generalities. We drew inspiration from him. And I was happy to appoint him as honorary president.'

That congenial period came to an end when Laporta stepped down in July 2010. Johan did not see eye to eye with the new president Sandro Rosell. Before long he ended his honorary presidency of FC Barcelona. He stayed away from Camp Nou from then on and followed the matches on television.

Cruyff didn't need to sit still for long. His supporters at Ajax were calling him. He answered their call. Because while Barça may have been his great footballing love, Ajax was his footballing family and he could never leave it. 'Ajax was clearly more

strongly influenced by Johan than Barcelona,' says midfielder
of the time Roger García. In 1995 Roger, as he was known
in football, had made his debut at Barça at the age of eighteen
thanks to Johan. In 2006 he played in Amsterdam for a year
on Cruyff's recommendation. 'At Ajax, Johan was ubiquitous,'
the Catalan says. 'As if his spirit was still walking the dressing
rooms. He was repeatedly mentioned in conversations as an
example of how you should deal with something. In Barcelona
that was rather less the case; that club is far bigger and other
influences are always noticeable.'

At that time, in 2010, Ajax were bobbing about on waves
of short-sightedness and opportunism. Since the move to
Amsterdam-Zuidoost and the stock-market flotation in 1998,
the club had become larger and more complex, a public limited
company with all the accompanying procedures, while retain-
ing some of its former characteristics. The culture of gossip and
backbiting lived on at the De Toekomst sport complex and in
the new stadium, Arena, and made the working environment
feel unsafe. The first eleven achieved little on the international
stage. Directors and coaches engaged in a running battle and the
name 'Johan' was enough to decide an argument in your favour.

Some, such as Piet Keizer and Rolf Grootenboer, actually inspired fear when they walked into the canteen at De
Toekomst. Not because they held high positions, but because
they talked to Johan. 'I assiduously kept him up to date on
everything that was going on at Ajax,' says Grootenboer. 'I was
in a position to know. I've always been attached to the club, as
a leader and as youth coach. Even when Johan and Danny were
on Mauritius in January, I'd send them a fax with the results
for all the teams. They'd go through it in bed on the Sunday
morning. If I'd forgotten to include a result for the B1 juniors,
Johan would ring me. "How did B1 do?"'

Ajax was deep inside him. So deep that based on what
Grootenboer and other sources told him, he kept up on who
might be doing things wrong – in other words, not in the

Cruyffian way. 'So you had to watch what you said when Rolf was around,' says team manager at the time David Endt. 'Other people deliberately went over to talk with him to mutter about someone they didn't like. That way Johan often arrived at his opinions on Ajax from hearsay, and they were extremely one-sided.'

Cruyff unexpectedly turned up at meetings, at the AGM for example, to which he was invited as an honorary member, and in September 2010 he wrote in his now notorious *Telegraaf* column, 'This is no longer Ajax.' The team was playing badly, both tactically and technically, under the leadership of coach Martin Jol (Van Basten had resigned in 2009). 'It's even worse than the team from the period before Rinus Michels came to the club in 1965.' A humiliating 2-0 defeat in Bernabéu against Real Madrid (it could have been 8-0) was reason enough to clear the decks, according to Cruyff. In other words, the entire club leadership must be dismissed right away. Ajax was getting it all wrong. It was a mess.

For a start, the members' council, the club parliament, had hardly any former players on it. That was naturally unaccept-able, Cruyff believed, and when several seats on the council became vacant, he used his influence to get a number of former players elected to it. There followed a series of squabbles at Ajax that soon became known as the 'Velvet Revolution'. Feedback groups were introduced, as were investigative committees and nominating committees, reports were drawn up, accusations and smears flew. Directors, officials and trainers left, as did team leaders, doctors and physiotherapists. They were replaced by people who agreed with the 'Cruyff Plan', or said they did. It looked like a war. 'We weren't intending to let it get to that point,' remembers former Ajax player Keje Molenaar, who acted as Cruyff's assistant in that turbulent time. 'We were only con-cerned about the technical side, the youth training, the coaching staff, the selection policy. It all needed reforming to get Ajax back to the top in Europe.'

In periods of make or break, Cruyff did not shrink from personally putting those in charge under pressure. In this 'revolution', intended to make football the key focus in all departments of the club, everything was permitted. Cruyff walked into directors' rooms and made clear to his quaking listeners that they must hightail it out of there because they didn't understand 'anything' and were bringing the club to rack and ruin. Anyone who didn't obey might be 'destroyed' by *De Telegraaf*, he said.

In late March 2011 Cruyff appeared at Arena in the evening darkness. His followers Dennis Bergkamp and Wim Jonk were with him, two former players who 'got it' and would help to bring about the necessary changes. The three men, in leather jackets, looked intimidating, like marauders come to stage a coup. In reality they wanted to convince the members' council (and the club leadership) of their points of view. The idea was that Jonk and Bergkamp would form the 'technical heart' of the club along with the new coach Frank de Boer, which is indeed what happened. 'We understand what we're doing,' Cruyff explained to the assembled press. 'And if you submit plans, you want them to be implemented properly. But it's not a matter of imposing your will. It's just that we're upfront and hands-on. You have to be, if you want to change things.'

The next day *De Telegraaf* – the only newspaper read by everyone at Ajax – published a photo on its front page showing the Ajax managers and officials who had suddenly resigned. They had red crosses printed across their faces. It looked almost as if, rather than resigning, they had been liquidated. 'The thing escalated,' Molenaar recalls. '*De Telegraaf* was full-square behind Cruyff and it covered the matter as if it was a coup. For reporter Jaap de Groot, who was on top of it all and as Johan's ghost writer sometimes used to dramatise Johan's opinion in his columns, journalism was a form of power play. Everything was magnified. Johan's opponents talked to the *Algemeen Dagblad* and threw mud back.'

In July 2011 a new supervisory board was appointed, with, as its most attention-grabbing member, Johan Cruyff. At Ajax, in accordance with his wishes, former virtuoso players were teaching youngsters to kick and head the ball better, while the newly appointed technical heart governed footballing matters within the club, cutting across the existing hierarchy. But more was needed, so Cruyff became a member of the supervisory board of AFC Ajax NV. The fun was short-lived. In late March 2012 the board resigned, including the 'club phenomenon'. The intervening nine months are best described as a major misunderstanding.

First of all, Cruyff, who hated meetings, had to sit round a table with a lawyer (Marjan Olfers), an organisational adviser (Steven ten Have), a television producer (Paul Römer) and former player Edgar Davids. He arrived late to the first meeting of the supervisory board in Landgoed Duin & Kruidberg, a hotel in Santpoort. He also took his adviser Rutger Koopmans with him, unannounced. The main item on the agenda was the appointment of a new managing director. Cruyff had already made his decision. They must appoint Tscheu La Ling.

The other board members were shocked by this vigorous approach. Someone muttered something about a selection procedure. 'No,' said Cruyff, according to the notes that Paul Römer made during a different meeting, in which the dispute was discussed. 'You've got it wrong. It's going to be Ling.' He also knew who would be the technical director: Mark Overmars, another former star player. Steven ten Have, chair of the board and at that point also a board member at the ABN AMRO Bank, who had written a thesis on the management of change in large international companies, stared uneasily into space.

Thirty-eight-year-old Edgar Davids was the only person present who did not quake before the international icon. 'This is sloppy,' he said.

Cruyff did not engage with that. He stood up and, followed in silence by his adviser, walked to the exit.

*

It wasn't long before *De Telegraaf* reported that Ling and Overmars were highly likely to become directors at Ajax. The board members inquired about Ling and concluded that the former Ajax right-winger was running an unknown professional club in Slovakia and dealing in nutritional supplements. There was a rumour, moreover, that he was mixing in dubious circles. Most of the board could not reconcile this kind of information with their attempts to ensure good governance. Cruyff saw things differently. To the extent that he attended meetings at all, he stuck to his view. 'Ling will be managing director.'

If Davids said anything against Ling, Cruyff would say something unpleasant about Davids' past. If the chairman said anything against Ling, Cruyff would say, 'You're a hundred per cent wrongly connected.' Before adding in front of all those present, 'You lot come from a different world from me. You just don't get it.'

Meanwhile, the technical heart, unimpeded by any organisational experience, had enthusiastically begun firing people. Rumours of a culture of fear reached the board members; staff were said to be walking the corridors in tears. There was a desperate need for the management of day-to-day business, but the Ling issue was holding everything up. The problem was broached during a telephone conference call. In the heat of the battle, Cruyff told Marjan Olfers that she was there only because she was a woman. Davids, born in Paramaribo, Suriname, was told he'd been appointed to the board purely because of his skin colour.

'He's risen up above everything,' said Piet Keizer of his former friend in *Het Parool*. 'He's lost touch with the ground under his feet. Because of all the things his past brings with it, he's happier among people he can trust, who are eager to do what he says.' Keizer distanced himself from Cruyff. 'A one point Johan said, "I'd do it myself." I said, "Go ahead, but without me."'

Cruyff had previously quarrelled with Tscheu La Ling. He had more or less driven the winger out of De Meer in 1982 and

there is everything to suggest that in 2011 he had barely looked
into the man's background. But ultimately that wasn't relevant.
He had put Ling's name forward, so there was no way back.
Just like the time he had refused to wear those three stripes as
a player, this was a matter of power. In August 2011 he put his
cards on the table. The board members plus several representatives of Ajax travelled to Barcelona, and in the Spanish office of
the Cruyff Foundation they were told, 'If Ling isn't appointed,
I lose. And when you lose, you lose authority and respect and
then you're lost.' A lot of further discussion went on that day
and when the delegation left, Cruyff impressed upon them, 'It
has to be Ling.'

A month later Ling turned up unannounced at a meeting.
Bergkamp and Jonk of the technical heart were suddenly there
too, surprising the other board members. It was a violation of
protocol. The chairman refused to declare the meeting official;
there was merely some informal talk and argument. The stale-
mate continued. In television programmes Cruyff was given
every opportunity to express his opinion and in November 2011
the board members decided to dismantle the whole thing. They
were planning to surprise Cruyff with the name of Louis van
Gaal, in the expectation that the club phenomenon would at last
withdraw and a managing director could be appointed. Shortly
before the meeting started, Johan sent his apologies. The board
announced that Van Gaal would be managing director of Ajax
as of 1 July 2012. Until that time, former FC Utrecht chairman
Martin Sturkenboom would be interim director. Former player
Danny Blind would be technical director.

The Cruyff camp exploded. It filed a lawsuit, and the most
fanatical Ajax supporters were mobilised. On Christmas Eve
2011, Cruyff rang Ruud van Dijk, a prominent member of what
was known as the 'hard core', and a 'diehard Cruyffian'. The
hard core had been pro-Cruyff for a long time. Nostalgic banners with his face on them had been hung at Arena. Van Dijk
had sent several emails to Barcelona, according to his column

on ajaxshowtime.com, but was astonished when the celebrity responded to them. Cruyff had never shown much interest in the hard core. Now he did. Several of his accomplices within Ajax are said to have whipped up the supporters and the consequences were dramatic. In January 2012 a group of hooligans used threatening language against the interim director late at night at the Sturkenbooms' house. His wife and children needed to watch out too, they shouted. The shocked interim director reported the threats to the police.

In February 2012 the appointment of Van Gaal and Sturkenboom was declared invalid on appeal, because it had taken place without the knowledge of board member Cruyff. A month later the entire supervisory board resigned, including Johan. The revolt had succeeded. For the umpteenth time, Cruyff had got his way in a manner that was inelegant but effective. A supervisory board was appointed that would act in his spirit. Former players Marc Overmars and Edwin van der Sar would be directors – Ling was out – and football itself would be key at all levels. Once again, it cut both ways. Cruyff had meanwhile set up the Cruyff Institute, a commercial company that would guide Ajax – and after that possibly many other professional clubs – on their way to attractive football played according to the 'Cruyff philosophy'. Dozens of Ajax staff members were obliged to take courses at the Cruyff Institute. Co-founder of the institute was Todd Beane, the new husband of Cruyff's daughter Chantal. The American Beane didn't have deep roots in soccer, but he was enthusiastic and Johan remained, even now that he'd reached retirement age, a family man.

Not for the first time, Cruyff had aroused suspicions that he thought very much in terms of self-interest. 'I'm convinced that Johan wanted above all to help his old club,' says Van 't Schip. 'But he simply found his own ideas so good that Ajax could only gain from the deployment of the Cruyff Institute.'

With Ajax as its standard bearer, the Cruyff Institute was out to conquer the world. The offensive began at Chivas

Guadalajara, a popular but declining club in Mexico. Cruyff advised his son-in-law Beane to approach John van 't Schip, who liked the idea and became coach at Chivas. 'Johan immediately started connecting a whole lot of people together,' Van 't Schip recalls. 'He saw it all before him. But the owner's wife turned out to call the shots at Chivas and she had appointed all sorts of people who knew nothing about soccer. So Johan told her to get rid of them. It wasn't that simple, naturally, and moreover Johan put in an appearance there far less often than the club had hoped. Since I didn't speak Spanish – although of course Johan did – people felt we were showing insufficient respect for Mexican culture. Various Dutch people came to reorganise the youth training. That didn't work.'

After eight months the contract with adviser Cruyff was terminated. A month later, in early January 2013, the rest of the Dutch people there were asked to leave too. Other top clubs did not apply to the Cruyff Institute. 'Once again it was clear that Johan had insufficient understanding of complexities off the pitch,' says Van 't Schip.

At Ajax too the 'revolution' did not turn out as anticipated. Cruyff assumed that former professional footballers would understand one another under all circumstances and as old mates would go for gold – as if the feeling of sharing a changing room continued when you pored over paperwork together. In reality the ex-players were soon at each other's throats; there was a lack of proper communication and one after another they called it a day. New managerial crises were the result. Little came of the idea of having the first eleven made up almost entirely of players who had trained in Ajax youth teams, supplemented by a few 'targeted purchases'.

Cruyff, who continued to work as an adviser, noticed after a while that he had 'no influence', as he later put it in *My Turn*. On closer inspection the former players who were now in charge – Van der Sar, Overmars and Bergkamp – had insufficient understanding of his tactics to be able to implement the Cruyff Plan successfully. Precisely because he had health problems from 2013 onwards, it was important that the new generation could flesh out the plan independently of him. But Ajax were playing with too many 'backward and lateral passes' and their positional play was pathetic, he believed. In short, it was a matter of 'bad technical policy'. There was no such thing as coincidence, so this was all 'deliberate'. There was 'no point' being involved any longer, Cruyff said. 'Nobody wants to listen.' To make things worse, on 10 November 2015 Wim Jonk, 'the only one who implemented the essence of the Cruyff Plan', was dismissed by Ajax.

Five days later, Cruyff had had enough. The door to Ajax was pulled shut. His former teammate Theo van Duivenbode and fellow Betondorp lad Leo van Wijk (both on the board), the former apple of his eye Dennis Bergkamp and a whole bunch of others were now on their own. Johan's world shrank further.

Fortunately, he still had his family, his anchor in life. Chantal had six children, two by her first husband Jesús Angoy and another four by Todd Beane. Chantal was Johan's right hand at the foundation, while horse-loving Susila did some work for the foundation on a freelance basis and Jordi was pursuing a career as technical director at Maccabi Tel Aviv. Cruyff was proud of his relationship with his children, which had remained close over the years despite the pressure that his fame had placed on the family.

He carried on imperturbably with his foundation and his academy. He gave interviews to magazines and appeared on television programmes on condition his organisations were given a mention. In the television show *Sterren op het Doek*, recorded in 2015, he appeared in a simple jacket and a light blue shirt that was a little tight around his waist. The 68-year-old was no longer truly skinny. He remained funny and engaging, though. He freely admitted to presenter Hanneke Groenteman – who in 1965 had been one of his first interviewers, on the occasion of a sale in the Spijkerbroekenhuis in the centre of Amsterdam – that he was bad at 'writing things down, remembering things, the paperwork'. But, he said, 'I have a wife who's good at it. I've been married for forty-six years now, so without her I wouldn't have made it. She's taken very good care of all the stupid things I've done.'

She was still doing that, incidentally. Johan was no longer allowed to put his name to business transactions. With his impulsivity he was in danger of causing himself financial damage. 'That was his Achilles heel,' according to *Cruyff & Johan*, a book by his business partner Ferenc van der Vlies, published in 2019. 'As soon as Cruyff started to like someone, he put his trust in them, even if they didn't have his best interests at heart.'

In *Sterren op het Doek* he was asked to choose his favourite of the three portraits painted of him. Cruyff chose the 'most unusual' one, because, he said, 'It's as if you're looking at the inside of me, without skin.' The winning artist, Kuin Heuff, demonstrated excellent powers of observation when she said of her model, 'There's something calm and friendly about him, but there's a whole layer of gunpowder underneath.'

On 24 September 2015 Cruyff paid his last visit to his academy. He was due to open the third of its Dutch branches, in Groningen. He arrived in the late morning in his black Audi, just on time. His passengers looked pale when they got out, probably because they'd had to undergo his battle against traffic lights. But otherwise it was an enjoyable afternoon there on the Zernikeplein. Cruyff endeared himself to the students with his relaxed attitude and his interest in the passions of youth. If a young man was outstanding at wakeboarding, then he wanted to know all about the sport. A girl who specialised in golf was bombarded with questions from him about the correct stance. In the packed hall he talked about diplomas. He'd gone through his life without any, Cruyff said, to underline once more the

importance of his academy. And, yes, of course he still remembered his debut match in Groningen, on 15 November 1964. It
was windy and he'd scored – but how, he couldn't really recall
any longer.

As usual, he left much later than planned. The students
wanted to know all kinds of things from him and he still found
it impossible to say no.

The organisers said he had looked fit, but that was merely a
facade. He was getting tired more quickly than normal. 'Johan
thought it might be because of cardiac arrhythmia, which he'd
suffered from before,' his friend Rolf Grootenboer later told
Voetbal International. 'It wasn't that.' Danny urged him to go to
the hospital for tests, but he refused. When she kept insisting, he
went. On 22 October 2015 it was announced that he had lung
cancer. He was given chemotherapy, but afterwards he quickly
felt better and was able to go to Tangiers in Morocco for a few
days with Rolf and Danny. In January he flew to Mauritius as
usual for a week with the family.

'Johan still seemed to be doing well,' Grootenboer told *Voetbal
International*. 'Every morning he came to wake me up with a cup
of tea. And two biscuits. That was the tradition. He'd always
say the same thing. "Hey, deadman, are you awake? In half an
hour we're up and running." Johan always called me "deadman" because I'm not all that talkative. For those few days it
was almost the way it used to be. The chemotherapy seemed
to be working and we were positive about the future. Johan
was cheerful. Another couple of courses of treatment and it'll
be behind us, we told each other. Because of those favourable
prospects, we never had any in-depth conversations about his
illness. We were convinced everything was going to be fine.'

Keje Molenaar had engaged in a long telephone conversation
with Cruyff that autumn, partly about his break with Ajax.
'It turned out later that he'd just heard he had cancer,' says
Molenaar. 'I asked him why he hadn't said anything about

it and he said, "Oh, they're working on it; they know what they're doing."'

Phone calls kept coming from all sides at the villa on the corner of the Carrer de Margenat and the Carrer de les Escoles Pies. But again Danny was the filter between him and the outside world. She had sometimes been scoffed at for her protective attitude, but now it won her respect. There was a remarkable silence, however, from his 'football family' in Amsterdam-Zuidoost. 'On the day I spoke to him for the last time, in early March, he had the feeling that many friends were no longer there for him,' said Jaap de Groot later in *Nieuwe Revu*. 'In the end Johan was in touch only with Wim Jonk. He heard nothing from the rest. That caused him a lot of distress.' Fortunately, he was still in touch with FC Barcelona. His last formal signature was on a co-operation agreement between Barça and his foundation.

In this period Johan and Danny made one last visit to Club de Golf Montanya on the slopes of the mountain outside Barcelona, not far from their summer house. Cruyff was mad keen on golf. Not that he was particularly good at it. He lacked the inner tranquillity needed to made a good shot. He also lacked the patience to listen to the advice of top exponents of the game. In 1986 he had met Severiano Ballesteros, the Cruyff among golfers. The conversation between them became muddled; it was unclear which of them ought to admire the other more. Johan and Danny regularly lunched in the golf club restaurant before playing a round. In the fifteenth-century country clubhouse, surrounded by nature reserves and luxuriant sloping lawns, they enjoyed local dishes. Johan also frequently had meetings there with followers like Pep Guardiola; they often went to sit and talk in a private corner, with a good bottle of red. Johan sometimes went to the clubhouse to watch football in the evenings, too, sitting among the other club members.

One day Johan heard there were children who would like to

learn golf but couldn't afford the club fees. He went straight to see manager Jordi Puig. Was it true? It was true, Puig admitted. Johan thought up a plan on the spot. You let those children play golf here for a reduced fee, he told the manager, on condition they do little jobs around the clubhouse. It'll keep them off the streets. Puig nodded. A week later Cruyff asked whether the plan had been put into effect. A week later he asked again. This is Catalonia, Puig stammered, not the Netherlands. Things take time. Then we'll arrange it ourselves, said Johan, and he immediately named people who could assist the manager. Sure enough, the plan became a reality.

Now, in February 2016, after months of absence, Johan and Danny turned up in the attractive, stone-built *masia*. Manager Puig and chef Joan Font were shocked by Johan's puffy face. He barely seemed able to lift his wine glass. The manager and the chef felt powerless and sad. They would never see him again.

On 2 March 2016 Cruyff finally visited Max Verstappen on the Barcelona-Catalunya Circuit, where the racing driver was testing his latest Formula 1 car. Cruyff had been forced to cancel the first two meetings because he'd felt so sick from the chemotherapy. Now he was able to come. His face swollen due to the side effects of the prednisone he was taking, he posed next to the young driver. Two prodigies, two problem children side by side, the sick old man and the young tearaway, both lovers of risk, of going on the attack and of striking out on new paths. Both with a tendency to irritate the establishment. They clicked immediately.

On the circuit Cruyff told the press that after his chemotherapy he'd felt as if he'd been 'beaten up'. So what did he do? 'Lots of walking, lots of this, lots of that.'

Three days later Johan and Danny flew to Tel Aviv for a week to visit Jordi. They stayed at the Herods Hotel on the boulevard, close to the marina. Cruyff loved to call in at Maccabi to watch the squad training. He would sit on a bench in the sun to chat with technical director Jordi and coach Peter Bosz. Fifty-two-year-old Bosz already knew that Cruyff would come to the club every day that week. 'Then he's away from my mother for a bit,' Jordi confided to him with a wink. As soon as Bosz saw his idol approaching, he would leave the training to his assistant. The Dutch coach had been studying Cruyff's ideas for years, and he too believed fervently in attacking football. So now he listened to Johan every afternoon, sometimes along with Jordi, about game patterns, ball technique, anticipatory passes. 'I didn't understand everything he said, and he'd often go off at a tangent,' Bosz remembers. 'But all the same it was extremely inspiring.'

Inspiring. That was in fact the legacy of the sick man there in the Israeli sun: a collection of great ideas; a 'philosophy' but, to the regret of Bosz and many others, without any theoretical framework. All attempts to put Cruyff's thoughts about football down on paper as a coherent whole, including efforts by his football mate Wim Jansen, had failed. What remained was imagination, faith in attacking tactics on the pitch, faith in young people, all of it in the knowledge that with good technique and clever teamwork you could get the better of the musclemen and sprinters. If you could only see it – and if you dared to turn what you saw into action immediately, radical and resolute. Long live the adventure we call football.

One day Johan and Danny asked whether the coach and his wife Jolyn would like to have lunch with them. 'We were in a fish restaurant on the beach,' Bosz remembers. 'It was a great afternoon. My assistant Hendrie Krüzen and his wife came too. We hadn't been there for fifteen minutes before the owner, who must have been alerted, walked up to us with his son who was studying at the Cruyff Academy. Could he have his picture taken with Cruyff? Yes, certainly, said Johan, already pushing his chair back to pose. Danny shook her head. "This is how it always goes," she said loudly in an Amsterdam accent. "You could just say that it's not a good moment, couldn't you? We

never get a chance for a quiet meal." A little after that, the minister of sport turned up. The same scene was repeated. Outside,
the reporters were gathering.'

Cruyff told Bosz frankly about his illness. 'It wasn't just lung
cancer, as many people thought,' says Bosz. 'The lumps were
everywhere by then, including his back. He remained positive,
because he had blind faith in the specialists. He was going to
make it, he was sure of that. He was an incredible optimist.'

On the plane from Tel Aviv to Barcelona, Johan was troubled
by pressure in his chest. When they arrived at El Prat airport
they rang a doctor immediately. He advised them to come
round just to make sure. The situation was alarming. The next
morning, at breakfast, Cruyff found himself unable to move his
hands. He was taken to hospital and this time he stayed there.
'Johan got a terrible pain in his head,' Grootenboer told *Voetbal
International*. 'Scans showed there were secondary tumours
in there, of the most aggressive kind. We could tell from the
doctor's face that it was bad. It wasn't possible to operate. From
that point on Johan declined very rapidly. I found it dreadfully
difficult to see him lying in bed like that. At the end it went so
quickly that we had to call the family together. His daughters
Susila and Chantal were already there, but Jordi was on his way
to Canada, to see the owner of Maccabi Tel Aviv. Jordi flew
back straight away on the same plane. Fortunately, he was in
time. I think Johan really did wait until his family was complete.
Amid all the sorrow, that was something beautiful. It was how
it had to be.'

Johan Cruyff could not go on. The player who had never
been able to accept losing now had to give up. He died on the
morning of Thursday 24 March 2016. His death made world
news. Countless newspapers quoted one of his most celebrated
sayings, with which, in 1997, he had expressed his surprise about
what he saw as the ridiculous amount of attention that was paid
to his fiftieth birthday:

'In a certain sense I'm probably immortal.'

It was well said. In the days after his death – 'Johan *bedankt!*'
'*Gràcies* Johan!' 'Thanks Johan!' – and to judge by the many
tributes and declarations of love that followed, it would indeed
prove to be the case. But that was only logical.

ACKNOWLEDGEMENTS

I am grateful to several people in particular. First of all, of course, Robbert Ammerlaan, with whom I've already thought up so many plans for books and who was once again the first to show rock-solid faith in this undertaking. As with all my football books, Sytze de Boer was a wonderful fact-checker and brought me heaps of important information. With patience and accuracy, Sytze corrected me chapter by chapter, and then often again after reading new versions. Even when my descriptions did not correspond with his faith in the visionary Cruyff, he loyally carried on. Pablo Koch, Sam Porskamp and Bas de Wit also helped me tremendously in various ways with the research. Frans Oosterwijk was a great reader of the manuscript, and what to say about Dido Michielsen? Even more than with my previous books, my delightful wife was an indispensable fellow thinker and reader, a tireless corrector and an inspiration, every day of a long and difficult year of writing. Johan had his Danny, I have my Dido, my anchor in life.

Despite my criticisms of Cruyff, Dido came to feel a lot of affection for him. If all readers respond like that, then I'll have no complaints.

BIBLIOGRAPHY AND SOURCES

Archives
Ajax Archief, Amsterdam City Archives; Nederlands Instituut voor Beeld en Geluid, Hilversum; archives of Studio Sport, Hilversum.

Websites
youtube.com, footballia.net, geheugenvanoost.amsterdam.nl, afc-ajax.info, vi.nl, worldfootball.net.

Newspapers
Algemeen Dagblad, Leeuwarder Courant, Leidsch Dagblad, Limburgsch Dagblad, Nieuwsblad van het Noorden, NRC Handelsblad, Het Parool, De Telegraaf, Trouw, De Tijd, de Volkskrant, Het Vrije Volk.

Magazines
Elsevier, Hard Gras, HP/DeTijd, Johan, Nieuwe Revu, So foot, Voetbal International.

Documentaries and films
En un momento dado (2004), *Football's Greatest – Johan Cruyff* (2010), *Nummer 14* (1973), *L'Últim partit* (2014), *Wonderkind uit de Akkerstraat* (2013).

Psychological studies

Gemeentelijk Arbeidsbureau Amsterdam: 1959, as cited in *Boem – Hun levensverhaal verteld aan Jaap ter Haar.*

Psychologist and graphologist Jan Slikboer: reports 1965-7, as cited in *Mijn Ajax* by Salo Muller, *Trots van de wereld* by Menno de Galan and *Leerschool Ajax* by Rik Planting, and in an interview in *Het Parool* (11 March 1967).

Psychologist Dolf Grunwald: various reports 1967-71, with thanks to Menno de Galan and Dolf's son Jeroen Grunwald.

Psychiatrist Roelf Zeven (1967-71): based on conversations with his son Marius Zeven and interviews in *De Tijd* (17 November 1967), *Het Parool* (30 November 1967 and 14 March 1968) and *Trouw* (18 February 1969).

Books

Abrahams, Frits et al.: *Mijn Johan Cruijff.* Amsterdam, 2007.

Aert, Dolf van, Harry Hamer and Frans Nieuwenhof (eds.): *VI Legends – Johan Cruijff.* Utrecht, 2016.

Barend, Frits: *Topclub Ajax*, parts 1, 2 and 3. Amsterdam, 1970-2.

Barend, Frits, and Henk van Dorp: *Ajax Barcelona Cruijff.* Amsterdam 1997.

Barend, Frits, and Henk van Dorp: *Twee keer 45 minuten.* Amsterdam, 1978.

Barkman, Bas: *Rinus Michels.* Rotterdam, 2011.

Bax, Maarten, and Vrougje Fikke et al.: *Cruijff 14 – Bijzondere ontmoetingen met het fenomeen.* Diemen, 2018.

Bens, Felip, and José Luis García Nieves: *Historias del Levante UD.* Valencia, 2019.

Blaisse, Mark: *Baas boven baas.* Amsterdam, 2016.

Boer, Sytze de: *Het Amsterdam van Johan Cruijff.* Amsterdam, 2018.

Boer, Sytze de: *Johan Cruijff – Uitspraken.* Amsterdam, 2011.

Bonte, F.R.: *Oog in oog met Johan Cruyff.* Leiden, 1967.

Burns, Jimmy: *Barça – De passie van een volk.* Amsterdam, 2000.

Busken, Youri van den: *Jan Jongbloed – Aparteling*. Amsterdam, 2019.

Butter, Jan-Cees, and Ferenc van der Vlies: *Cruijff & Johan*. Amsterdam, 2019.

Cruyff, Johan, and Danny: *Boem – Hun levensverhaal verteld aan Jaap ter Haar*. Bussum, 1975.

Cruyff, Johan: *Cupstukken 71/72*. Haarlem, 1972.

Cruyff, Johan: *Ik houd van voetbal*. The Hague, 2002.

Cruyff, Johan: *Mijn verhaal – De autobiografie*. Amsterdam, 2016.

Cruyff, Johan: *My Turn – The autobiography*. London, 2016.

Cruyff, Johan: *Voetbal*. Amsterdam, 2012.

Cruyff, Johan: *Voetbal Plus*. Groningen, ca. 1980.

Davidse, Henk: *Je moet schieten, anders kun je niet scoren*. The Hague, 1998.

Derksen, Johan et al.: *Johan Cruijff*. Amsterdam, 2007.

Duizings, Martin W.: *Faas Wilkes – Een voetbalcarrière*. Baarn, 1951.

Egmond, Michel: *Kieft*. Amsterdam, 2014.

Endt, David, and Sytze van der Zee: *Ajax 1900-2000*. Bussum, 2000.

Galan, Menno de: *De coup van Cruijff – Hoe Johan de macht greep bij Ajax*. Amsterdam, 2012.

Galan, Menno de: *De trots van de wereld – Michels, Cruijff en het gouden Ajax van 1964-1974*. Amsterdam, 2006.

Graaf, Bram de: *Voetbalvrouwen – De glorietijd van Nederlandse voetbal 1970-1978*. Amsterdam, 2008.

Guardiola, Pep: *Een andere manier van winnen – Biografie*. Utrecht, 2012.

Heuvel, Mark van den: *Johnny Rep – Buitenbeentje*. Amsterdam, 2016.

Hiddema, Bert: *Cruijff! – Van Jopie tot Johan*. Amsterdam, 1996.

Hiddema, Bert: *El Cruijff!*. Amsterdam, 1997.

Hoof, Marcel van: *Een mooi huis in een grote tuin – De geschiedenis van het Ajax-stadion De Meer 1934-1996*. Baarn, 1996.

Horn, Leo: *Fluit*. Amsterdam, 1964.

Jong, Guus de, and Jaap Visser: *Johan Cruijff – De Ajacied*. Utrecht, 2003.

Kuiphof, Herman: *De aanvalsspits – Johan Cruyff*. Leiden, 1968.

Kuiphof, Herman: *Samenspel – Klaas Nuninga*. Leiden, 1967.

Luitzen, Jan, and Mik Schots: *Wie is Johan Cruijff?*. Amsterdam, 2007.

Mari, Henk de, and Sjaak Swart: *Sjaak Swart vertelt over ...* Bussum, 1969.

Mast, Johann: *Abe – Het levensverhaal van Nederlands eerste grote sportidool*. Baarn, 2007.

Meijer, Ischa: *Interviewen voor beginners*. Utrecht, 1987.

Michels, Rinus: *Het WK 1990 van Rinus Michels*. Kampen, 1990.

Michels, Rinus: *Teambuilding als route naar succes*. Leeuwarden, 2000.

Molby, Jan, and Grahame Lloyd: *Jan the Man – From Anfield to Vetch Field*. London, 2000.

Motley, Willard: *Klop maar op 'n deur*. The Hague, 1952.

Motley, Willard: *Knock on Any Door*. New York, 1947.

Muller, Lex, and Ruud Doevendans: *Jan van Beveren – 1948-2011*. Amsterdam, 2013.

Muller, Salo: *Mijn Ajax*. Antwerp, 2006.

Nederlof, Bert: *Don Leo – Het werd stil aan de overkant*. Deventer, 2015.

Nederlof, Bert: *Ronald Koeman*. Amsterdam, 2013.

Nieuwenhof, Frans van den: *Willem van Hanegem*. Amsterdam, 2018.

Os, Pieter van: *Johan Cruijff – De Amerikaanse jaren*. Amsterdam, 2007.

Planting, Rik: *Leerschool Ajax*. Amsterdam, 2001.

Praag, Marga van, and Ad van Liempt: *Jaap & Max – Het verhaal van de broers Van Praag*. Amsterdam, 2012.

Rexach, Carles: *Ara parlo jo*. Badalona, 2008.

Rözer, Marcel: *Beckenbauer & Cruijff – De keizer en de verlosser*. Antwerp, 2007.

Scheepmaker, Nico: *Ajax en de kunst van het voetballen*. Utrecht, 1993.

Scheepmaker, Nico: *Cruijff, Hendrik Johannes, fenomeen*. Amsterdam, 1972.

Verheul, Leo: *Frank Rijkaard – De biografie*. Utrecht, 2008.

Verkamman, Matty (ed.): *Het Nederlands elftal 1905-1989 – De historie van Oranje*. Amsterdam, 1989.

Verkamman, Matty et al.: *Johan Cruijff – De legende 1947-2016*. Rotterdam, 2016.

Vermeer, Evert: *95 jaar Ajax 1900-1995*. Amsterdam, 1996.

Vermeer, Evert: *We are the Champions*. Amsterdam, 1998.

Visser, Jaap: *Johan Neeskens – Wereldvoetballer*. Rotterdam, 2017.

Vos, Maarten de: *De Ajacieden*. Baarn, 1971.

Wardt, Jules van der: *Arie Haan – Terug naar Finsterwolde*. Deventer, 2018.

Wilson, Jonathan: *Inverting the Pyramid: The history of football tactics*. London, 2008.

Winkels, Edwin: *Johan Cruijff in Barcelona – De mythe van de verlosser*. Amsterdam, 2016.

Winsemius, Pieter: *Je gaat het pas zien als je het doorhebt – Over Cruijff en leiderschap*. Amsterdam, 2004.

Winsemius, Pieter: *Toeval is logisch*. Amsterdam, 2012.

Interviewees

Guillermo Amor, Jesús Angoy, Poul Annema, Herman Arendse, Frits Barend, Herman Beidschat, Ramon Besa, Rob Bianchi, Mark Blaisse, André Boeken, Levie Boektje, Jan de Boer Jr, Peter Bosz, Joukje Breitsma, Bob Bremer, Ruud Bröring, Chris Buitelaar, Tinie Burgers, Rob Cohen, Chema Corbella, John Damgard, Johan Derksen, Jan de Deugd, Pim Donkersloot, Ruud Draaijer, Jan van Drecht, Leo Driessen, Theo van Duivenbode, Arie van Eijden, Davied Eliasar, David Endt, Frans van Essen, Tonny Eyk, Tom Fadrhonc, Francisco Fenollosa, Maarten Fontein, Bernard and Carla Frank, Bob Friedländer, Louis van Gaal, Menno de Galan, José Luis García,

Roger García, Juan Gaspart, Dennis Gebbink, Martin van Geel, Charlie George, André Gieling, Ramón Gieling, Roel Glasbeek, George Graham, Yvonne Gransjean, Paul Grijpma, Hans Groen, Hans de Groot, Henk Groot, Rolf Grootenboer, Miep ter Haak, Arie Haan, Günther de Haan, Martin Hamburg, Corrie and Leo Happé, Gees Hazendonk, Ben Hazewindus, Henny Heerland, Evert van den Heuvel, Bert Hiddema, Michah Hony, Wim Hoopman, Miki and Daan Horstman, Adriaan Huigen, Benno Huve, Bert IJsebrands, Rinus Israël, Kees Jansma, Arie and Bep Jaring, Martin Kamminga, Willy and René van de Kerkhof, Riet Kerssen-Glashouwer, Wim Kieft, Michael Kinsbergen, Kees Kist, Henk Koenders, Cees Koppelaar, Ria Lagrand, Sanny Lampie, Jaume Langa, Joan Laporta, Vicente Latorre, Aad Leenheer, Benno Leeser, Dick Luijendijk, Frank McLintock, Marjolijn van der Meer, Harrie van Mens, Richard de Metz, Dorie de Meyer, Keje Molenaar, Jan Mulder, Bennie Muller, Salo Muller, André Naber, Bobby Nees, Cees van Nieuwenhuizen, Rob Nolet, Bert Nuis, Klaas Nuninga, Heini Otto, Piet Ouderland, Loek Overweel, Hub Pfennings, Dick Piet, Roger Pop, Marga van Praag, Fermí Puig, Peter van Rees, Carles Rexach, Miguel Rico, Don van Riel, Bep Ritchi, Paul Römer, Sjirk de Romph, Thomas Rongen, Nel Schellingerhout, John van 't Schip, Dick Schneider, Dick Schoenaker, Sonny Silooy, Philippe Smit, Cor Spaanderman, Nelleke Spee, Bertus and Sien Strijks, Heinz Stuy, Ruud Suurendonk, Sjaak Swart, Ed Tanis, Charles Taylor, Eddy Terstall, Siem Tijm, Tineke and Toon Timmers, Jo Toennaer, Ferran Torrent, Vicent Chilet Torrent, Rob Verburg, Dick van Vlierden, Hans de Vos, Sierd de Vos, Jan Wardenburg, Karl van der Wel, Jan Peter Wever, Sies Wever, Leo van Wijk, Hans van Willigenburg, Bob Wilson, David Winner, Pieter Winsemius, Theun de Winter, Wim de Wit, Marius Zeven.

I have also made use of my notes from older interviews about Cruyff with Fred Blankemeijer, Henny Cruyff, Henk Duut,

André Hoekstra, Barry Hulshoff, Gerrie Splinter, Henk Timman and Jany van der Veen.

And with thanks to:
Alex Alferink, Paulien Berkelaar, Ruud Boelens, Frans Bonte, Marcel van den Bos, Ria Bremer, Jaap Choufour, Henk Davidse, Jan Donkers, Cock Frederking, José Luis García, Dennis Gebbink, Juul Geleick, Leo Groenteman, Jeroen Grunwald, Jo Haen, Hubert Hermans, Hans Heus, Laura Heuvel, Dick Heuvelman, Henk G. Hilders, Ivo van Hilvoorde, Guus van Holland, Jan Hondius, Bas Kammenga, Frans de Klerk, Dick Kluiver, Henk Kok, Sander de Kramer, Jan Luitzen, Johann Mast, Frans Oosterwijk, Pieter van Os, Erwin van de Pol, Frank Ritmeester, Mariëlle van Roekel, Geert-Jan van der Sangen, Anne Scheepmaker, Jaap Schoufour, Edwin Smulders, Jon Spurling, John Swelsen, Paul Verheij, Leo Verheul, Jaap Visser, Hans Vos, Hans de Weerd, Bibian Weggelaar, Edwin Winkels.

INDEX

JC indicates Johan Cruyff.